DEFINING SPACES IN IRON AGE NORTHUMBERLAND

EXCAVATIONS AT MORLEY HILL AND LOWER CALLERTON

JOSH GAUNT, CLAIRE CHRISTIE AND CANDY HATHERLEY

With contributions by
Hugo Anderson-Whymark, Alex Croom, Julie Franklin, Derek Hamilton,
Fraser Hunter, Patrick Quinn and Michael Wallace
Illustrations by Rafael Maya Torcelly

Edited by Alex Smith

OXBOW | books
Oxford & Philadelphia

Published in the United Kingdom in 2023 by
OXBOW BOOKS
The Old Music Hall, 106–108 Cowley Road, Oxford, OX4 1JE

and in the United States by
OXBOW BOOKS
1950 Lawrence Road, Havertown, PA 19083

© Oxbow Books and the individual authors 2023

Paperback Edition: ISBN 978-1-78925-856-1
Digital Edition: ISBN 978-1-78925-857-8 (epub)

A CIP record for this book is available from the British Library

Library of Congress Control Number: 2022946206

All rights reserved. No part of this book may be reproduced or transmitted in any form or by any means, electronic or mechanical including photocopying, recording or by any information storage and retrieval system, without permission from the publisher in writing.

Printed in the United Kingdom by Severn Print

Typeset in India by Lapiz Digital Services, Chennai.

For a complete list of Oxbow titles, please contact:

UNITED KINGDOM
Oxbow Books
Telephone (01865) 241249
Email: oxbow@oxbowbooks.com
www.oxbowbooks.com

UNITED STATES OF AMERICA
Oxbow Books
Telephone (610) 853-9131, Fax (610) 853-9146
Email: queries@casemateacademic.com
www.casemateacademic.com/oxbow

Oxbow Books is part of the Casemate Group

Cover: Artist's reconstruction of the site at Lower Callerton (created by Eleanor Winter)

Contents

List of illustrations

List of tables

Acknowledgements

The excavations at Morley Hill were funded by the Banks Group and at Lower Callerton by Bellway Homes. Both excavations followed the specifications prepared by Tyne and Wear County Archaeology Service and we are grateful for their curatorial guidance and support.

Thanks must first be given to the fieldwork teams who worked tirelessly to complete the archaeological program. The field team comprised: Mareike Ahlers, Steve Cox, Magnar Dalland, Steve Digney, Aisling Fitzpatrick-Sinclair, Kimberley Gaunt, Robert Howarth, Gemma Jurado, Michail Kaikas, Rafa Maya-Torcelly, Julia Maxwell, Claire McCabe, Fraser McFarlane, Rachel McMullan, James Miller, Angus Milne, Mark Newey, Asta Pavilionyte, Isaac Penaluna, Phil Roberts, Steven Roe, Nela Scholma-Mason, Owain Scholma-Mason, Glyn Sheldrick, Ben Sorrill, Anthony Taylor and Don Wilson. The excavations were directed by Steve Cox and Josh Gaunt at Morley Hill and by Josh Gaunt at Lower Callerton. Candy Hatherley was Project Manager for both excavations and played a major role in the post-excavation programme and in the production of this monograph.

A number of individuals contributed to the project during post-excavation beyond the named specialists. Thanks must go to the entire post-excavation team from initial processing to archiving including Amy Koonce, Steve Roe and Megan Roberts. Special thanks to the specialists who contributed at various stages including Julie Franklin, Julie Lochrie, Amy Koonce, Rebecca Devaney, Aisling Fitzpatrick, Susan Ramsey, Angela Walker and Laura Bailey. The post-excavation analysis was managed by Claire Christie with additional editing undertaken by Alex Smith to whom thanks are also given for providing comments on the Roman section. Many thanks go to Nick Hodgson for providing insightful comments on the draft manuscript.

Thanks must also be given to the the Society of Antiquaries of Newcastle upon Tyne and Pre-construct Archaeology for kindly granting permission to reproduce images. Throughout the monograph the archaeology has been brought to life by the illustrations created by Rafael Maya Torcelly and the wonderful reconstructions by Eleanor Winter.

1

Introduction

The Northumberland Coastal Plain extends from Berwick-upon-Tweed in the north to the River Tyne in the south and boasts a rich and diverse archaeological record. The Iron Age settlements of the Northumberland Coastal Plain are particularly distinctive, comprising roundhouses surrounded by monumental enclosures potentially with associated banks. Research into the function, structure and development of these settlements has rapidly expanded in part due to developer-funded excavations in the commercial archaeological sector. There is increasing recognition of the diversity and complexity of such sites along with questions regarding their development and decline. Over the past ten years, Headland Archaeology (UK) Ltd has been involved in several large-scale excavations of Iron Age enclosed settlements in Northumberland. The excavations have produced important datasets for furthering our understanding of Iron Age Northumberland and its varied social, cultural and architectural traditions. In 2017 and 2019 Headland Archaeology excavated two substantial settlements located only six miles apart at Morley Hill and Lower Callerton (Fig. 1.1). The results of these archaeological investigations are described and discussed in this volume.

The excavated sites were in an area with an underlying geology comprising Westphalian strata of the Pennine Middle Coal Measures Formation that is overlain by Devensian diamicton till (NERC 2019; Fig. 1.2). Morley Hill and Lower Callerton fit into the distinctive Iron Age presence on the south-east Northumberland coastal plain where a substantial corpus of Iron Age ditched enclosure and palisaded settlements have been identified. These include sites such as Pegswood Moor (Proctor 2009), East and West Brunton (Hodgson *et al.* 2012), Blagdon Park (*ibid.*), Shotton (*ibid.*), East Wideopen (Archaeological Services Durham University 2014b; Northern Archaeological Associates 2016) and Brenkley Lane Open Mine (van Wessel and Wilson 2020). The region has a long history of research, yet questions remain regarding settlement

development, longevity and tempo, social organisation and identity, roundhouse architecture, and the impact of contact with the Roman world.

Morley Hill and Lower Callerton: discovery and excavation

Morley Hill, located on the northern outskirts of Newcastle upon Tyne adjacent to the A1 and Newcastle Airport, forms part of a cluster of Iron Age sites within a 2 km radius (centred on NZ 2265 7229). The upstanding banks of a large enclosure adjacent to Morley Hill Farm were identified during aerial surveys conducted in the 1960s along with two further cropmarks at Hazlerigg South (McCord and Jobey 1968; 1971). At Morley Hill Farm, three enclosures, located on slightly elevated ground, became designated as Morley Hill Enclosures 1, 2 and 3 (HER: 1330). A proposed housing development prompted further investigations including aerial, LiDAR and geophysical surveys and a small-scale evaluation in 2015 (AD Archaeology 2013, 2014 and 2015; ASDU 2017a). The earlier investigations informed the Headland Archaeology excavation strategy for approximately 2 ha of land centred on Morley Hill Enclosures 2 and 3 (Fig. 1.3). The excavations at Morley Hill Enclosure 2 (Area A) revealed a rectilinear enclosure surrounding four circular structures with a further boundary extending to the north-west. Morley Hill Enclosure 3 was located 165 m to the east of Enclosure 2 (Areas C and D) and comprised a further enclosure surrounding eight circular structures and an unenclosed settlement of 13 circular structures. Morley Hill Enclosure 3 appeared to be a more complex multiperiod site.

A further extensive settlement, of different character, was excavated at Lower Callerton situated west of Newcastle, directly north of the A69, west of North Walbottle Road and within 300 m of Hadrian's Wall, which lay to the south (centred on NZ 1712 6734). The extensive Iron Age settlement at Lower Callerton was first identified on

Figure 1.1 Location of Morley Hill and Lower Callerton

aerial photography as a large sub-square enclosure similar in form to several Iron Age enclosures recorded across the region (ASDU 2013; Hodgson *et al.* 2012). The extent of the site was established through a geophysical survey (ASDU 2013; 2014a) and a trial trench evaluation (ASDU 2015) which confirmed the presence of the Iron Age enclosures, numerous structures and further settlement activity to the south and east. Following this, Headland Archaeology undertook the excavation of three areas totalling 7 ha (Fig. 1.4). Area 2 was designed to target the later prehistoric settlement activity associated with the sub-square enclosure; Area 1 targeted the peripheral activity identified to the south of the main enclosure, and Area 3 was designed to target the Walbottle Moor Waggonway (Headland Archaeology 2020; Gaunt *et al.* forthcoming).

The excavation of Areas 1 and 2 revealed a rich prehistoric landscape with evidence for earlier activity in addition to multiple phases of Iron Age settlement. A total of 53 structures, substantial boundaries, enclosures and associated features were uncovered. The enclosures and structures displayed evidence for several phases of development with the preferential preservation conditions allowing for a suite of 70 radiocarbon dates to be taken. The form of the settlement differed from that at Morley Hill, presenting the opportunity to explore the development of both large-scale settlements and smaller enclosed

settlements in the region, along with their potential connectivity, community and status.

Archaeological background

There is a relatively long history of archaeological investigation, at varying scales and using a wide variety of techniques, into settlements of the Northumberland Iron Age. Extensive earthwork surveys were undertaken in the 1850s and 60s by antiquarian Henry MacLauchlan (1858) on the behalf of the Duke of Northumberland, which began the early mapping and classification of sites. In the 1960s to 1990s, George Jobey took up the mantle of investigating and excavating Iron Age settlement across lowland and upland Northumberland. The excavation and survey of several significant enclosure settlements, including High Knowes (Jobey and Tait 1966), Burradon (Jobey 1970), Boggle Hill (Jobey 1984) and West Brandon, Durham (Jobey 1962), formed the basis of early understanding of these settlement types and how they might be classified. In 1968 McCord and Jobey (1968; 1971) undertook a series of aerial investigations to identify and map the location and distribution of cropmark sites, many of which had distinctly familiar outlines to previously excavated enclosure settlements. Many of these sites are scheduled to this day, including

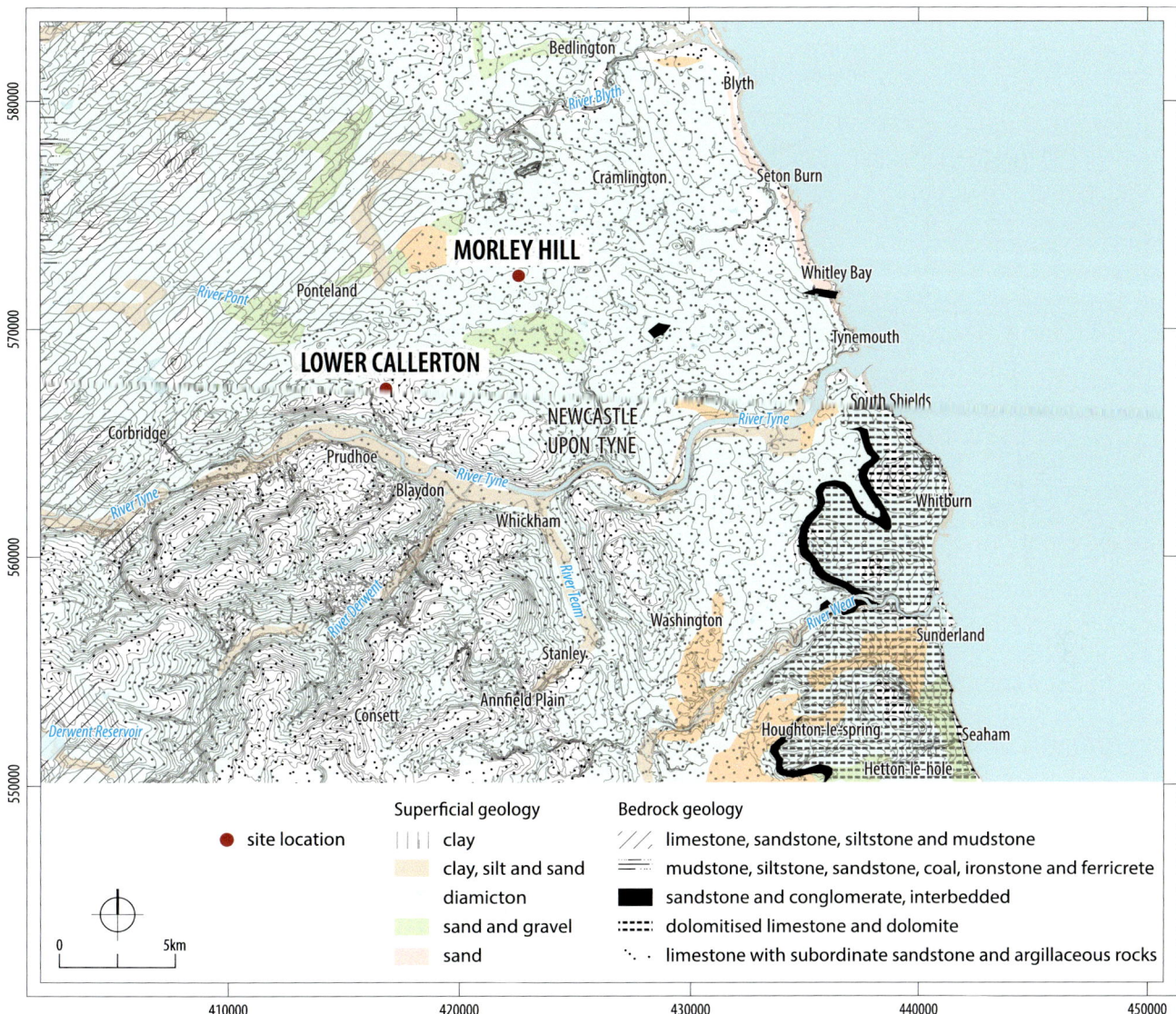

Figure 1.2 Location of Morley Hill and Lower Callerton in their geological context

the two enclosures identified at Hazlerigg South, 700 m to the south-east of the Morley Hill enclosures. Jobey excavated several sites, including Burradon, North Tyneside and Hartburn, with evidence for multiple phases of development interpreted as pre-Roman enclosures overlain by Roman enclosures, likely dating to the late first or second century AD (Jobey 1970; 1973). The relationship between the ordered rectangular enclosures and Roman military activity proposed during these early works pervaded many subsequent interpretations. Whilst archaeological thought has moved away from some of the interpretations and conclusions reached from his early work, the ideas and theories posed by Jobey have formed a strong foundation for our current understanding of the region and its archaeological complexity.

In recent years developer-funded archaeology has enabled an unprecedented view of the entire footprints of larger enclosure settlements and the surrounding landscape. Through this work, the characterisation of rectangular enclosures as the archetypal settlement form for the Northumberland Coastal Plain in the first millennium BC was firmly established (Haselgrove 1984; Welfare 1992; Proctor 2009). The lowland settlements, contemporary with the hillforts of the uplands, were viewed as predominantly agricultural in nature and were thought to continue into the Roman period, including those sites identified close to Hadrian's wall (Gates 2004).

The seminal work of Hodgson, McKelvey and Muncaster (2012) on the sites of Blagdon Park, East Brunton, West Brunton, and Shotton, along with data from other development-led excavations, has provided new perspectives on Iron Age settlement development. The review of sites revealed increasing evidence for the longevity of settlement development with Blagdon Park 2, East Brunton and Shotton all displaying evidence for Bronze Age activity (Hodgson *et al.* 2012, 184).

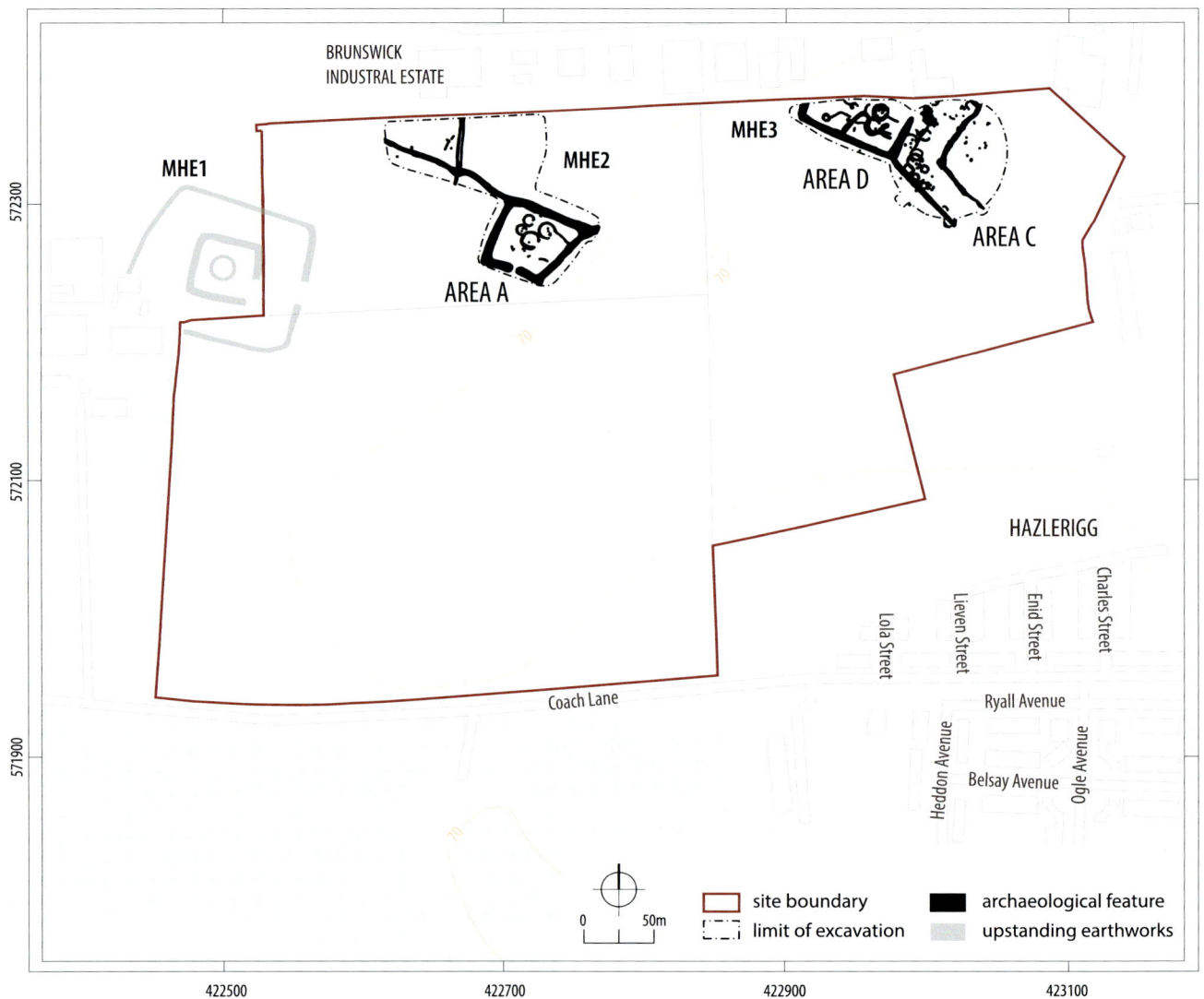

Figure 1.3 Site plan of Morley Hill Enclosure 2 and Enclosure 3

Analysis of these sites confirmed Jobey's (1973, 50) earlier hypothesis that unenclosed settlements dating to the early–mid Iron Age, potentially comprising large numbers of roundhouses, underlay many of the later rectilinear enclosures (Hodgson *et al.* 2012, 186–8). The rectilinear enclosures appear to have been established at all sites during the late Iron Age, matching the widely recognised trend towards enclosure in the later Iron Age witnessed across Britain (Haselgrove 2009, 230; Romankiewicz 2019). Hodgson *et al.*'s 2012 work firmly established the expected pattern of the development with initial palisaded settlements becoming open before the rectilinear enclosures were established in the later Iron Age.

While rectilinear enclosures have come to the fore, other late Iron Age settlement forms are increasingly being recognised, adding further complexity to the expected pattern of settlement development. Sites with seemingly episodic occupation with agglomerations of

fields, sub-enclosures, droveways and associated ditches have been excavated at Blagdon Park 1 (Hodgson *et al.* 2012, 192), Pegswood Moor, north of Morpeth (Proctor 2009) and now Lower Callerton. The suite of radiocarbon dates from Pegswood Moor indicated occupation in the first centuries BC and AD (Hamilton 2010; 2012), thereby suggesting that these expansive sites were potentially contemporary with the rectilinear enclosed settlements. The identification of an increasing diversity of settlement forms raises questions about the date, longevity, tempo and connectivity of occupation sites.

Research aims and objectives

A series of key research questions for the Morley Hill and Lower Callerton sites arose from a review of current literature, the project research aims and objectives outlined in the Specifications by Tyne and Wear Archaeology Service (Morrison 2016; 2017) and the regional research

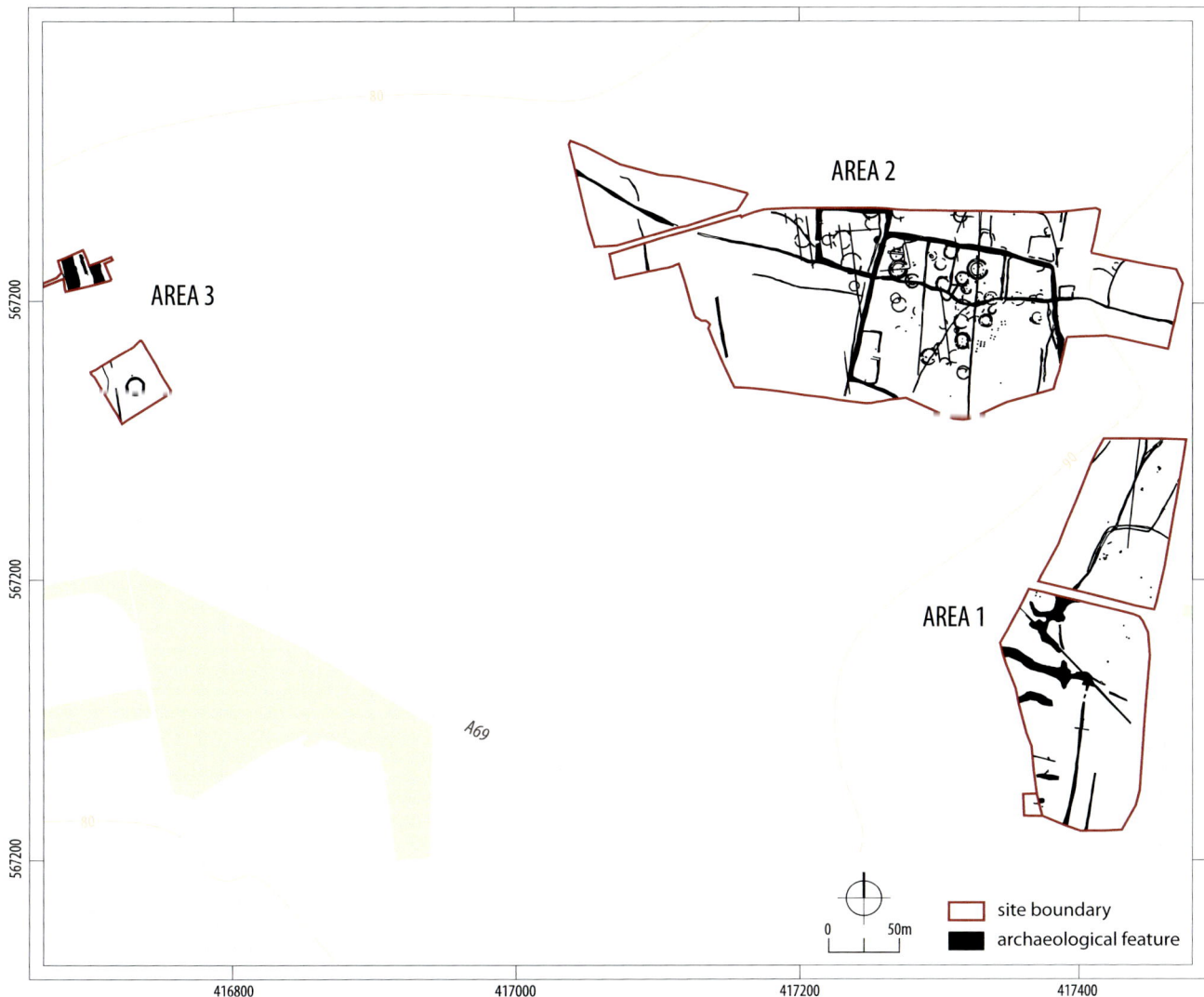

Figure 1.4 Site plan of Lower Callerton Areas 1, 2 and 3

framework (Petts and Gerrard 2006). Although the core research focus remains on Iron Age settlement, recent excavations in the region have highlighted evidence for an earlier prehistoric presence on many sites. The identification and understanding of the earlier prehistoric activity, Mesolithic to Bronze Age, has the potential to contribute to questions regarding the distribution and nature of activity in areas masked by the intensity of later prehistoric activity. This volume aims to explore the evidence for activity in the Mesolithic, Neolithic and Bronze Age and how these fit into the current corpus of data for the earlier prehistoric period in the lowlands of the region. The evidence of earlier prehistoric activity is presented in Chapter 2 detailing the identified features and highlighting those 'hidden' within the later settlement. Artefacts have been analysed, and the application of isotopic analysis of early prehistoric cereals grains from Lower Callerton has offered the chance to explore subsistence strategies from this time.

The core research aims are focused on the potential contribution of Iron Age settlements at Morley Hill and Lower Callerton. These settlements differ significantly in size and complexity providing the opportunity to compare sites located only 7 km apart. This monograph aims to present an exploration of the development of both these large-scale settlements and the smaller enclosures in the region, along with their potential connectivity, community and status. The comparative analysis of enclosed settlement sites of Iron Age date across the region will allow for a better understanding of settlement patterns and farming practices and how these sites fit into both the settlement morphology and the developing chronological frameworks for later prehistoric settlement on the Northumberland coastal plain. The pattern of settlement development at Lower Callerton could be better defined due to the comprehensive suite of radiocarbon dates and subsequent Bayesian modelling.

In addition to questions on overall settlement development, the large numbers of structures at each site can assist in defining aspects of architectural type and potentially function. As is typical for the region, many are represented by a single narrow gully with few internal features. More can potentially be surmised about the construction and form of the complex larger structures with a wide outer and narrow inner curvilinear ditch, an arrangement which has been observed on other similar lowland Iron Age sites on the Northumberland Coastal Plain (*e.g.* Blagdon Park 2; Hodgson *et al.* 2012). Further research on similar forms of roundhouses in the region and beyond will assist in developing a better understanding of the potential forms of these structures and their longevity.

Finally, the impact of direct and indirect interaction with the Roman world must be considered. The Roman military would have become an increasingly overbearing force in the area since the first campaigns into Scotland in the AD 70s (Harding 2017, 227), while the establishment of Hadrian's Wall from *c.* AD 122, close to both sites, is increasingly seen as having a catastrophic effect upon native settlement in a band to the north of the wall with sites rapidly abandoned following its construction (Hodgson *et al.* 2012, 212). The programme of radiocarbon dating at Lower Callerton, and the broader consideration of the available evidence, will aim to explore the date of decline and expand upon the potential influences on settlement abandonment.

To conclude, the key research questions can be summarised as:

- What evidence is there for the chronology of settlement development in each site? Iron Age settlement development follows complex trajectories that appear to vary across the North-East. How do Lower Callerton and Morley Hill Farm fit into existing models for settlement development in the region?
- Can we begin to define social organisation, social role and cultural identity on either site? Can the chronology and architecture of the roundhouses assist here?
- What can we say about the agricultural landscape of the sites; *i.e.* how land was divided up and used? Can we see similarities with other lowland settlements in the region? What wider role could these complex lowland sites have played in the contemporary Iron Age landscape?
- Contemporary environment and subsistence economy: Do the sites exhibit preferences for particular crops, and to what extent does crop choice conform with contemporary regional trends?
- When were the sites abandoned, and could the Roman presence in the region (*e.g.* the Roman Conquest, military presence along the Stanegate 'frontier' and the construction of Dere Street and Hadrian's Wall) be a factor?

Monograph structure and conventions

The monograph will first present the evidence for earlier prehistoric activity at Morley Hill and Lower Callerton. Chapter 2 presents the evidence for Mesolithic to Bronze Age activity from both sites including the limited artefactual assemblage. The preservation of cereal grains in several of the earlier features at Lower Callerton presented the opportunity to explore subsistence strategies and crop management practices through isotopic analysis.

The results of the excavation of the Iron Age settlements are presented in Chapters 3 and 4. In presenting the results, the term 'structure' is used to capture the range of architectural forms, ambiguity in the function of the structures, and the variable levels of preservation – all of which is explored further in the discussion. Chapter 3 details the results of the excavations at Morley Hill, presented chronologically by area – first a wider chronology of the four areas of settlement is established, then the results are discussed chronologically within these wider phases of activity. This is followed by analysis and discussion of the finds assemblage. Chapter 4 presents the results of the extensive excavations at Lower Callerton. The chapter starts with a discussion of the phasing and chronology of site, including a discussion of the sample selection process for radiocarbon dating. The excavation results are then presented by phase with this being structured through the development of the boundaries and enclosures. Finds and environmental analyses follow, including the results of further isotopic analysis and Bayesian modelling, which feed into the wider discussion of the Lower Callerton site.

A discussion of the Iron Age activity throughout the region, and how these sites fit into the wider physical and social landscape, is presented in Chapter 5. The themes include settlement development; the form and function of enclosures and roundhouses; settlement identity and social organisation; contact with the Roman world; and the decline of Iron Age settlement on the Northumberland Coastal Plain.

In keeping with previous research into Iron Age settlement in Northumberland (Proctor 2009; Hodgson *et al.* 2012), the following definitions of the archaeological periods will be employed:

Late Bronze Age	*c.* 1000–700 BC
Early Iron Age	*c.* 700–450 BC
Middle Iron Age	*c.* 450–200 BC
Late Iron Age	*c.* 200 BC–AD 50
Roman Iron Age	*c.* AD 50–200

All radiocarbon dates presented in the text are presented as calibrated dates at 95% confidence (unless otherwise stated) rounded outward to ten years. All dates were calibrated using the internationally agreed terrestrial calibration curve (IntCal20) of Reimer *et al.* (2020) and the OxCal v4.4 computer program (Bronk Ramsey 2009).

Earlier prehistoric activity at Morley Hill and Lower Callerton

Evidence for earlier prehistoric activity in the vicinity of Iron Age settlements is common in the north-east region, and the sites of Morley Hill and Lower Callerton are no exceptions. Pre-Iron Age activity tends to be scattered and smaller in scale, often appearing as a series of discrete pits, only identified through period-specific finds such as stone tools or pottery. Evidence of a Mesolithic to Bronze Age presence was identified at Morley Hill with a range of artefacts recovered from pits and later features. Greater evidence of prehistoric activity was uncovered at Lower Callerton, comprising Neolithic pits and Bronze Age boundaries.

Morley Hill

Mesolithic lithics were recovered from several features within Morley Hill Enclosure 3 and the unenclosed settlement (Fig. 2.1). The earliest of these, dating from the later Mesolithic (8500–4000 BC), were recovered from later Structures 7 and 20. An intact microlith was found in the ring-gully along with a small platform core in the southern entrance post-hole of Structure 7. A further broken microlith was recovered from the ring-gully of Structure 20. Undiagnostic flakes and chips were also recovered from the ring-gullies of Structure 1 (unenclosed settlement), Structure 14 and Structure 15 (MHE2). The lithics indicate a Mesolithic presence at the site, but with the residual nature of the depositions limiting further interpretation.

Neolithic and Bronze Age artefacts were recovered from features within Morley Hill Enclosure 2, including from a Neolithic pit and possible Bronze Age gully (Fig. 2.2). Pit 0137 was located to the north of the later structures within the enclosure. The irregular-shaped pit measured 9 m in length, 0.64 m in width and 0.17 m in depth with a single dark grey silty clay fill. The fill contained fragments of hazel nutshell and a small flaked and ground axehead. The axehead was manufactured from Langdale Tuff, a rock quarried in Cumbria, providing an early to mid-Neolithic date of c. 3800–3300 BC (Bradley

et al. 2019). The pit is comparable to the more extensive distribution of early Neolithic pits uncovered at Lower Callerton.

Limited activity in the early Bronze Age was indicated by the recovery of a barbed and tanged arrowhead from the western terminus of a short gully to the south of the later structures within Morley Hill Enclosure 2. The 6 m long gully, Gully 0178, varied in width from 0.3–0.4 m and was between 0.12 m and 0.26 m deep. It is unclear if this artefact is residual or if this feature is related to Bronze Age activity on the site.

Lower Callerton

In contrast to Morley Hill, extensive evidence of earlier prehistoric activity was uncovered across Areas 1 and 2 at Lower Callerton (Fig. 2.3). Area 1 was located to the south of the main Iron Age enclosure settlement and south of an east–west running stream. Features across this area were pre-Iron Age in date and included several clusters of Neolithic and Bronze Age pits, and ditches potentially dating to the Bronze Age. The earlier prehistoric activity identified within Area 2 was hidden amongst the extensive Iron Age settlement, comprising a discrete group of three pits and a curvilinear gully. The exploration of the earlier prehistoric features has illuminated aspects of earlier subsistence strategy including the use of both wild and domestic resources. Isotopic analysis of the cereal grains recovered from Neolithic pits at Lower Callerton has added further detail to the picture of a diverse early prehistoric landscape, while linear boundaries, possibly of Bronze Age date, uncovered at Lower Callerton hint at the potential influence of earlier land use patterns on later settlement.

Area 1

In total 15 pits were located within Area 1 including Neolithic pits containing relatively rich artefactual and

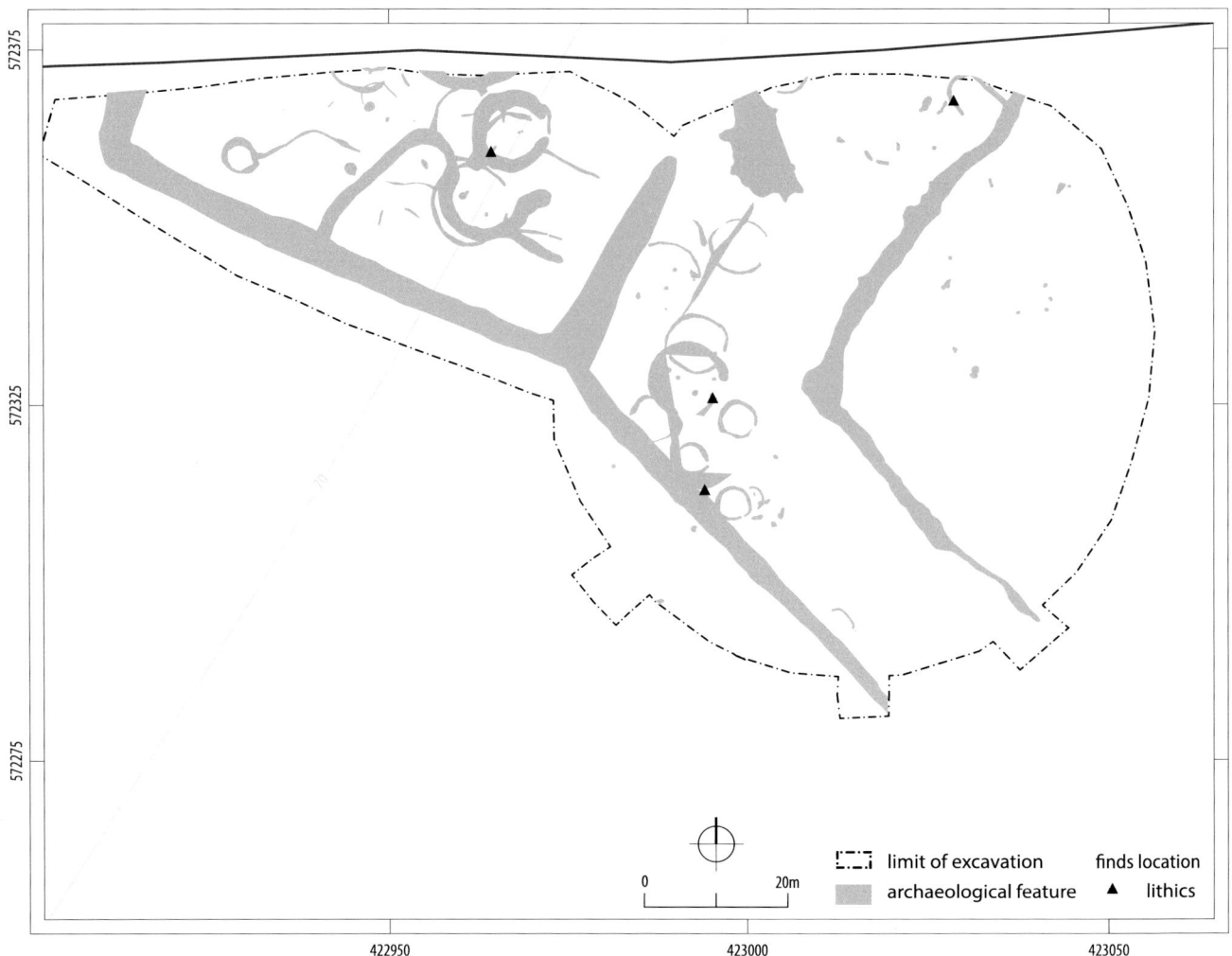

Figure 2.1 Earlier prehistoric activity at Morley Hill Enclosure 3

environmental assemblages (Fig. 2.4). The Neolithic pits form two distinct clusters of activity with further possible prehistoric pits to the south. A group of four Neolithic pits, 0183, 0189, 0195 and 0196, and three associated pits, 0153, 0155 and 0178, were located at the centre of the site. The Neolithic pits were similar in form, measuring 0.4–0.85 m in diameter and up to 0.18 m in depth, with gently sloping curved sides and flat bases. They contained single backfilled deposits comprising loose mid-orangish to greyish-black fine sandy silts. A total of 30 lithics were recovered from pits 0189 and 0195 comprising chips, flakes and a single bladelet from Pit 0195. Pits 0196 and 0189 contained sherds of Neolithic organic-tempered pottery, whilst Pit 0195 contained scraps of granitic-tempered pottery and four sherds of fine black pottery. In addition to the artefacts, the environmental samples revealed an abundance of hazel nutshell, barley and emmer wheat. Carbonised barley grain from Pit 0189 returned a radiocarbon date of 3760–3640 cal BC (SUERC-95781). The sample from Pit 0195 returned a similar date of 3700–3630 cal BC (SUERC-95783) placing both pits in the early

Neolithic. The three further pits (0153, 0155 and 0178) to the north of the cluster measured 0.4–0.9 m in diameter and up to 0.15 m in depth, with similar profiles and fills. While no definitive dating material was recovered, their proximity and the similarities in form suggest they may be associated.

A further cluster of Neolithic features was located towards the north-eastern corner of Area 1, comprising Pit 0167 and associated deposits 0175 and 0176. Pit 0167 measured 1.09 m in length, 0.86 m in width and 0.66 m in depth and was sub-circular in plan with a flat base (Fig. 2.5). The charcoal rich lower fill (0169) was overlain by redeposited natural (0170) followed by a sequence of further charcoal rich fills. The upper fills, (0171)–(0174), contained large quantities of oak charcoal along with hazel, alder and hazel nutshell. The composition of fills is suggestive of hearth waste resulting from multiple episodes of deposition. Deposits 0175 and 0176 sat within slight scoops or depressions adjacent to the pit and contained shallow layers of burnt material. The deposits measured 0.65 m in extent and up

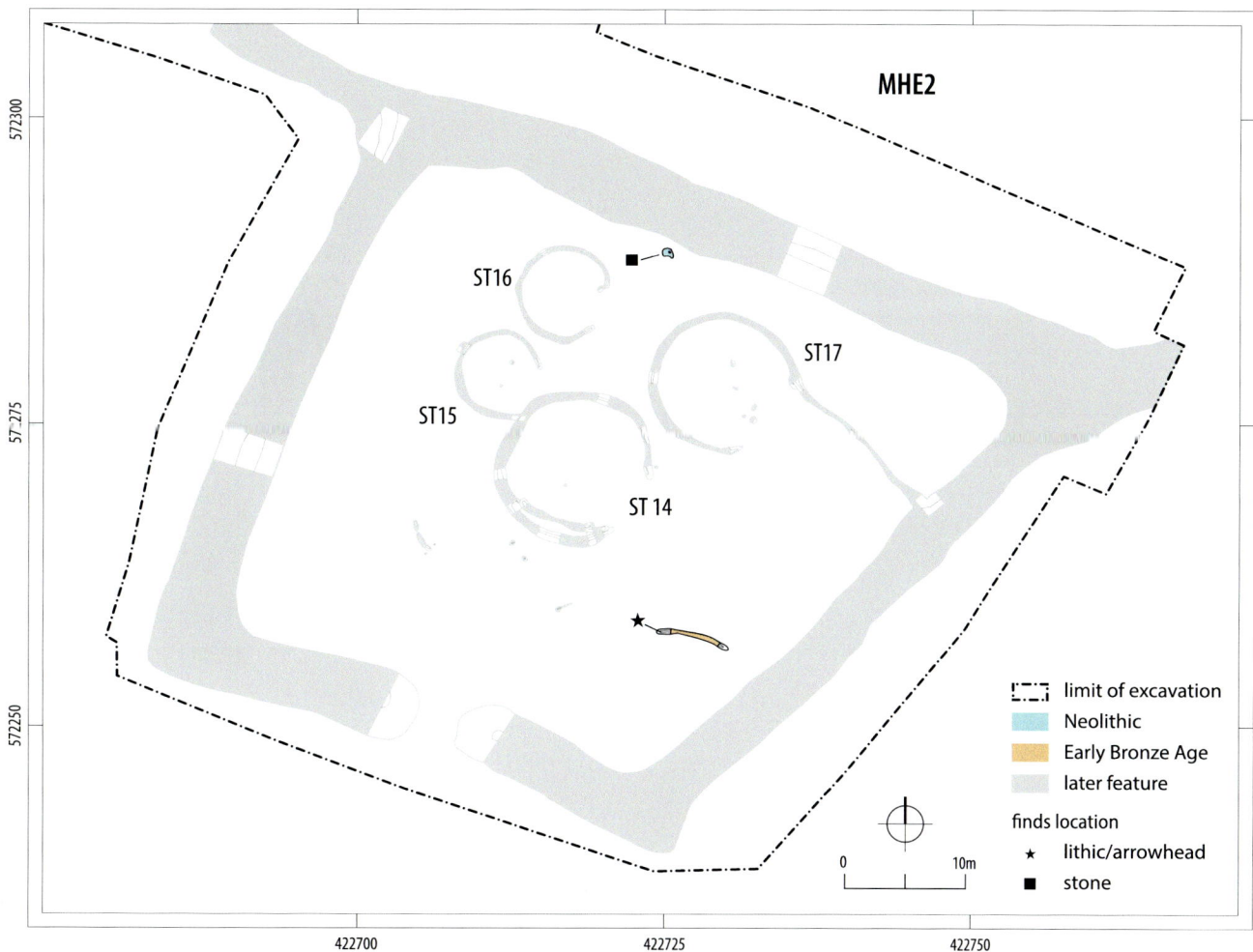

Figure 2.2 Earlier prehistoric activity at Morley Hill Enclosure 2

to 0.10 m in depth, with no clear cut. A small assemblage of artefacts was recovered from Deposit 0175 which included four sherds of granitic-tempered pottery dating to the Neolithic and three lithic flakes and chips. The features have been interpreted as surviving hearth bases from which material may have been dumped into Pit 0167. A sample of hazel charcoal from Deposit 0175 was radiocarbon dated to 3640–3520 cal BC (SUERC-95777) placing the activity within the same timeframe as Pit Cluster A (Fig. 2.4).

A further group of pits, potentially dating to the Neolithic or earlier prehistoric period, was located to the south. The southernmost pit, Pit 0049, measured 0.84 m in diameter and 0.10 m in depth containing a single fill from which 11 lithic flakes and chips were recovered. A single chip was recovered from Pit 0073 to the north, while no lithics were recovered from the nearby pits 0058 and 0060. The pits may relate to prehistoric activity but cannot be closely dated.

A single Bronze Age pit was uncovered to the west of the group of four Neolithic pits and east of the possible Bronze Age boundary. Pit 0191 measured 0.6 m

in diameter and 0.2 m in depth, with gently sloping curved sides and a flat base. The single fill of loose mid-orangish silt contained hazel and willow charcoal, alongside hazel nutshells and four lithic chips. Cereal grain from the pit was radiocarbon dated to 1940–1740 cal BC (SUERC-95782).

The ditch to the west of the pit forms part of a wider network of linear boundaries. The earliest boundary, cut by all others, was Ditch 0177 which ran north–south before turning east at its northern extent. The ditch measured 38.7 m long, up to 0.37 m wide and varied in depth from 0.13 to 0.5 m. No artefacts were recovered from the ditch, which appeared to have gradually infilled with dark grey fine sandy silt. Ditch 0177 was cut by ditches 0086 and 0182 which formed the main ditch running through the centre of Area 1. Ditch 0086 ran north–south and was truncated by the later Ditch 0182 located on the same alignment of which only a few sections remained. Ditch 0086 measured 0.68–0.75 m in width and 0.15–0.40 m in depth with a single mid-brownish grey silty fine sand fill. The ditch extended southwards beyond the central modern hedge-line as Ditch 0042. Ditch 0042 curved

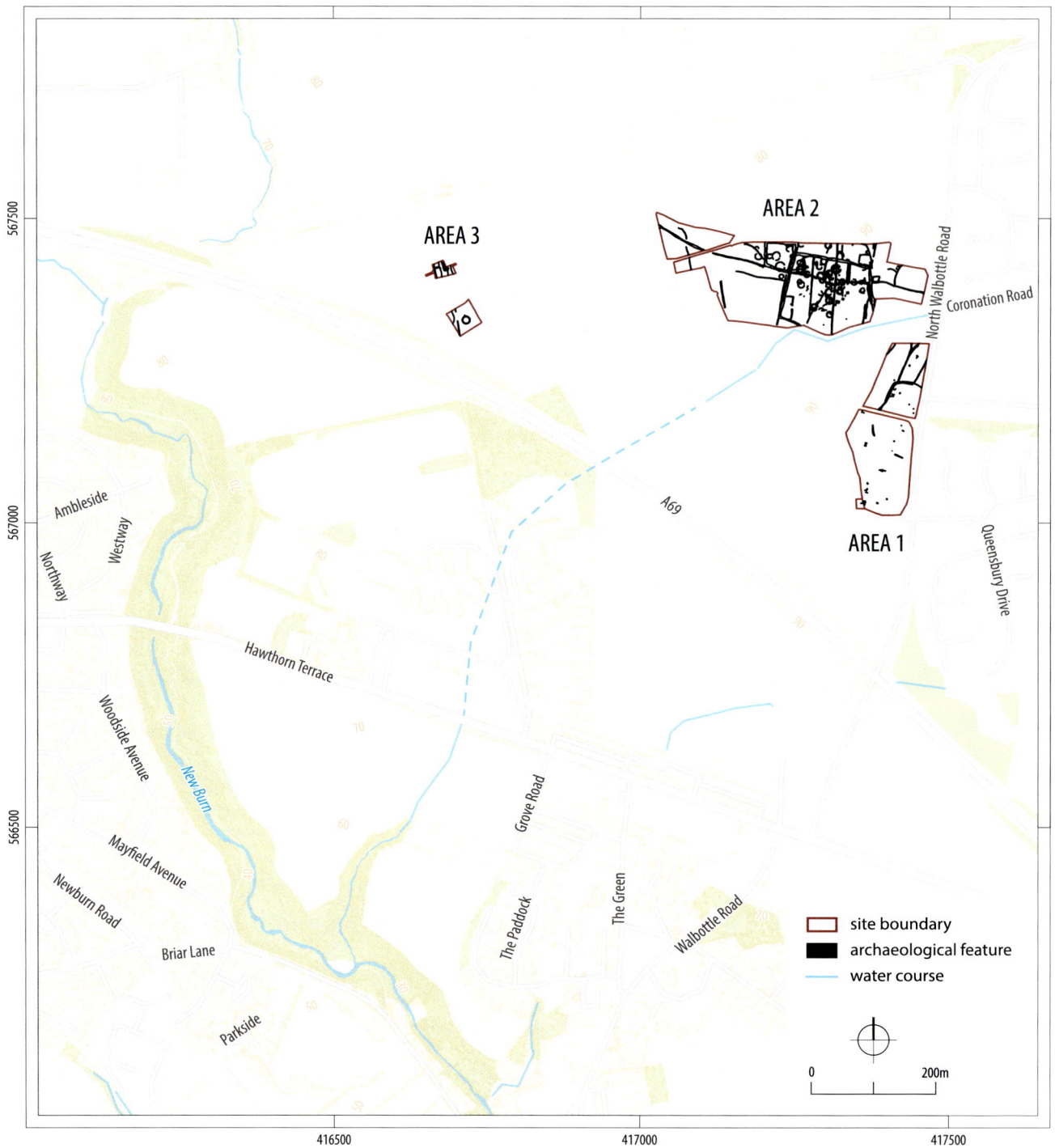

Figure 2.3 Lower Callerton in its local context

slightly eastward, perhaps forming the start of a return of an enclosure, which would bound an area of 0.6 ha within the limits of excavation. Ditch 0182 ran 126 m north-east to south-west, extending across the northern section of Area 1 and likely beyond the limit of excavation to the north. It measured 0.60–2.35 m in width at its widest point, 0.09–0.35 m in depth, with several phases of recutting evident along its length. The recuts did not appear to be continuous along the length of the ditch, suggesting ongoing maintenance and clearance of particular sections, possibly due to heavy silting. The fills along the length of Ditch 0182 comprised a series of natural silting events consisting of friable mid-brownish-grey silty fine sands. The fill of the ditch contained gradually accumulated material resulting from the surrounding activity. As such two samples were selected for radiocarbon dating

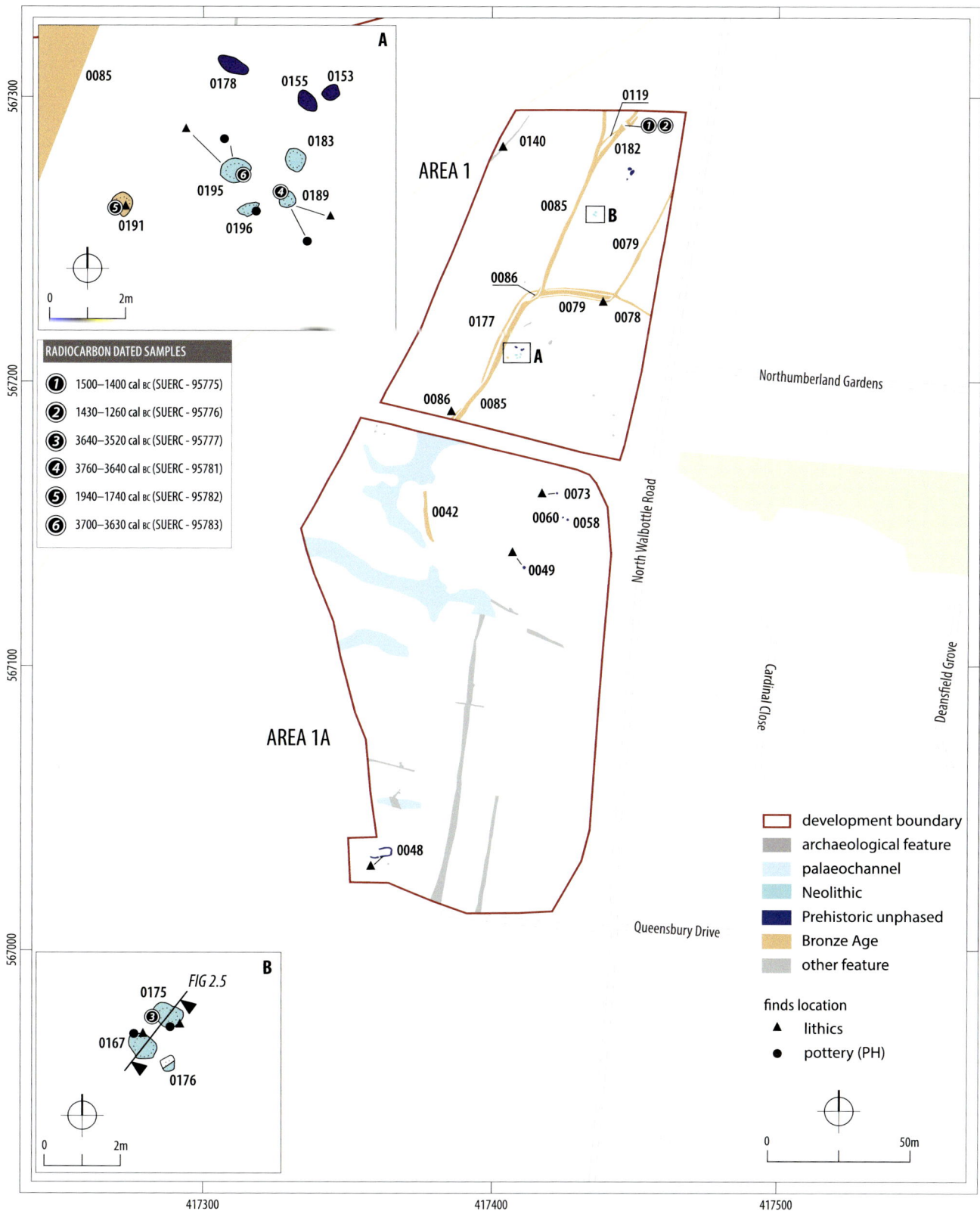

Figure 2.4 Earlier prehistoric activity at Lower Callerton Area 1

from the same context within the northernmost section of Ditch 0182. The samples provided complimentary middle Bronze Age dates of 1500–1400 cal BC (SUERC-95775) and 1430–1260 cal BC (SUERC-95776). The dates provide a broad chronological framework for the ditches and surrounding activity.

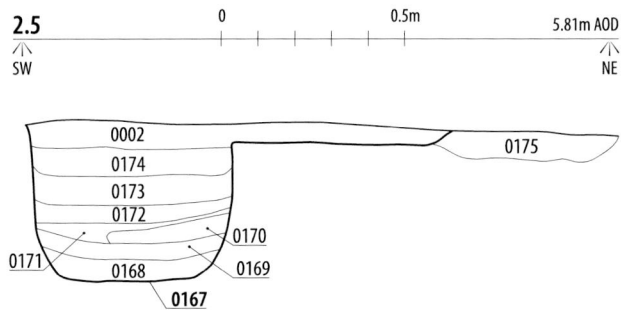

Figure 2.5 South-east-facing section of Pit 0167

Further boundaries, ditches 0079 and 0078, extended to the east of Ditch 0182. Ditch 0079 ran east–west from the eastern edge of Ditch 0182 before turning to the north-east to form the eastern extent of a sub-enclosure. Ditch 0079 measured 70 m in length and 0.45–0.75 m in width with gently sloping sides with a flat base. Its fills were composed primarily of friable mid-brownish-grey silt resulting from natural silting. Ditch 0078 appeared very similar in form to Ditch 0079 and ran roughly east–west terminating 0.92m east of Ditch 0182. It measured 38.3 m in length, 0.88 m in width and 0.2 m in depth, shallowing to 0.06 m at its western terminus. The ditch was filled with dark-brownish-grey coarse sandy silt. Ditch 0078 cut sub-enclosure ditch 0079 and was likely a later recut, extending the sub-enclosure to the east.

An isolated enclosure extends the area of possible prehistoric activity to the south of the central paleo-channel. Enclosure 0048 was located in the south-west corner of Area 1 and was heavily truncated. The enclosure was formed of three gully segments forming a small D-shaped enclosure. A break measuring 0.2 m in width was identified between the northern gully segment (5.2 m in length) and southern gully segments (5.4 m in length). All three gully segments were filled with firm orange-grey silty clay from which a small quantity of industrial waste (slag and magnetic residue) along with a single lithic chip were recovered. The assessment of the environmental samples identified the presence of a small amount of hazel, cherry type and oak charcoal (Headland Archaeology 2020, 80). While the gullies appear to have formed a small enclosed space, the function and date for this feature remain unclear.

The prehistoric features across Area 1 attest to the longevity of occupation at Lower Callerton, indicating not only significant Neolithic activity but potentially the establishment of boundaries in the Bronze Age prior to the construction of the extensive Iron Age settlement. As is apparent in the discussion of the prehistoric features in Area 2 such evidence is often hidden and obscured by the intensity of later settlement.

Area 2

Within the bounds of the main Iron Age enclosure settlement, a series of features were identified as pre-Iron Age in origin, including a cluster of three pits, isolated pits and a curvilinear gully (Fig. 2.6). The features were found to predominantly date to the Neolithic with some evidence of early Bronze Age activity. No features could be clearly linked to the middle Bronze Age ditches to the south-east within Area 1. However, it must be considered that some of the more ephemeral severely truncated boundaries, which cannot easily be dated, may relate to this earlier phase of activity.

A group of three pits containing rich artefactual and environmental assemblages, located at the centre of the site, represent the earliest prehistoric features uncovered. Pits 1775, 1798 and 1803 form a distinct cluster which despite their location were not truncated by later features. Pit 1775 was oval in plan and measured 0.8 × 0.6 m in diameter and 0.1 m in depth with gently sloping sides and a flat base. It contained a single backfilled deposit of mid-greyish-orange silty clay with charcoal flecks, lithics and three sherds of Neolithic pottery. Oak and alder charcoal and hazel nutshell were retrieved from the fill with the radiocarbon dating of a sample of alder charcoal returning an early Neolithic date of 3640–3510 cal BC (SUERC-95784). Pit 1798 was located immediately south of Pit 1775 and was similar in form and contents. The pit was also oval in plan and measured 0.7 × 0.5 m in diameter and 0.06 m in depth with steep sides and a flat base. It contained a single fill of mid-orangey-grey clayey-silt with occasional small charcoal fragments, primarily oak with some alder and hazel charcoal, in addition to 136 fragments of hazel nutshell. Five sherds of Neolithic pottery, similar to that from Pit 1775, were also recovered from the fill. The final pit in this group, Pit 1803, was located 1.5 m to the north-west and was circular in shape measuring 5 m in diameter and 0.15 m in depth (Fig. 2.7). It had steep sides and a flat base and contained two fills. The primary deposit was 0.08 m thick and composed of dark greyish-brown silt with frequent small charcoal flecks and occasional small sub-angular stones. A total of 13 sherds of Neolithic pottery were recovered from the primary fill. This was overlain by a secondary deposit of light orange-grey clayey-silt with occasional oak charcoal. A significant quantity (138 fragments) of hazel nutshells were retrieved from the fills along with ten lithic chips and flakes. A charcoal sample from the primary fill returned an early Neolithic date of 3700–3630 cal BC (SUERC-95785) grouping the activities with those represented by the other pits in this group. The clustering of these pits along with the similarities in size, shape and fill all contribute to assigning them to a contemporary cluster. The comparable finds and environmental assemblages, which included oak charcoal, hazel nutshells, pottery of similar

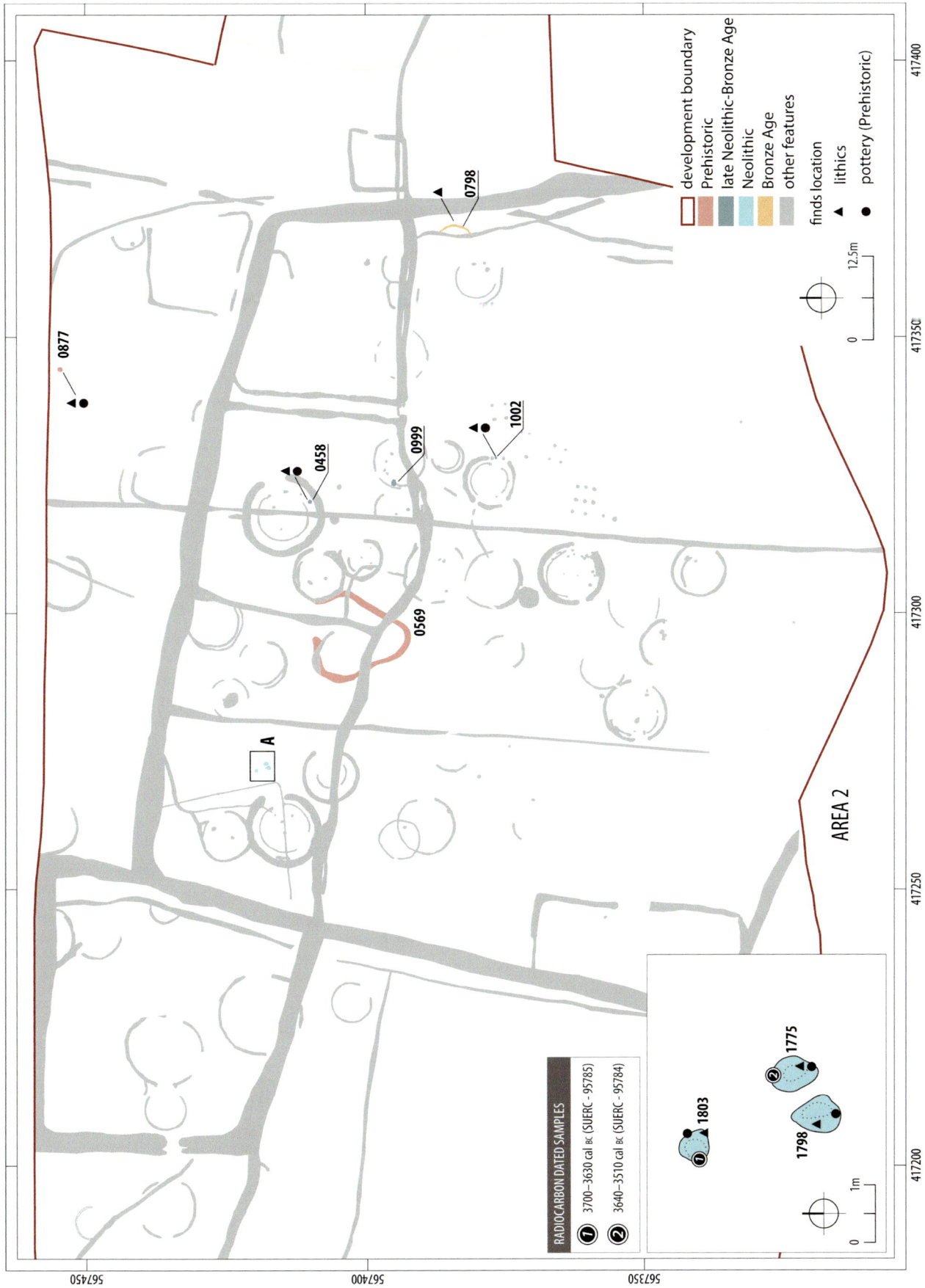

Figure 2.6 Earlier prehistoric activity across Lower Callerton Area 2

fabrics and lithic debitage, along with the radiocarbon dates firmly place the pits in the early Neolithic.

Further potentially early Neolithic pits were identified hidden amongst the later features, in some cases within the footprint of structures. Pit 1002 was located within the south-east entrance of Structure 22. The small circular pit measured 0.32 m in diameter and 0.12 m in depth with a curved base and sides. It contained a single backfill deposit (1003) comprising light-grey silt with rare angular stones and charcoal. A single sherd of dolerite-tempered pottery was also recovered. The fill contained a relative abundance of alder, hazel, oak and hazel nutshells, suggestive of hearth waste. Two samples of hazel charcoal were radiocarbon dated to 3640–3520 cal BC (SUERC-98225) and 3630–3370 cal BC (SUERC-98226) again dating the pit to the early Neolithic.

A further pit, Pit 0999, was located within the footprint of the later Structure 23. Pit 0999 measured 1.06 × 0.83 m in plan and 0.11 m in depth, with gently sloping sides and a flat base. The fill of hearth waste (0997) comprised frequent ash and small oak and hazel charcoal fragments along with hazel nutshell. An assemblage of 102 lithics and 11 sherds of prehistoric pottery were recovered from the fill. The pottery comprised dolerite- and pebble-tempered fabrics with incised decoration, whilst the lithics were primarily chips with a few flakes, many of which were burnt and broken. The decoration of the pottery suggests a late Neolithic–Bronze Age date with two samples of hazel charcoal radiocarbon dated to 2880–2580 cal BC (SUERC-98227) and 2870–2500 cal BC (SUERC-98228).

Pit 0458 was located between the inner gully and outer ditch of Structure 2 and measured 0.59 m in length, 0.57 m in width and 0.20 m in depth. It contained a single fill (0459) from which three sherds of pottery with external decoration, indicative of a late Neolithic–Bronze Age date, were recovered. A further two lithic flakes, three sieved chips and a dense, undiagnostic lump of slag were found in the fill. As with the other earlier prehistoric pits, the fill contained large amounts of oak charcoal together with a smaller amount of hazel.

Figure 2.7 South-facing photograph of Pit 1803

The final pit, Pit 0877, was located to the north of the later large enclosure at the northern edge of the excavated area. The fill contained very large quantities of charcoal, with oak, alder and hazel all represented together with fragments of hazel nutshell. This deposit is probably hearth waste that has been deliberately deposited into this pit. The presence of hazel nutshells and the similarity to the other prehistoric pits suggests this is of a similar date.

A further two features, Gully 0798 and Ditch 569, also appeared to be pre-Iron Age in date and exemplify the difficulties in identifying earlier occupation. Gully 0798 defined a possible circular structure, Structure 20, with a projected diameter of 6.7 m which was heavily truncated on its western side. The curvilinear gully measured 0.11–0.25 m in width and 0.06–0.10 m in depth. An early Bronze Age barbed and tanged arrowhead was recovered from the single fill introducing the possibility that this gully constituted the remains of a Bronze Age structure. However, the arrowhead may be residual indicating no more than early Bronze Age activity in the area. The location of the gully, within 2 m of the main enclosure, and the similarities in form to later structures suggests that this structure may be associated with the later settlement.

A sinuous ditch at the centre of the excavated area, Ditch 0569, also predates the Iron Age settlement. Ditch 0569 was truncated by later Iron Age sub-enclosures 2 and 3, as well as structures 3, 11, 12 and 56. It formed an irregularly shaped enclosure measuring 16 × 14 m with a possible north-facing entrance. The ditch measured 16 m in length, 1.26 m in width, 0.40 m in depth and contained a series of natural infilling deposits. No dating evidence was recovered from this feature. Due to its stratigraphic relationships and the presence of surrounding earlier activity, it has been designated as part of the pre-Iron Age settlement despite its location within the bounds of the main enclosure.

Residual evidence for earlier activity was also found associated with features more confidently assigned to later periods. Single samples from Enclosure 1422, the inner gully of Structure 28, and a post-hole of Structure 13 returned earlier than anticipated radiocarbon dates. During the evaluation phase, a trench was excavated over the southern terminus of Enclosure 1422 with a sample from the fill radiocarbon dated to 2341–2147 cal BC (95% probability; SUERC-76861; Muncaster 2015). As discussed further in Chapter 4 this enclosure was interpreted as a subdivision typical of the later Iron Age settlement. As such the date may result from residual material from earlier activity washed into the ditch. An early Bronze Age date was also received from the inner gully, Gully 1072, of Structure 28. Two samples were submitted for radiocarbon dating returning differing dates: 360–150 cal BC (SUERC-98245) and 2580–2460 cal BC (SUERC-95805) suggesting a level of disturbance and residual material. The earlier date is comparable to the date from residual material in Enclosure 1422. Finally, a sample of hazel charcoal from the north-western post-hole of the Structure 13 was dated to 3010–2880 cal BC

(SUERC-98237). While Neolithic post-built structures are known from Northumberland the structure closely resembles a typical Iron Age four-post structure. The contexts of the dates will be explored in more detail within the analysis of the structures presented in Chapter 4 (see Table 4.8).

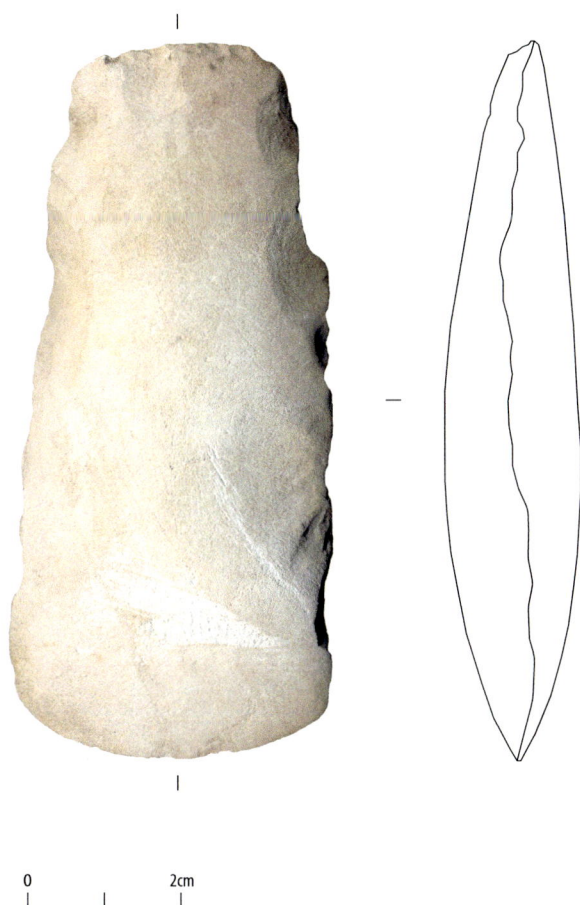

Figure 2.8 Morley Hill Neolithic axehead

Earlier prehistoric finds

The small prehistoric assemblage from Morley Hill and Lower Callerton indicates a range of activities over several millennia, spanning the Mesolithic, Neolithic and early Bronze Age. The limited lithics assemblage from Morley Hill provides evidence of a Mesolithic presence, while a Neolithic axehead and an early Bronze Age barbed and tanged arrowhead indicate later activity. The prehistoric assemblage from Lower Callerton, comprising lithics and pottery, was primarily recovered from pits across the site.

Lithics
Hugo Anderson-Whymark[1]
Morley Hill

A total of seven flaked lithic artefacts and a flaked and ground stone axehead was recovered during the excavations at Morley Hill (Table 2.1). Diagnostic artefacts indicate that this small assemblage derives from activity over several millennia, spanning the Mesolithic, Neolithic and early Bronze Age. The earliest artefacts are two flint narrow-blade isosceles triangle microliths (Jacobi 1978, form 2a), dating from the later Mesolithic (*c.* 8500–4000 cal BC) recovered from later structures. The first, an intact microlith from Structure 7, is in fresh condition and measures $13.9 \times 4 \times 2.2$ mm, while a second example with a broken tip recovered from Structure 20 measures $9 + \times 4.2 \times 1.9$ mm and retains its bulb. A small single platform core producing narrow flakes, from Post-hole 5031 of Structure 7, may also date from the Mesolithic, although a Neolithic date is possible.

A small flaked and ground axehead dating to the Neolithic was found in Pit 0137 within Morley Hill Enclosure 2 (Fig. 2.8). This artefact, which measures $78.7 \times 34.1 \times 14.8$ mm, exhibits a heavily weathered white surface but a small area of recent damage reveals the original grey-green colour of the rock. The fine texture and colour

Table 2.1 Lithics by context for Morley Hill

Feature	Cut	Quantity	Weight (g)	Material	Object	Period
Morley Hill Enclosure 2						
Structure 14	Ditch 0013	1	0	Flint	Chip	Prehistoric
Structure 17	Gully 0081	1	0	Chert	Chip	-
	Curvilinear 0178/0143	1	1	Flint	Arrowhead	Early Bronze Age
Pit	Pit 137	1		Langdale tuff	Axehead	Neolithic
Morley Hill Enclosure 3						
Structure 20	Ditch 5445	1	0	Flint	Microlith: Isoleces triangle	Mesolithic
Unenclosed Settlement						
Structure 7	Post-hole 5031	1	6	Flint	Single platform flake core	Mesolithic – early Neolithic
Structure 7	Ditch 5002	1	0	Flint	Microlith: Isoleces triangle	Mesolithic
Structure 1	Gully 5277	1	0	Flint	Flake	Prehistoric

indicate this artefact is manufactured from Langdale tuff, a rock extensively quarried in Cumbria during the early and middle Neolithic, 3800–3300 BC (Bradley *et al.* 2019). Axeheads of Langdale tuff are widely distributed across Britain (Bradley and Edmonds 1993).

A barbed and tanged arrowhead indicates a presence in the local landscape during the early Bronze Age, albeit potentially fleeting. The arrowhead exhibits semi-invasive retouch, with a squared tang and one rounded barb; the second barb is broken (Sutton Type B; Green 1980). The arrowhead has impact damage to its tip and its surviving dimensions are 18.6 + × 18.7 + × 3.3 mm (Fig. 2.9). The arrowhead was recovered from the terminus of curvilinear Gully 0178 located within Morley Hill Enclosure 2. In addition to the diagnostic artefacts, a fragmentary bipolar flint flake (Structure 1), a flint chip (Structure 14) and a black chert chip (Structure 17) was recovered.

These lithics indicate activity in the local landscape during the later Mesolithic, Neolithic and early Bronze Age, but the limited size of the assemblage precludes any detailed interpretation of the nature of the activity. The

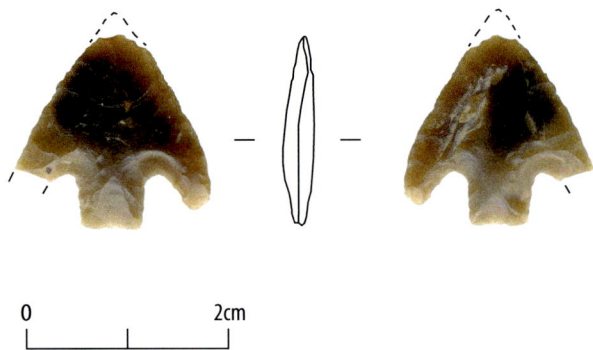

0   2cm

Figure 2.9 Morley Hill barbed and tanged arrowhead

deposition of a Neolithic axehead in a pit is characteristic of ritualised deposition practices during the period, with many of these deposits related to periods of occupation (Anderson-Whymark and Thomas 2012).

Lower Callerton

The excavations recovered 239 struck lithics and ten pieces (3 g) of burnt unworked flint. The greater part of the lithic assemblage was recovered from the charcoal-rich fills of pits, including several which were radiocarbon dated to the early Neolithic (*c.* 3700–3500 BC). A small number of struck lithics were recovered from chronologically later ditches, gullies and post-holes and are residual artefacts. An early Bronze Age barbed and tanged arrowhead recovered from an Iron Age curvilinear ditch forming part of Structure 20 is the only notable artefact from the latter contexts (Table 2.2).

RAW MATERIAL

The lithics assemblage is dominated by flint but includes two flakes of burnt black chert and a flake and a chip of Langdale tuff. The latter originates from the Great Langdale Neolithic quarries in Cumbria, for example on Scafell Pike, that supplied raw materials for axeheads in the early and middle Neolithic, *c.* 3800–3300 cal BC (Bradley and Edmonds 1993; Bradley *et al.* 2019). The black chert is too burnt to determine its source.

The flint is predominantly light to mid-brown, although grey and orange pieces were recorded. The cortex, where present, is generally water-worn indicating most of the raw material was obtained from a secondary source, such as river gravels. A small number of flints exhibit a chalky cortex up to 3 mm thick and this raw material may have been obtained from a chalk region.

*Table 2.2 Summary of lithics by lithic category and feature type. The lithic assemblage is all flint except: [1] two flakes of black chert (Structure 17– Post-hole 0710, Structure 42 – Ring-ditch 1535) and * a flake and chip of Langdale tuff in Pit 1803.*

Lithic category	Pits	Feature type Ditches/gullies	Post-holes	Grand Total
Flake	22*	8[1]	3[1]	33
Blade-like flake	2			2
Blade		1		1
Bladelet	1		1	2
Chip	157*	30	10	197
Irregular waste	1			1
Barbed and tanged arrowhead		1		1
End scraper	1			1
Flake from ground implement	1			1
Grand Total	**185**	**40**	**14**	**239**
No. burnt artefacts	84 (45.4%)	15 (37.5%)	5 (35.7%)	104 (43.5%)
No. broken artefacts	79 (42.7%)	25 (62.5%)	8 (57.1%)	112 (46.9%)
Burnt unworked flint	5	2	3	10

A flake from a polished flint implement is manufactured from a distinctive opaque mid-grey flint with small light grey inclusions and black speckles; this raw material may have originated from a more distant region, such as North Yorkshire.

CONDITION

The lithic artefacts are generally free from post-depositional edge-damage and are unlikely to have moved far from their original place of deposition. A high proportion of the assemblage is burnt (43.5% of the total assemblage), with many pieces calcined white. A similar proportion of artefacts are broken (46.9%), with burning responsible for the majority of breaks. All the unburnt pieces are free from surface cortication.

PROVENANCE

Struck lithics artefacts were recovered from 65 archaeological features, including pits, post-holes and ditches. The ditches and post-holes yielded just one or two flints per feature, with the exception of Post-hole 0710 (Structure 17) that yielded a flake and three chips. These artefacts are probably residual; the only notable artefact was an early

Bronze Age barbed and tanged arrowhead from curvilinear Ditch 0782 that forms part of Structure 20. The greater part of the assemblage was recovered from 19 pits, but the assemblages from each feature were generally small with only five pits yielding more than five lithics (Tables 2.3 and 2.4). Seven pits containing lithics were located in three discrete pit clusters that have been radiocarbon dated to the early Neolithic; a further pair of pits (0468 and 0498) yielded a small number of lithics and early Neolithic pottery. In addition, ten isolated pits yielded struck lithics and it is probably that some of these are also Neolithic features, particularly those with charcoal-rich fills and more than one or two artefacts (*e.g.* pits 0049, 0454, 0458 and 0999; Table 2.4), although some may be Iron Age or later in date and contain residual finds.

TECHNOLOGY AND TYPOLOGY

The technology of the struck lithics is consistent across the site and the assemblage will be considered as a whole, due to the limited number of artefacts from individual features. The low proportion of blades indicates a flake-orientated reduction strategy, but the presence of several narrow blade-like flakes with regular dorsal scars and platform-edge

Table 2.3 Summary of lithics from pit pairs and clusters by lithic category

| Lithic category | Area 1 | | | | Area 2 | | | | | |
	0167	0175	0189	0195	0191	0468	0498	1775	1803	Total
Flake		2	1	6		1			1	11
Blade-like flake								1		1
Bladelet				1						1
Chip	1	1	2	19	4	2	1		9	39
End scraper				1						1
Grand Total	**1**	**3**	**3**	**27**	**4**	**3**	**1**	**1**	**10**	**53**
No. burnt artefacts		3	2	25	1	1			2	34 (64.2%)
No. broken artefacts	1	3	2	1	3	2			7	19 (35.4%)
Burnt unworked flint			1	2						3

Table 2.4 Summary of lithics from isolated pits by lithic category

| Lithic category | Area 1 | | | | Area 2 | | | | | | |
	0049	0073	0516	0454	0458	0877	0907	0999	1495	1326	Total
Flake	3			1	1			5		1	11
Blade-like flake									1		1
Chips	8	1	1	2	6	2	1	97			118
Irregular waste										1	1
Flake from a ground implement					1						1
Grand Total	**11**	**1**	**1**	**3**	**8**	**2**	**1**	**102**	**1**	**2**	**132**
No. burnt artefacts	1	1	1	1	5		1	37	1	2	50 (37.9%)
No. broken artefacts	8	1	1	1	7		1	38	1	2	60 (45.5%)
Burnt unworked flint	1							1			2

Figure 2.10 Lower Callerton end scraper

Figure 2.11 Lower Callerton barbed and tanged arrowhead

abrasion demonstrates a careful and considered approach to reduction. The presence of cortex on several flakes indicates the working of small pebbles and cobbles with limited core preparation. The large number of chips include pieces of larger flakes damaged by fire and micro-debitage. The latter demonstrates that some knapping was undertaken on site, but the small quantity of debitage indicates knapping was probably limited to removing flakes for immediate use or modification into simple retouched flake tools. The reduction technology is consistent with the early Neolithic radiocarbon dates for some of the pits.

The assemblage contains two retouched artefacts and a flake from a polished flint implement. A small, burnt, regularly retouched end scraper was recovered from Pit 0195; scrapers are not closely datable but the regular form of the flake blank is consistent with the early Neolithic date for the feature (Fig. 2.10). The second retouched artefact is a regularly retouched early Bronze Age barbed and tanged arrowhead of Green's (1980) Sutton type B, with a squared tang and one rounded and one pointed barb, measuring 18 mm long × 18.8 mm wide and 3.1 mm thick (Fig. 2.11)

The flake from a polished implement was recovered from Pit 0458 and appears to have been struck from the side of polished axehead with slight edge facets. As previously noted, the raw material for this artefact is likely to have been imported and this flake may reflect the reworking of a broken implement as a core. The flake and chip of Langdale tuff show no traces of polish to indicate they were once part of polished implements, although it is conceivable that they were produced by reworking an axehead as not all flakes will retain part of the polished surface.

DISCUSSION

While comparatively small, the lithic assemblage from Lower Callerton provides some indication of the activities undertaken at this location in the early Neolithic. The presence of micro-debitage in many pit deposits indicates limited flint

knapping was undertaken, perhaps the production of a few tools for a specific task. This activity was undertaken close to a fire, or the waste was deliberately burnt, before the flint and the charred deposit was swept or scooped up and deposited in a pit. The pit deposits at this site reflect a pattern seen across Britain indicating a common ritualised practice, probably related to periods of occupation (Anderson-Whymark and Thomas 2012). The pairing and grouping of pits is common in many parts of Britain, with some evidence of sequential excavation and deposition, for example at Kilverstone, Norfolk, and Cotswold Community, Wiltshire (Garrow *et al.* 2005; Lamdin-Whymark 2010; Anderson-Whymark 2012). The presence of Langdale tuff from Cumbria and a flake from a polished implement of 'Yorkshire'-type flint, indicate wider networks of contact and movement. The early Bronze Age arrowhead represents an isolated stray find, but with the example from Morley Hill it indicates an enduring, if ephemeral, presence in the landscape.

Pottery
Alex Croom

The ceramic assemblage from Morley Hill contained no earlier prehistoric vessels with 80% of the assemblage dated to the mid- to late Bronze Age–Iron Age. As such the assemblage is discussed in relation to the later phases of activity (see Chapter 3). The prehistoric assemblage from Lower Callerton consists of 46 sherds of prehistoric pottery weighing 0.237 kg. Although only a small assemblage by weight, there were at least 12 prehistoric vessels. The pottery was quantified in its fabric categories by weight, sherd count and estimated vessel equivalents (EVEs, *i.e.* percentages of surviving rim diameters). The catalogue numbers refer to the entire Lower Callerton assemblage with the prehistoric pottery included as catalogue numbers 1–16.

Location and distribution

The majority of the prehistoric pottery was recovered from pits either isolated or within pit groups (Table 2.5). Only a

Table 2.5 Prehistoric pottery by feature

Feature	Fill	Cat No.	Fabric	Wt	No.
Area 1					
Pit 0175	0175	12	granitic	15	3
Pit 0195	0187	16	fine black	8	4
Pit 0195	0187	15	granitic	6	0
Pit 0196	0188	2	organic	9	2
Pit 0189	0190	3	organic	9	2
Area 2					
Pit 1775	1776	5	dolerite	20	1
Pit 1775	1776	14	granitic	6	2
Pit 1798	1799	11	granitic	21	3
Pit 1798	1799	4	dolerite	7	2
Pit 1803	1804	1	organic	46	10
Pit 1803	1804	13	granitic	6	2
Pit 1002	1003	6	dolerite	1	1
Pit 0999	0997	9	dolerite & pebble	47	8
Pit 0999	0997	10	pebble	3	1
Pit 0999	0997	7	dolerite & pebble	13	2
Pit 0458	0459	8	dolerite & pebble	20	3

Table 2.6 Prehistoric pottery by fabric

Fabric	Wt (g)	No. of Sherds	EVE
Organic-tempered	0.064	14	14
Dolerite-tempered	0.028	4	
Dolerite- and pebble-tempered	0.08	13	5
Pebble-tempered	0.003	1	2
Granitic-tempered	0.054	10	
Fine black	0.008	4	
TOTAL	**0.237**	**46**	**21**

single abraded sherd was recovered from the fill of a later post-hole. In Area 1 pottery was recovered from four pits forming two pit clusters. Three very small body sherds of granitic-tempered ware (Catalogue No. 12) were recovered from Pit 0175. To the south, prehistoric pottery was also recovered from a group of three pits, 0195, 0196 and 0189. Four very small body sherds of fine black ware (Catalogue No. 16), and scraps of granitic-tempered ware (Catalogue No. 15) were recovered from Pit 0195. Two small body sherds of organic-tempered ware (Catalogue No. 2) were found in Pit 0196 with a further two small body sherds of organic-tempered ware (Catalogue No. 3) from Pit 0189.

In Area 2, the prehistoric assemblage was primarily recovered from a single pit group clustered in amongst the later structures. One body sherd of dolerite-tempered ware (Catalogue No. 5) and two body sherds of granitic-tempered ware (Catalogue No. 14) were recovered from

Pit 1775. Three body sherds of granitic-tempered ware (Catalogue No. 11), and two body sherds of dolerite-tempered ware (Catalogue No. 4) were found in Pit 1798. The largest quantity was recovered from Pit 1803 totalling ten rim and body sherds of organic-tempered ware (Catalogue No.1), and two very small sherds of granitic-tempered ware (Catalogue No.13).

A small assemblage was also recovered from Pit 1002 located within the entranceway to Structure 22. The pit contained a single very small body sherd of dolerite-tempered ware (Catalogue No. 6) with the fill of the pit radiocarbon dated to the early Neolithic. A larger assemblage was recovered from Pit 0999 located within Structure 23, comprising a rim and body sherd of dolerite-tempered ware (Catalogue No. 7), eight small base and body sherds of dolerite- and pebble-tempered ware (Catalogue No. 9), and a rim of pebble-tempered ware (Catalogue No. 10). This pit was radiocarbon dated to the late Neolithic. Finally, a small assemblage, comprising three small body sherds of dolerite- and pebble-tempered ware (Catalogue No. 8), was recovered from Pit 0458 located within Structure 2.

Neolithic – Bronze Age fabrics

ORGANIC-TEMPERED

Fine black fabric with brown surfaces, some dolerite inclusions up to 2 mm long, and plentiful voids on the surfaces from burnt-out organic material and some surviving charred organic material within the fabric, some of which appear 'woody' (see petrographic analysis). The

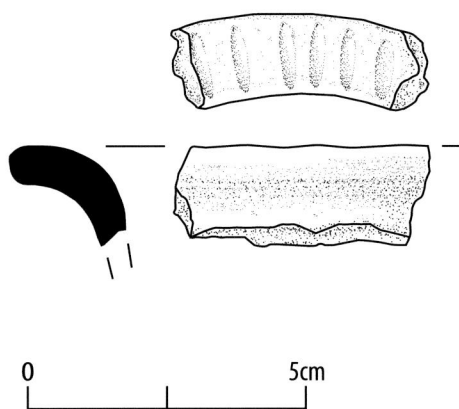

Figure 2.12 Lower Callerton rim sherd with impressed transverse lines (Cat. No. 1)

voids are both semicircular and sub-rectangular and up to *c.* 3 mm long. It is generally thin-walled (up to *c.* 7 mm). Organic-tempered ware with a similar 'corky' appearance was used from the early Neolithic period until the Bronze Age (an S-profile bowl at Thirlings: Miket *et al.* 2008, 57; Millson 2013, 192, 214, 218).

Catalogue No. 1. (Fig 2.12) Three rim sherds, seven body sherds and scraps. The rim is everted and the upper surface has impressed transverse lines. Everted rims were used for bowls and other wide-mouthed vessels in the early Neolithic period (*cf.* Thirlings: Miket *et al.* 2008, fig. 21, nos. 20.1, 45). The decoration is unusual as decoration is very rare at this period, although finger-rippling or fluting on rims was sometimes used (*ibid.,* 48, no. 45; Millson *et al.* 2011, 11). About 14% of the rim survives as three sherds, but as they do not join the size of the pot is approximate (1804). Wt: 46 g.
Catalogue No. 2. Two small body sherds (up to 30 mm in length) plus scraps; exterior surface orange in part (0188). Wt.: 9 g.
Catalogue No. 3. Two small body sherds (up to 36 mm) plus scraps (0190). Wt: 9 g.

CRUSHED ROCK TEMPERS
The use of local crushed rock fragments up to *c.* 5 mm ('small' to 'large': Millson *et al.* 2011, 10, fig. 4) continued from the Neolithic through to the Iron Age and Roman periods, although the exact type of stone used for the temper varied according to local resources. At Lower Callerton dolerite was most commonly used, being easily available locally (see petrographic analysis below).

Dolerite-tempered
Micaceous black fabric with an oxidised exterior, sometimes patchy and a wall thickness of *c.* 7–8 mm. The dolerite temper is small to large (up to *c.* 5 mm) and does not have the 'extremely large' fragments (up to *c.* 12 mm) used from the late Bronze Age to Roman periods

(see Chapter 3, Morley Hill, fabric 1.1), and the temper does not project from the surfaces. On this site, this fabric was used in the early Neolithic period, and although body sherds were also found in later phases, it is impossible to say if they were contemporary or residual.

Catalogue No. 4. Two body sherds. Black fabric with brown exterior surface. This surface is very rough, but the sherd is too small to see if this was intentional or just an eroded surface (1799). Wt: 7 g.
Catalogue No. 5. One body sherd and scraps. Black fabric with patchy oxidised exterior (1776). Wt: 20 g.
Catalogue No. 6. One very small, thin-walled (5 mm) body sherd. Black fabric with oxidised exterior; worn-looking sherd (1003). Wt: 1 g.

Dolerite- and pebble-tempered
Hard black fabric or core, with both self-coloured and oxidised surfaces, with a wall thickness of *c.* 7–10 mm. As well as small to large (up to *c.* 5 mm) dolerite inclusions, there can be soft, rounded black inclusions (up to 3 mm) and a range of other occasional ill-sorted material such as quartz, light grey, pink and red pebbles up to 9 mm across. Its hard feel and a usually rough, pitted or even cracked surface make the fabric very distinct from the dolerite-tempered ware. The presence of decoration suggests a late Neolithic to Bronze Age date.

Catalogue No. 7. (Fig. 2.13) Rim and body sherd in oxidised fabric, from a bucket-shaped vessel. The rim is plain and tapers noticeably to the top (10 mm thick wall), and the exterior has rustication or other form of random impressed decoration. The body sherd has two incised lines, possibly from vertical zigzag decoration. This form of rim was in use from the late Neolithic to the Roman period (see Chapter 3, Morley Hill, vessels 2–3), but the presence of decoration suggests a late Neolithic date rather than a later one (*cf.* Thirlings: Miket *et al.* 2008, fig. 32, nos. 114.1, 114.2; also fig. 28, no. 69.3). As only about 5% of the rim remains the diameter of the vessel is uncertain, but the piece as it survives suggests a diameter in the region of 200 mm (997). Wt: 13 g.
Catalogue No. 8. (Fig. 2.14) Three small body sherds and scraps. One has two lightly incised parallel lines below diagonal lines, although a rough surface means details are not clear. Dark brown/black fabric with light brown surfaces (459). Wt: 20 g.
Catalogue No. 9. (Fig. 2.15) One base, seven small body sherds (up to 30 mm long) and scraps in black fabric with slightly brown surfaces. Some of the sherds have lightly incised line decoration, and some probable random impressions, although their small size and uneven surface make details unclear. One has two parallel grooves and diagonal lines, and one has possible cross-hatching or lattice (997). Wt: 47 g.

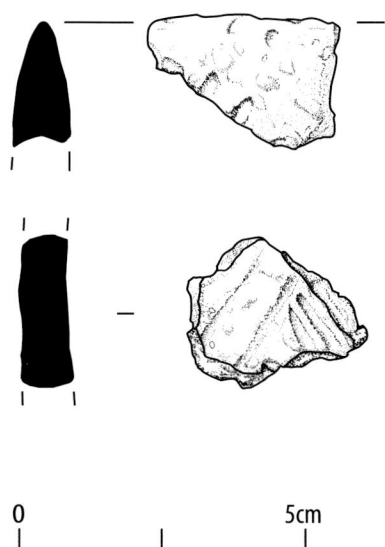

Figure 2.13 Lower Callerton decorated rim and body sherd (Cat. No. 7)

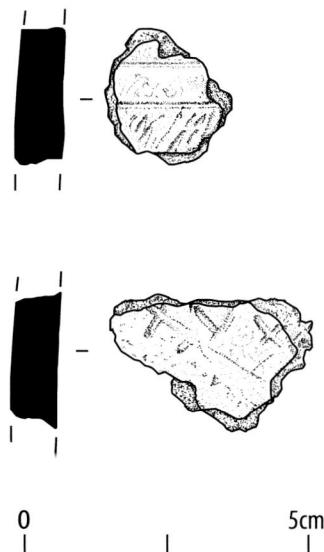

Figure 2.15 Lower Callerton incised line decorated sherds (Cat. No. 9)

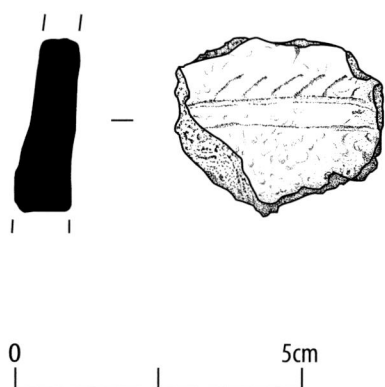

Figure 2.14 Lower Callerton body sherds with incised lines (Cat. No. 8)

Figure 2.16 Lower Callerton flat-topped rim sherd (Cat. No. 10)

Pebble-tempered

A single sherd of sightly soapy black fabric, with some angular hard grey stone inclusions (up to 3 mm). The sherd is so small it is possible it originally had other temper as well.

Catalogue No. 10. (Fig. 2.16) Flat-topped rim with diagonal lines incised with a stick or similar 1 mm wide on one of the three surviving faces. It is possible that it comes from a flat-topped bowl projecting slightly on the interior, with the decoration on the exterior, but the sherd is only 25 mm long and may be misleading. There are traces of a white material surviving in two of the grooves. White paste inlay is most often found on beakers but has also been found on a funerary cup and food vessels (Wilkin 2013, 151; Hallam 2017, 234). Such vessels are usually oxidised,

and this sherd is fully reduced, but there is at least one vessel with inlay that has a deliberately blackened exterior (Hallam 2017, 102). While the exact form of the vessel is unclear, the presence of inlay suggests a late Neolithic/early Bronze Age date. Black fabric through-out (997). Wt: 3 g.

Granitic-tempered

Black or dark grey fabric, sometimes with an oxidised exterior surface, with a wall thickness *c.* 8 mm. A clean matrix with common ill-sorted angular granitic inclusions up to 5 mm across, although generally smaller (*c.* 2 mm). The rock is usually crushed so that individual angular crystals of white and colourless quartz and black mica plates are visible. Granite would have been available at a source such as Cheviot in Northumberland, but it is unclear if it was collected at source or from glacial erratics (Hodgson *et al.* 2012, 133). Pottery tempered in this way was still used locally in the Iron Age at West Brunton, approximately 7 km from Lower Callerton (*ibid.*, fig. 83, nos. 10, 14), but here the fabric appears to be used only in the early Neolithic.

Catalogue No. 11. Three body sherds and scraps. Brown fabric, with brown or orange exterior and black interior (1799). Wt: 21 g.

Catalogue No. 12. Three very small body sherds (up to 25 mm) and scraps. Black fabric (0175). Wt: 15 g.

Catalogue No. 13. Two very small sherds (up to 20 mm). The same colouration as V11 and could easily be from the same vessel (1804). Wt: 6 g.

Catalogue No. 14. Two small body sherds and scraps. Black fabric with brown exterior (1776). Wt: 6 g.

Catalogue No. 15. Scraps (very small fragments with only one surviving face). Black fabric (0187). Wt: 6 g.

FINE BLACK

This was recovered from a single context only, dating to the early Neolithic period. It is a fine, non-micaceous black fabric with very small buff inclusions, often linear, most less than 1 mm in length. There are occasional soft black rounded inclusions with a void round them. The outer surface is white. Wall thickness: *c.* 7 mm.

Catalogue No. 16. Four very small body sherds (up to 23 mm), plus scraps. The exterior surface is pockmarked like some of the dolerite-tempered ware, and may have random impressions, but the sherds are too small for certainty. There are the remains of burnt material on the interior surface (0187). Wt: 8 g.

Discussion

Although small and very fragmentary this is an important assemblage as no Neolithic pottery has been found in the immediate area. Most examples of Neolithic pottery in the region come from sites in northern Northumberland, while most of the pottery in the Tyne Valley and coastal plain (mainly complete or substantially complete vessels from burials) is Bronze Age in date (Millson 2013, maps 1.2, 6.1–8; Miket *et al.* 2008, fig. 40; Miket 1984, map 3).

The early Neolithic material consists of wares tempered with organic and granitic material and dolerite. Organic-tempered material is known from the northern Northumberland sites, but is rare: at Thirlings there were just two vessels and at Lanton Quarry only one, and it is possible they represent vessels brought in from elsewhere (Miket *et al.* 2008, 57; Tinsley and Waddington 2009, 5). The petrographic analysis of the Lower Callerton vessel suggests it could have been made locally, although the small size of the assemblage means it is impossible to say if organic-tempered ware was more common locally than further north, and if the use of rim decoration was typical for this area. It has been suggested that the use of some tempers had a symbolic meaning beyond their practical function in clay preparation (Cootes and Quinn 2017, 687) and it is possible that the use of organic-tempered clay was also unusual locally, and it had been chosen specifically for a vessel intended for some special function.

Three of the four vessels with wall decoration come from pits spread across the site and are likely to be late Neolithic or Bronze Age in date, while the fourth decorated sherd is from Pit 0458 (Catalogue No. 8) is likely to be residual in that context. Most are in a distinctive hard dolerite-tempered ware with more pebble inclusions than the earlier dolerite-tempered fabric.

Petrographic analysis of organic-tempered ware
Patrick Quinn

Petrographic analysis was undertaken on a sherd from Vessel 1, recovered from Pit 1803, to confirm the fabric was organic-tempered rather than tempered with something that had since leached out, and to find out if the vessel was made in the local area.

Methodology

The sherd was prepared as a 30 μm petrographic thin section using a modification of the standard geological technique (Quinn 2013, 23–30). It was then examined under the polarising light microscope and characterised in terms of its raw materials and manufacturing technology. The composition of the sherd was compared to the local and regional geology, as well as with analyses of contemporaneous prehistoric sherds from the same general area. Photomicrographs of the prepared thin section are presented in Figure 2.17.

Results

The sherd is composed in thin section of coarse somewhat heterogeneous fabric characterised by the presence of igneous rock fragments and charred organic matter in a non-calcareous clay matrix with moderate porosity (Fig. 2.17). The conspicuous igneous rock inclusions reach 2 mm in the prepared thin section and are of basic igneous composition. They are composed of fine radiating plagioclase and less common orthoclase feldspar laths, clinopyroxene and opaques (Figs 2.17A and B). Some of the examples are small and exhibit weathering, nevertheless, all appear to come from a similar rock, which was some sort of equigranular basalt. The inclusions vary in size and are sub-angular to angular. Other mineralised inclusions are rare in the sample and rather fine grained. These are composed mainly of sparse silt-sized quartz, mica and opaques. That the basalt rock fragments are much larger than these suggests that the former was added as temper. This interpretation is supported by their angular shape and varied size. The sherd also contains some larger laminar opaque inclusions that have a somewhat woody appearance (Figs 2.17B and C). It is not clear whether they are of organic origin or are iron-rich. A concentration of definite charred organic matter does however occur at the edge of the sample (Fig. 2.17D). These inclusions have a cellular appearance and are associated with voids

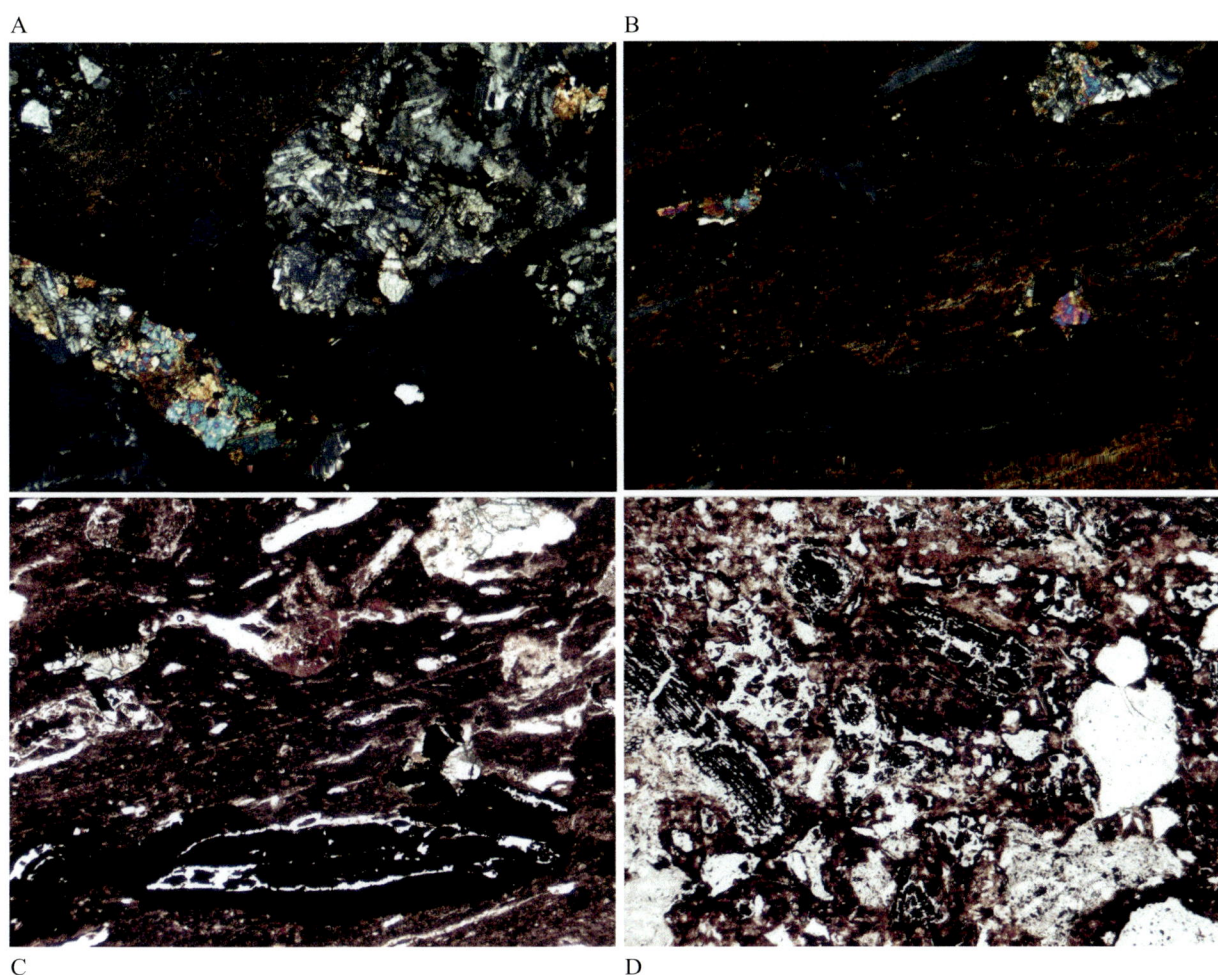

Figure 2.17 Thin section photomicrographs of the prehistoric sherd from Lower Callerton, near Newcastle upon Tyne, analysed in this report. Images A and B taken in crossed polars and C and D in plane polarised light. Image width = 2.9 mm, except D = 1.45 mm

from the degradation of the organic material during firing. The clay matrix of the sample is non-calcareous and relatively clean. The sherd is moderately porous due to the presence of meso- and macro-elongate voids. While some of these are cracks between crumbs of clay, others appear to have been left by the destruction of some sort of inclusion, perhaps organic in origin. Some have been infilled post-depositionally by phosphate.

Discussion

The petrographic analysis above reveals that the sherd was indeed tempered with some sort of woody plant matter that has charred during firing but still remains in the ceramic. There is no evidence in the prepared thin section for any inclusions, nor remains thereof, or inclusions that could have leached out, for example calcite or gypsum.

The most informative inclusion type in respect of the source of the clay is the basic igneous rock. The geology of the area local to the site is dominated by sedimentary rock of the Pennine Lower Coal Measures Formation, including sandstone, siltstone, mudstone and coal (Stone

et al. 2010). Nevertheless, an isolated lone igneous intrusion of basic igneous composition crops out *c.* 1.6 km from the site. This body, referred to as the Walbottle Dyke, is described as being of 'microgabbro' and was quarried in the past. Microgabbro is used as an alternative name to dolerite, a medium-grained basic igneous rock. Though the inclusions in the Lower Callerton sherd have crystals sizes <1 mm and should strictly be classified as basalt, they also have a basic igneous composition and are thus in keeping with the Walbottle Dyke. Igneous intrusions often contain variation in grain size due to differences in cooling rate. It is therefore feasible that the sherd could have been locally produced by the addition of weathered and potentially crushed material from the dyke.

Much of the bedrock in the local area is covered with glacial till and fluvioglacial sediment. This might contain igneous clasts from the Walbottle Dyke or other intrusions eroded by ice. It is therefore possible that the potter who made the vessel selected specific inclusions from the till and used this as temper. The intentional addition of basic igneous rock temper to prehistoric British ceramics has been recorded in several studies, including Williams and Jenkins (1999), Cootes and Quinn (2017) and Flaherty *et al.* (2020). Igneous rock has a similar thermal expansion coefficient to fired ceramic when heated due to the presence of abundant feldspars (Rye 1976), making it an ideal filler for coarse ware cooking vessels (Freestone 1992; Sheridan 1997). However, its presence within urns and beakers seem to suggest that the use of this temper type may also have served non-utilitarian functions (Cootes and Quinn 2017). It could have been imbued with symbolic meaning that cannot be understood in terms of its physical or behavioural characteristics (Woodward 2008). Such an idea has been proposed for the production of Bronze Age pottery from Wales by Williams and Jenkins (1999) and the Peak District by Cootes and Quinn (2017), both of which are overwhelmingly tempered with basalt and dolerite. The author is not aware of any prehistoric ceramics from the same general area as the Lower Callerton sherd that were also tempered with basalt, though fabrics characterised by the presence of angular granitic igneous inclusions are common among Anglo-Saxon and prehistoric pottery in the north of England and the Midlands (*e.g.* Freestone and Middleton 1991; Wardle 1992; Vince 2005; Ixer and Vince 2009; Quinn 2011).

The palaeoenvironmental assemblage
Michael Wallace

Area 1 at Lower Callerton contained several sparsely distributed linear and pit features. Many of these were of known post-medieval or modern date, whilst others were of unknown date at the time of excavation. Radiocarbon dating determined that the pits span the earliest Neolithic through to the Bronze Age – Iron Age transition.

The pre-Iron Age charcoal assemblage of the ditches and gullies was notable for its diversity of taxa present. Pits, on the other hand, yielded a more constrained assemblage, with an emphasis on oak (*Quercus* sp.) and, to a lesser extent, alder (*Alnus* cf. *glutinosa*) and hazelnut (*Corylus* cf. *avellana*). Unusually, the charcoal assemblage from Pit 0191 was dominated by willow (*Salix* sp.). Taken as a whole, the charcoal assemblage attests to a complex and substantial utilisation of mixed-deciduous woodland. There is no direct evidence that the pits contain architectural material, though some of the taxa represented do have potential for such use including oak as timbers, and birch and willow as wattle. Oak charcoal is dominant in the Neolithic features, a trend that is widely attested in northern England and Scotland (Barclay *et al.* 2003). Whilst this can be partly explained by the robustness of charcoal, and its consequential propensity to be preserved, it may also indicate preferential use of oak. The basis of this preference may be utilitarian, owing to oak's suitability for heavy architectural duties, or cultural, perhaps associated with the prominence or longevity of oak trees (Thomas 1991).

Within Area 1B, a cluster of eight pits was found, four of which (0189, 0191, 0195 and 0196) contained appreciable quantities of cereal grains. Pit 0189 had the largest assemblage, comprising roughly equivalent amounts of barley (105 grains) and wheat (124 grains, including 60 emmer – *Triticum dicoccum* – and 74 indeterminate – *Triticum* spp. – grains). There were as many grains again (197) of cereal indeterminate (likely *Triticum/Hordeum* spp.), making estimation of the true barley-wheat ratio unreliable. Preservation was poorer in Pit 0195, which contained 27 wheat grains (*Triticum* cf. *discoccum* and *Triticum* spp.), 12 barley grains (including cf. *Hordeum vulgare*) and 43 indeterminate cereal grains. The remaining two pits contained fewer than ten grains, with Pit 0191 containing barley and cereal indet. and Pit 0196 wheat and cereal indet. No chaff or wild seeds were recovered from these or any other pre-Iron Age features at the site.

The Lower Callerton Neolithic cereal assemblage is small in absolute terms (four pits, 537 grains). Northern England, however, lacks rich archaeobotanical assemblages in comparison with those for southern England and Scotland. The extent to which this is a taphonomic factor (*e.g.* the suitability of soils for the preservation of plant remains) or a human behavioural factor (*e.g.* a reduced dependence on cereals or a scarcity of evidence for domestic occupation) is unclear. Indeed, both may combine to the detriment of archaeobotanical study.

There is an evident change in the staple basis of food economies in Britain, with sites in southern England moderately wheat-dominated (*e.g.* Fairbairn, 2000) and those in Scotland strongly barley-dominated (*e.g.* Bishop *et al.* 2010). The relative dearth of archaeobotanical data for the central latitudes of Britain means it is not possible to define the timing, distribution and nature of this transition. The Lower Callerton assemblage contributes to the filling this gap, showing that wheat remained a substantial part of the Neolithic crop assemblage of Britain to the 55th parallel north.

Stable isotope analysis of Neolithic crops

In recent years the interpretative value of biological remains has been extended through stable isotope analysis. The ratio of stable isotopes in an organism relate to the conditions under which it grew, its life history, and so can provide evidence for past environment (*e.g.* climate) and human activities (*e.g.* farming) on the level of individual samples (an overview is provided by Fiorentino *et al.* 2015). The formation of isotope ratios in cereal crops has been outlined extensively (Araus *et al.* 1993; 1997; 1999; Bogaard *et al.* 2007; Voltas *et al.* 2008; Fraser *et al.* 2013; Wallace *et al.* 2013; Nitsch *et al.* 2015). In summary, stable carbon isotope ratios indicate the level of stomatal conductance, which is commonly associated with the water availability (*i.e.*

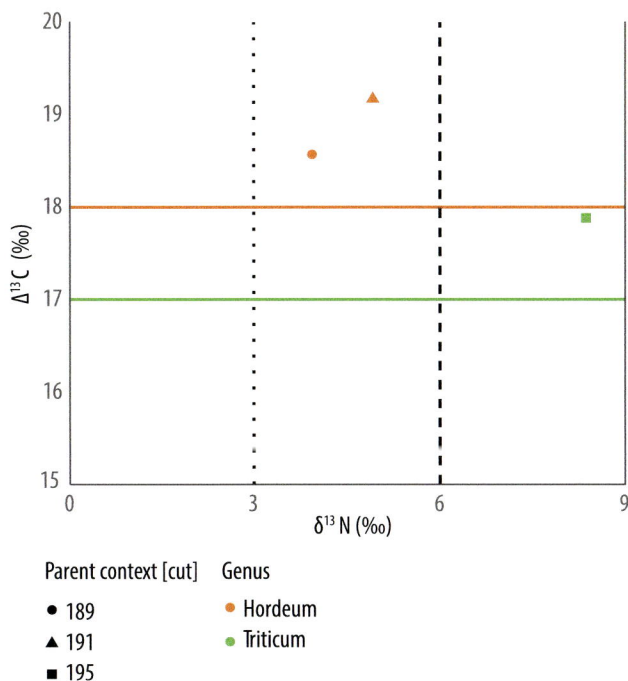

Figure 2.18 Δ¹³C and δ¹⁵N results for Neolithic cereal grain samples from Lower Callerton. Lines indicate indicative thresholds for interpreting crop status (see text for explanation): dotted line indicates transition from low to medium intensity manuring, dashed line indicates transition from medium to high intensity manuring, above green line indicates well-watered wheat crops, and above orange line indicates well-watered barley crops

$\Delta^{13}C$, calculated from $\delta^{13}C$ to account for changes in atmospheric CO_2 (Ferrio *et al.* 2005) values are greater in wetter conditions), though other environmental factors do influence ratios. Stable nitrogen isotopes represent the uptake of nitrogen compounds, and their isotopic ratio is dependant on the position in the food chain from which they derive. For each step in the food chain the trophic level (equivalent to 3–4‰) rises, such that vegetation has lower values than herbivores, which have lower values than carnivores. The application of animal dung serves to raise the $\delta^{15}N$ of soil compounds, and by extension plants grown on manured soils will have elevated $\delta^{15}N$ values. The reality of both the carbon and nitrogen systems is more complex than this, nevertheless the above relationships provide a basic interpretative framework.

Cereal grain samples (including those from Iron Age deposits – see Chapter 4) were submitted to Iso-Analytical for Elemental Analysis – Isotope Ratio Mass Spectrometry. The reference material used for $\delta^{13}C$ and $\delta^{15}N$ analysis was IA-R001 (wheat flour, $\delta^{13}C_{V\text{-}PDB}$ = -26.43‰, $\delta^{15}N_{AIR}$ = 2.55‰) calibrated against IAEA-CH-6 (sucrose, $\delta^{13}C$V-PDB = -10.449‰) and IAEA-N-1 (ammonium sulphate, $\delta^{15}N_{AIR}$ = 0.40‰). The analytical precision was

0.02‰ for $\delta^{13}C$ and 0.06‰ for $\delta^{15}N$. Grains were not chemically pre-treated prior to analysis. Post-mortem diagenesis – principally charring and contamination – can cause the original isotopic values of plant remains to be altered (Fraser *et al.* 2011; 2013; Wallace *et al.* 2013; Vaiglova *et al.* 2014). For $\delta^{13}C$, repeated experimentation and archaeological application has demonstrated that isotopic values are rarely altered post-mortem (Fraser *et al.* 2013). In the case of $\delta^{15}N$, both charring and contamination (Fraser *et al.* 2011; 2013; Styring *et al.* 2013; Vaiglova *et al.* 2014) have been shown to increase values, with untreated samples tending to be around 1‰ higher than those pre-treated (Fraser *et al.* 2013; Vaiglova *et al.* 2014). It is always preferable to take account of a site's unique depositional environment, but at Lower Callerton no depositional conditions were encountered that might indicate likely high levels of contamination. The results from untreated Lower Callerton samples can be considered robust in relative terms and if compared, in absolute terms, to other sites the $\delta^{15}N$ values should be considered slightly elevated.

The $\Delta^{13}C$ results for the three Neolithic samples show values around 19‰ for barley and 18‰ for wheat (Fig. 2.18). Experimental studies have demonstrated that $\Delta^{13}C$ above 17‰ for wheat and 18‰ for barley indicate crops for which water availability was a non-limited growth factor, and likely indicate that the plant was not stressed (Araus *et al.* 1997; Wallace *et al.* 2013). All three Neolithic samples from Lower Callerton provide values above these thresholds. For nitrogen, whilst the base level of soil $\delta^{15}N$ is unknown, it is often in region of 0–2‰ (Bakels 2019), and so plant values of greater than 3–4‰ have been taken as indicative of some manuring and values greater than 6–7‰ of intensive manuring. At Lower Callerton, the barley sits in the moderate manuring range, and the wheat samples are in the higher range (Fig. 2.18). Whilst the sample size here is very limited the results do correspond well to the broader picture of Neolithic agriculture. The prevailing view of Neolithic agriculture in north-west Europe is one of intensive practices (also known as 'garden agriculture') in which large amounts of time (*e.g.* tillage, weeding) and resources (*e.g.* manure, water) are invested to ensure a good yield (Bogaard 2004; 2005). This can be thought of as a highly attentive approach to farming, in which food security is linked to the careful tending of crops, which in turn necessities high amounts of human (rather than animal) labour and occupation in close proximity to arable land. This model contrasts with extensive agriculture, in which attentiveness is sacrificed for the cultivation of larger areas, usually with a greater assistance of animal labour. The Lower Callerton isotope results indicate that crops were not under water stress and were manured, with wheat likely benefitting more so than barley.

The palaeoenvironmental record's context

The precise chronology that emerged from the radiocarbon dating of cereal grains from the pit cluster provided some unexpected results. Pits 0189 (3760–3640 cal BC) and 0195 (3700–3630 cal BC) date to the earliest Neolithic in the northern England, associated with the Carinated Bowl phase of Neolithic expansion. Pit 0191 sits slightly to the east of the other pits in the same cluster, but dates to around two millennia later (1940–1740 cal BC). This places this one pit to the late Neolithic – early Bronze Age transition. This small number of pits thus seems to encompass the entire span of the British Neolithic. The absence of middle Neolithic evidence is also of note given the argued collapse of crop agriculture following the early Neolithic boom, from which recovery was not until the late Neolithic (Stevens and Fuller 2012; 2015; Timpson *et al.* 2014; Whitehouse *et al.* 2014; Bevan *et al.* 2017). The extent to which this 'collapse' is an artefact of research bias, however, remains uncertain (Bishop 2015a; 2015b).

The similarity of the cereal assemblage at Lower Callerton for the earlier Neolithic pits to that of southern England is, given the early date, not unexpected. The initial wave that brought Neolithic activities to Britain is thought to have swept up the eastern seaboard of England rapidly. An intense debate continues as to whether this wave was propagated by pioneer settlers from continental Europe or adoption by native inhabitants (Bogaard and Jones 2007; Sheridan 2010), with the ferocity of this debate recently inflamed by ancient DNA evidence interpreted as indicating large-scale population replacement at the start of the Neolithic (Brace *et al.* 2019). In either case, given the rapidity with which domesticated crops were introduced means there was little opportunity for agriculture to be acclimatised to the environments of Britain, and so it may be premature to expect to see changes in the composition of the crops that were cultivated.

The coincidence of a late Neolithic pit being placed in close proximity to a cluster of early Neolithic pits is difficult to ignore. Whilst an analytical error, and erroneous date, cannot be entirely excluded, there is presently no reason to suspect the veracity of the dates. And yet, the implication that a pit was added to the cluster some two millennia later is extraordinary. The pits do appear to have cultural significance, in that their form and contents are consistent with the British picture of pits having been places of deliberate deposition. The contents of these pits are seemingly mundane, representing the normal detritus of unexceptional activities (Ray and Thomas 2018, 180–4). Yet the diversity and nature of the contents hints that these features are contexts of deliberate placement, rather than happenstance deposits of waste. For example, amongst the plant remains only crop *product* (grains – the consumed part) are present, and the less valuable by-products (chaff and weed seeds) are absent. This contrasts with the abundance of hazel nutshell, the by-product of this wild resource.

The interpretation and nature of Neolithic pits varies across Britain, and they likely represent the material remains of varied behaviours and processes (*e.g.* Garrow 2011). Neolithic pits do, however, often share an apparent association with consumption (Ray and Thomas 2018, 178), including possible associations with commensality (Hayden 2001). The inter-mixing of non-food associated artefacts may, however, indicate that deposits in pits represent shared experience in a broader sense. Perhaps representing the coming together of distinct groups for finite periods, and the deposits representing the output of that collaborative encounter. If true, the revisiting of the deposits some two millennia later implies a persistence in the cultural value of this place. Perhaps the later deposits commemorated the past (albeit probably unknown) events evidenced by the first pits, creating layers of narrative upon the landscape.

Palaeoenvironmental summary

The Neolithic plant remains of Lower Callerton attest to complex human-plant interactions from the early beginnings of the Neolithic in Britain. The composition of cereal crops and stable isotope evidence provide rare glimpses of agricultural activity in northern England's Neolithic. Though the sample size is modest, the range of crops and their management is consistent with economies to the south – relying on a mix of wheat and barley, both of which are grown under intensive regimes. Both wild and domesticated plant resources are used and seemingly, purposefully deposited. Whilst the initial acts of deposition were themselves likely imbued with cultural significance, there is the tantalising possibility that this significance was maintained or resurrected long into the Neolithic future.

Prehistoric pits and hidden features

The recovery of a small quantity of Mesolithic lithics from Morley Hill attests to the potential longevity of activity developing into the Neolithic. Prehistoric activity at Morley Hill spanned three main periods represented by a scatter of Mesolithic flints and cherts, a Neolithic axehead, and an early Bronze Age barbed and tanged arrowhead. These all suggest a general level of activity, whilst not providing any solid evidence of related features beyond the pit into which the axehead was intentionally deposited. The majority of pre-Iron Age activity comprised residual material likely left scattered on the ground surface until incorporated into Iron Age features. This contrasts with the group of pits and ditches identified at Lower Callerton which indicate repeated episodes of deposition and potentially the longer-term development of boundaries. The identification of hidden earlier prehistoric features at sites with intense and complex phases of later settlement is problematic. At both Morley Hill and Lower Callerton their identification relied on limited chronologically distinctive artefacts and the detailed programme of radiocarbon dating.

The Neolithic pits at Lower Callerton are comparable with those found across Britain and exemplify the duality of pits as both signifiers of occupation but also common ritualised practise (Anderson-Whymark and Thomas 2012). The pits in Area 1 and Area 2 are grouped and appear to represent repeated visitations to the same location to conduct a similar range of activities from the early to later Neolithic. The pits contained pottery, lithics and rich environmental assemblages with both cereals and wild resources. The inclusion of both wild resources and cereals, including barley and in some cases emmer wheat, is a common feature of pits across the region (Waddington 2011, 296). The isotopic analysis of cereal grains from the pits indicated that the Neolithic occupants at Lower Callerton were engaging in complex subsistence strategies involving cultivation regimes that included manuring. The importance of cereal cultivation may be reflected in the depositions with only grains recovered from the pits. The ritualised aspect of the pits is reflected in the artefacts with the early Neolithic assemblage including rare examples of the use of organic temper. The seemingly purposeful deposition of selected material within the pits may indicate they are linked to specific activities or significant events.

The picture of Neolithic Northumberland has largely been built on the discoveries made to the north in the Tweed Valley, particularly the Midfield Basin, with sites such as Cheviot Quarry, Thirlings and Lanton Quarry coming to the fore when discussing settlement (Waddington 2011). A range of pits have been identified including those associated with small lightweight post-built structures at Thirling (Miket *et al.* 2008), Bolam Lake (Waddington and Davies 2002), Cheviot Quarry North and South (Johnson *et al.* 2008) and Lanton Quarry (Waddington 2009). The extent to which these sites represent activity across the region is uncertain with the diversity of Neolithic activities likely reflecting the variety of upland and lowland landscapes. On the Northumberland Coastal Plain, the prehistoric features uncovered at St Georges Hospital, Morpeth, are comparable to those at Lower Callerton. The excavation of an extensive Iron Age site at St Georges Hospital, Morpeth, revealed an early Neolithic pit, a late Neolithic pit containing Grooved Ware,

a Beaker pit and a group of early Bronze Age pits. The group of seven closely spaced early Bronze Age pits contained coarse-ware pottery with carbonised food residues adhering to the exteriors (ARS Ltd 2016, 19). The pits were interpreted as midden pits resulting from repeated deposition representing longer-term activity or episodic visitation (*ibid.*). Across the Northumberland Coastal Plain the extent to which the Neolithic pits represent the fleeting visitations of mobile groups, seasonal occupation or more long-term settlement is unclear.

In addition to the prehistoric pits, an earlier enclosure was also identified at St Georges Hospital. Enclosure 1, interpreted as an early Bronze Age stock enclosure, measured 9 × 19 m in diameter and was radiocarbon dated to 1751–1621 cal BC (SUERC-66312; ARS Ltd 2016, 20). The enclosure is similar in form to the smaller truncated enclosure, Enclosure 0048, within Area 1 at Lower Callerton, which was also ovoid in shape but measured *c.* 7 × 3 m in diameter. Further boundaries were also identified within Area 1 interpreted as Bronze Age in date representing the earliest phase of land division. The tentative identification of Bronze Age boundaries may link activities occurring on the coastal plain with changes in land division more clearly observed in upland areas (Frodsham 2004, 27). The identification of early boundaries on the Northumberland Coastal Plain is difficult but late Bronze Age pit alignments have been excavated at Iron Age sites including Shotton Northeast, Blagdon Park and Fox Covert (Hodgson *et al.* 2012, 185). The extent to which Iron Age settlement aligned to pre-existing boundaries is debatable but in several instances there appears to be a relationship (*ibid.*). While no pit alignments were identified at Lower Callerton or St Georges Hospital, the presence of earlier features indicates the long-term significance of specific locations. The long-term significance of some locations, in the case of Lower Callerton from the early Neolithic, adds further intrigue to the eventual abandonment of many sites in the later Iron Age.

Note

1 Note on authorship: The lithic assemblage was catalogued and assessed by Rebecca Devaney. Hugo Anderson-Whymark prepared the publication text.

3

The Iron Age settlements at Morley Hill

The Iron Age settlement at Morley Hill Farm comprises three sites: Morley Hill Enclosure 1 (MHE1), Morley Hill Enclosure 2 (MHE2: Area A), and Morley Hill Enclosure 3 (MHE3: Area D) with neighbouring unenclosed settlement (Area C; Fig. 3.1). The sites were subject to a series of investigations which included the excavation of trial trenches between MHE2 and MHE3 to identify further possible boundaries (Headland Archaeology 2018; Fig. 3.2). The presence of several areas of activity offered the opportunity to explore not only individual site development but relational chronologies between neighbouring enclosures. The construction of detailed chronological frameworks was challenging due to limited stratigraphic relationships, artefactual evidence and poor organic preservation. The programme of radiocarbon dating was intended to target the structures, enclosure ditches and other significant features, with the aim of constructing comparable chronological frameworks for the individual enclosures. Unfortunately, very limited material suitable for radiocarbon dating was recovered due to the poor preservation of carbonised material. During the initial assessment, a total of 19 samples, comprising a variety of materials, were sent to the Scottish Universities Environmental Research Centre (SUERC). Of the 19 samples, 11 failed due to insufficient carbon, reflecting the poor quality of organic preservation across the sites (Table 3.1).

Upon review of the available evidence and with comparison to sites across the region, the sites were determined to have been in use in the following order:

Morley Hill Enclosure 2

↓

Morley Hill Enclosure 1

↓

Morley Hill Enclosure 3

The evidence suggests that Morley Hill Enclosure 2 is potentially the earliest in the sequence. The relationship between Enclosures 1 and 3 is less certain as the chronological evidence is unclear and paired broadly contemporary settlements are not uncommon across the region (Hodgson *et al.* 2012). The nuances are discussed in more detail in this chapter, where the excavation results are presented in the proposed order in an effort to show the changing and developing picture of settlement activity at Morley Hill.

Morley Hill Enclosure 2

Morley Hill Enclosure 2 was identified during earlier phases of geophysical survey and trial trenching as a rectilinear enclosure surrounding a series of four structures and associated features (AD Archaeology 2013; 2014; 2015; ASDU 2017a). Topsoil was removed from a 0.96 ha area to reveal the entire enclosure and partially expose a length of ditch extending to the north-west from the main enclosure (Fig. 3.3). The excavations revealed evidence for Iron Age occupation with structures of varying sizes. The palaeoenvironmental samples contained a limited quantity of material suitable for radiocarbon dating resulting in only two dates from the site.

Rectilinear enclosure and associated ditches

Morley Hill Enclosure 2 was defined by a sub-square enclosure ditch surrounding an area of 1760 m² (Fig. 3.4). The 3.5 m wide entrance was centrally located along the southern side of the enclosure providing the only access point to the interior. The enclosure ditch measured 3.5–5.5 m in width and survived to an average depth of 1.7 m. The excavation of five main sections revealed a similar profile with steep sides and a rounded base. The ditch initially infilled gradually, likely the result of erosion and water-borne silting, before being almost completely backfilled by a series of possible slumping events (Figs 3.5 and 3.6). The lower ditch fills were primarily composed of silty clays from which a small assemblage of animal bone

Table 3.1 Samples from Morley Hill submitted to SUERC for radiocarbon dating

Lab ID	Feature	Context	Material Type	Radiocarbon Age (BP)	δ¹³C (‰)	Calibrated date (95% confidence)
Morley Hill Enclosure 2						
SUERC-83347 (GU49591)	Structure 14	(0018) Uppermost fill of gully [0013]	Cereal Grain: indeterminate	2165 ± 29	−25.3%	360–60 cal BC
SUERC-83348 (GU49592)	Structure 17	(0034) Single fill of gully [0033]	Charcoal: non-oak	6843 ± 29	−27.5%	5800–5650 cal BC
Morley Hill Enclosure 3						
SUERC-83345 (GU49589)	Terminus of enclosure ditch of MHE3	(05067) Secondary fill of enclosure ditch [5065]	Cereal Grain *Hordeum vulgare* (Barley)	2014 ± 29	−25.0%	100 cal BC–cal AD 110
SUERC-83346 (GU49590)	Small pit, could be associated with Structure 19 or Structure 21	(5456) Fill of pit [5455]	Burnt bone: animal	2484 ± 29	−29.8%	780–480 cal BC
SUERC-83350 (GU49594)	Post-hole within Structure 5	(5201) Fill of post-hole [5200]	Burnt bone: animal	1868 ± 29	−19.7%	cal AD 80–240
SUERC-83351 (GU49603)	Isolated feature possibly extension of gully [5344]	(5337) Fill of gully [5336]	Cereal Grain: *Triticum dioccum* (Emmer wheat)	2033 ± 29	−21.9%	150 cal BC – cal AD 70
SUERC-83355 (GU49604)	Structure 18	(5349) Fill of gully [5348]	Cereal Grain: *Triticum dioccum* (Emmer wheat)	38421 ± 330	−22.0%	40770–40210 cal BC
SUERC-87249 (GU51566)	Burnt residue from pottery recovered from the fill	(5339) Fill of hollow [5338] by Structure 18	Burnt residue from pottery	2972 ± 24	−28.1%	1280–1110 cal BC

was recovered. The animal bone assemblage included long bone fragments with possible butchery marks, recovered from the eastern terminus. The initial fills were overlain by a series of redeposited clay layers consisting of compact mottled mid-orangish brown and mid-blueish grey sandy clay. The presence of a corresponding bank comprising upcast ditch material is proposed similar to the bank visible at MHE1. The bank may have formed the source of the redeposited material which slumped back into the ditch following the abandonment of the site. However, no distinctive tip or slump lines were identified at either side of the ditch during the excavations.

Two contemporary ditches extended outwards from the north-western and eastern corners of the main enclosure. These ditches were shallower and narrower in depth than those of the main enclosure, and may have aided in drainage and functioned as boundaries. The presence of ditches adjoining settlement enclosures is noted at other sites in the region such as Phase 4 at Pegswood Moor (Proctor 2009) and East Wideopen (ASDU 2014b). These potentially served a function in the wider landscape for navigation and forming networks of interconnected settlements, both literally and figuratively connecting these communities.

Structures

The interior of the main enclosure was heavily plough-truncated, however, the remains of four ring-gullies survived, comprising the last traces of structures 14, 15, 16 and 17. Several pits, post-holes and truncated gully segments were also identified within and around these structures. There is little evidence to suggest which, if any, of these structures may have been contemporary or whether they were all constructed independently.

Structures 15 and 16

Structure 15 was defined by a ring-gully encircling an area 6.5 m in diameter with a south-east-facing entrance. The ring-gully measured 0.44 m in width and 0.19 m in depth with a regular, steep-sided profile. It contained two fills of sandy clay with the lower containing rare charcoal inclusions and a small amount of undiagnostic abraded fired clay. Two shallow pits were recorded within Structure 15 which do not clearly relate to the structure. Structure 15 was identified as the earliest structure within MHE2 as the southern terminus was truncated by the ring-gully of Structure 14.

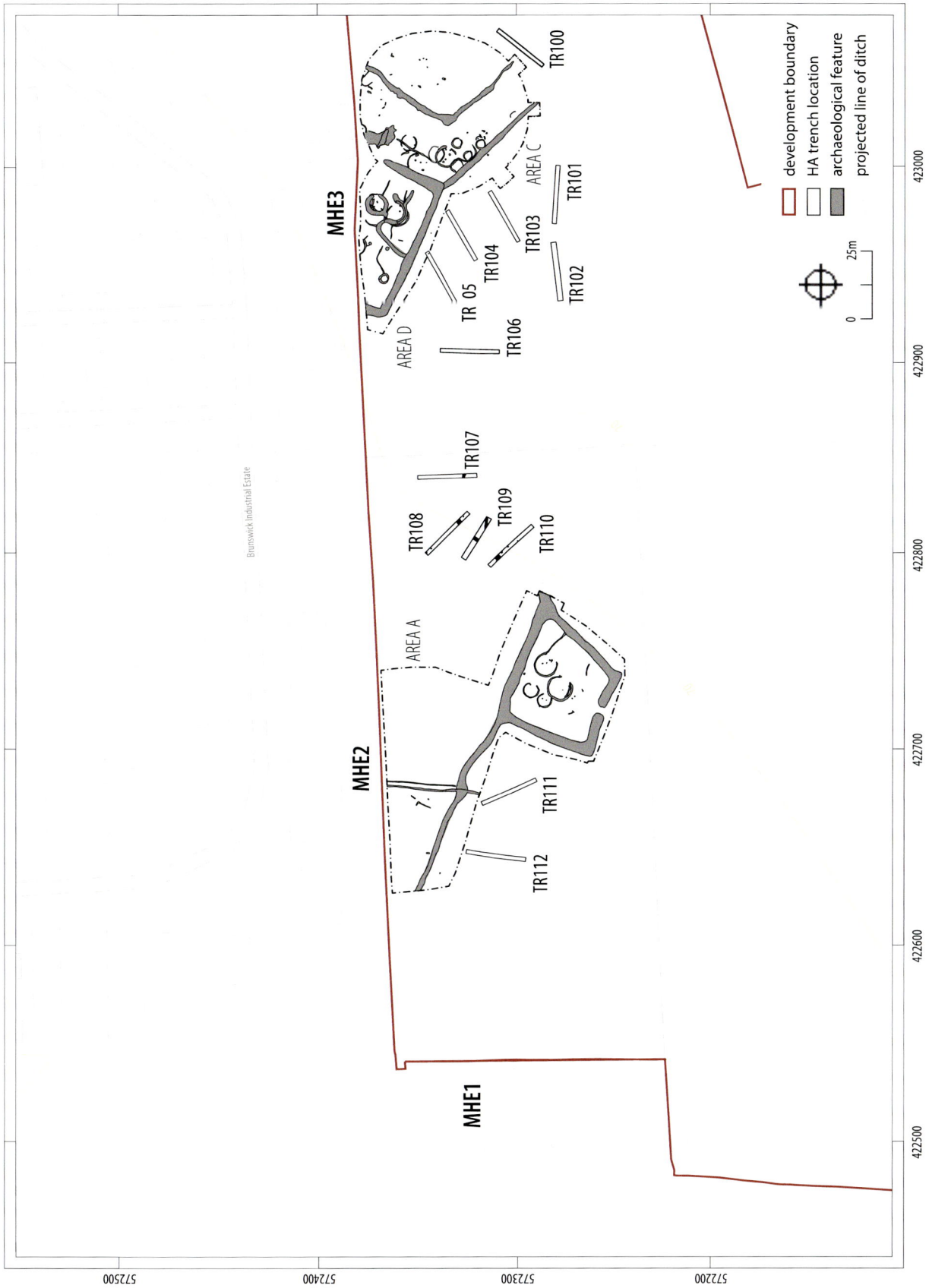

Figure 3.1 Site plan of Morley Hill

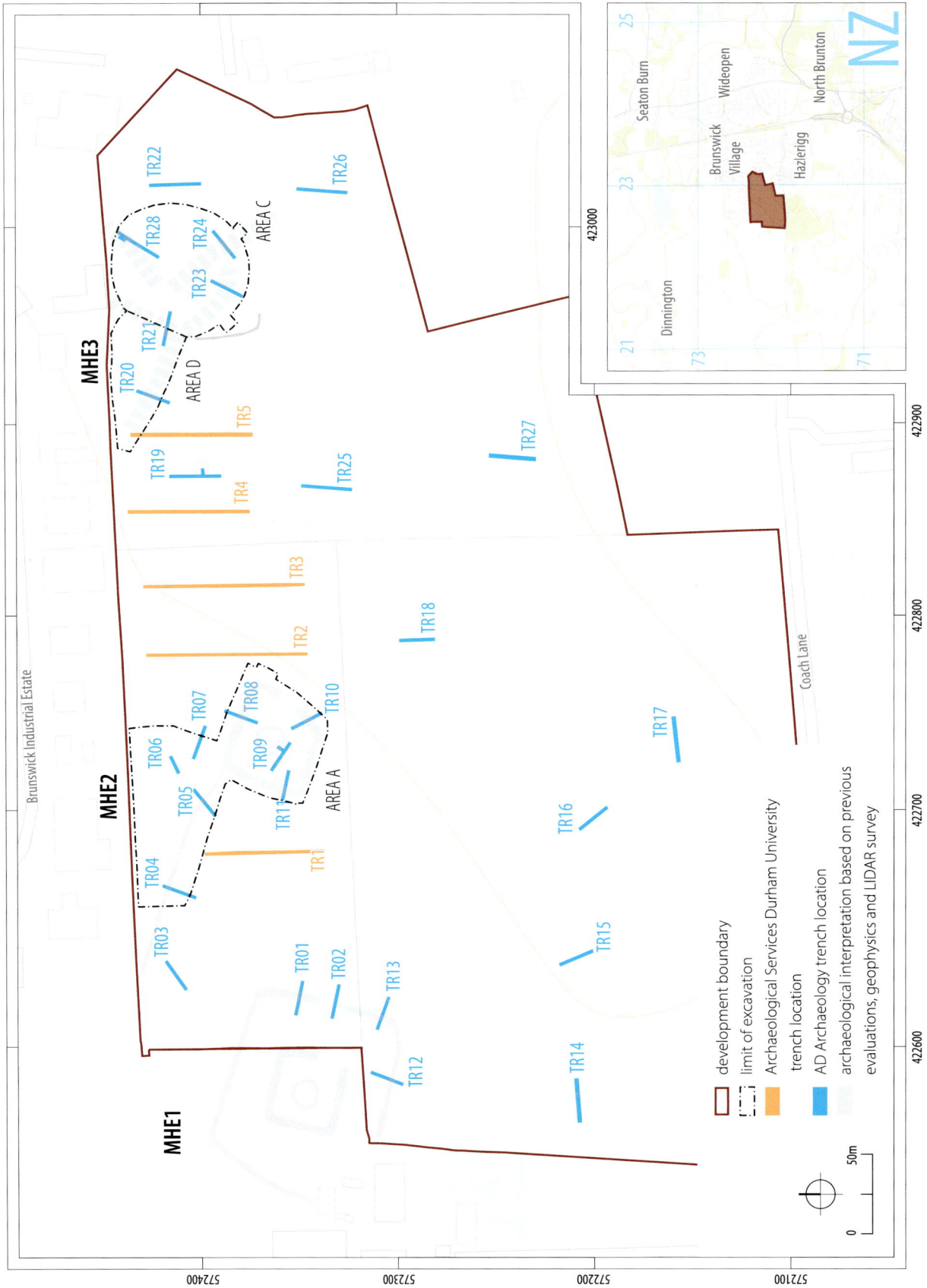

Figure 3.2 Previous investigations at Morley Hill

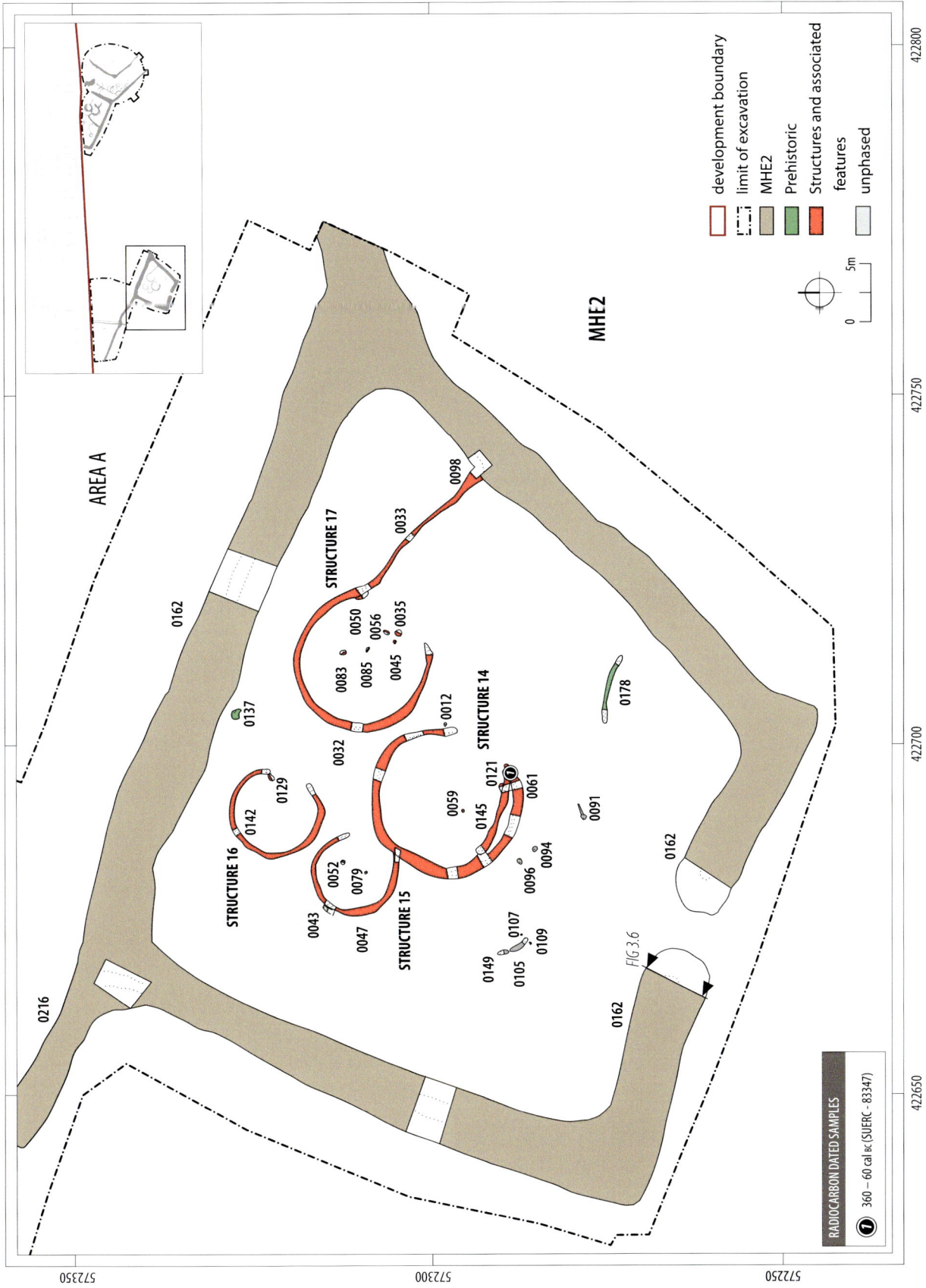

Figure 3.3 Morley Hill Enclosure 2

Figure 3.4 East-facing view of Morley Hill Enclosure 2

Structure 16 was located 0.8 m to the north-east of Structure 15 and was very similar in form. It comprised a penannular ring-gully enclosing an area 7.1 m in diameter also with a 3.3 m wide south-east-facing entrance. The ring-gully measured 0.44 m in width and 0.2 m in depth with a U-shaped profile and contained fills of brown silty clay. A single small post-hole that measured 0.7 × 0.19 m in diameter and 0.21 m in depth, was located immediately adjacent to the northern ditch terminus. It is unclear whether the structures formed a contemporary phase of activity due to the lack of stratigraphic relationship. As Structure 15 is truncated by the larger Structure 14 it is possible they represent an earlier phase of activity or the relationship is more complex with each representing a smaller paired structure located off-centre within the enclosure.

Structure 14

Structure 14 was the largest within MHE2, was located centrally within the enclosure, and measured 12.5 m in diameter with a south-east-facing entrance 4.8 m in width (Fig. 3.7). The ring-gully measured 0.4–1 m in width and 0.3–0.5 m in depth with a U-shaped profile. The sequence of fills appeared to indicate a process of deliberate backfilling as opposed to gradual infilling due to water-borne erosion. An assemblage of animal bone

and teeth was recovered from the fill of the ditch along with a small amount of fired clay. The southern edge of the structure showed signs of a realignment or repair, with a length of curvilinear gully, Gully 0145, overlying the main ring-gully. No internal features or post-holes were evident.

Two radiocarbon dates were taken from material found within this secondary gully during the initial evaluation and the excavation. A charred cereal grain produced a radiocarbon date of 360–60 cal BC (SUERC-83347) and a fragment of hazel nutshell returned a date of 375–180 cal BC (SUERC-61974; AD Archaeology 2015). The consistency of these dates is helpful in securing the phasing of this enclosure, assuming this central structure, potentially a roundhouse, formed the focal point of the enclosure.

Structure 17

Structure 17 was located to the north-east of Structure 14 and comprised a ring-gully measuring 10.4 m in diameter with a south-east-facing 4.6 m wide entrance. The gully measured up to 0.8 m in width, 0.33 m in depth and contained two deposits of gradually infilled sediment. The gully extended for 13.5 m downslope from the northern terminus, truncating a small post-hole, to connect with the main enclosure ditch. The

Figure 3.5 West-facing view of eastern terminal of enclosure ditch MHE2

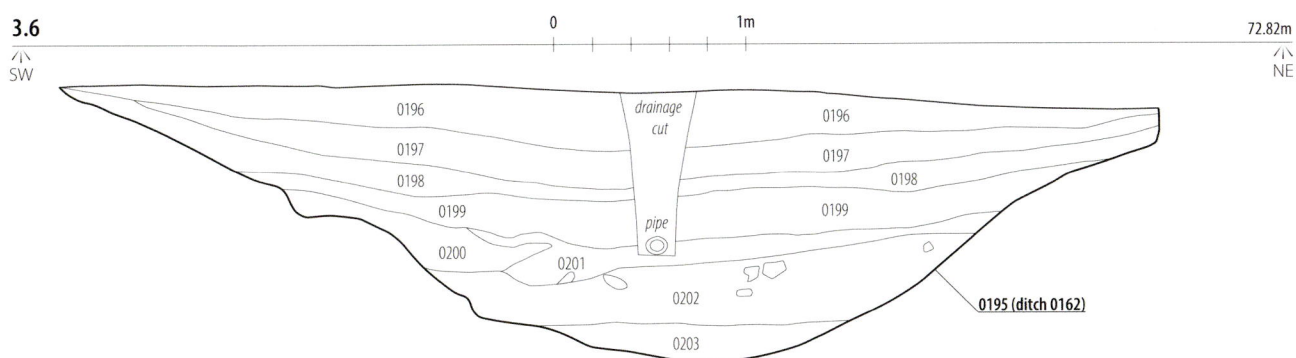

Figure 3.6 Section through Ditch 0162 (MHE2)

extension appears to have functioned as a drainage channel diverting water away from the structure or working area. The shallower gully of Structure 17 may be the drip-gully of a further roundhouse or define a working area perhaps surrounding a small structure or wind-break. Two post-holes were identified within the structure along with three shallow pits. Post-hole 0035

was located at the centre of the entranceway and measured 0.5 m in diameter and 0.35 m in depth (Fig. 3.8). A post-pipe was visible in the section along with angular stones potentially used for packing. A further post-hole, 0083, was located to the north within the structure. The three shallow pits contained fills of grey silty clay from which no finds were recovered giving no indication of

Figure 3.7 North-west-facing view of Structure 14

Figure 3.8 North-west-facing view of Post-hole 0035

their function or whether they represented activities relating to the structure.

Other features

Three post-holes and three short ditch sections were recorded to the south of Structure 14. These features may have been fences and small animal pens used to segregate livestock from dwellings and activity areas. However, the truncated and disparate nature of the evidence precludes any certainty.

Summary

Stratigraphically only one relationship could be identified between the structures within Morley Hill Enclosure 2, with the gully of Structure 14 truncating that of Structure 15. Due to the paucity of stratigraphic and dating material, a more precise phasing was not possible to establish. It is possible that the structures were constructed as pairs comprising the main structure and an ancillary structure or space. The placement of Structure 14 at the centre of the enclosure mirrors the configuration of settlements identified at Burradon (Jobey 1970), West Brunton and East Brunton (Hodgson *et al.* 2012) amongst many other settlements across the region. Structure 17 was also interpreted as contemporary with the main enclosure due to its likely functional interaction in managing water around this structure. However, the alignment of the structure entrances is highly unusual as none are aligned to the south-west-facing entrance of the enclosure. Typically, the entrances of contemporary structures are aligned to that of the surrounding enclosure (Hodgson *et al.* 2012). Several explanations can be proposed, including the possibility that the structures are not contemporary with the enclosure, the entranceway was relocated during the life of the settlement, or another influence taking precedent over the alignment of the structures. Given the lack of stratigraphic and dating evidence it is possible that the structures are either earlier than the enclosure or a later addition. There are examples of enclosures without structures, such as Shotton North-East (Hodgson *et al.* 2012, 97–103), however, given the placement of Structure 14 and the gully of Structure 17 at some point they appear to be contemporary. There is no excavated evidence for the relocation of the entranceway but as settlements are not static and there is no evidence for the longevity of occupation here it cannot be fully discounted. The alignment of all four structures with south-east-facing entrances is typical of this period (Pope 2003, 175) and is the trend across all three settlements at Morley Hill. The alignment of the structures may simply reflect prevailing wind or light as opposed to conforming to the enclosure alignment.

Morley Hill Enclosure 1

Morley Hill Enclosure 1 survives as an upstanding earthwork and was not excavated as part of archaeological investigations conducted by Headland Archaeology. The site has been extensively surveyed and was subject to trial trench excavations by AD Archaeology in 2015 (2013; 2015; Fig. 3.2). The results of this work are summarised here to allow the site to be compared to the neighbouring enclosures.

The geophysical survey (magnetometry) conducted in 2013 by AD Archaeology produced magnetic anomalies matching the features identified on the ground and in aerial photography (AD Archaeology 2013, 7). The double rectilinear enclosure was clear with the inner ditch found to measure *c.* 11 m in width with a *c.* 4 m wide external bank. The outer ditch measured *c.* 7 m in width and could be traced to the north (*ibid.*). A semi-circular feature, *c.* 8.3 m in diameter, was identified within the inner enclosure with an adjoining gully, reminiscent of Structure 7 (MHE2), extending to the main enclosure ditch. A further smaller curvilinear feature was also identified along with five fragmentary curvilinear features between the inner and outer enclosure (*ibid.*).

The outer enclosure ditch was further explored during the trial trench evaluation, with four trenches excavated across the ditch (1, 2, 12 and 13; AD Archaeology 2015). The excavation revealed the external ditch to measure 4–5 m in width and 1.30–2 m in depth with a series of clayey silt fills (*ibid.*). A sample of charcoal from the lower fill (Deposit 107, Trench 1) was radiocarbon dated to 47 cal BC–cal AD 120 (95.4% probability; SUERC-61970; *ibid.*, 5). A layer of scattered stone or cobbles was identified in Trench 2 located over the entranceway of the outer enclosure indicating the presence of a metalled or cobbled surface (*ibid.*, 7). Two features were identified outside the enclosure ditch, a gully with a shallow U-shaped profile

and a cut containing lenses of burnt clay with flecks of charcoal (*ibid.*, 8). The features outside the enclosure hint at activity extending to the east towards MHE2.

The enclosure is similar in form to Morley Hill Enclosure 2 with the settlement interpreted as farmstead rather than a larger village-type settlement. The single radiocarbon date suggests the site may broadly date to the later Iron Age and may post-date MHE2. However, this is far from conclusive with the chronological development of the site and the relationship to MHE2 remaining unclear. No further excavation was undertaken for Morley Hill Enclosure 1 as it was outside the footprint of the development works. It remains an upstanding earthwork within the landscape providing insights into features that do not survive at other sites, primarily the presence of an external bank.

Morley Hill Enclosure 3

Morley Hill Enclosure 3 was located 165 m to the east of Morley Hill Enclosure 2, with a large portion of the projected site truncated to the north by a modern industrial estate (Fig. 3.9). The site was identified during the trial trench evaluation (AD Archaeology 2015; ASDU 2017a; Fig. 3.2) with the subsequent excavations by Headland Archaeology uncovering a *c.* 0.82 ha area. The excavation revealed the main enclosure, associated ditches and a series of structures. Further ditches were identified to the east overlain by a series of structures, pits, post-holes and gullies relating to an unenclosed phase of settlement. Samples taken from features across the site provided a total of six successful radiocarbon dates from the enclosure ditch and structures. The enclosure ditch and associated ditches will first be described before presenting the multiple phases of structure development within the enclosure.

Rectilinear enclosure and associated ditches

The main enclosure ditch was excavated at four sections and measured *c.* 4–5m in width and 1.5 m in depth with steep sides and a rounded base (Fig. 3.10). The ditch contained a sequence of silting events with the primary fill characterised as mid-greenish-grey clay overlain by a series of grey sandy clay deposits. Cereal grain retrieved from the fill (5067) of the entrance terminus of the ditch yielded a single radiocarbon date of 100 cal BC–cal AD 110 (SUERC-83345; Fig. 3.11). The date provides a broad marker for activity associated with the enclosure.

The entrance to the enclosure was located along the south-eastern side, with only the southern terminus seen within the limits of the excavation. A large shallow hollow containing a layer of stones, Surface 5060, was located immediately to the east of the entrance (Fig. 3.12). The feature may represent the remains of a surface which served to provide ground stability for the increased flow of activity across the main route to and from the enclosure. Similar surfaces were observed

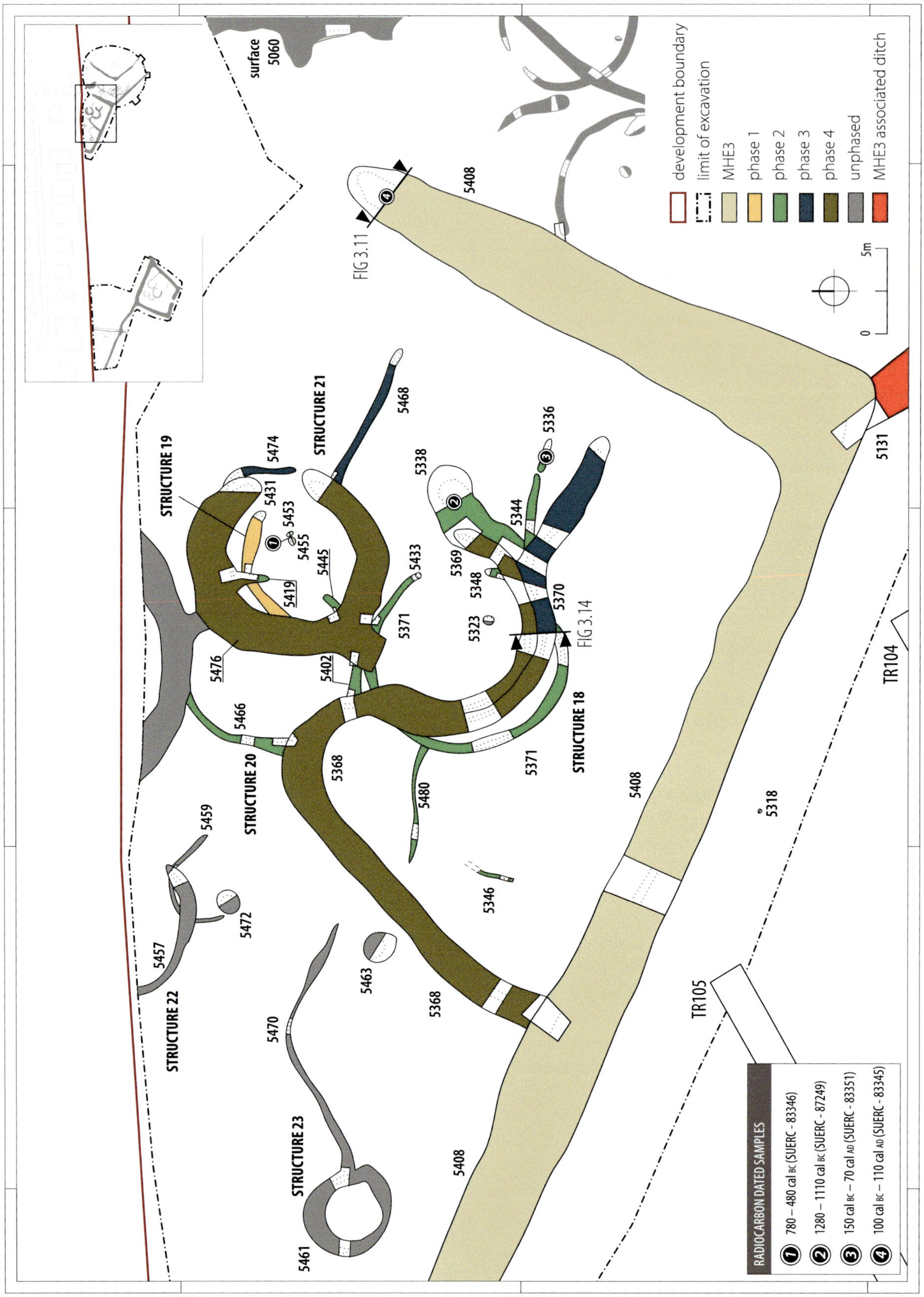

surface 5060

5408

FIG 3.11

development boundary
limit of excavation
MHE3
phase 1
phase 2
phase 3
phase 4
unphased
MHE3 associated ditch

5m

0

5131

STRUCTURE 21

5468

5474

STRUCTURE 19

5431

5453

5455

5445

5419

5476

5402

5466

STRUCTURE 20

5433

5371

5368

5459

5472

5457

STRUCTURE 22

5470

5463

STRUCTURE 23

5368

5461

5338

5336

5344

5369

5348

5370

5323

FIG 3.14

STRUCTURE 18

5371

5480

5346

5408

5318

TR104

5408

TR105

RADIOCARBON DATED SAMPLES

1 780 – 480 cal BC (SUERC - 83346)
2 1280 – 1110 cal BC (SUERC - 87249)
3 150 cal BC – 70 cal AD (SUERC - 83351)
4 100 cal BC – 110 cal AD (SUERC - 83345)

Figure 3.9 Morley Hill Enclosure 3

422980

422970

422950

422930

572340

572340

572330

Figure 3.10 East-facing view of Morley Hill Enclosure 3

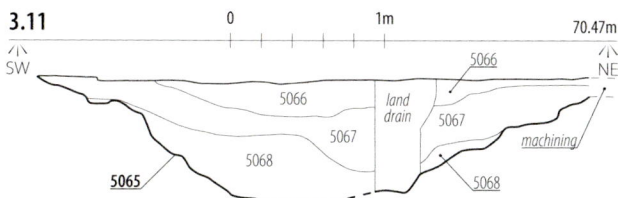

Figure 3.11 North-east-facing section through MHE3 main enclosure ditch southern entrance terminus

Figure 3.12 West-facing section of the metalled surface at MHE3

at the entrance to the main enclosure of Morley Hill Enclosure 1 (AD Archaeology 2015) and the entrance to sub-enclosure C at Blagdon Park 2 (Hodgson *et al.* 2012, 35).

A large linear ditch, 5131, adjoined the south-eastern corner of the main enclosure ditch extending for *c.* 63 m to the south-east beyond the limit of excavation. The ditch measured *c.* 3 m in width and 0.4 m in depth, significantly shallower than the main enclosure ditch. As at MHE2, the ditch may be contemporary extending the settlement or pointing to wider landscape boundaries. The ditch may have also functioned as an overflow for the main enclosure, directing excess water downslope away from the

settlement. At the intersection between this ditch and the main enclosure, this ditch was cut higher, which would have had the effect of causing the retention of water to a certain level within the main enclosure, before acting as an overflow. This would indicate that a level of water retention within the enclosure ditch was intentional and sought after.

An additional ditch to the east appeared to mirror the L-shape formed by the east side of the main enclosure ditch and Ditch 5131 (see Fig. 3.16). Ditch 5072 measured 95 m in length, 0.6 m in depth and was irregular in width, averaging 1.7 m. The ditch petered out to the east with no clear-cut terminus identified which may be due to truncation or design. No dating evidence was recovered from the silty clay fills but as it reflected the outline of the ditch to the west, these may have been contemporary features. The function of the ditch was unclear but as a defined L-shaped feature it may have been paired with the ditch to the west to control livestock and direct movement directly towards the enclosure entrance. If the ditches both extended further beyond the excavated area they may have acted to delineate spaces and movement within the wider landscape. Many similar sites such as Brenkley, West Brunton and Morley Hill Enclosure 1 show signs of double-ditched enclosures, with the outer ditches of some extending far beyond the bounds of the inner enclosure. Due to the truncation of MHE3 and its surrounding landscape to the north, it is difficult to ascertain whether this site followed a similar pattern, but it is likely that it is related to the wider landscape division at MHE3.

Structures

The remains of eight structures were extant within the interior of the main enclosure, and are assumed to relate to the enclosure phase of MHE3 (Fig. 3.9). The stratigraphy suggests multiple building events and indicates the majority of structures did not exist concurrently. Several phases of structure construction were identified, with Structure 19 appearing to be the earliest (Phase 1) truncated by Structure 20 which was stratigraphically phased with Structure 18 (Phase 2). Overlying and intercutting several of the structures, were a series of linear and curvilinear gullies (Phase 3). The fourth and final phase of activity within MHE3 comprised Structure 21 which was defined by the widest ring-ditch. A number of structures, gullies and discrete features were also identified within the enclosure, primarily located to the north-west of the phased features. They remained unphased due to a lack of stratigraphic relationships with ground conditions precluding further excavation. Structures 22 and 23 fell into this category, as well as the two unexcavated structures.

Phase 1
STRUCTURE 19

Structure 19 was defined by a short, c. 7 m long, shallow curvilinear gully c. 0.6 m wide and 0.2 m deep. This gully was interpreted to be the northern edge of a structure, c.7 m in diameter, with an entrance to the east. Truncation by later phases made the further analysis of this structure difficult. Structure 19 was truncated by both Structure 20 and Structure 21 and appears to be stratigraphically the earliest structure of MHE3.

Phase 2
STRUCTURE 18

Structure 18 comprised a narrow, shallow ring-gully 0.45–0.6 m wide and 0.16–0.24 m deep enclosing a space just over 10 m in diameter with an east-facing entrance 3.8 m in width (Figs 3.13 and 3.14). The fragments of animal bone recovered from the brownish-grey silty clay fill (5335) exhibited butchery marks. Cereal grain retrieved from the fill of the southern terminus was radiocarbon dated to 40770–40210 cal BC (SUERC-83355) providing an erroneous date and no indication of the date of the feature. Animal bone retrieved from the ring-gully failed to yield a radiocarbon date due to insufficient carbon (GU49600). A sub-circular post-hole, 5433, was identified within the northern terminus of the gully.

A series of gullies extending from Structure 18 suggest the presence of small internal enclosures directly associated with the structure. A narrow gully, 5480, extended for c. 7 m from the western side of Structure 18, which along with Ditch 5346, potentially formed a small rectangular enclosure. Ditch 5346, aligned north–south, was heavily truncated with no direct relationship to Gully 5480. To the east of Structure 18 were a further two gullies, 5344 and 5336, that formed the eastern section of the small enclosure. Gully 5344 measured 0.47 m in width, 0.2 m in depth and 4 m in length with its relationship to Structure 18 truncated by later phases. Gully 5336 measured 1.42 m in length, 0.33 m in width and 0.27 m in depth and contained degraded wood fragments within the single fill. Cereal grain from the fill yielded a radiocarbon date of 150 cal BC–cal AD 70 (SUERC-83351).

Pit 5338 was located immediately east of the entrance to Structure 18 and comprised a large shallow hollow measuring 6.58 m by 2.52 m and 0.1 m in depth. It contained a very stony mid-orangey-brown clayey-sand fill (5339) from which indeterminate burnt and unburnt animal bone and a significant quantity of dolerite-tempered pottery were recovered. Burnt residues from a sherd of an almond-rimmed jar were radiocarbon dated to the middle to late Bronze Age 1280–1110 cal BC (SUERC-87249). This raises the possibility that the pit, and at least some of the pottery recovered from the site, relates to an earlier phase of activity. The pottery form and fabric are long-lived and in use from the late Bronze Age through the Iron Age and potentially later. The pottery could be considered residual with the hollow representing the remains of a surface covering an eroded area in the front of the structure.

STRUCTURE 20

Structure 20 was located directly north of Structure 18 and comprised a narrow, shallow ring-gully similar in form and size to Structure 18. It measured c. 0.6 m wide and

Figure 3.13 South-east-facing section of gullies relating to Structure 18 and curvilinear ditches 5368 and 5370

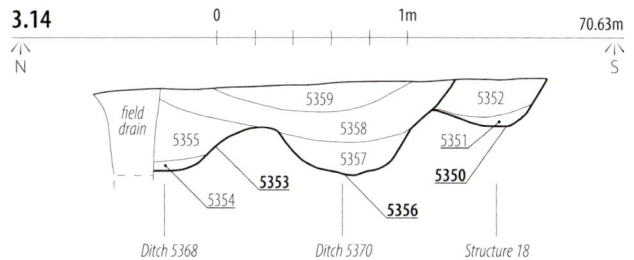

Figure 3.14 West-facing section through Structure 18 and curvilinear ditches 5368 and 5370

0.2 m deep encircling an area 9.7 m in diameter with an east-facing entrance 3.5 m in width. It was truncated by Structure 21 and showed no similar signs of elaboration as seen from Structure 18.

Phase 3

Phase 3 comprised a series of gullies that truncated the earlier structures and were in turn severely truncated by later structures. Curvilinear Ditch 5370 truncated Structure 18 and may represent an earlier phase of a drainage channel (Figs 3.13 and 3.14). The ditch measured 1.6–1.86 m in width and 0.67 m in depth and was visible curving for *c.* 11 m before extending straight and terminating to the east. The ditch contained between two and five fills of grey clay resulting from water erosion. Animal bone retrieved from three separate contexts within the ditch all failed to yield radiocarbon dates due to insufficient carbon (GU49597; GU49598; GU49599). Three sherds of pottery and fired clay were recovered from the backfill (5340) of the ditch, and included fragments with vitrified surfaces indicating they may be from a hearth or furnace lining. The ditch was truncated by Ditch 5368 which continued until it funnelled into the main enclosure ditch to the south-west. Ditch 5370 may represent an earlier drainage channel recut in later phases surrounding an open area or workspace.

To the north of Gully 5370 was a linear gully truncated by Structure 21 (Phase 4). Gully 5468 measured 8.5 m in length, 0.52 m in width and 0.18 m in depth, running slightly off an east to west line, in rough alignment with the earlier Gully 5344. It terminated prior to reaching the enclosure ditch, leaving an opening 5.5 m in width. Immediately north was a further small section of gully situated to the east of structures 19 and 20 and truncated by Structure 21. Gully 5474 measured 3.7 m in length,

0.55 m in width and 0.28 m in depth and along with Gully 5470 may indicate the presence of further enclosure or divisions within the main enclosure.

Phase 4

STRUCTURE 21

Structure 21 was located to the north of Structure 18 and truncated structures 19 and 20 (Fig. 3.15). It comprised a wide curvilinear ditch measuring up to 2.4 m in width, 0.5 m in depth and encircling an area 7.7 m in diameter, with an east-facing entrance, 2.6 m in width. The ditch was significantly wider than the earlier gullies potentially suggesting a different type of roundhouse or structure. A very limited artefactual assemblage was recovered from the fill of the ditch comprising fired clay fragments, fuel ash slag and two sherds of pottery. Two pits were located within the area of the structure, both measuring approximately 0.5 m by 0.3 m in diameter and 0.2 m in depth. Pit 5455 contained fired clay and burnt animal bone which yielded a single radiocarbon date of 780–480 cal BC (SUERC-83346) indicating the pits may relate to an earlier structure, not Structure 21. No gullies, post-rings or internal features were identified to aid in understanding this structure further.

DITCH 5368

Structure 18 was truncated by two curvilinear ditches, 5368 and 5369. These curvilinear ditches converged and formed a reverse S-shape in plan (Fig. 3.15), before turning south-west to join up with the main enclosure, replacing the curvilinear Ditch 5370 of phase 3. These ditches may relate to water management in the later phases of the enclosure, diverting water from within the enclosure into the main enclosure ditch, draining the water away downslope to the south-east.

Unphased

STRUCTURE 22

Structure 22 was located *c.* 8 m west of Structure 20 and extended beyond the limit of excavation to the north. It comprised a shallow curvilinear gully that measured 0.6 m in width, widening to 1 m in width towards the

Figure 3.15 Pre-excavation plan shot of structures 18–21 with S-shaped gully

southern terminal, and 0.3 m in depth. It had a projected diameter of 8.5 m with a south-east-facing entrance. In form the structure is reminiscent of structures 18 and 20 suggesting it may have formed part of the same phase of activity.

The ring-gully cut a C-shaped gully, 5459, which may have functioned as an earlier wind-break type structure. Another probable ring-gully was located immediately to the north of Structure 22, continuing beyond the limits of the excavation. This structure was not investigated due to flooding in this area.

STRUCTURE 23

Structure 23 was located 15 m south-west of Structure 22 and comprised a circular ring-gully up to 1m wide, 0.5 m deep and surrounding an area 3.5 m in diameter with no apparent entrance. This feature has been interpreted as a possible auxiliary structure or building relating to agricultural activities as it would likely have been too small in diameter to act as a dwelling and was isolated from other structures.

Gully 5470 extended 16 m eastwards from the ring-gully and may have functioned as a boundary in a similar fashion to those identified in Phases 2 and 3, delineating internal spaces within the enclosure.

OTHER FEATURES

Several other pits and small sections of linear gullies were identified throughout the enclosure that could not be linked directly to any of the phases of settlement activity. They may have resulted from a myriad of settlement activities and structures; however, their exact function has remained elusive.

Summary

Morley Hill Enclosure 3 showed a level of increased complexity and variety in both its structures and internal layout, suggesting this phase of activity comprised more than just a single farmstead or dwelling, but rather had multiple phases with multiple, complex activities ongoing at the same time. If the missing 60% of the interior of the enclosure had contained a similar density of archaeological remains, it would have indeed been a highly active settlement with a complex system of water management, zoning of activity and structural continuity.

Unenclosed settlement

A series of twelve ring-gullies and related pits, post-holes and linear gullies were located to the east of Morley Hill Enclosure 3 (Fig. 3.16). These features were bounded

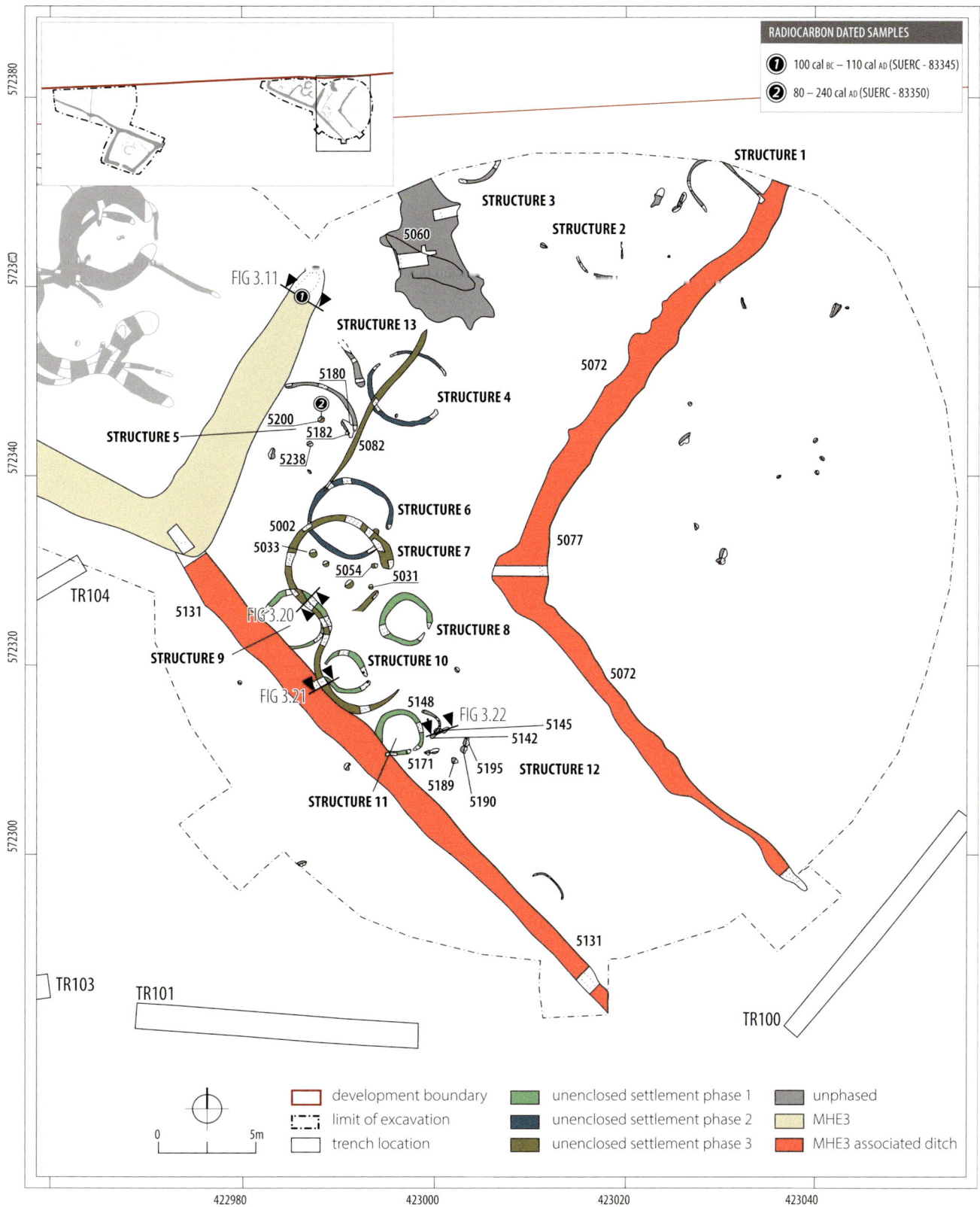

Figure 3.16 Morley Hill unenclosed settlement

between the main MHE3 enclosure, the adjoining ditch and the parallel L-shaped ditch, which formed a 20–30 m wide corridor heading north-east and south-east. The area was heavily plough truncated and many of the curvilinear gullies were shallow, indistinct and often difficult to identify on the ground due to the similarity of the fills to the natural silt and clay deposits in the area. While a large number of the stratigraphic relationships are unclear, three broad phases of activity are proposed. Phase 1 comprised a cluster of four small structures, structures 8–11, which have been interpreted as specialist or ancillary structures. Two larger structures, 4 and 6, located to the north of the Phase 1 structures formed Phase 2. Phase 3 consisted of a single large structure, Structure 7, and a connected curvilinear ditch segment and associated linear ditch extending north-east from the structure. Several pits were identified within Structure 7, and post-holes were found within its entrance. Unphased activity included a series of curvilinear ditches, at least one identified as a structure (Structure 5), and a series of post-holes forming Structure 12.

Phase 1: Structures 8–11

Structures 8–11 were circular or oval features, smaller and less regular in plan than those of later phases. This group of features were characterised by extremely narrow entranceways often under 1 m wide. The form of the structures is unusual and perhaps indicative of an ancillary or specialist function. There is a level of ambiguity in the phasing of this group as the relationship with Ditch 5131 is unclear due to plough truncation. The features could belong to an earlier initial phase of unenclosed settlement pre-dating the rectilinear enclosure and adjoining ditches. However, they could also plausibly relate to this later phase of settlement as a distinct group of ancillary structures.

Structure 8 comprised a circular ring-gully enclosing an area 4.5 m in diameter with a south-east-facing entrance measuring 1.29 m wide. The ring-gully measured 0.7 m in width, 0.15 m in depth and contained a deposit of gradually infilled silty clay. The ditch termini contained large stones which were unusual for deposits across the site. The ring-gully was truncated by ploughing, particularly to the south, with no relationships to other structures present.

Structure 9 was located to the west of Structure 8 and was heavily truncated by Structure 7 but survived as a sub-circular gully surrounding an area 6 m in diameter. It appeared to have a west-facing entrance but the full plan of the structure was not clear due to the presence of Ditch 5131 on its southern side. The ring-gully measured 0.7 m in width, 0.38 m in depth, and contained two silty clay deposits. The irregularity of the gully indicated that it did not form the perimeter of a roundhouse but may nonetheless have acted as a slot for a fence to bound a small working area.

Structure 10 was located to the south-east of Structure 9 and comprised two heavily truncated gullies forming a sub-circular space 3.6 m in diameter with a possible east-facing entrance measuring 0.4 m in width. These gullies averaged 0.6 m in width and 0.15 m in depth and contained silty clay deposits with occasional charcoal inclusions. Post-holes were located within the terminal ends of each gully indicating the presence of entrance posts. The small post-holes measured c. 0.20 m by 0.11–0.16 m in diameter and 0.17–0.23 m in depth. The southern side of the structure was truncated by Structure 7 and a modern field drain.

Structure 11 was located to the south-east of Structure 10 and comprised a circular ring-gully 4 m in diameter. The structure had a south-east-facing entrance measuring 0.2 m in width, though this gap may not have been wide enough to act as a functional entrance (Fig. 3.17). The gully measured 0.5 m in width and 0.2 m depth with silty clay fills. The structure's relationship to Ditch 5131 was unclear due to similarities in the fills, raising the question as to whether this structure may have pre-dated MHE3. A curvilinear gully, 5148, was located to the east of Structure 11, which may have formed a small semicircular extension to the structure, however, no direct evidence of association was present.

Phase 2: Structures 4 and 6

Structure 4 comprised a ring-gully formed from two sections which together enclosed a space 7 m in diameter. It had an east-facing entrance which measured 3.8 m in width, with a further gap separating the two gully segments to the north-west, created by modern plough truncation. The gully measured 0.5 m in width and 0.2 m in depth and contained two water-lain deposits of sandy clay. A single pit was identified within the interior of the structure but showed no evidence of function. Structure 4 was cut by Gully 5082, a narrow linear gully that related to Phase 3 activity.

Structure 6 was located to the south of Structure 4 and comprised a narrow, shallow ring-gully 7.5 m in diameter, with a south-east-facing entrance measuring c. 1.5 m in width. The ring-gully measured 0.3 m in width, 0.1 m in depth and contained silty clay fills with occasional daub fragments. It was very similar in size and shape to Structure 4, suggesting these may have been contemporary structures. Structure 6 was cut by linear Gully 5082 to the north-west and the ring-gully of Structure 7 to the south.

Phase 3: Structure 7

Structure 7 comprised a curvilinear ditch measuring c. 9.5 m diameter, with an east-facing entrance measuring 2.5 m in width (Fig. 3.18). The ditch measured up to 0.8 m in width, 0.4 m in depth and contained silted deposits that contained sherds of a Roman cooking pot, alongside an intrusive Mesolithic microlith. Two post-holes, 5054 and 5031, located within and parallel to the entrance of the structure indicate the presence of internal structural features in contrast to the surrounding structures.

Figure 3.17 Entrance of Structure 11

Figure 3.18 North-west-facing pre-excavation shot of Structure 7

Three further pits were located within the interior of the Structure. Pit 5033 was the most significant measuring 0.84 m by 0.82 m and 0.16 m deep with two sandy fills. The upper fill contained burnt daub possibly resulting from the destruction of the structure. Structure 7's gully cut the ring-gullies of Structure 6, structures 9 (Figs 3.19 and 3.20) and 10, and Ditch 5131 (Fig. 3.21).

To the north of Structure 7 was a linear ditch starting 2.5 m from its northern edge. Ditch 5082 measured 20 m in length, 0.87 m in width and 0.27 m in depth, tapering off towards its north-eastern end. It is possible that this ditch functioned to move water down the slight slope to the north, away from Structure 7. It showed signs of similarity in plan to the fence lines identified within MHE3, however, it was much wider and less steeply sided. To the south, a curvilinear ditch appeared to adjoin to the ring-gully potentially forming an external space delineated by the ditch. This truncated Structure 10 and Ditch 5131 suggesting that Structure 7 may have been a later phase addition outside the main enclosure or post-dates the main phase of enclosure activity.

Unphased

Structures 1, 2 and 3

Structures 1, 2 and 3 were located at the northern edge of the stripped area, showing no clear association to the main cluster of structures or each other. All contained single natural infilling deposits.

Structure 1 comprised a narrow, shallow ring-gully 0.4 m in width, 0.3 m in depth and enclosing a space 4.4 m in diameter. The northern gully extended beyond the main structure, leading into Ditch 5072 indicating its function in moving water and keeping the inner space dry. This supported the idea that this may have formed

an external area for activity within the bounds of the gully, though any evidence of tasks or structure within has been lost.

Structure 2, to the south-west of Structure 1, comprised the heavily truncated remains of a ring-gully formed of several shorter segments, with a projected diameter of *c.* 4 m. The gully measured 0.21 m in width and 0.07 m in depth and showed no clear indication of function – it was too truncated to ascertain whether this definitively formed the footprint of a structure.

Structure 3, to the north-west of Structure 2, was a section of narrow ring-gully measuring 0.4 m in width and 0.2 m in depth which continued beyond the northern limit of excavation and appeared to have a south-west-facing entrance. It had an estimated diameter of 5.5 m. Structure 3 showed more similarities to the structures of the main cluster to the south, likely representing a structural gully similar to Structures 4 and 6, albeit at a smaller scale.

Structure 5

Structure 5 was located to the south-west of Structure 4 and comprised a C-shaped gully section which is thought to have been the heavily truncated remnants of a roundhouse with a projected diameter of 10 m. It measured 0.3 m in width, 0.1 m in depth and contained a natural silting deposit with mammal bone fragments.

A post-hole at the eastern end of the gully indicated that the entrance to the roundhouse may have been east facing. Three further post-holes and two pits were

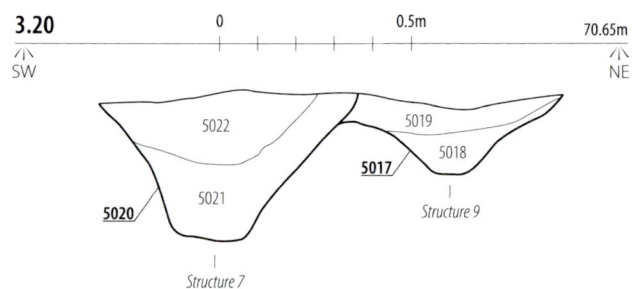

Figure 3.20 South-east-facing section through Structure 7 and Structure 9

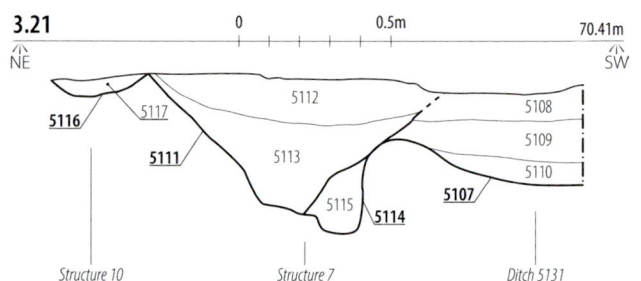

Figure 3.21 North-west-facing section through Structure 7, Structure 10 and Ditch 5131

Figure 3.19 North-east-facing shot of Structure 7 and its intersection with Structure 9

located to the south of the gully within the footprint of the structure and formed no definite pattern; it is possible that post-holes 5182, 5200 and 5238 formed two sides of a four-post structure with a 2.5 m spacing, though the missing fourth post was not present to form the south-eastern corner – this may be coincidental and would preclude these posts from relating to Structure 5. Animal bone retrieved from the fill (5201) of post-hole 5200 yielded a single radiocarbon date of cal AD 80–240 (SUERC-83350), though the relationship of these post-holes to the structure was not certain, and as such this date cannot be used to ascertain the date of Structure 5.

Structure 12

To the south-east of Structure 11 and located at the furthest extent of the unenclosed settlement were seven pits. The pits were grouped as intercutting pairs potentially defining a square or sub-circular area. These were roughly sub-circular in plan and may have indicated the location of two phases of a small four-poster structure (Fig. 3.22) with the irregular shape due to episodes the recutting and replacement. However, no definitive signs of posts or characteristic post-holes were identified. As such, the feature can only be considered a speculative four-poster structure, similar to that proposed within Structure 5.

Other features

Another short gully identified as Structure 13 was located to the west of Structure 4, measuring 5 m in length, 1 m in width and 0.35 m in depth. It is possible that this gully was the truncated remains of a roundhouse, with some similarity to Structure 7, although the extent of the truncation made this difficult to ascertain. If it had completed a full ring it would have intersected with the footprint of Structure 5 and potentially the main enclosure of MHE3.

To the east of the unenclosed settlement and beyond the L-shaped Ditch 5072 were 13 heavily truncated pits of various sizes and shapes, showing no clear function,

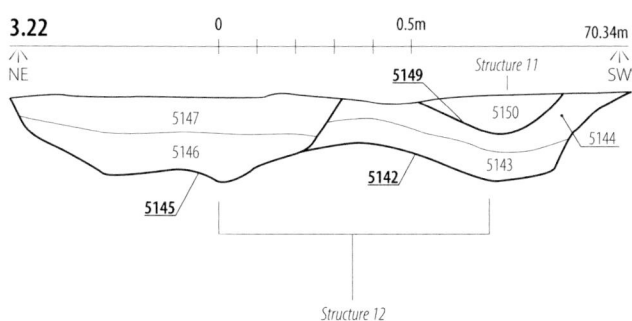

Figure 3.22 North-facing section of pits 5142, 5145 of Structure 12 and Gully 5149 of Structure 11

dating material or association to the settlement activity to their west.

Summary

The structures located outside the enclosure present a challenge in defining the chronological and spatial relationships. The features have been broadly grouped as an unenclosed settlement, yet several scenarios can be proposed to explore their relationship to the main enclosure. Firstly, it is possible that several of the features pre-date the enclosure and relate to an earlier phase of unenclosed settlement. The relationship between the Phase 1 structures and Ditch 5131 is unclear and the projected circumference of Structure 5 places it against the edge of the enclosure. The location of Structure 5 would place it under an external bank if the presence of such a feature is proposed. If the presence of an external bank is considered the majority of the structures would be located beyond the bank and potentially aligned to it (Structure 9, Structure 7, Structure 6 and Structure 4). The linear north-east to south-west alignment of the structures is striking as all are located *c.* 7.5 m from the enclosure ditch edge. This leads to the second proposal in which several of the structures are potentially contemporary with the use of the enclosure representing an extension of activity or ancillary structures passed before entering the main enclosure. Finally, a limited number of features likely post-date the main phase of activity at the enclosure, perhaps truncating now shallow ditches and eroding but visible banks. This phase is best indicated by Structure 7 from which 59 sherds of Roman pottery, dating to the first or early second century, were recovered. The late date from the post-hole within Structure 5 may hint at further features potentially cut into an eroded or no longer visible bank. The structures undoubtedly represent several phases of development with the broad phasing and summary providing some interpretive possibilities and challenges.

The finds assemblage

The finds assemblage from Morley Hill was limited, comprising a small amount of pottery, fragments of fired clay and industrial waste.

Pottery

Alex Croom

The assemblage from Morley Hill consists of 66 sherds of local traditional ware weighing 2.993 kg and 59 sherds of Roman pottery, weighing 0.114 kg. There was a minimum of eight late Bronze Age – Iron Age pots and a single Roman vessel. The pottery was quantified in its fabric categories by weight, sherd count and estimated vessel equivalents (EVEs, *i.e.* percentages of surviving rim diameters).

Table 3.2 Pottery by context

Feature	Fill	Cat. No.	Fabric	Wt (kg)	No.
Morley Hill Enclosure 3					
Pit 5338	5339	1	dolerite-tempered	0.820	21
		3	dolerite-tempered	0.224	6
		4	dolerite-tempered	0.048	1
Ditch 5370	5329	12	quartz-tempered	0.001	1
	5332	7	dolerite-tempered	0.008	1
	5342	9	dolerite-tempered	0.010	1
Structure 19	5475	13	quartz-tempered	0.002	1
	5475	6	dolerite-tempered	0.036	1
Structure 21	5440	10	dolerite-tempered	<0.001	1
	5443	14	pebble-tempered	0.014	1
Morley Hill Enclosure 3: Unenclosed Settlement					
Ditch 5131 [5107]	5108	8	dolerite-tempered	0.077	1
Structure 3	5089	5	dolerite-tempered	0.338	6
Structure 7	5006	11	dolerite- and quartz-tempered	0.007	1
	5014	2	dolerite-tempered	1.388	24
	5014, 5015	15	Roman Grey Ware	0.114	59

Location and distribution

The pottery from Morley Hill was predominantly recovered from Morley Hill Enclosure 3 from features within and outside the enclosure. The largest quantity of sherds from within the enclosure was recovered from Pit 5338. A total of 28 sherds from a jar with an almond-shaped rim, a jar with a plain rim, and a jar with a flat-topped plain rim (Catalogue Nos. 1, 3, 4) were recovered. A limited number of sherds were recovered from Ditch 5370 immediately to the south. A scrap of a possible quartz-tempered local ware sherd (Catalogue No. 12) and two body sherds of dolerite-tempered local ware were recovered (Catalogue Nos. 7 and 9).

Further sherds were recovered from the sequence of structures to the north, with a single body sherd of dolerite-tempered ware and a sherd of quartz-tempered local ware (Catalogue Nos. 6 and 13) recovered from Structure 19. A very small sherd of Dolerite-tempered local ware (Catalogue No. 10) and a single body sherd of pebble-tempered local ware (Catalogue No. 14) were recovered from Structure 21 which truncated Structure 19.

To the east of the site, outside the enclosure, a single body sherd of dolerite-tempered local ware (Catalogue No. 8) was recovered from Ditch 5131 with a further six body sherds (Catalogue No. 5) recovered from Structure 3. A large quantity of sherds totalling one body sherd of dolerite- and quartz-tempered local ware (Catalogue No. 11) and 24 sherds from a jar with an incurved plain rim of dolerite-tempered local ware were (Catalogue No. 2)

were recovered from Structure 7. A further 59 sherds of a Roman grey ware cooking pot (Catalogue No. 15) were also recovered from Structure 7.

Late Bronze Age to Iron Age wares

The use of coarse fabrics tempered with very large fragments of crushed rock (usually up to *c.* 12 mm) to make simple-rimmed vessels with little or no decoration first started in the late Bronze Age and continued through the Iron Age and into the Roman period (Johnson *et al.* 2008, 216–17). Most of the vessel forms produced did not alter over the whole of this period and so cannot be closely dated. The pottery was probably mainly made by individual settlements for their own use and therefore came from numerous different sources of clay, but as there was a widespread practice of using particular forms of temper the fabrics can be allocated to distinct 'groups' that followed the same tempering traditions whilst coming from different geographical locations. Although four fabric groups are represented in the assemblage, 94% by sherd count is in fabric 1.1.

LOCAL TRADITIONAL WARE FABRIC 1.1, DOLERITE-TEMPERED

Handmade black micaceous fabric, usually with one or both surfaces oxidised, with ill-sorted angular fragments of dolerite, up to 12 mm across, that frequently project from the surface. Frequently used for large, thick-walled vessels (*c.* 15–20 mm thick).

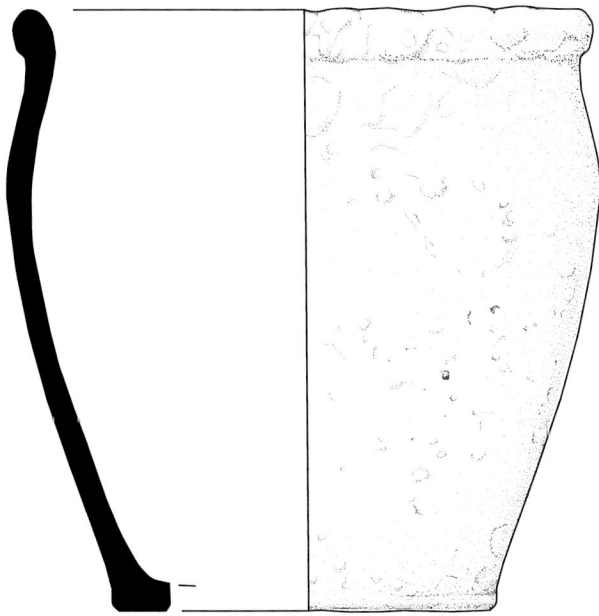

Figure 3.23 Jar with almond-shaped rim (Cat. No. 1)

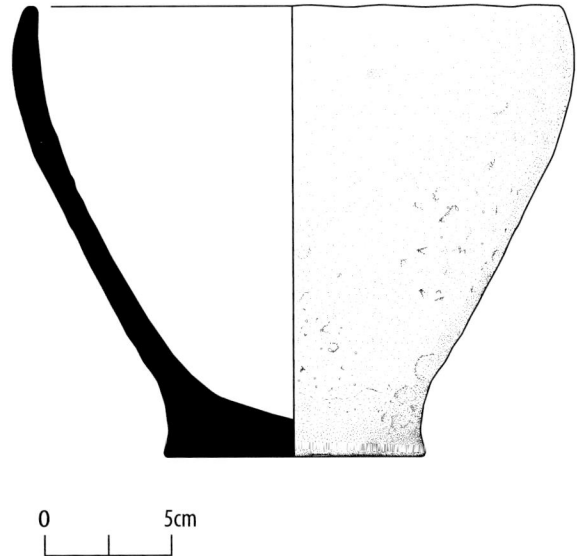

Figure 3.24 Jar with incurved plain rim (Cat. No. 2)

Catalogue No. 1. (Fig. 3.23) Jar with an almond-shaped rim. The temper is well-sorted and plentiful, without any of the extremely large fragments common in this fabric. The colouring is patchy, but is generally more oxidised near the base; a couple of sherds have a thin black layer on the interior, and there are heavily burnt remains on the exterior of the rim and upper body. There are twenty-one rim, body and base sherds, mainly making up three large fragments, which do not join. Only about 10% of the rim survives, which means the diameter and sit of the pot are only approximate (5339). Wt: 0.820 kg.

Catalogue No. 2. (Fig. 3.24) Jar with incurved plain rim. About half of the base and lower walls survive, but only about a third of the rim. The fragments do not join, but the profile can be reconstructed; for the combination of tapering incurved rim and flared base see Murton High Crags: Jobey and Jobey 1987, fig. 10, no. 4). Oxidised exterior surface near the base, which becomes more patchy towards the rim; there are also heavy burnt deposits on the upper part of the vessel. Twenty-four rim, body and base sherds, mainly making up two large fragments (5014). Wt: 1.388 kg.

Catalogue No. 3. (Fig. 3.25) Jar with plain rim and with a smoothed exterior surface. The interior surface is oxidised, apart from a narrow zone below the rim; the exterior is reduced, with some burnt deposits. This is a thick-walled vessel and there are a further four body

sherds 20 mm thick from the same context that might belong to this vessel, although these are oxidised on the exterior. Two rim sherds; less than 10% survives, so the diameter and sit of the vessel are approximate (5339). Wt: 0.244 kg.

Catalogue No. 4 (Fig. 3.26) Jar with a flat-topped plain rim. The exterior is buff/brown exterior and the interior pale orange and cream with the inclusions burnt red. There are some grass/straw impressions on the surfaces, especially on the exterior. One rim sherd; less than 10% of it survives so the original diameter is uncertain (5339). Wt: 0.048 kg.

Catalogue No. 5. Six thick-walled body sherds (18 mm), with some large inclusions up to 18 mm long (5089). Wt: 0.338 kg.

Catalogue No. 6. Thick-walled body sherd (max W: 23 mm) with oxidised exterior, light grey core and black interior surface (5475). Wt: 0.036 kg.

Catalogue No. 7. Thin-walled (12 mm) body sherd with oxidised exterior, buff margins and mid-grey core and interior (5332). Wt: 0.008 kg.

Catalogue No. 8. Body sherd with oxidised exterior. Heavy burnt deposits on interior (5108). Wt: 0.077 kg.

Catalogue No. 9. One base sherd, slightly flared (*cf.* no. 2 above). Oxidised exterior (5342). Wt: 0.010 kg.

Catalogue No. 10. Minute scrap, possible of fabric 1.1, but too small for certainty (5440). Wt: <0.001 kg.

LOCAL TRADITIONAL WARE FABRIC 3.1, DOLERITE- AND QUARTZ-TEMPERED

Black or dark grey fabric, often with one or both surfaces oxidised. As well as dolerite fragments there are smaller quartz inclusions, so the fabric has a glittering appearance due to the fine to very fine grains.

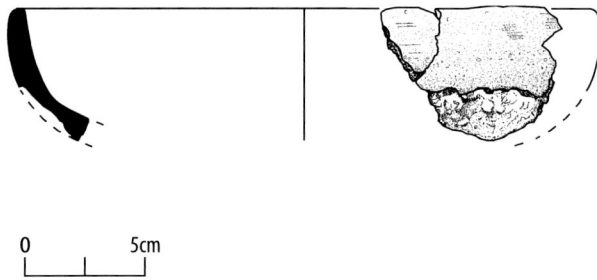

Figure 3.25 Jar with plain rim and with a smoothed exterior surface (Cat. No. 3)

Figure 3.26 Jar with a flat-topped plain rim (Cat. No.4)

Catalogue No. 11. Body sherd with oxidised exterior surface (5006). Wt: 0.007 kg.

LOCAL TRADITIONAL WARE FABRIC 4.1,
QUARTZ-TEMPERED

Fairly soft fabric, with dark grey core and brown to buff surfaces. White or semi-translucent quartz inclusions, including large fragments up to 7 mm across. The inclusions often break through the surface.

Catalogue No. 12. Scrap of quartz-tempered ware, probably fabric 4.1 (5329). Wt: 0.00 kg.
Catalogue No. 13. Small, thin-walled (8 mm) sherd with oxidised exterior (5475). Wt: 0.002 kg.

LOCAL TRADITIONAL WARE FABRIC 5.2,
PEBBLE-TEMPERED

Black or dark grey fabric, sometimes with one of both surfaces oxidised, with grey or black pebbles or angular stone fragments as temper. Other than the form of temper, it is similar in appearance to fabric 1.1, being usually thick-walled with often roughly finished surfaces and large fragments of projecting temper.

Catalogue No. 14. Body sherd (5443). Wt: 0.014 kg.

Roman wares

GREY WARE

Soft, sandy fabric with mid-grey exterior and core, cream interior margin and the patchy remains of the original mid-grey interior surface.

Catalogue No. 15. Up to 59 rim and body sherds of a grey ware cooking pot. First or early second century in date (*cf.* Carlisle: Swan *et al.* 2009, fig. 307, no. 152). The walls are very thin and in poor condition and many of the small pieces come from shattered sherds (5014, 5015). Wt: 0.114 kg.

Hearth or furnace lining

There is a small fragment of highly fired clay with one vitrified glossy black surface (5342).

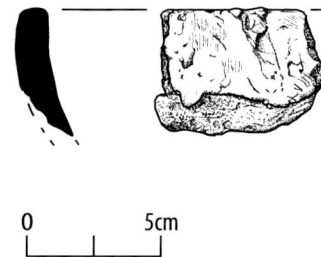

Discussion

Over 80% of the pottery came from just two features; large pieces of an almond-rimmed jar and sherds from two other vessels from the trampled area defined by Pit 5338 (MHE3) in phase 2 and large parts of a plain-rimmed jar and a Roman cooking pot from the ring-gully of Structure 7 in phase 3 of the unenclosed settlement. Both features contained vessels in dolerite-tempered ware (1.1), which appears in all phases, and is the only one of the local traditional fabrics to have produced substantial parts of vessels, including rim sherds. The other fabrics are only represented by body sherds and although it is assumed they are of a similar date to fabric 1.1, those without the distinctive use of large crushed rock temper could potentially be earlier in date.

Burnt residues on the almond-rimmed jar (Cat. No. 1) have been dated to the mid/late Bronze Age (Table 3.1). Like many vessel types of this period, it is a long-lived form, in use during both the late Bronze Age and Iron Age, and potentially longer. The rim form is not common and is more typical on Iron Age sites south of the River Wear (although still within the region where dolerite was commonly used for temper) than north of the Tyne (Evans 1995, fig. 5.6, form Hi; 50; there is also a more angular variant from Stanwick: Willis 2016, fig. 11.1, no. 2).

The other vessels (Cat. Nos. 2–4) are more typical forms, being wide-mouthed, thick-walled barrel- or bucket-shaped jars with incurving and flat-topped rims. These are the most common vessel form on late Bronze Age/Iron Age sites in the region (such as the local sites at East and West Brunton, Blagdon and Burradon: Hodgson *et al.* 2012, fig. 83; fig. 84, nos. 26, 28; Jobey 1970, fig. 8, nos. 4–6; fig. 9).

The presence of only a small quantity of Roman pottery is also typical of sites in the region that survived into the first or second century AD. While the occupants of the settlements acquired some Roman pottery they had no desire to use it in large quantities, and the Roman vessels never show the heavy encrustation of burnt materials so often found on the hand-built pottery, including many sherds in this assemblage. This may be because the Roman pottery was brought in simply as containers for some other commodity such as foodstuffs, or because its rarity within the settlement made it more suitable for use as tableware. It is also possible the small size or restricted shapes of the Roman vessels

Table 3.3 Pottery by fabric

Fabric	Fabric Group	Weight (kg)	No	EVE
Local traditional ware (LTW)				
Dolerite-tempered	1.1	2.969	62	64
Dolerite- and quartz-tempered	3.1	0.007	1	
Quartz-tempered	4.1	0.003	2	
Pebble-tempered	5.2	0.014	1	
Roman				
Grey ware		0.114	59	68
Total		3.107	125	132

were not suitable for the same purposes the hand-built vessels were intended for. Although they may have been used for cooking food, it is equally possible they were used for potentially messy activities that required larger, more open vessels, such as purifying animal fat or beeswax, the preparation of lanolin or soap, and the manufacture of adhesives from animal products or from birch bark tar (which may have also been used to line vessels).

Fired clay
Julie Franklin

A total of 134 fragments (438 g) of fired clay was recovered from features across the site (Table 3.4). The assemblage comprised undiagnostic abraded fragments with a limited number of identifiable fragments recovered from fill 5340 in Ditch 5370 and Structure 7. A fragment from Ditch 5370, located within Morley Hill Enclosure 3, had a vitrified surface indicating it may be from a hearth or furnace lining. A further fragment was identified as a possible hearth support. A fragment of a possible hearth support was also recovered from the fill of the ring-gully of Structure 7 located within the unenclosed settlement.

The assemblage was principally recovered from ring-gullies and gullies associated with the major structures. The undiagnostic sherds are similar in fabric and likely result from fired wattle and daub structures or pit linings.

Industrial waste
Julie Franklin

The industrial waste recovered from across the site comprised 36 g of vitrified fragments and <0.5 g of magnetic residues. The vitrified fragments can be characterised as fuel ash slags created through burning in the presence of siliceous material. Fuel ash slag can result from domestic hearths, ovens and industrial activity. The presence of magnetised gravel is representative of burning with the limited quantity of hammerscale and slag spheres, created during smithing or smelting, indicating no foci of industrial activity.

The palaeoenvironmental evidence
Michael Wallace

The Morley Hill palaeoenvironmental assemblage derived from 78 assessed samples and hand-collected remains. This yielded fewer than ten cereal grains, including barley (*Hordeum* sp.), spelt wheat (*Triticum spelta*), bread/club wheat (*Triticum* cf. *aestivo-compactum*) as well as cereal indeterminate grains. No chaff was recovered. A few weed seeds were found, which included mixed grasses (Poaceae) that likely represent weedy contaminants of cereal crop, and sedges (*Carex* sp.) and knotweeds (Polygonanceae) which are hardy seeds from plants most typically found in wet ground. The latter taxa may be weeds, but could have been collected in their own right as food, fodder or medicine (Cheij 1984; Chevallier 1996; Ertuğ 2000; Neef *et al.* 2012). A few other remains hint at a diverse economic base, including charred hazel (*Corylus avellana*) nutshell, indeterminate tuber fragments and indeterminate tree buds. Wood charcoal was dominated by oak, with the taxonomic identification of non-oak impossible due to impregnation with mineral deposits. The faunal assemblage was similarly constrained, with 30 features yielding an assemblage dominated by sheep/goat. Appreciable amounts of cattle were also present. Bones were of low and middle utility, and most likely represent butchery processing discard. Finally, a single horse tooth and two marine shells were also recovered. A combined discussion of the palaeoenvironmental evidence from both Morley Hill and Lower Callerton is presented in Chapter 4, further informed by the isotopic analysis.

Table 3.4 Quantification of fired clay by feature

Feature	Description	Total Weight (g)	Total Quantity
Morley Hill Enclosure 2			
Structure 14	Fired Clay	4	12
Structure 15	Fired Clay	7	14
Curvilinear Gully 0143	Fired Clay	0	1
Morley Hill Enclosure 3			
Ditch 5370	Fragment of hearth or furnace lining with vitrified surface.	8	1
	Fragment of possible hearth support with rounded edge.	16	1
	Fired Clay	175	22
Ditch 5368	Fired Clay	0	1
Ditch 5369	Fired Clay	46	4
Trample Area/Pit 5338	Fired Clay	26	5
Gully 5344	Fired Clay	24	1
Structure 18	Fired Clay	30	1
Structure 19	Fired Clay	9	10
Structure 20	Fired Clay	2	1
Structure 21	Fired Clay	7	6
Structure 22	Fired Clay	4	2
Pit 5455	Fired Clay	2	3
Pit 5462	Fired Clay	15	7
Gully 5474	Fired Clay	0	1
Morley Hill Enclosure 3: Unenclosed Settlement			
Structure 3	Fired Clay	14	8
Structure 4	Fired Clay	6	4
Structure 6	Fired Clay	7	9
Structure 7	Fired Clay	7	8
	Fragment of possible hearth support with right-angled edge.	18	3
Pit 5033	Fired Clay	1	4
Structure 8	Fired Clay	1	1
Ditch 5072	Fired Clay	9	1

4

The Iron Age settlements at Lower Callerton

The excavations at Lower Callerton revealed a multi-phase Iron Age settlement consisting of 53 structures, multiple enclosures and linear boundaries which extended beyond the excavated area (Fig. 4.1). The activity was concentrated within Area 2, which measured *c.* 4.6 ha, with the removal of the topsoil revealing a settlement extending over 2 ha. In addition to the large enclosure, a variety of structures were uncovered ranging from ephemeral ring-gullies to large ring-ditch defined structures displaying differing architectural traits (Fig. 4.2). The settlement pattern differs from that observed at Morley Hill, and others in the region, with no central rectilinear enclosure and few intercutting structures. A surprisingly limited artefactual assemblage was recovered as the site was found to be largely aceramic with the stone tool assemblage providing some insights into the activities taking place. The environmental assemblage, which included charred cereals, a diverse range of wood charcoal, and animal bone, was also relatively sparse. Despite this cereal grain samples recovered from the structures were subject to isotopic analysis, with the results offering further insights into agricultural strategies.

The expansive scale of settlement and the preservation conditions at Lower Callerton offered an opportunity to explore key questions of settlement development, tempo and longevity. An iterative programme of radiocarbon dating was employed resulting in a suite of 70 radiocarbon dates from targeted contexts (see Table 4.8). The sample selection process reviewed both the suitability of the material and the security of the context. The initial selection sought to target contexts representing events or specific activities, such as hearths, where the act of deposition, source of the material and therefore the interpretation of the date could be more closely defined. However, the number of such contexts was extremely limited. Samples from the enclosure ditches and ring-gullies were selected with the distribution dictated by the availability of suitable material. Where possible, samples were selected from roundhouses with stratigraphic relationships to aid in building relational chronologies. As the source of the infilled material in such contexts is less defined, multiple dates were obtained from features to combat questions of contextual security and provide a more robust chronological framework. The charcoal assemblage from the site was dominated by oak (*Quercus* spp) which was avoided, except in circumstances were roundwood could be identified, due to concerns surrounding old wood effect. Samples of alder (*Alnus* cf. *glutinosa*), hazel (*Corylus* cf. *avellana*) and birch (*Betula* spp.) were radiocarbon dated alongside samples of shorter-lived heather (*Calluna vulgaris*) and cereal grains (charcoal assemblage summarised in *The palaeoenvironmental evidence*).

Three broad phases of activity have been identified at Lower Callerton, based upon the limited stratigraphic sequences, spatial relationships and the results of the Bayesian modelling. Despite a large number of features, very few stratigraphic relationships could be established with many structures assigned to phases, particularly those relating to the pre-enclosure phase of activity, primarily through morphological similarities and location in relation to the main enclosure.

The model of development proposed for Lower Callerton comprises a pre-enclosure settlement (Phase 1) followed by the main enclosed settlement (Phase 2) with a final phase of modification and occupation (Phase 3; Fig. 4.3). The three phases of settlement identified follow the typical model of settlement development proposed for sites across the Northumberland coastal plain with sites moving from unenclosed to enclosed (Hodgson *et al.* 2012). The application of Bayesian modelling provides greater insights into the longevity of occupation allowing for a more nuanced interpretation of the main phase of settlement.

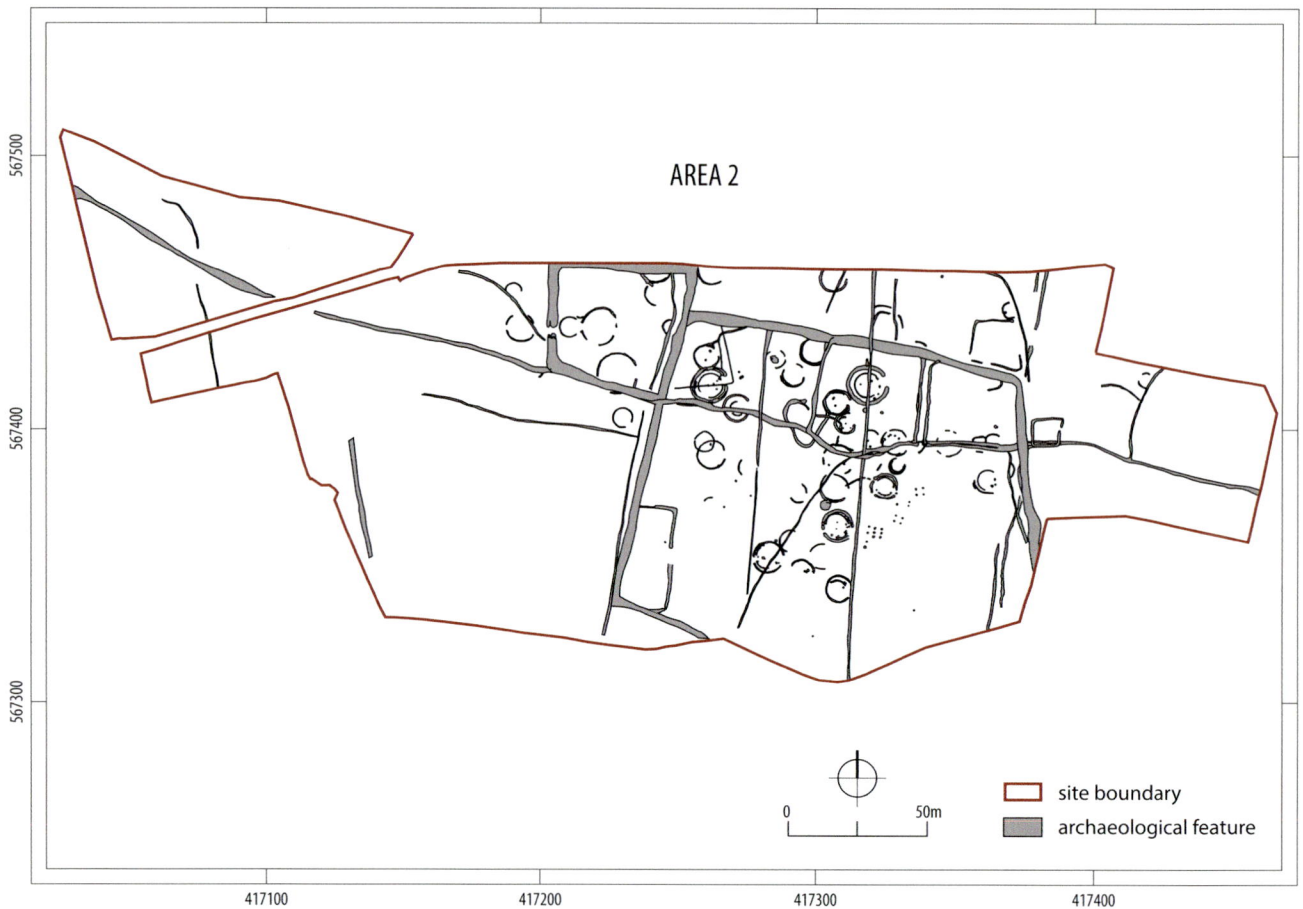

Figure 4.1 Lower Callerton site plan

Phase 1: Pre-enclosure settlement

The earliest Iron Age settlement appears to have developed across the northern portion of the site focused along the higher ground. A total of 17 structures, defined by narrow ring-gullies, have been grouped as part of this phase along with a possible palisade (Fig. 4.4). These structures have been interpreted as smaller scale precursor settlement activity to the main enclosure phase. The initial linear boundary which extends east–west across the entire excavated area also appears to relate to this early phase of settlement. While these features have been broadly grouped with the same phase they likely represent multiple episodes of occupation, activity and settlement organisation.

Structures

The majority of structures within this phase of activity were relatively simple single- or double-ringed ring-gullies with no internal or associated features. They were formed of narrow gullies naturally infilled primarily with silty clays. As the structures are grouped to the north outside the later enclosure few are truncated by later Iron Age features. However, all show signs of heavy truncation from modern agricultural activities. Of particular interest

was Structure 47 showing double entrances and signs of an adjoining structure incorporated into its plan. The structures will be described from east to west across the site grouped by location or similarities in form.

Structures 6 and 19

Structure 6 was located at the eastern extent of the site, to the north-east of the main enclosure. The structure consisted of two heavily truncated segments of curvilinear gullies which would have originally formed a single ring-gully 5.6 m in diameter. The sections measured *c.* 0.35 m in width and measured 2.6–3.5 m in length. Structure 6 possibly formed the remnants of a roundhouse, although no associated or internal features were identified.

Structure 19 was located 50 m to the west of Structure 6, truncated by the north-eastern corner of the main enclosure. It comprised a single curvilinear gully terminating at its south-western end. Its sub-circular plan precluded the estimation of a diameter. The gully measured 0.55 m in width and 6.6 m in length. The U-shaped plan of Structure 19 may indicate that it functioned as a windbreak or screen to delineate a working area as opposed to a roundhouse or more substantial structure. The gully showed signs of heavy truncation from modern agriculture.

Figure 4.2 Drone photograph of Lower Callerton Area 2

Structures 7 and 8

Structures 7 and 8 were in close proximity and are truncated by Sub-enclosure 1 (Phase 2b) and potentially the linear boundary if Ditch 1038 is accepted as an extension of this. The structures were small and slightly irregular in plan, indicating they may have formed structures or boundaries less permanent or well-built than a roundhouse – possibly storage areas or temporary shelters. Structure 7 comprised a 5.7 m length of curvilinear gully which terminated in rounded terminals at each end. It measured 0.4 m in width, 0.11 m in depth, with gently sloping sides, a flat base and contained a single fill. A short length of gully to the south may have also been associated with Structure 7. Structure 8 was a C-shaped gully located immediately to the east of Structure 7. It measured 5.2 m in diameter, up to 0.64 m in width, 0.20 m in depth and had gently sloping sides, a flat base and contained a single dark grey silt fill.

Structure 21

Structure 21 was located to the west of structures 7 and 8 and was also truncated by Sub-enclosure 1 (Phase 2b) and Ditch 1038. The heavily truncated ring-gully survived as five very shallow segments. The gully defined an area 9 m in diameter and measured 0.10 m in width and 0.04 m in depth, with gently sloping sides, a rounded base and

with a single fill. A short section of gully was located at the southern edge of the ring-gully, with a slight change in positioning to the south. It measured 1.85 m in length, 0.30 m in width and 0.04–0.05 m in depth, with gently sloping sides, a rounded base and contained a single deposit. This secondary gully may have formed a recutting, repair or alteration of the original gully.

Structure 44

Structure 44 was located to the west of Structure 21 and was truncated by both the main enclosure ditch and Sub-enclosure 2 (Phase 2b) (Fig. 4.5). It was formed of two concentric curvilinear gullies, with the initial outer being cut by a later inner. The initial curvilinear gully, 1612, showed signs of heavy truncation, only measuring a maximum of 0.05 m in depth. This was cut by the second gully, 1613, which was deeper, at up to 0.2 m in depth, and had a similar steep profile. If complete, the structure would have had a diameter of *c.* 10 m. No entrance was evident likely due to the truncation of the eastern side of the structure.

Structure 27

Structure 27 was located to the north of the large enclosure and continued beyond the northern limit of excavation. It

Figure 4.3 Lower Callerton Area 2 phased plan

AREA 2

ST6
0254
0488
0415
0489

ST19
ST21
ST7
STE
1038

ST27
ST44

1712
1671
ST40
ST49
ST54
ST47
ST51
ST50
ST52
ST48
ST55
ST53

2006

site boundary
pre-Iron Age settlement
Iron Age settlement Phase 1
other feature

0   25m

417100
417200
417300
417400

567300
567400
567500

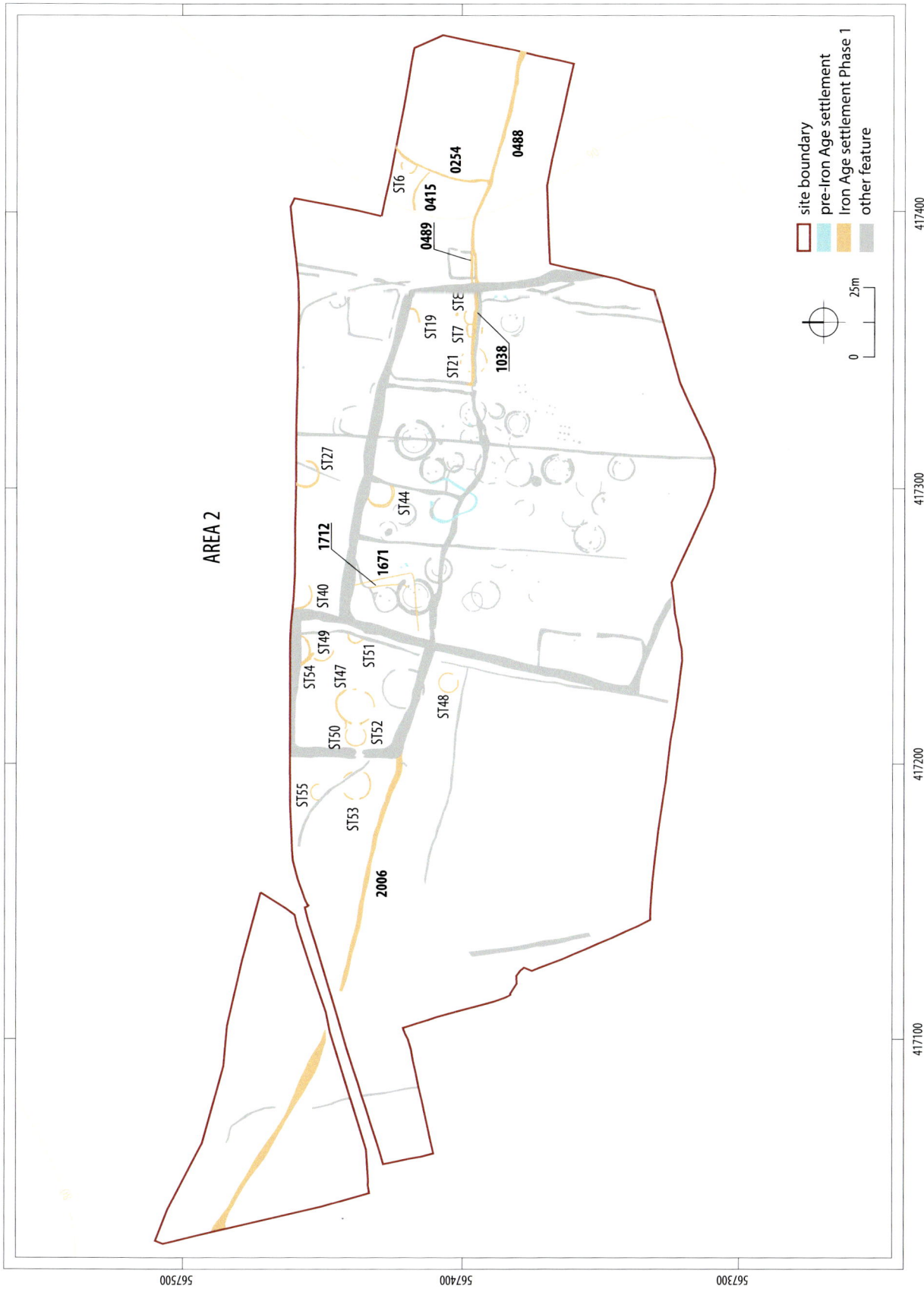

Figure 4.4 Lower Callerton Area 2 pre-enclosure settlement

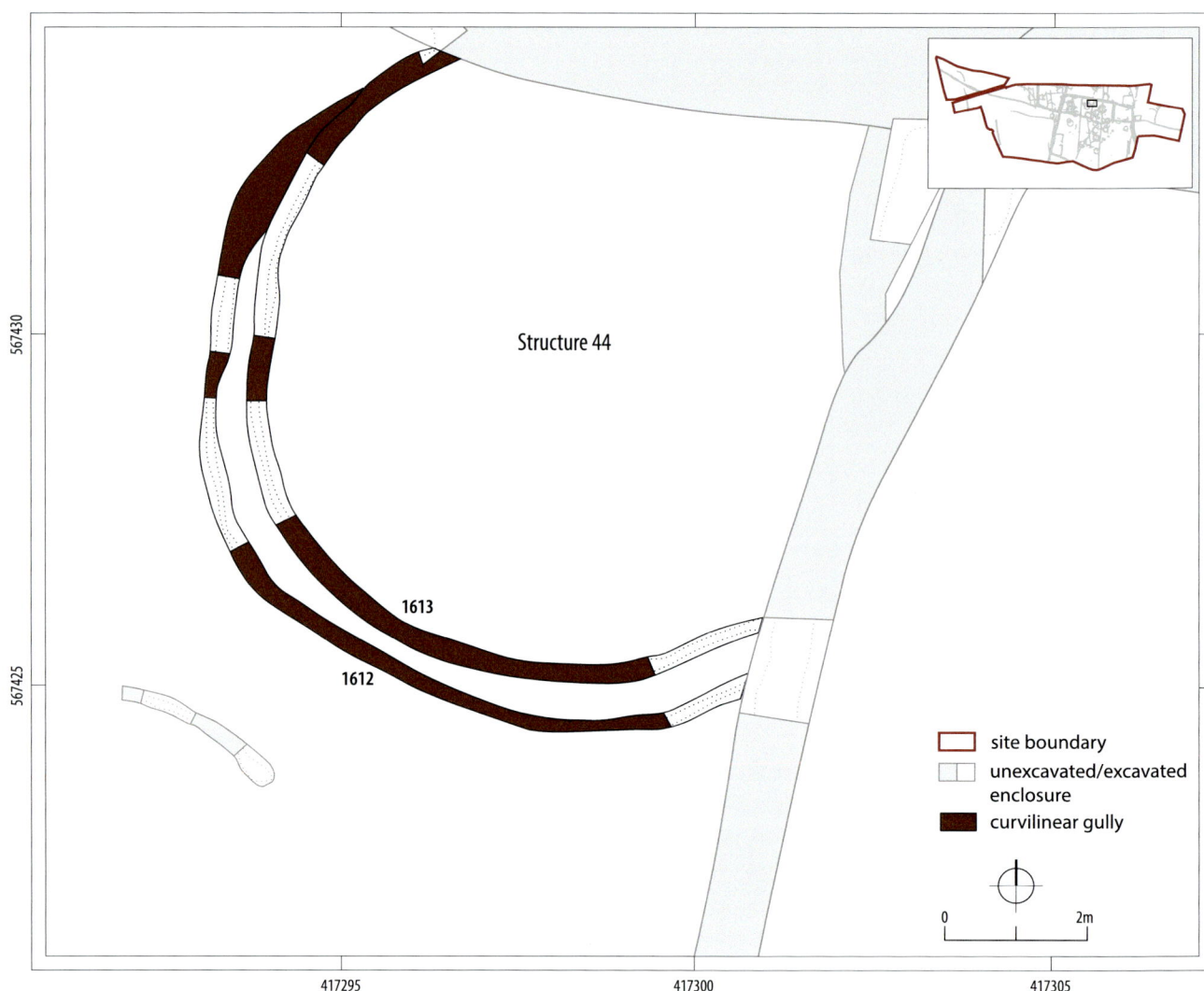

Figure 4.5 Plan of Structure 44

measured 10 m in diameter and comprised two curvilinear gullies – a primary gully and later recut. The initial gully was identified within the base of the secondary gully and appeared to be an earlier iteration of the structure. It measured 6.1 m in length, 0.46 m in width and 0.22 m in depth, with steep sides, rounded base and with a single fill of mid-greyish-brown silty clay. The secondary gully measured up to 0.7 m in width, 0.2 m in depth and had steep sides, rounded base and a single fill of dark-greyish-brown silty clay with rare large sub-angular stones. Despite extending beyond the limit of excavation, an east-facing entrance was evident.

Structures 40 and 54

Structure 40 was located to the north of the main enclosure (Fig. 4.6). It was truncated by the later Enclosure 0776 and extended northwards beyond the limits of excavation. The curvilinear gully and its recut measured 12 m in length with a projected diameter of 10 m. A more complex structure, Structure 54, was located 10 m to the west and was also cut by the northern edge of Enclosure 0776. It comprised the southern half of a structure which measured a projected 12 m in diameter and was defined by two intercutting gullies. The primary curvilinear gully, Gully 1902, measured up to 0.30 m in width and 0.25 m in depth with steep sides and a natural infilling deposit. This gully was cut to the west by Gully 1965 with both cut by Gully 1988. Gully 1988 following the same alignment as Gully 1902 with similar dimensions and profile suggesting phases of repair.

Structures 49 and 51

Structure 49 was located within the north-east corner of Enclosure 0776 immediately to the south of Structure 54 (Fig 4.7). It comprised a heavily truncated curvilinear gully forming the western edge of a probable circular structure with a projected diameter of 8.6 m. It measured up to 0.44 m in width and 0.24 m in depth. It had

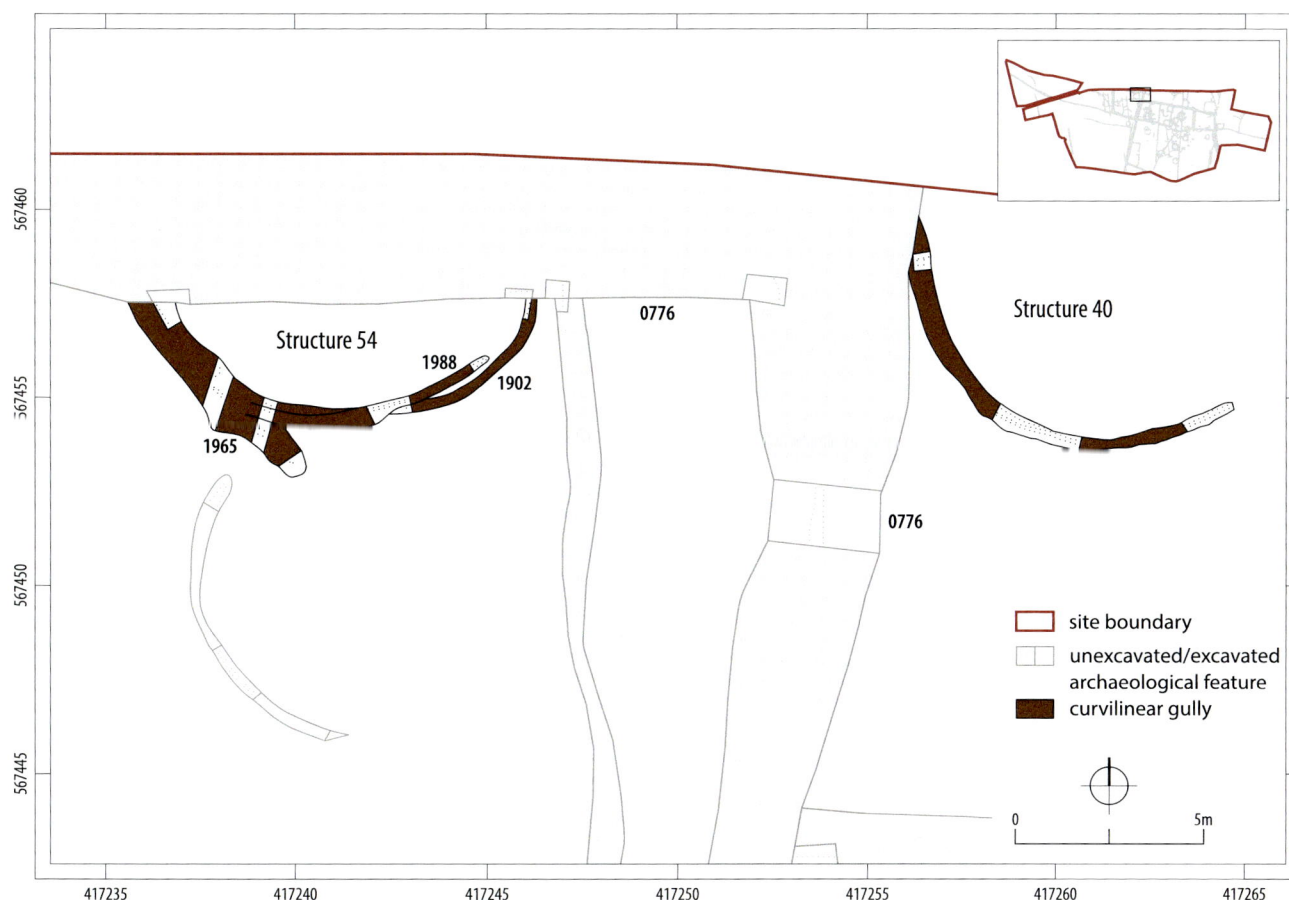

Figure 4.6 Plan of structures 40 and 54

steep sides, flat base and contained a single naturally infilled deposit. A possible terminus was identified at its northern end that may have suggested a north-west facing entrance.

Structure 51 was located within the eastern area of the later Enclosure 0776. It was heavily truncated by ploughing, with only the western side remaining, and was cut by a post-medieval ditch further obscuring its original form and function. It comprised a single curvilinear gully with a projected diameter of 5.4 m. The ditch measured up to 0.41 m in width, 0.19 m in depth with steep sides, a flat base and with a single naturally infilled fill of mid-orange-brown silty clay.

Structures 47, 50 and 52

Structures 47, 50 and 52 were located within the later Enclosure 0776 to the west of the main enclosure (Fig. 4.7). Due to their location blocking the entrance into the enclosure they have been interpreted as either pre- or post-dating its construction and use (Fig. 4.8).

The largest of the three structures, Structure 47, was located to the east of the group and consisted of two segments of curvilinear gully forming a circle with a diameter 13.7 m. The northern gully segment measured up to 0.57 m in width, 0.14 m in depth with gently sloping sides, a rounded base and with a single naturally infilled deposit of grey silty clay. The southern gully segment measured up to 0.43 m in width, 0.16 m in depth with gently sloping sides, a rounded base and contained a similar single naturally infilled deposit. Structure 47 had two entrances – a south-east facing entrance that measured 3.2 m in width and a west-facing entrance measuring 2.7 m in width. Two post-holes, 1875 and 1885, were excavated adjacent to the west of the of gully terminals forming the western entrance. Post-hole 1875 had an unclear relationship with the western end of the southern gully terminus. It measured 0.64 × 0.40 m in diameter and 0.16 m in depth with steep sides, a flat base and with a single fill. Post-hole 1885 cut the western end of the northern gully terminus and measured 0.43 × 0.30 m in diameter, 0.15 m in depth with gently sloping sides, rounded base and with a single fill. The addition of these posts after the construction of the gully could indicate the late modification of the entrance perhaps related to Structure 52.

Structure 52 comprised a curvilinear gully that measured 7.4 m in diameter with an east-facing entrance. The width of the entrance was obscured by modern field-drain

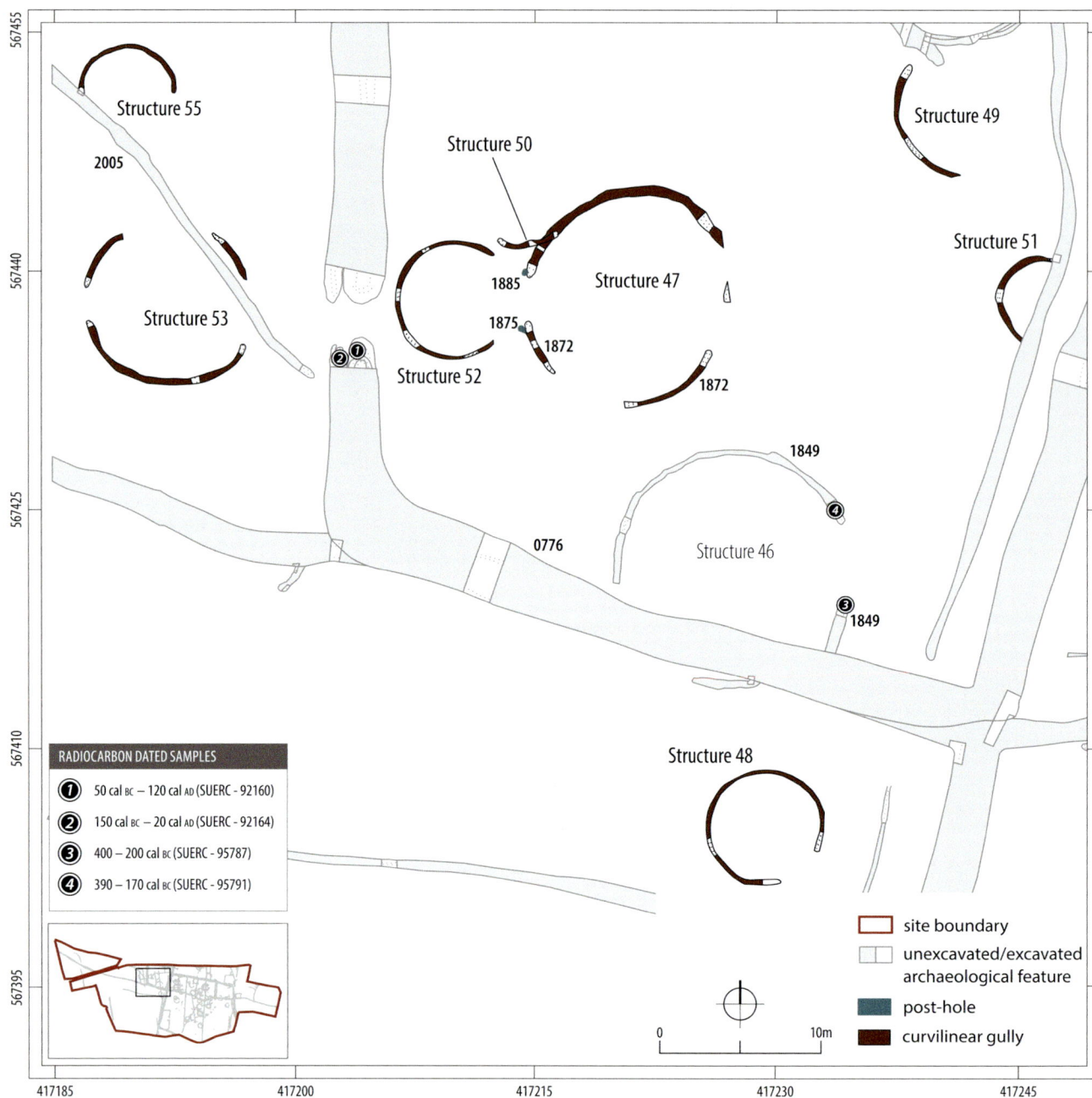

Figure 4.7 Plan of structures 47, 48, 49, 50, 51, 52, 53 and 55

and plough truncation of the southern terminus. The gully measured up to 0.25 m in width, 0.09 m in depth with gently sloping sides, rounded base and with a single fill. The relationship between Structure 52 and Structure 47 is unclear. Due to the potential alignment of entranceways, it is hypothesised that the two structures may have been linked.

The northern gully of Structure 47 was cut by Structure 50 at its western edge. Structure 50 comprised a short 4 m length of curvilinear gully that measured 0.30 m in width, 0.12 m in depth with steep sides, flat base and with a single mixed fill of orange and grey silty clay.

Structure 53

Structure 53 was located to the west of Enclosure 0776, *c.* 9 m from Structure 52. It was truncated and comprised three segments of a curvilinear gully forming a ring-gully 9.7 m in diameter. The gully segments measured 0.3–0.4 m in width, 0.06–0.09 m in depth and had steep sides, a flat base and contained a naturally infilled deposit of silty clay. Two entrances were identified, an east-facing entrance measuring 4 m in width and a west-facing entrance measuring 2 m in width. The opposing entrances were similar in alignment to Structure 47, indicating a possible similar function, or potentially allowing passage through this structure.

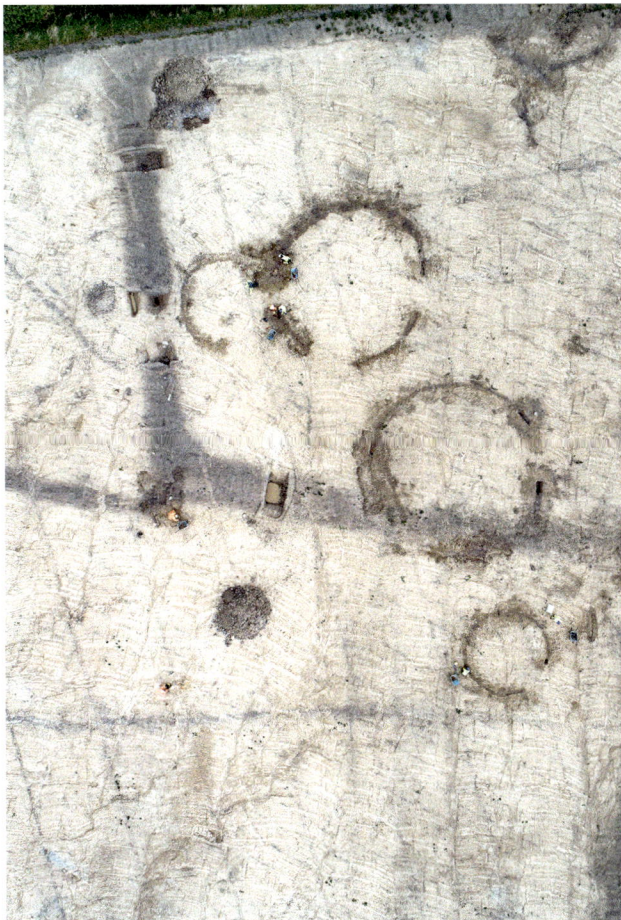

Figure 4.8 Drone photograph of structures 46–50 and 52 during excavation

Structure 55

Structure 55 was located to the north of Structure 53. It comprised a 7 m long curvilinear gully that had a projected diameter of 5.8 m, with a possible south-east-facing entrance. The gully measured 0.24 m in width and 0.09 m in depth, with a flat base, steep sides and contained a single naturally infilled deposit. It was truncated to the south-west by Ditch 2005.

Structure 48

Structure 48 was located to the south of Enclosure 0776. It consisted of a sub-circular gully with a diameter of 7.4 m and a south-east-facing entrance measuring 3 m in width. The gully measured 0.27 m in width and 0.10 m in depth, with a flat base, steep sides and with a single naturally infilled deposit. Its regular shape and entranceway were indicative of this forming a small roundhouse.

Palisade and linear boundary

A possible palisade formed of a narrow ditch (1671) was located to the north-west (Fig. 4.9). The palisade ditch measured 42 m in total length, up to 0.17 m in width and

0.13 m in depth. The cut was steep to vertically sided with a rounded irregular base and contained a single naturally deposited silty clay fill. Ditch 1712 ran parallel to the palisade ditch for 14.3 m terminating in a rounded terminus at its southern end. The ditch measured 25 m in width and 0.25 m in depth with steep sides and contained a naturally deposited silty clay infilling. The steep sides, irregular bases and widths of these ditches were indicative of their function as cuts for palisades or fence-lines delineating space to their north-west, though the shallowness and truncation of these features obscured the full extent and associations of this enclosed space with other features. It most likely acted as a phase of palisaded settlement prior to the construction of the later enclosure settlement. The palisade and the associated ditch were truncated by later structures, and whilst a relationship with the main enclosure was not evident during excavation it is probable that it pre-dated the main phase of enclosed settlement.

The settlement at Lower Callerton appears to have developed along a linear boundary defined by Ditch 0448 to the east, with potential fragments surviving under the later sub-enclosures as Ditch 1038 and continuing westward as Ditch 2006. Ditch 0488 measured approximately 165 m in length and ran from the eastern limit of excavation westwards into the area occupied by the main enclosure (Fig. 4.10). It was roughly linear, curving slightly south-east as it headed east. It measured up to 0.8 m in width and 0.40 m in depth, with several silting events and localised recutting events suggesting a level of maintenance over time. Further field boundaries associated with the ditch to the north-east are indicated by ditches 0254 and 0415. Ditch 0448 pre-dated the main enclosure ditch and the majority of associated features that crossed its path, suggesting that it formed a significant early boundary that may have influenced the later organisation of the site. The later enclosures within the main rectangular enclosure follow its alignment as does the southern edge of Enclosure 0776. Ditch 0448 continued beyond Enclosure 0776 as Ditch 2006, which extended in a north-western direction for a further 185m. Ditch 2006 measured 1.16–1.50 m in width, 0.38–0.60 m in depth and had steep sides, a flat base and sharp break of slope, containing two to four natural silting deposits. Several slots within this ditch showed signs of recutting, suggesting a level of maintenance or re-establishment of this boundary over time.

Summary

The structures of the pre-enclosure settlement phase almost exclusively were formed of single ring-gullies, indicating a simpler form than later phases of construction, although structures 47 and 53 showed some signs of more complexity and possibly pairing of structures to form larger dwellings. The designation of these features to the pre-enclosure phase is to some extent speculative due to the lack of concrete dating or evidence, however,

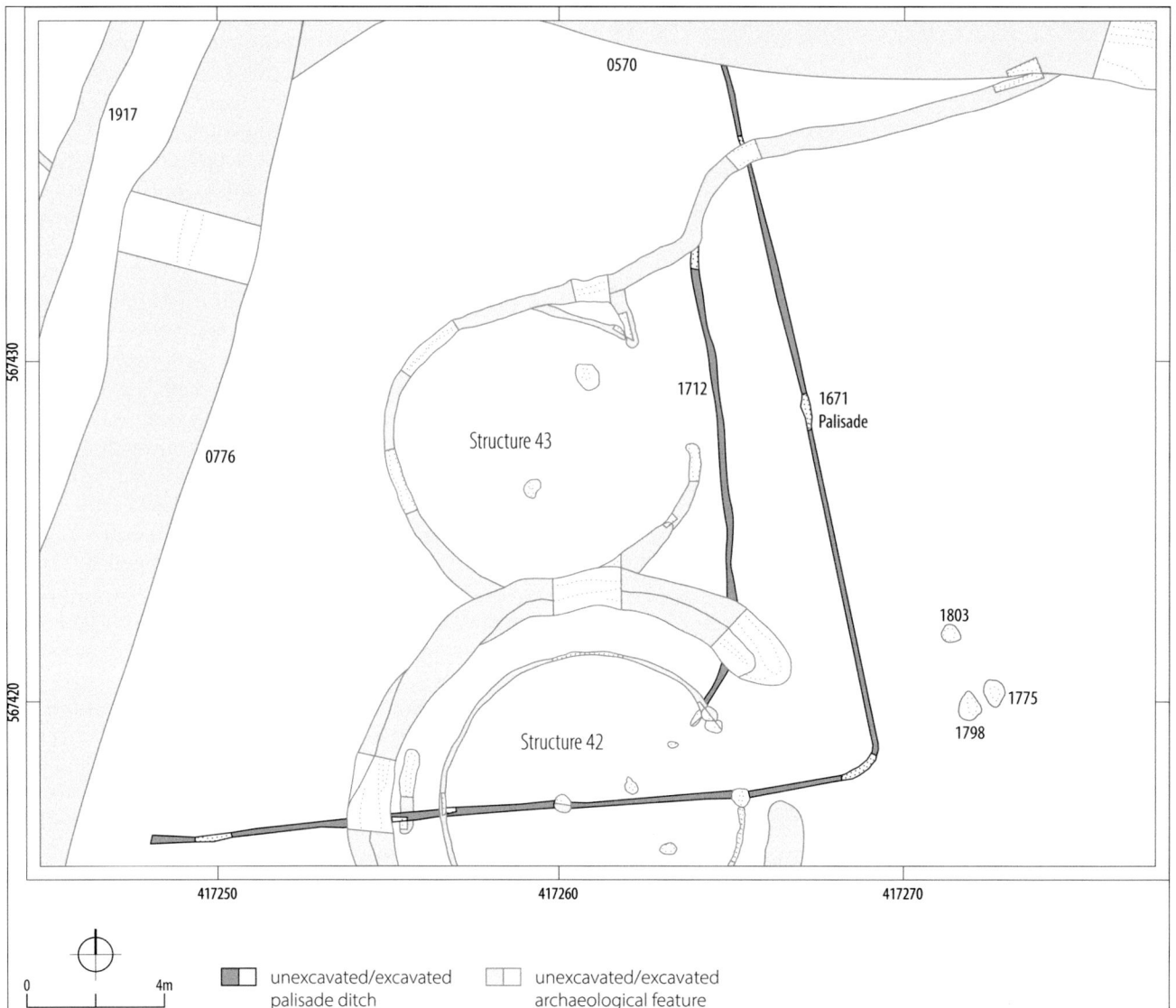

Figure 4.9 Plan of the palisade ditches

the morphology of the gullies and spatial relationships between structures provided evidence of a cluster of structures located to the north and north-west of the main enclosure, as well as the occasional structure further to the east.

The linear boundary running east–west through the site may have formed a focal line for the location of both this phase and later settlement, forming a reference point between the phases of settlement, and between communities in the wider landscape. The earlier palisades showed no clear link to any other structures, though they pre-dated the main enclosure phase. Defining the limits and connections between these disparate settlement elements without the unifying presence of a clear boundary or enclosure was difficult to ascertain with certainty.

Phase 2: enclosed settlement

The main phase of settlement activity at Lower Callerton was primarily defined by a large rectangular enclosure surrounding 33 structures, including three post-built structures, alongside various internal sub-enclosures (Fig. 4.11). Two smaller sub-square enclosures were located immediately to the exterior of the main enclosure ditch which may also relate to this phase. The lack of stratigraphic relationships between the structures results in difficulties in assigning phases, particularly as this phase almost certainly represented a continuous phase of settlement, with old buildings being abandoned or dismantled whilst new structures were erected, depending on the requirements of the settlement. The stratigraphic evidence, finds and Bayesian modelling indicate three broad

Figure 4.10 West-facing photograph of Ditch 0488

sub-phases or groups – early (phase 2a), late (Phase 2b) and undetermined (Phase 2). Phase 2a comprised seven structures, Phase 2b comprised 13 structures including the post-built Structure 17, and Phase 2 comprised 13 structures including two four-post structures. The results of the excavation of the enclosure will be presented first before discussing the structural sequences (2a, 2b and 2). As with the preceding section, structures will be presented from east to west across the site.

Rectangular enclosure

The rectangular enclosure was defined by Ditch 0570 which measured 135 m east–west and 110 m north–south, measuring a total of 340 m in length (Fig. 4.12). The northern and western sides of the enclosure were completely exposed within the excavation area while the eastern and southern sides were only partially exposed, with both ditches on these sides continuing beyond the limits of the excavation.

The ditch measured 2–4.8 m in width and 0.45–1.3 m in depth, with steep sides, a rounded base and sharp breaks of slope, containing an additional step towards the base of the ditch in some areas (Fig. 4.13). It contained

a sequence of five fills throughout most of its length, comprising phases of natural infilling with silts and clays, with no clear evidence of slumping or backfilling from an adjacent bank. The likelihood of a corresponding bank is increased by the sheer volume of upcast material that would have been produced from the initial excavation of the ditch. The final upper deposit of ploughed-in topsoil from more recent agricultural activities indicates this enclosure remained visible in the landscape until the land was intensively farmed long after its abandonment. Charcoal retrieved during the evaluation appears to have been taken from an upper fill and returned a radiocarbon date of cal AD 550–640 (SUERC-76860; ASDU 2015). The date relates to post-abandonment activity and while of little value in dating activity on site further supports the interpretation of the ditches having gradually back-filled. The southern side of the enclosure was truncated further as the land dipped towards the watercourse located immediately beyond the southern limit of excavation. It is unclear if the southern edge of the enclosure had ever formed a complete square joining up with the eastern edge, or if the watercourse had played a role in defining the southern edge of the enclosure. During the later phases (Phase 2b), four sub-enclosures were constructed

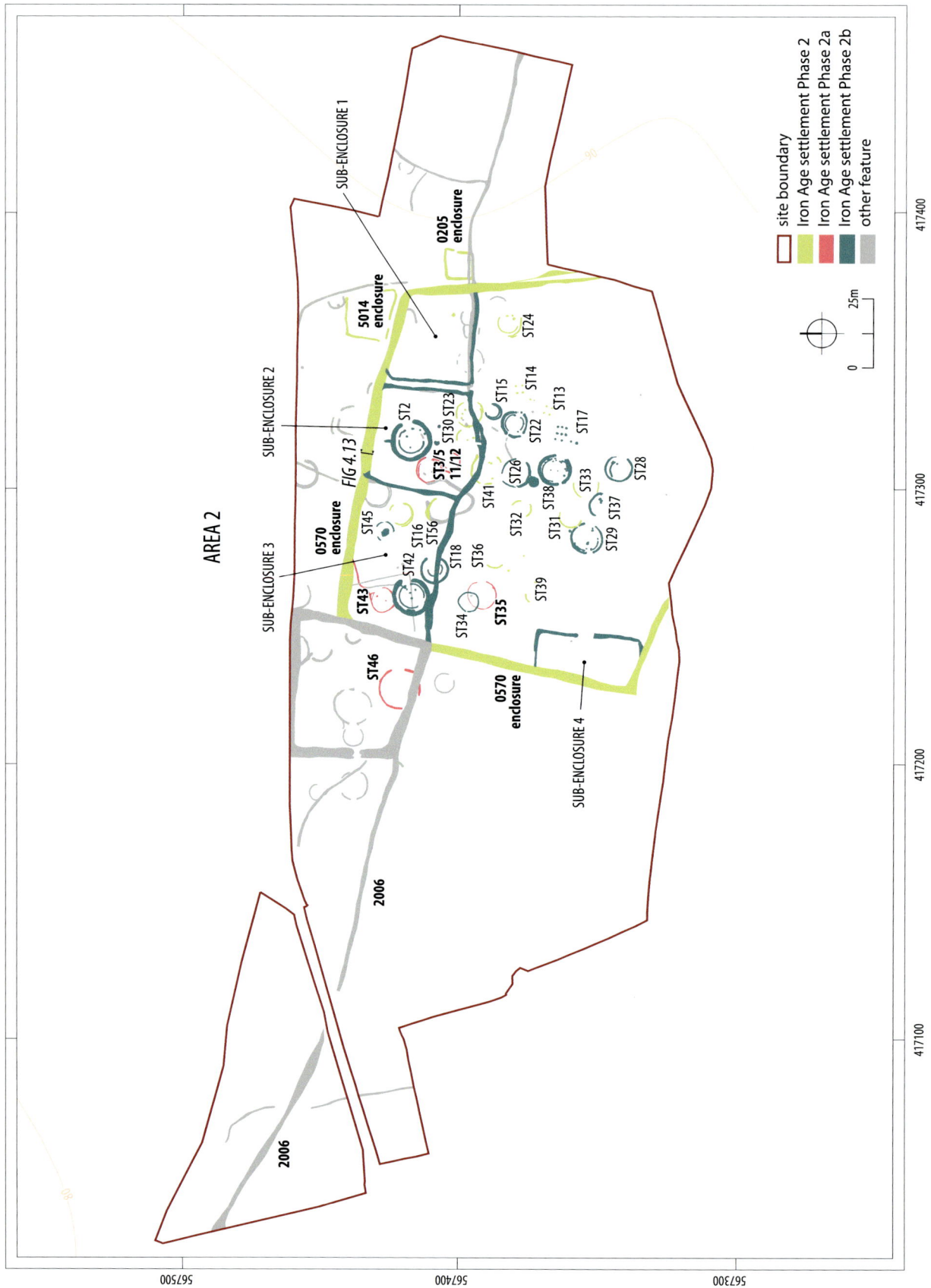

AREA 2

SUB-ENCLOSURE 1

0205 enclosure

5014 enclosure

SUB-ENCLOSURE 2

FIG 4.13

ST24

ST15
ST14
ST13
ST17

ST2
ST30 ST23

ST3/5
11/12

ST41
ST26
ST22
ST33
ST28
ST38
ST31
ST29 ST37
ST32

0570 enclosure

SUB-ENCLOSURE 3

ST45
ST16
ST56
ST18
ST36
ST42
ST34
ST35

ST43

SUB-ENCLOSURE 4

0570 enclosure

ST46

ST39

2006

2006

site boundary
Iron Age settlement Phase 2
Iron Age settlement Phase 2a
Iron Age settlement Phase 2b
other feature

0   25m

417400   417300   417200   417100

567500   567400   567300

Figure 4.11 Lower Callerton Area 2 – enclosed settlement

Figure 4.12 Photograph of Ditch 0570 during excavation looking east

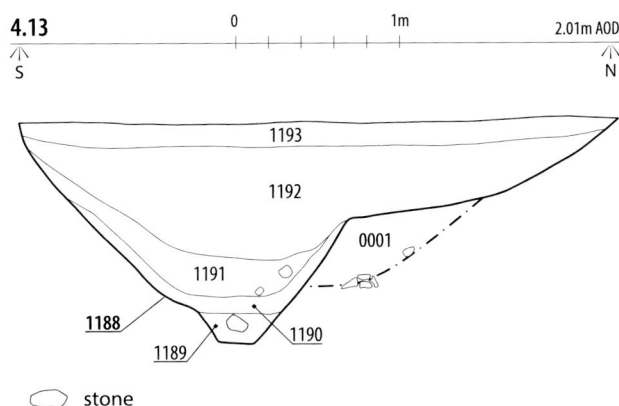

4.13 0   1m   2.01m AOD

S   N

1193

1192

0001

1191

1188 1190

1189

◯ stone

Figure 4.13 East-facing section of Ditch 0570 (section 1188 located at the centre of the northern edge)

within the rectangular enclosure. Sub-enclosures 1–3 were located along the northern edge whilst Sub-enclosure 4 was constructed to the south. The later radiocarbon date from Sub-enclosure 4 and its alignment to the main ditch supports the interpretation that Ditch 0570 must have been in existence before this date.

Phase 2a

Phase 2a defines the earliest phase of the enclosed settlement (Fig. 4.11). A limited number of features could

confidently be attributed to this phase, with structures 3 and 5 providing a set of earlier radiocarbon dates. Other structures in this phase, such as Structure 43, are truncated by later features providing some stratigraphic clarity. This section presents the structures from east to west beginning with the central cluster of intercutting roundhouses.

Structures 3, 11 and 12

Structures 3, 11 and 12 formed a set of three intercutting structures roughly central within the northern area of the enclosure (Fig. 4.14). These structures measured *c.* 9 m in diameter with east-facing entrances *c.* 2 m wide. The earliest structure in this sequence was Structure 11 which survived as only a short length of curvilinear gully, Gully 0442, on the southern side of the building. It was cut by both structures 3 and 12 obscuring its width and extent. Structure 12 survived as a curvilinear gully, Gully 0443, which was visible only at the south-east, south-west and north side of the structure. It measured 0.16–0.50 m in width and 0.07–0.20 m in depth with steep sides and a rounded base. It contained a single naturally infilled deposit of silty sand.

Structure 3 was directly built over structures 11 and 12 and cut the northern edge of Structure 5 located to the south (Figs 4.15 and 4.16). Structure 3 was formed of a single curvilinear gully with an east-facing entrance

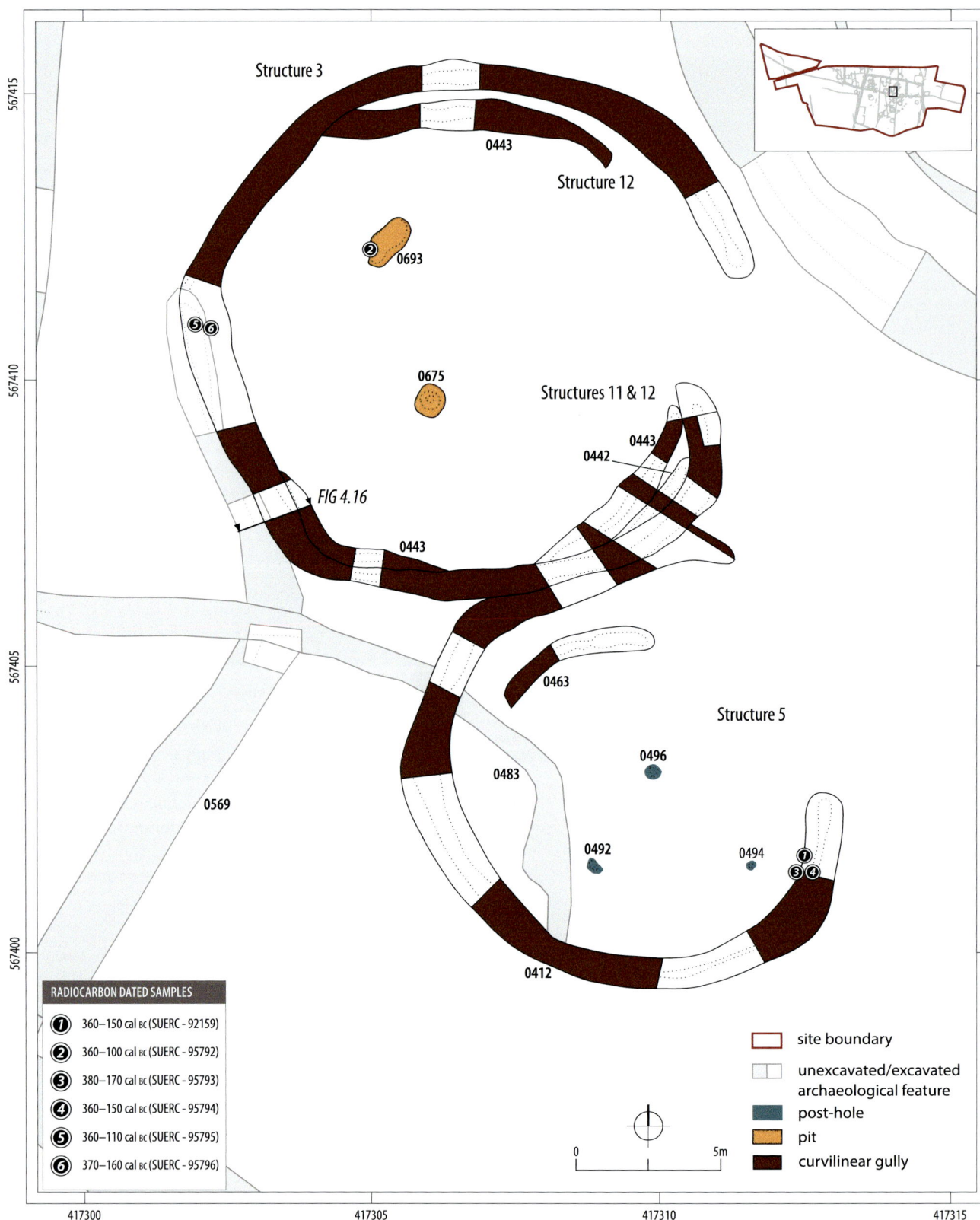

Figure 4.14 Plan of structures 3, 5, 11 and 12

formed by two rounded terminals *c.* 2 m apart. It measured 0.21–0.80 m in width, 0.08–0.28 m in depth and had steep sides and a rounded base. It contained fills of silty sand from which a stone rubber from a small saddle quern was recovered. Two similar radiocarbon dates were retrieved from charcoal within the fills of the gully, dating to 360–110 cal BC (SUERC-95795) and 370–160 cal BC (SUERC-95796).

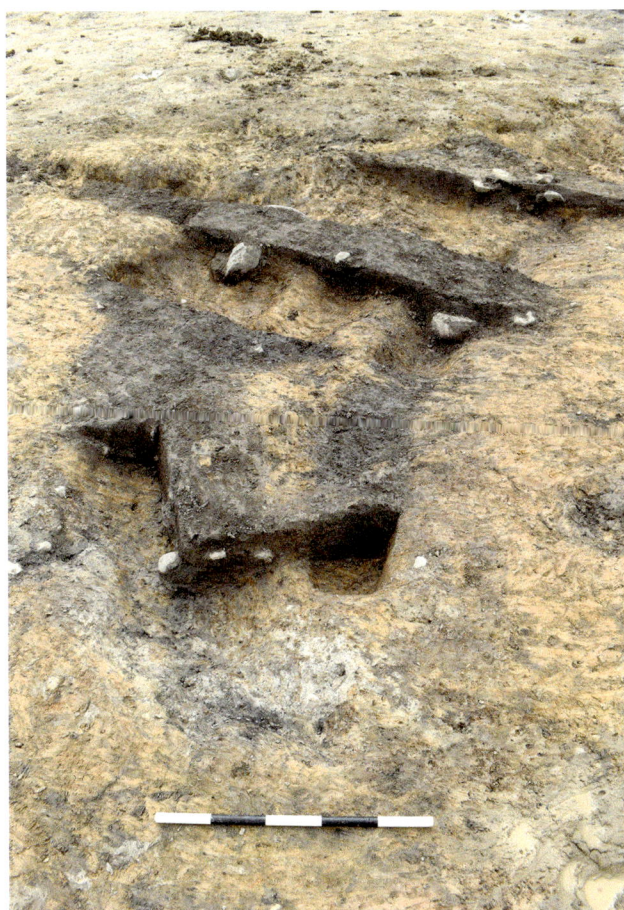

Figure 4.15 South-west-facing photograph of the intercutting ditches of structures 3, 11 and 12

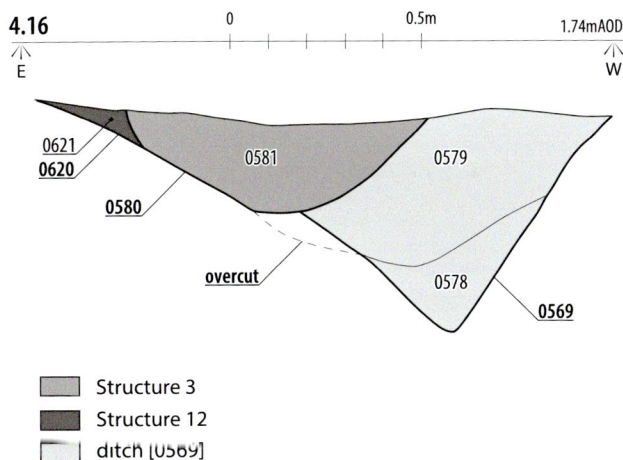

Figure 4.16 North-west-facing section showing the relationship between structures 3, 12 and Ditch 0569

Two pits were located within the interior of structures 3, 11 and 12. It was not possible to associate them to a specific structure. Pit 0675 measured 0.55 × 0.50 m in plan and 0.15 m in depth, circular in plan and rounded base. It contained a backfilled deposit of dark grey silty-sand with frequent large sub-angular stones. Pit 0693 measured 0.99 × 0.48 m in plan and 0.06 m in depth. It was ovoid in plan and had vertical sides, a flat base and gradual break of slope. It contained a single backfilled deposit of brown silty sand with moderate quantities of small burnt stones, occasional small charcoal fragments, and rare fired clay fragments. A radiocarbon date was retrieved from the charcoal within this fill, dating to 360–100 cal BC (SUERC-95792), similar to the dates from Structure 3. Neither pit had a clear function, though they likely related to a phase of internal domestic activity within one of the roundhouses.

Structure 5

Structure 5 was located to the south of Structure 3 (Figs 4.14 and 4.17) It comprised a single curvilinear gully with a diameter of *c.* 7.5 m and an east-facing entrance *c.* 4.3 m in width. A short section of curvilinear gully and

three post-holes were located within the interior of the structure. The main gully measured 0.43–0.97 m in width, 0.08–0.25 m in depth and had steep sides, a rounded base and gradual breaks of slope. It contained a single fill of mid-orange and brownish-grey silty sand with charcoal inclusions. Three radiocarbon dates were obtained from charcoal and cereal grain from the fill (0360): 360–150 cal BC (SUERC-92159), 380–170 cal BC (SUERC-95793) and 360–150 cal BC (SUERC-95794).

The inner gully, Gully 0463, was 2.8 m in length and was located on the inner northern edge of the main gully of the structure, following a similar alignment. It was heavily truncated and where it survived measured 0.35 m in width and 0.05 m in depth, containing a single fill of mottled orange-grey silty sand. It may represent a smaller earlier phase of the structure. Three post-holes were located within the interior of Structure 5 and formed no apparent alignment. They measured 0.20–0.33 m in diameter, 0.04–0.08 m in depth, all with steep sides, rounded bases and containing silting deposits containing charcoal flecks. Post-hole 0496 contained a large sandstone block at its base which may have formed a post-pad. Structure 5 cut an inverted L-shaped gully, 0483, that measured *c.* 10 m in length. The gully showed no clear function and could not be definitively assigned to a phase.

Structure 35

Structure 35 was located towards the western edge of the main enclosure and comprised a curvilinear gully with a diameter of 10.6 m and east-facing entrance measuring 3.15 m in width (Fig. 4.18). The gully measured up to 0.43 m in width and 0.27 m in depth, deepest towards the southern terminus and shallowing out towards the northern terminus. It had gently sloping sides, a rounded base and contained two deposits formed through the natural silting of the feature during and after its use. The primary fill (1346) comprised mottled greyish-brown fine sandy clay

Figure 4.17 South-west-facing photograph of Structure 5

overlain by dark greyish-brown fine sandy clay (1347). Charcoal from the primary fill was radiocarbon dated to 370–170 cal BC (SUERC-95813) and 390–170 cal BC (SUERC-95854). Structure 35 was truncated by Structure 34 (Phase 2b) to the north-west.

Two pits were associated with the roundhouse. Pit 1353 was cut into the southern edge of Structure 35 and measured 0.75 × 0.51 m in diameter and 0.08 m in depth. It had steep sides, flat base and gradual breaks of slope. It contained a single fill of greyish-brown sandy clay and was of unknown function. Pit 1397 was located in the overlapping space between structures 34 and 35. It measured 0.60 × 0.46 m in diameter, 0.14 m in depth and had steep sides, an irregular base and gentle breaks of slope. It contained a single backfilled deposit comprising dark brownish-grey silty sand with occasional burnt stones, charcoal and burnt bone fragments throughout. Due to its positioning, it was unclear which roundhouse this may have related to – if any.

Structure 43

Structure 43 was located within the north-eastern corner of the main enclosure (Fig. 4.19). The sub-circular structure, formed of two gullies, had an east-facing entrance and a projected diameter of *c*. 9 m. The initial gully only survived in two short lengths located in the northern

side of the structure and at the southern terminus of the entrance. This gully was between 0.26–0.83 m in width, 0.04–0.12 m in depth and had regular gently sloping sides, rounded base and with a single fill of brownish-grey silty sand with small stones and rare charcoal. The initial gully was heavily truncated by a secondary more substantial sub-circular gully. The measured 0.26–1.02 m in width and 0.11–0.28 m in depth with regular gently sloping sides, rounded base, and was filled by brownish-grey silty fine sand with rare charcoal inclusions. Charcoal from the ring-gully was radiocarbon dated to 380–170 cal BC (SUERC-98224). The rounded northern terminal was cut by a gully, Gully 1764, that ran towards the main enclosure ditch to the north-east, indicating either function as a drainage gully, or a fence-line to delineate space around the roundhouse. To the south, the terminal appeared to have been extended perhaps indicating a further phase of modification. Along its southern edge Structure 43 was cut by later Structure 42 (Phase 2b).

Two pits, 1722 and 1773, were located within Structure 43 which may be related to activities occurring within the boundaries of the structure. The function of either pit was not immediately evident with both being somewhat irregular and containing deposits with small charcoal inclusions. A very small scrap of grass-tempered pottery was recovered from Pit 1722. Two radiocarbon dates

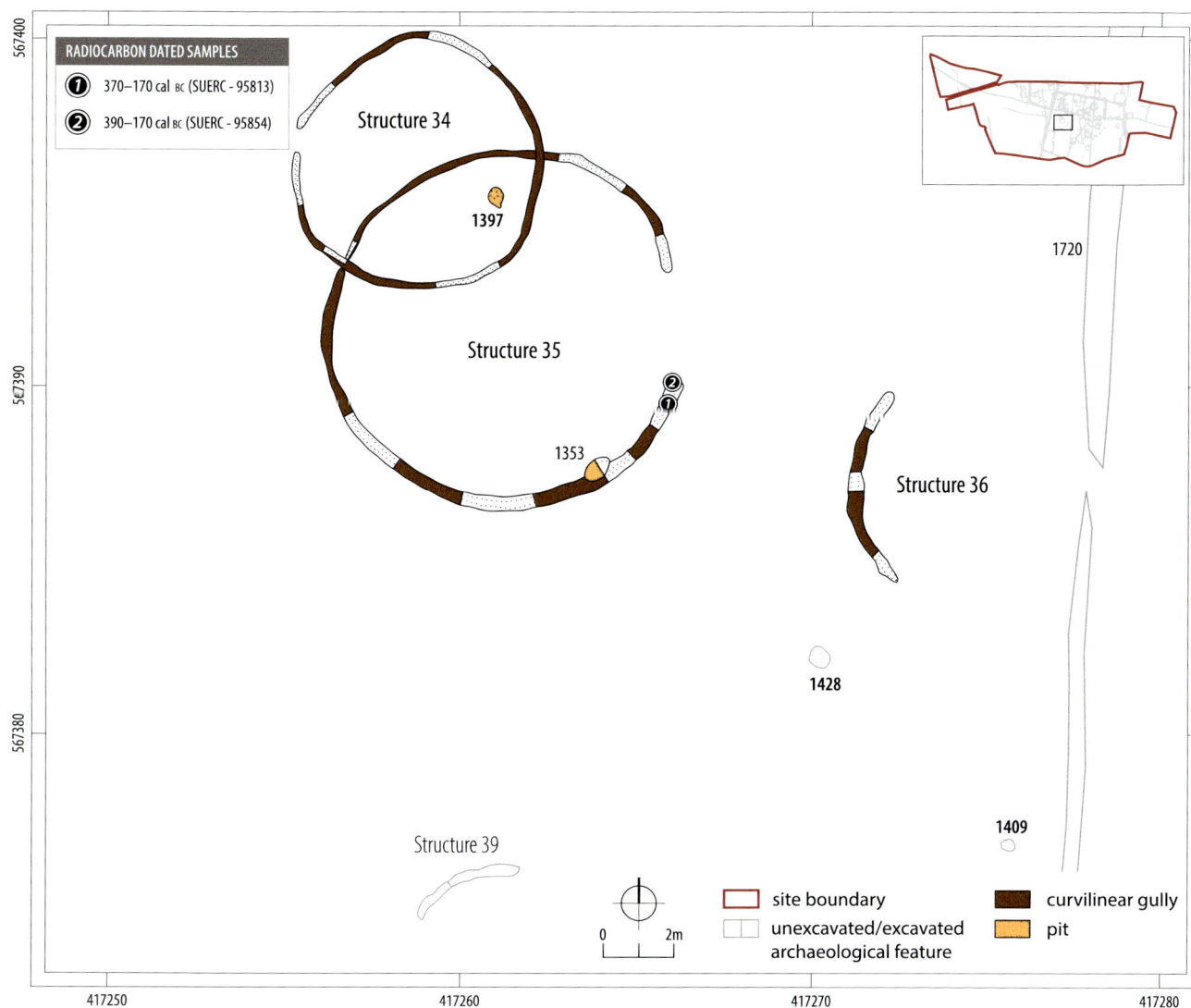

Figure 4.18 Plan of Structure 35 with structures 34 and 36

were retrieved from Pit 1722, dating to 390–190 cal BC (SUERC-95825) and 360–100 cal BC (SUERC-95826).

Structure 46

Structure 46 was located to the west of the main enclosure (Fig. 4.20). It consisted of a single curvilinear gully, Gully 1849, defining an area 15 m in diameter with an east-facing entrance measuring 4.7 m in width. The gully measured 0.27–0.66 m in width and up to 0.30 m in depth with a flat base, gently sloping sides and sharp breaks of slope. The fill comprised dark grey silty clay with charcoal inclusions from which two radiocarbon dates were retrieved from the terminal ends dating to 400–200 cal BC (SUERC-95787) and 390–170 cal BC (SUERC-95791).

The diameter of the ring-gully makes this one of the largest on site raising the question as to whether a gully this large could support a roundhouse roof without internal post-holes or a supporting bank of some description – of which there was no surviving evidence. The presence of a large structure outside the main enclosure suggests associated surrounding activity and highlights the difficulty in assigning a date to seemingly unenclosed features with limited stratigraphic or chronological resolution.

Phase 2b

The concentration of structures from this phase was centrally located within the enclosures with some peripheral activity (Fig. 4.11). The structures which have been grouped as part of this phase most clearly present later activity likely dating to the second century cal BC. Internal enclosures developed during this phase across the northern portion of the enclosures indicating the greater division of space. Several large roundhouses were attributed to this phase with outer ditches surrounding an inner gully with internal features exemplified by Structure 2 and Structure 42. Structures 22 and 29 were of particular interest, with

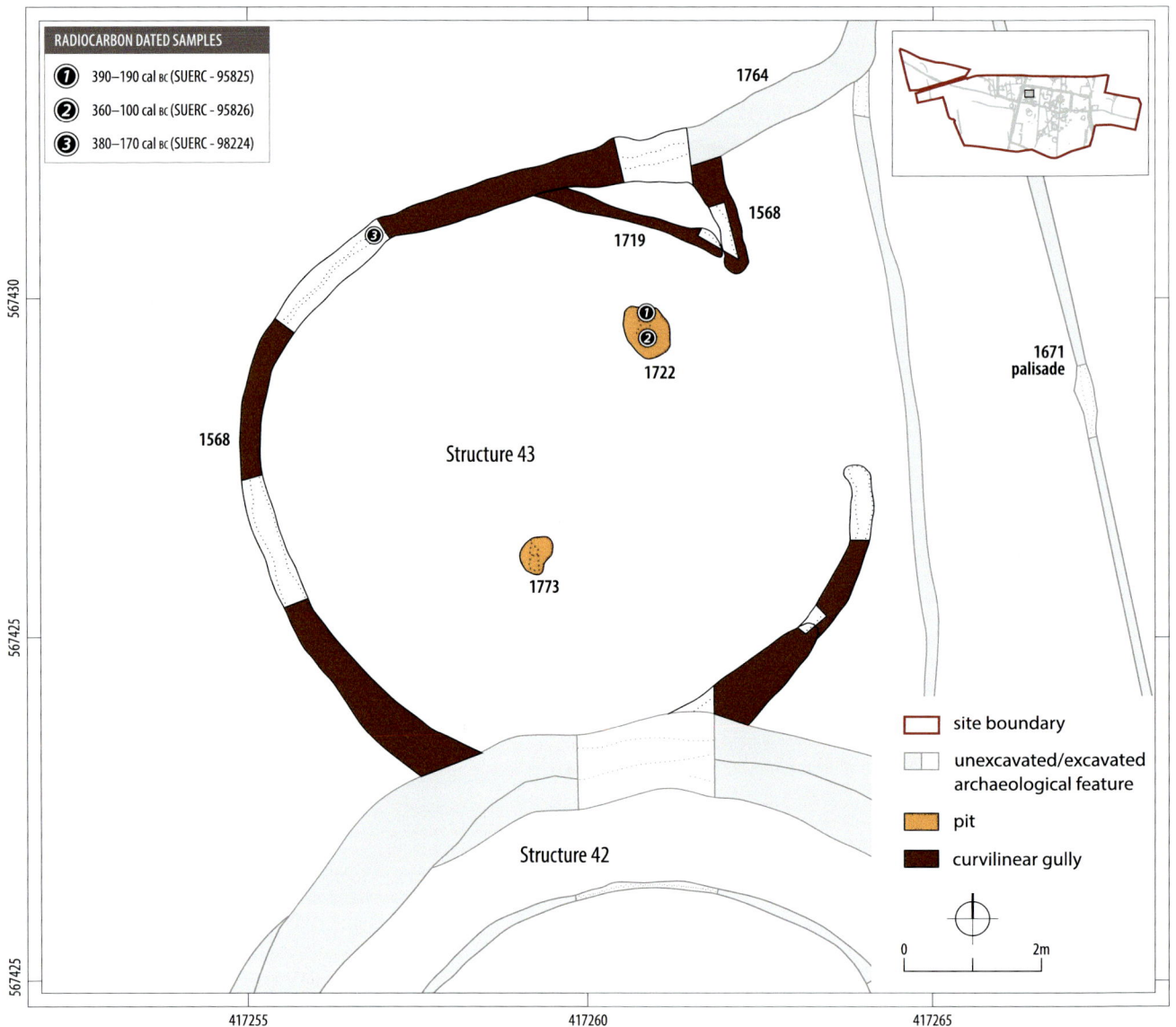

Figure 4.19 Plan of Structure 43

their inner gullies, outer ditches and multiple entrances indicating a greater complexity of design than witnessed at other structures. As the key development of this phase the sub-enclosures will be presented before the structures are described from east to west across the site.

Sub-enclosures

The ditches which form the internal enclosures have been grouped from east to west forming three distinct spaces (Fig. 4.21). The 2 m space between sub-enclosures 1 and 2 may have formed a trackway with a gate or entrance feature at the southern end. Sub-enclosure 3 was delineated to the south by Ditch 1777 which aligned to the earlier linear boundary. Sub-enclosure 4, located in the south-west corner of the main enclosure, has also been placed in phase 2b but its connection to the rest of the site

is unclear. A single radiocarbon date from the fill of this sub-enclosure ditch falls within the later period of the site.

SUB-ENCLOSURES 1 AND 2

Sub-enclosure 1 was located within the north-eastern corner of the main enclosure (Fig. 4.21). The square enclosure was defined by an L-shaped ditch, Ditch 1037, along its western and southern edge creating an enclosure measuring *c.* 30 × 25 m in diameter (750 m²). Ditch 1037 measured 62 m in length, up to 1.36 m in width, 0.33 m in depth, with steep sides, a flat base and with a fill of mid-brown to orange grey silty clay. The western edge of the enclosure also formed part of the droveway into the main enclosure, suggesting a dual purpose, and indicating the internal space related to livestock enclosure. No contemporary features were identified within the interior of the enclosure.

Figure 4.20 Plan of Structure 46

Sub-enclosure 2 was formed of two ditches, defining an area *c*. 35 × 37 m (1241 m²). The square enclosure was defined along its southern and western edge by an L-shaped ditch, 0958, that measured 88 m in length, up to 1.70 m in width and 0.49 m in depth. The short section of ditch, 0959, uncovered underneath its southern edge may be a surviving fragment of the linear boundary established earlier in the settlement. Ditch 0958 terminated at the south-eastern corner of the enclosure. The eastern edge of the enclosure, running parallel to Sub-enclosure 1, was defined by Ditch 1285. The ditch cut the main enclosure ditch to the north and

terminated in a rounded terminal abutting Ditch 0958 to the south.

The gap between Sub-enclosures 1 and 2 measured *c*. 2 m in width and potentially formed a trackway, though no clear access out of the main enclosure was evident to the north. A linear gully, 0677, located across the southern entrance into this passage may have defined a gate or fence at this location.

Sub-enclosure 3

A further rectangular enclosure, *c*. 50 × 30 m in diameter (1535 m²), was created to the west through the recutting

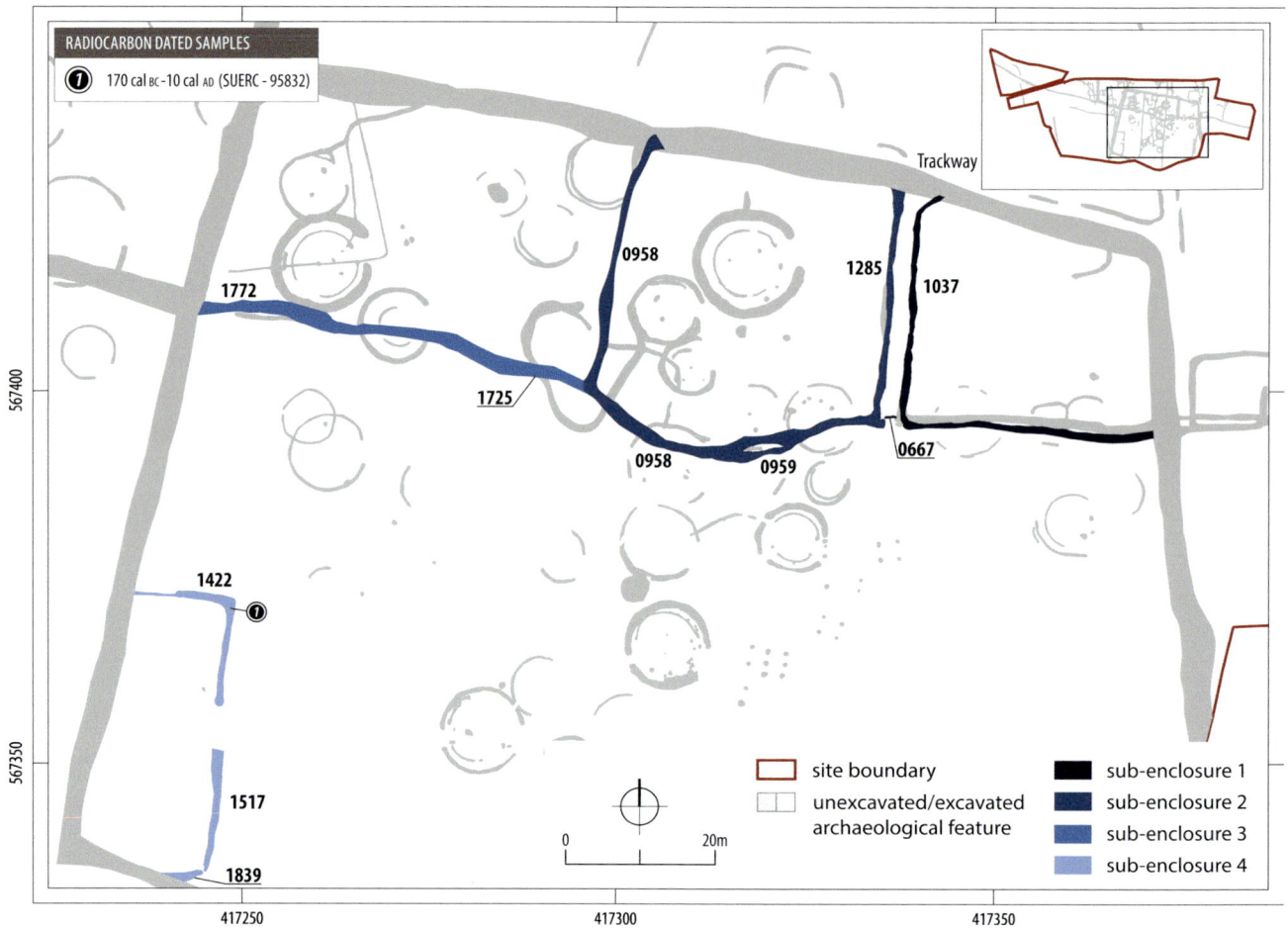

Figure 4.21 Plan of Phase 2b sub-enclosures

of the main east–west linear boundary (Fig. 4.21). Ditch 1772 appears to have been recut and maintained although the sequence was not clear in the field. The ditch measured *c.* 50 m in length, 1.19–1.90 m in width and 0.23–0.48 m in depth, with gently sloping sides, a flat base and gradual break of slope. A base stone from a saddle quern was recovered from the ditch with a post-hole recorded in the base of section 1725. Post-hole 1728 measured 0.23 m in diameter, 0.31 m in depth with vertical sides, a flat base and sharp breaks of slope. It contained a single fill (1729) comprising mid-brown gravelly clay with occasional small charcoal flecks. Evidence for recutting of the ditch was also discovered in this section with a 1.47 m wide and 0.29 m deep cut identified. Similarities in the composition of the fills made it difficult in the field to distinguish between the fills of intercutting features.

SUB-ENCLOSURE 4

Sub-enclosure 4 was located in the south-west corner of the main enclosure and abutted the main enclosure ditches to the south and west (Fig. 4.21). The enclosure was rectangular with an entrance to the east measuring 4 m in width. The ditch bounded an area of 37 × 14 m (476 m²),

containing one pit within its interior which showed no clear signs of function or associations with other features.

The northern ditch section, Ditch 1422, measured 27.6 m in length, 1.0–1.9 m in width, 0.48–0.54 m in depth, and narrowed towards the west to a width of 0.40 m and depth of 0.33 m. Its relationship to the main enclosure was inconclusive from stratigraphic evidence due to truncation from a modern field drain. Four sections were excavated across the ditch which identified a sequence of fills with a primary silting event (1451) comprising mid-brownish-grey silty sand with rare iron panning throughout, overlain by a sequence of three later deposits (1452, 1453 and 1454). The secondary fill (1452) comprised grey silty clay with rare charcoal inclusions, with the upper fills of greyish brown silty clay with stone inclusions.

The southern ditch section, Ditch 1517, measured 17.5 m in length, 0.90 m in width and 0.35 m in depth; it had steep sides, and a flat base and contained a similar sequence of fills to the northern ditch section. A rounded terminus was located the southern end of the ditch, 6 m from the southern ditch of the main enclosure. A length of ditch, Ditch 1839, located to the south of this terminus appeared to bridge the gap between the southern ditch

Figure 4.22 Drone photograph of Sub-enclosure 2 and Structure 2 during excavation

and the main enclosure ditch to the south. This curvi-linear ditch measured 5.4 m in length, 1.28 m in width and 0.30 m in depth and contained a single deposit. Its relationship with the main enclosure was unclear due to similar silting deposits within each.

This enclosure clearly respected the alignment and positioning of the main enclosure, and likely acted as an animal enclosure, though little associated evidence was identified. Two radiocarbon dates were retrieved from the enclosure ditches, the first during the during the evaluation provided a dated of 2341–2417 cal BC (SUERC-76861; ASDU 2015); while a further sample of charcoal retrieved from the northern enclosure (fill 1452) during the excavation returned a radiocarbon date of between 170 cal BC–cal AD 10 (SUERC-95832). Due to the sub-enclosures' association to the main enclosure the latter date is more in keeping with the overarching chronology and evidence available.

Structures

STRUCTURE 2

Structure 2 was located centrally within internal Enclosure 1285 (Figs 4.23 and 4.24). It comprised an outer ring-ditch with a diameter of 13.2 m and an east-facing entrance measuring 3.9 m in width. The outer ditch was mirrored by an inner ditch enclosing a space 8.6 m in diameter. A series of eight pits and post-holes were identified within the structure.

The outer ditch measured up to 1.38 m in width, 0.60 m in depth and had vertical sides, a flat base and sharp breaks of slope. A single naturally infilled deposit of brown to grey silty clay with rare charcoal inclusions was present within the majority of the ditch. The terminal ends of the ditch had differing sequences of deposits. The northern terminus of the ditch contained a sequence of five fills. Its primary fill (0236) was formed through slumping of redeposited natural subsoil and comprised light grey silty clay, overlain by a charcoal-rich backfilling event. Charcoal recovered from the secondary deposit (0237) yielded a date of 380–170 cal BC (SUERC-92157). Overlying this was a second fill of redeposited natural (0238) slumped into the ditch from the inner edge. This was overlain by a series of topsoil and charcoal-rich silting events. The southern terminus contained four fills formed through natural silting. These fills varied from light bluish-yellow clays to mid-orange-grey sandy clays. Charcoal retrieved from deposit (0245) yielded a date of 360–100 cal BC (SUERC-92158).

The inner gully measured 0.21 m in width, 0.10 m in depth and had steep irregular sides, irregular base and contained a single deposit of brownish-grey sandy silt clay. It was consistently spaced *c.* 1.5 m from the outer

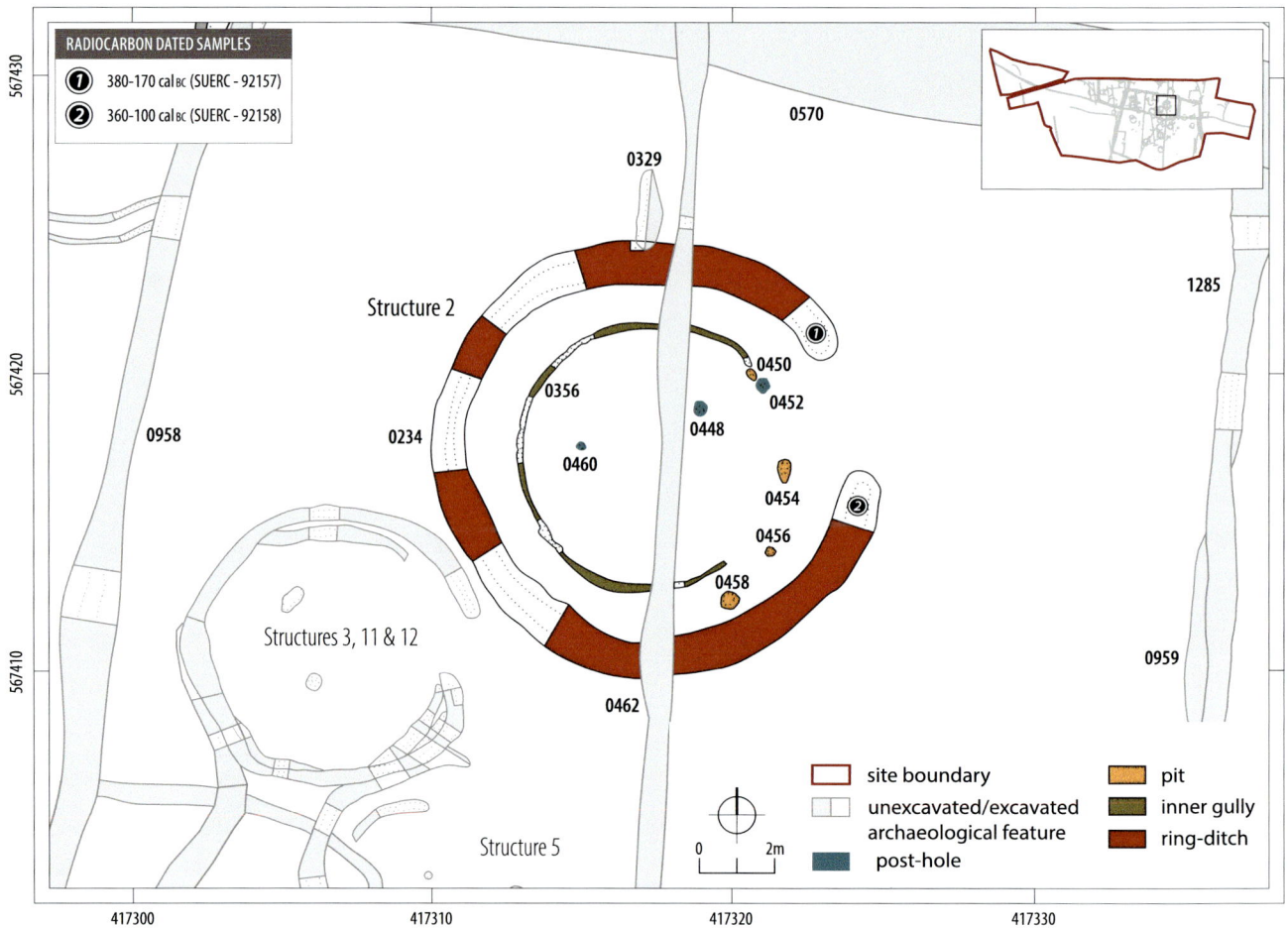

Figure 4.23 Plan of Structure 2

ditch. This gully may have formed a wall slot for the roundhouse – the irregular nature being created by the insertion of wall material directly into the ground. It is possible that this formed the inner retaining wall of a cob (subsoil) wall structure. The redeposited subsoil material identified within the northern terminus of the outer ditch was a key indicator of the use of cob as a construction material within the structure; and that the outer ditch was non-structural and open during the use of the structure. Structure 2 likely represents a complex roundhouse.

Seven discrete features were located within the structure. Pit 0450 and Post-hole 0452 were located adjacent to the northern terminus of the inner gully following its alignment. Post-hole 0452 and Pit 0454, located *c.* 2.3 m to the south, appear to flank the entranceway. The fill of Pit 0454 contained a diverse charcoal assemblage indicative of domestic hearth waste. A further small pit, 456, was located to the south between the inner gully and outer ditch. Two post-holes, 0448 and 0460, were located within the structure and may represent internal structural elements. A final pit, 0458, contained four sherds of Neolithic pottery (see Chapter 2).

Two additional pits were situated to the south of Structure 2. The pits appeared to have been deliberately backfilled with waste deposits of burnt material including heat-affected stones and charcoal. It is unclear if they are related to the activity associated with Structure 2. An elongated pit, 0329, was located to the north of the building and cut the outer ditch.

STRUCTURE 15

Structure 15 was located to the south of Structure 2 outside the sub-enclosure (Figs 4.25 and 4.26). It comprised an outer gully with a diameter of 5.8 m and an inner gully with a diameter of 4.6 m. The north-east-facing entrance was defined by rounded terminals with the outer entrance measuring 3.8 m in width. The outer gully measured 0.50 m in width, 0.20 m in depth and had steep sides, a flat base and sharp breaks of slope. It contained a single fill of brownish-grey silty clay with occasional sub-angular stones. The inner gully measured 0.20 m in width and 0.17 m in depth. It had steep to vertical sides, a flat base and gradual to sharp breaks of slope and contained a similar fill comprising brownish-grey silty clay. Two radiocarbon dates were retrieved from the fill of the outer

Figure 4.24 North-facing photograph of Structure 2

gully, dating to 360–50 cal BC (SUERC-95801) and 350–50 cal BC (SUERC-95802). There were no other features associated with this roundhouse.

STRUCTURE 22

Structure 22 was located to the south-east of Structure 15 (Figs 4.25 and 4.26). It was composed of three segments of outer curvilinear ditch and two segments of inner curvilinear gully. Seven post-holes were located either at the entrances to these gullies or within the bounds of the structure. This structure formed one of the most substantial and intact roundhouses of this phase, showing a higher level of complexity with multiple entrances and a possible porch structure.

The outer ditch enclosed a space measuring 9.7 m in diameter and had three clear entrances formed by rounded terminals: the south-east entrance which measured 3.5 m in width; the south-west entrance which measured 1 m in width; and the north-west entrance which measured 0.75 m in width. The three ditch segments were very similar in form with a higher degree of truncation towards the south. They measured 4.3–11 m in length, 0.55–0.89 m in width and 0.20–0.28 m in depth, with greater depth being noted at the terminal ends. They had steep sides, rounded bases and contained naturally infilled deposits comprising mid-grey silts and clays; two radiocarbon dates were retrieved from the southern section dating to 350–40 cal BC (SUERC-95803) and 360–50 cal BC (SUERC-95804).

The inner gully had a diameter of 6.2 m and was formed of a northern and southern segment with an entrance located to the east in line with the eastern entrance of the outer ditch. It was apparent that the western side of the gully had been truncated away. The northern section measured 0.20 m in width and 0.23 m in depth, with steep sides, a rounded base and gradual breaks of slope, with a single naturally accumulated silty clay fill. A post-hole may have originally been located at its eastern terminus. The southern gully section had a similar profile and fill. The western end of the southern gully segment ended in a rounded terminus, and a post-hole may have been located here as evidenced by the deeper, wider dimensions of the terminus. This would have formed a post-lined entrance-way into the internal space of the structure along with Post-hole 0946 located 1 m to the north-west. Post-hole 0946 measured 0.31 × 0.26 m in diameter and 0.17 m in depth, with vertical sides, a flat base and sharp break of slope. It contained a single backfilled deposit (0947) comprising mid-brownish-grey clayey silt which may have related to the packing of the post. The heavy truncation of the north-western corner of the structure masked the evidence showing a similar occurrence in the north-west corner's entrance, though it most likely followed the

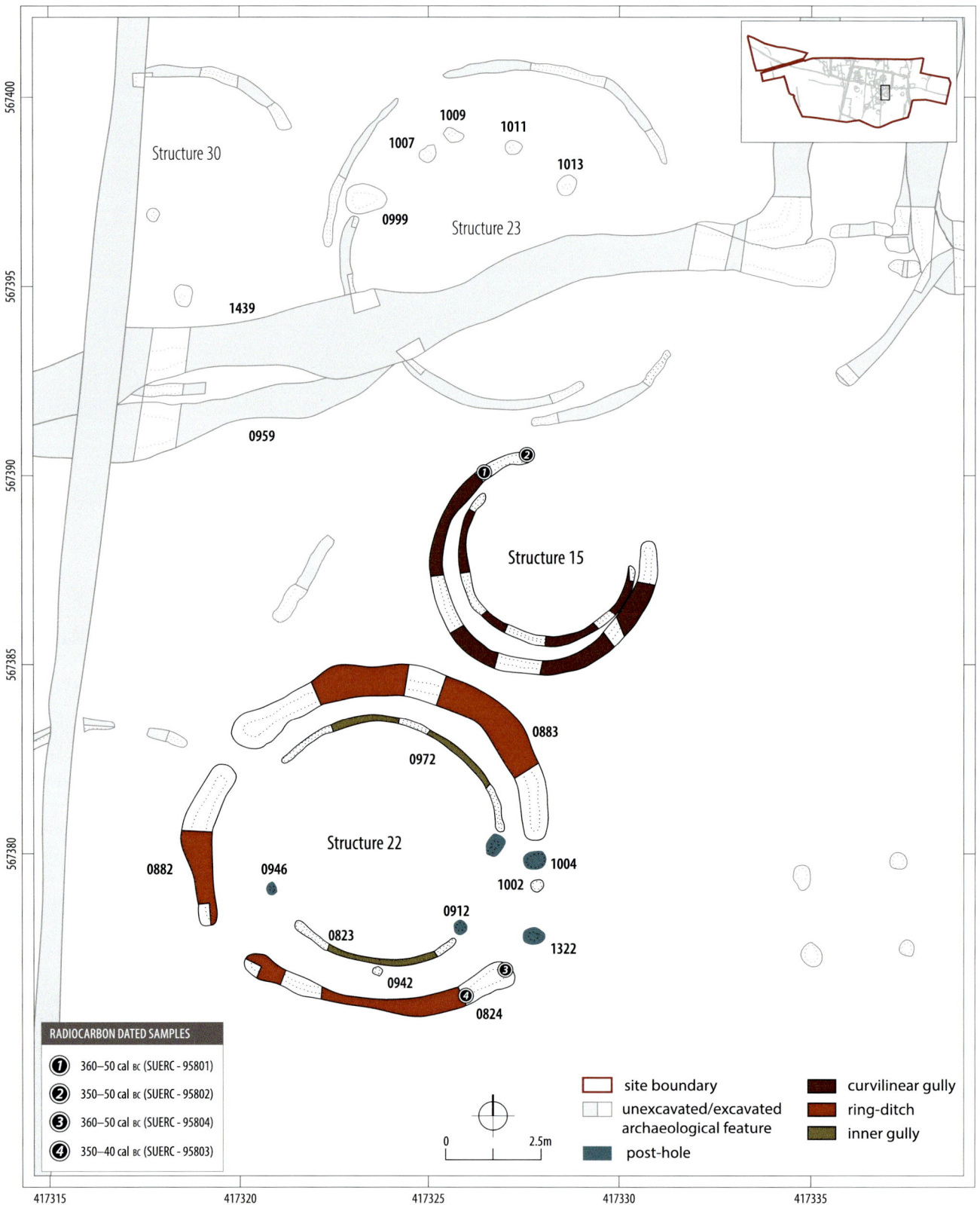

Figure 4.25 Plan of Structure 22 with structures 15 and 23

same pattern – with the inner gully mirroring the breaks in the outer gully.

The eastern entrance of the structure was defined by four post-holes aligned adjacent to the terminal ends of the inner gully and outer ditch. These post-holes measured 0.35–0.51 m in diameter and up to 0.42 m in depth and had steep sides, flat bases and sharp breaks of slope. They contained a series of initial backfilled deposits followed

Figure 4.26 Drone photograph of Structure 22 with structures 15 and 23

by later natural silting (relating to the removal of posts and abandonment of the structure). These posts formed a possible 'porch' area and indicated this entrance was the most substantial, and likely primary entrance to the roundhouse.

STRUCTURE 26

Structure 26 was located to the west of Structure 22. The original roundhouse was formed of two curvilinear gullies, defining an area *c.* 9 m in diameter, which were later cut by two further gullies on the southern side of the round-house, with another segment of curvilinear gully forming a north-eastern arc (Fig. 4.27). A further gully and a large, shallow pit were associated with the structure.

Curvilinear gullies 1052 and 1359 formed the southern arc of the structure, both with rounded terminals which

formed a south-facing entrance measuring 1.6 m in width. Gully 1052 measured 5.3 m in length, 0.66 m in width, 0.31 m in depth with steep sides and a flat base. It contained naturally infilled deposits of silty clays. A charcoal sample from the south-eastern terminus was radiocarbon dated to 350–50 cal BC (SUERC-98229). Gully 1359 measured 4 m in length, 0.7 m in width, 0.27 m in depth with steep sides and a flat base. It contained a single fill of orange-grey silty clay with small charcoal flecks. Gully 1360 was located across the south-facing entrance located between earlier gullies 1359 and 1052, effectively blocking this entrance off in later phases. It measured 0.32 m in width, 0.15 m in depth and had gently sloping sides and a rounded base. It contained a single fill of dark grey fine sandy clay. Gully 1363 to the north-west appeared to be a continuation of Gully 1359, cutting the

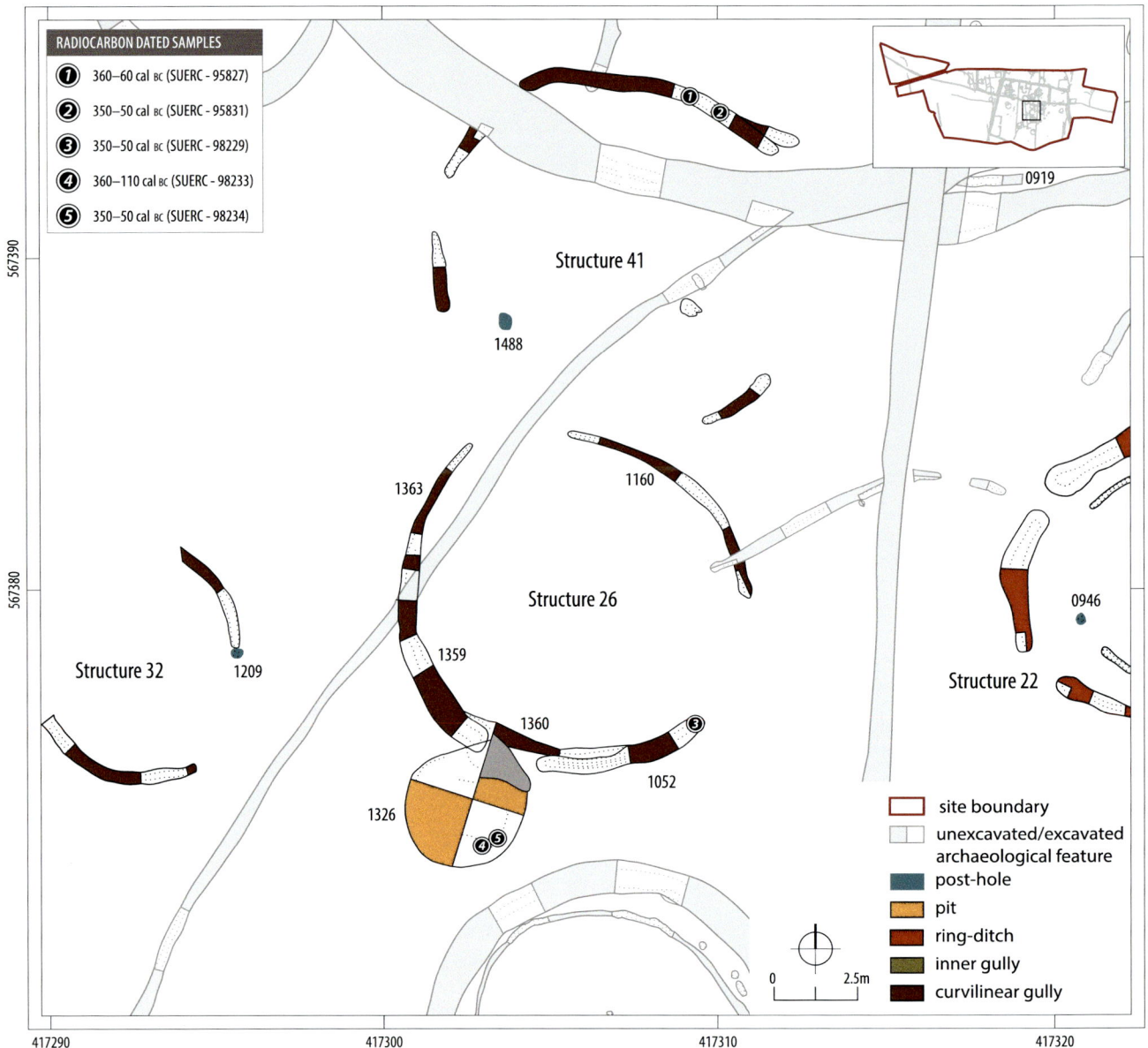

Figure 4.27 Plan of structures 26, 41 and 32

original gully and extending it to the north-east by *c.* 5 m. It measured 0.23 m in width and 0.10 m in depth and contained a single fill of mid to dark greyish-brown sandy silt. Gully 1160 was the north-east arc of the structure, with the rounded terminal at the southern end of the gully forming the east-facing entrance. It measured 7.4 m in length, 0.38 m in width and 0.04 m in depth with gently sloping sides and a rounded base. It was unclear whether Gully 1160 represented the initial construction of the building or the later phase.

Pit 1326 was located immediately to the south of Structure 26, cutting the earlier structural gullies of Structure 26. It measured 3.8 × 3.5 m in diameter, 0.15 m in depth and had gently sloping sides, a flat base and a gradual break of slope. It was filled by a sequence of mid- to dark grey silty clay deposits, suggesting an area of repeated activity adjacent to the structure. It also contained a slightly higher density of slag finds than other structures, suggesting a relationship to metalworking activities in the vicinity.

STRUCTURE 38

Structure 38 was located roughly centrally within the main enclosure, to the south of Structure 26, and was the most architecturally complex with two phases of construction identified (Figs 4.28 and 4.29). The first phase survived only as a very short length of a possible curvilinear ditch, 1511 and 1542, which was identified on the inner edge of the later structure's northern outer ditch. The second more substantial phase comprised two segments of an outer curvilinear ditch and two inner gully segments.

RADIOCARBON DATED SAMPLES

1. 2580–2460 cal BC (SUERC - 95805)
2. 360–60 cal BC (SUERC - 95806)
3. 340–40 cal BC (SUERC - 95807)
4. 380–170 cal BC (SUERC - 95811)
5. 360–100 cal BC (SUERC - 95812)
6. 170 cal BC – 10 cal AD (SUERC - 95814)
7. 340–40 cal BC (SUERC - 95815)
8. 180 cal BC –10 cal AD (SUERC - 95816)
9. 200–40 cal BC (SUERC - 95817)
10. 100 cal BC – 70 cal AD (SUERC - 95821)
11. 100 cal BC – 60 cal AD (SUERC - 95822)
12. 350–50 cal BC (SUERC - 95823)
13. 350–50 cal BC (SUERC - 95824)
14. 160 cal BC – 20 cal AD (SUERC - 98246)
15. 180–1 cal BC (SUERC - 98244)
16. 360–150 cal BC (SUERC - 98245)
17. 200–40 cal BC (SUERC - 98235)

Structure 38, Structure 31, Structure 29, Structure 33, Structure 37, Structure 28

Legend:
- site boundary
- unexcavated/excavated archaeological feature
- curvilinear gully
- post-hole
- pit
- ring-ditch
- inner gully

0 — 5m

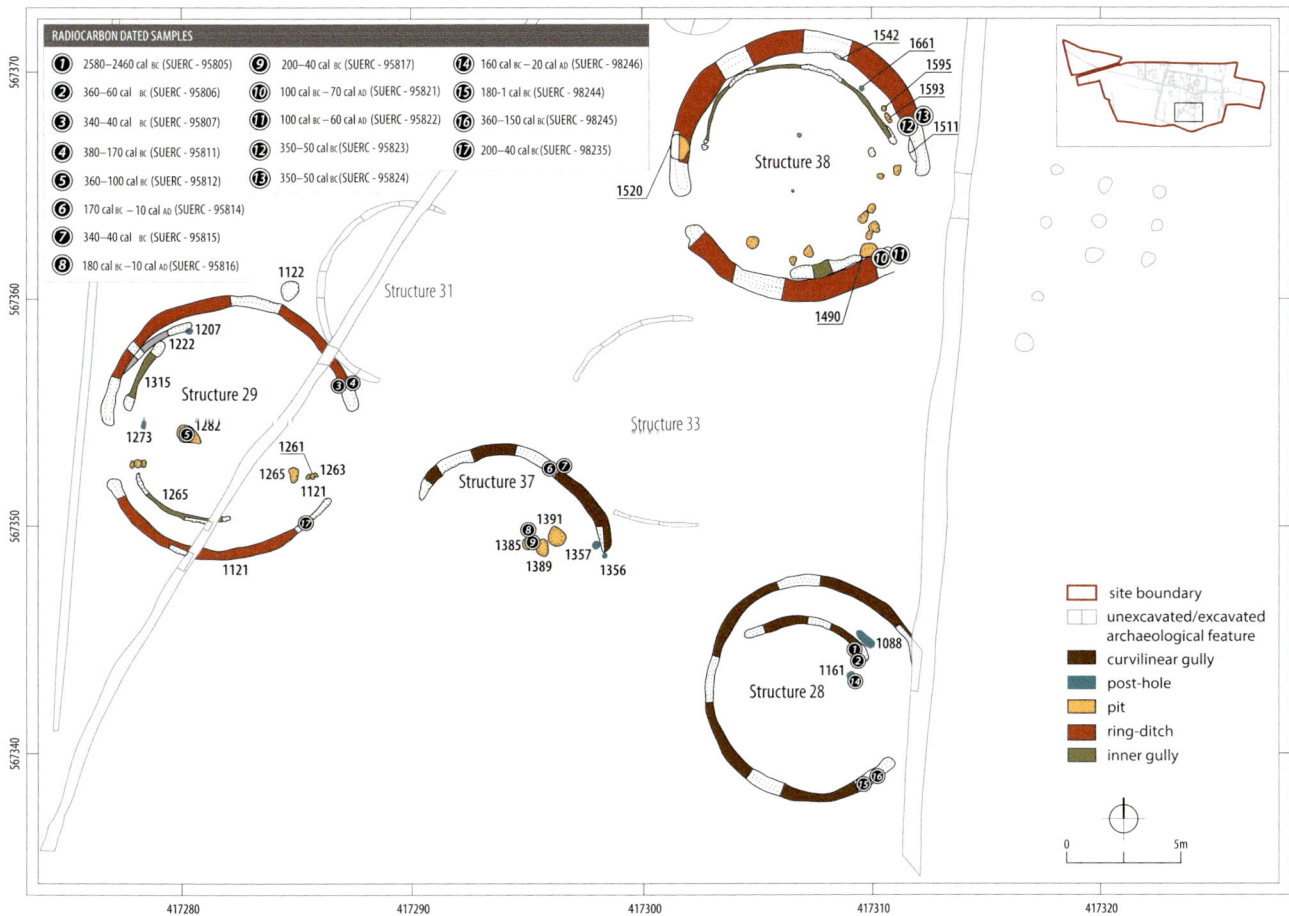

Figure 4.28 Plan of Structure 38 with Structure 28, Structure 37 and Structure 29

The two segments of outer ditch forming the later phase were located along the northern and southern arc, forming a structure with a diameter of 12 m. The outer ditches had two entrances; one at the south-west which measured 1.32 m in width and one to the south-east which measured 3.4 m in width, indicating the main entrance faced to the south-east. The northern outer ditch measured 0.69–1.01 m in width, 0.22–0.30 m in depth and had steep rounded sides, a rounded base, and contained a single deposit of mid-brownish-grey clayey silt with frequent poorly sorted stones, rare small fragments of charcoal and burnt stone – indicative of washed-in material from nearby activity. Two radiocarbon dates were retrieved from charcoal and cereal grain within this fill, dating to 350–50 cal BC (SUERC-95823) and 350–50 cal BC (SUERC-95824). The southern outer ditch measured up to 1.04 m in width, 0.44 m in depth and had steep rounded sides, rounded base, with a similar fill as the northern ditch, though with a lower quantity of charcoal and burnt stone inclusions, indicating less activity adjacent to this side of the structure. Two radiocarbon dates were retrieved from charcoal and cereal grain within this fill, dating to 100 cal BC–cal AD 70 (SUERC-95821) and 100 cal BC–cal AD 60 (SUERC-95822).

The inner curvilinear gully (1597), situated within the arc of the northern ditch, measured 12 m in length. The gully measured 0.08–0.27 m in width, 0.08–0.22 m in depth and had irregular steep sides, rounded irregular base and contained a single natural infilling deposit. A further inner gully (1598) of differing proportions was located to the south-east. This measured 3 m in length, 0.56–0.66 m in width, 0.10–0.17 m in depth and had gently sloping rounded sides, a flat base, and with a single fill of brownish-grey clayey silt with occasional small fragments of charcoal. Pit 1490 was located immediately to the east of the gully.

A series of pits and post-holes were located within this structure with several of them lining up or falling just within the projected entrance to the roundhouse. A post-hole, 1661, and two pits, 1595 and 1593, were located between the inner gully and outer ditch. No functions or alignments could be identified for these internal features. Pit 1520 that cut the outer ditch contained a sherd of post-medieval pot, suggesting a level of later intrusion by some of these features. Structure 38 was comparable to the later structures 2 and 42 in architectural style with an external boundary ditch and internal gully.

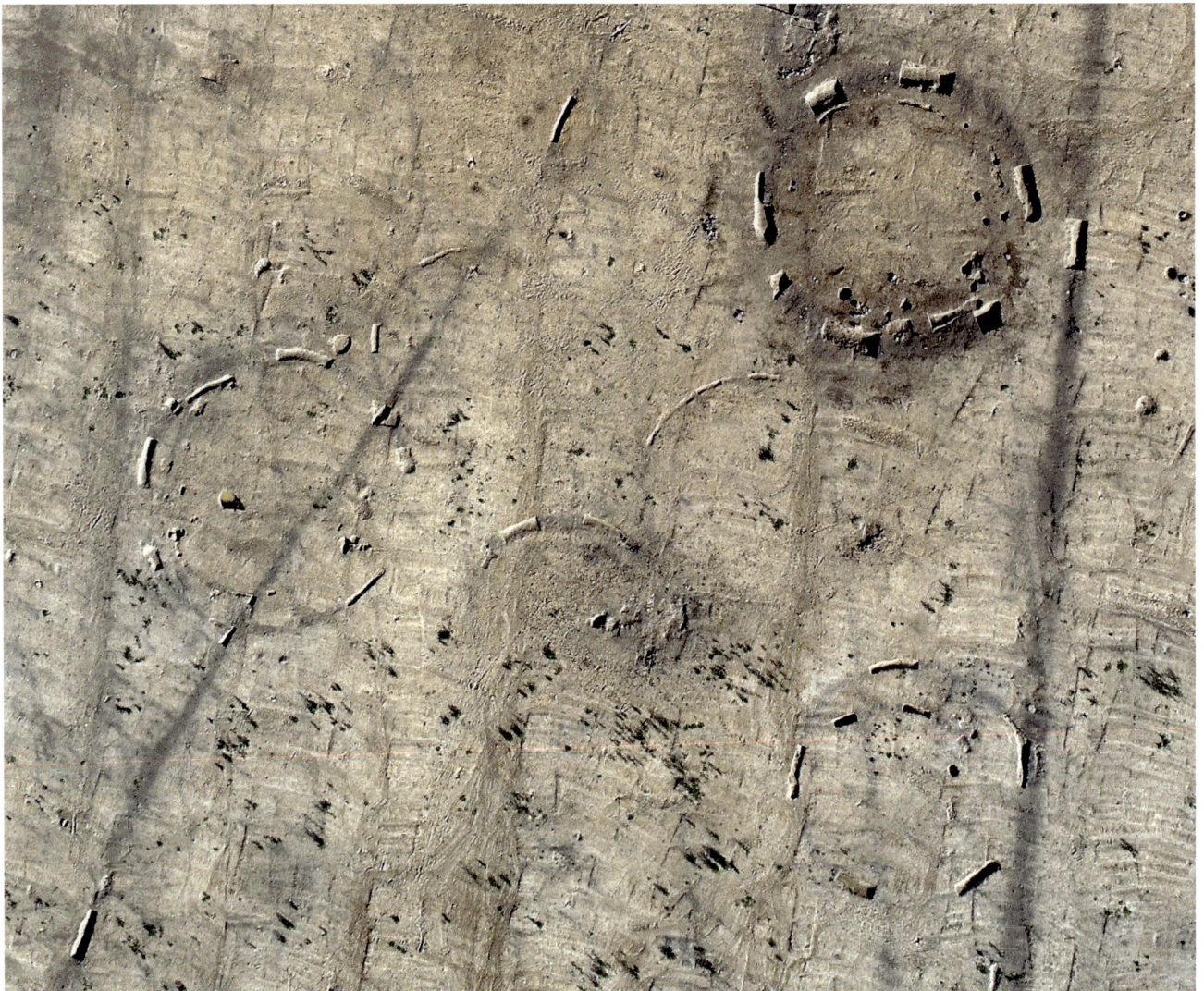

Figure 4.29 Drone photograph of Structure 38 with Structure 29, Structure 37 and Structure 28

STRUCTURE 28

Structure 28 was the most southerly possible roundhouse within the main enclosure, at the southern extent of the main cluster of structures (Figs 4.28 and 4.29). It comprised an outer curvilinear gully, an inner gully segment and two internal features. The outer gully measured 10 m in diameter, with an east-facing entrance measuring *c.* 3.6 m, truncated at its northern terminus by a modern ditch. The gully measured up to 0.59 m in width, 0.20 m in depth and had gently sloping sides, a rounded base and contained a natural infilled deposit of silty clay. Charcoal from the outer gully was radiocarbon dated to 360–150 cal BC (SUERC-98245) and 180–1 cal BC (SUERC-98244). A short section of gully, which terminated at each end, was located on the inner edge of the northern side of the outer gully. The inner gully measured 0.39 m in width, 0.30 m in depth and had steep sides, a rounded base and gradual breaks of slope. It contained two natural infilled deposits

comprising silty clays. Due to its differing alignment to the outer gully, it is possible this gully is unrelated to this roundhouse or acted to subdivide the internal space. Two radiocarbon dates were retrieved for this gully, with differing dates – 360–60 cal BC (SUERC-95806) and 2580–2460 cal BC (SUERC-95805) suggesting a level of disturbance of the feature regardless of its true age. The earlier date was similar to the intrusive date retrieved from Enclosure 1422, suggesting a possible phase of residual Neolithic activity across the southern part of site.

Post-hole 1161 was located within the interior of the structure. It measured 0.49 × 0.36 m in plan, 0.20 m in depth and had vertical sides, a flat base and sharp break of slope. It contained a primary packing fill overlain by an upper natural silting deposit. The post-hole contained a large quantity of birch charcoal which was radiocarbon dated to 160 cal BC–cal AD 20 (SUERC-98246). No other post-holes were identified within the vicinity, and as such its association to any phase or gully is uncertain. Pit 1088 was located adjacent to the eastern terminus of the inner gully. It measured 1.00 × 0.33 m in diameter and 0.08 m in depth with gently sloping sides, rounded base and contained a single natural infilling deposit. No function was evident for this pit.

STRUCTURE 37

Structure 37 was located between Structures 28 and 29 at the southern end of the enclosure (Figs 4.28 and 4.29). It was formed of a curvilinear gully comprising the northern arc with a series of pits and post-holes located internally. The gully measured 11.5 m in length and measured 0.48–0.50 m in width, 0.08–0.13 m in depth and had steep sides, a flat base and a single fill of dark orange-grey fine sandy silt. Two radiocarbon dates were retrieved from charcoal within the fill of this gully, dating to 170 cal BC–cal AD 10 (SUERC-95814) and 340–40 cal BC (SUERC-95815).

Post-holes 1356 and 1357 were situated adjacent to the eastern terminus of the gully. They measured 0.25–0.30 m in diameter and 0.04–0.05 m in depth, with steep sides, flat bases and gradual breaks of slope. A further cluster of three pits was located to the south of the gully. Pits 1389 and 1391 measured 0.64–0.88 m in diameter, 0.07–0.08 m in depth, with steep sides, flat bases and with natural infilled deposits. Pit 1385 measured 0.6 × 0.5 m in plan, and 0.23 m in depth. It had a flat base, steep sides and gradual breaks of slope, and contained three fills. Primary fill (1386) comprised a 0.05 m thick deposit of black silt with frequent charcoal flecks. Heat-affected natural forming the base of the pit indicated this burning event likely occurred in situ. This deposit was overlain by redeposited natural and sealed by natural infilling. This clear evidence of in situ burning alongside the irregularity of the gully in plan suggested this structure may not have been a roundhouse, but instead may have acted as a slot for an open wind-break type structure to shelter the burning activities within and may have been fairly temporary in function and construction. Two radiocarbon dates were retrieved (from charcoal and cereal grain respectively) within the fills of this pit, dating to 180 cal BC–cal AD 10 (SUERC-95816) and 200–40 cal BC (SUERC-95817), indicating a similar time frame as Structures 28 and 29.

STRUCTURE 29

Structure 29 was located to the west of Structure 28 (Figs 4.28 and 4.29). It consisted of two sections of an outer gully, two sections of an inner gully and ten internal features including pits and post-holes. The structure had a maximum diameter of *c.* 10.5 m. The outer gully cut an earlier gully, 1222, indicating the potential for an earlier phase or feature. The outer gully had two entrances, one to the east and one to the west, measuring 3.9 m and 2.3 m in width respectively. The inner gully had one entrance to the west which aligned with the entrance in the outer gully.

The southern outer gully measured approximately 11.5 m in length, 0.46 m in width and 0.13 m in depth with steep sides and a rounded base. It contained a single fill comprising sandy clay with occasional poorly sorted stones. The northern outer gully measured approximately 16.5 m in length, 0.52 m in width and 0.20 m in depth with gently sloping sides and a rounded to flat base. It contained two fills with a possible stone pot lid or disc recovered from the primary deposit. Two radiocarbon dates were retrieved from the northern terminus, dating to 340–40 cal BC (SUERC-95807) and 380–170 cal BC (SUERC-95811).

The southern inner gully measured approximately 5 m with a rounded terminal at each end. The gully measured 0.22 m in width and 0.08 m in depth with gently sloping sides, and an irregular rounded to flat base. The northern inner gully measured approximately 3.5 m in length, 0.38 m in width and 0.07 m in depth with gently sloping sides and a flat base. A sample of alder charcoal was dated to 200–40 cal BC (SUERC-98235) for the southern terminus of the outer ring-ditch.

Pit 1282 located within the roundhouse measured 1.1 m in length, 0.66 m in width and 0.35 m in depth. The pit contained two fills comprising grey silty clays from which a sample of charred cereal grain from the basal fill was radiocarbon dated to 360–100 cal BC (SUERC-95812). Two post-holes were also located within Structure 29. Post-hole 1207, which cut Gully 1222, and Post-hole 1273, located to the south-east of Gully 1315. The post-holes measured 0.3 m in length, 0.2 m in width and 0.2 m in depth. Six pits were also located within the building, though most of the internal pits or post-holes showed no clear indication of alignment or function. It is possible that pits 1261 and 1273 may have formed more significant entrance posts relating to the inner gully structure, however, truncation makes this assertion somewhat speculative.

STRUCTURE 34

Structure 34 was located to the north-west of Structure 29 and truncates Structure 35 (Phase 2a; Fig. 4.18). It comprised a curvilinear gully measuring 7.3 m in diameter, with a narrow west-facing entrance measuring 0.76 m in width (Fig. 4.31). The gully measured up to 0.20 m in width and 0.17 m in depth, with steep sides and rounded base. The narrow west-facing entrance is unusual and may indicate a differing function to this structure.

STRUCTURE 18

Structure 18 was located to the north of Structure 34, towards the north-west corner of the main enclosure (Fig. 4.30). The structure appeared to be truncated by Ditch 1772 of Sub-enclosure 3. Structure 18 has been

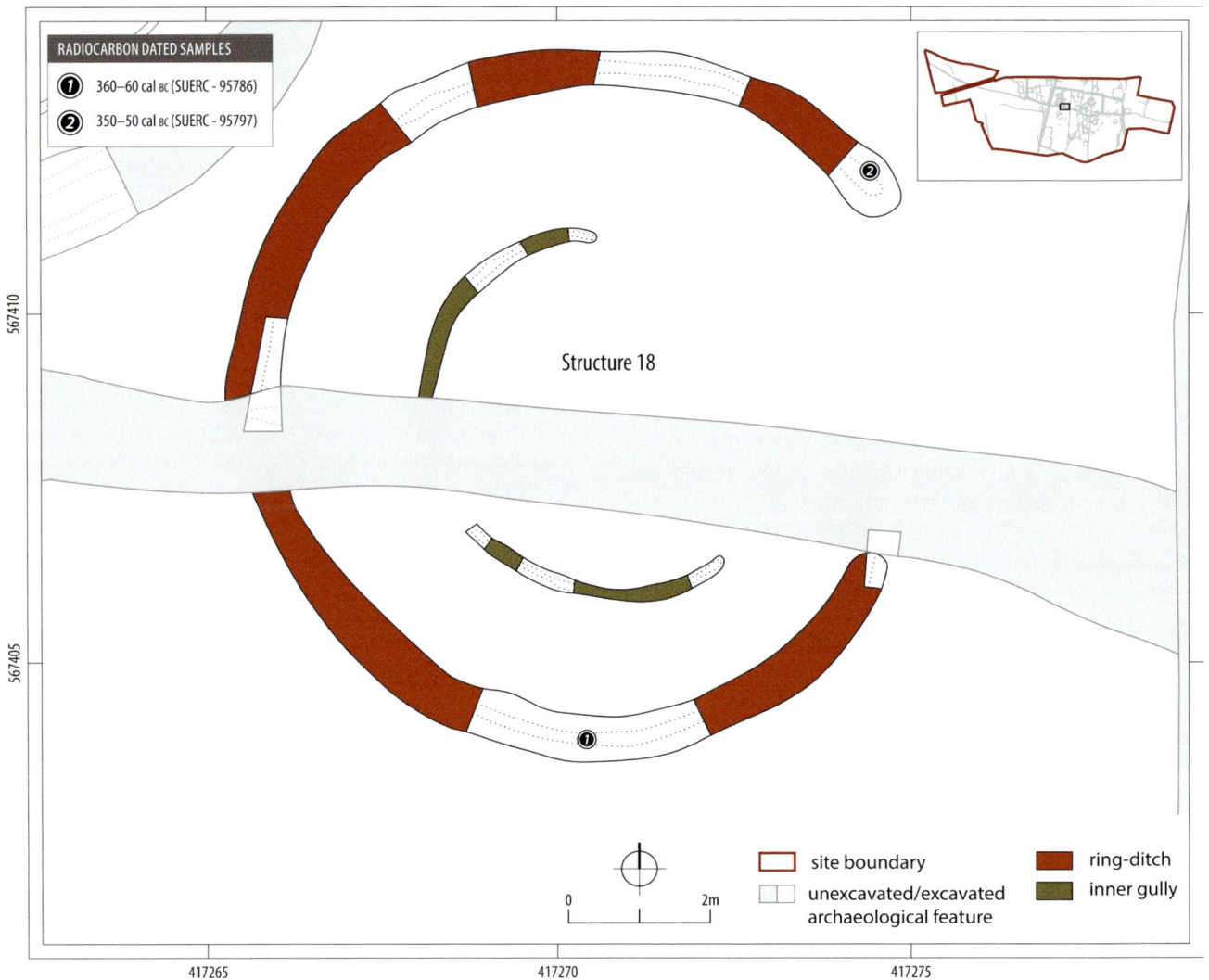

Figure 4.30 Plan of Structure 18

grouped within Phase 2b as its form and radiocarbon dates suggest that it is part of the later development of the site but its relationship to Sub-enclosure 3 is unclear. This ditch of Sub-enclosure 3 appeared to have been recut multiple times with the suggestion that it followed the line of an earlier linear boundary (see Sub-enclosure 3). The recutting of the ditch, truncating Structure 18, may have been later in the sequence of enclosure development perhaps to define the area surrounding Structure 42.

Structure 18 comprised two elements – an outer curvilinear ditch and an inner curvilinear gully spaced *c.* 2 m from the outer ditch. The outer ditch enclosed an area 10.4 m in diameter with an east-facing entrance measuring 4.5 m in width. This steep-sided ditch measured 0.65 m in width and up to 0.24 m in depth and contained a mid-greyish-brown clay fill. Due to the wide nature of this ditch, and its placement around the inner gully, it appeared to form an outer perimeter ditch to the roundhouse. Two radiocarbon dates were retrieved from charcoal within the fills of this ditch. A sample of willow charcoal from a

section of the outer ring-ditch was dated to 360–60 cal BC (SUERC-95786) with alder charcoal from the ditch terminus dated to 350–50 cal BC (SUERC-95797). The inner ring-ditch was heavily truncated but would originally have formed a circle with a diameter of 5 m. The steep-sided gully measured 0.2 m in width and 0.08 m in depth with a single clay fill. The steep sides and narrow width of the ditch suggests this may have defined a structural wall slot.

STRUCTURE 42

Structure 42 was located next to Structure 18, within Sub-enclosure 3, and truncated Structure 43 (Phase 2a). The structure also cut the pre-enclosure phase palisades and the edge of Sub-enclosure 3. Structure 42 was formed of a series of intercutting outer ditches with a diameter of *c.* 11 m and an inner gully with a *c.* 8.3 m diameter (Fig. 4.31). The primary outer ditch, 1571, had been almost completely recut by the secondary ditch and could only be identified in section in the northern terminus. The secondary ditch, 1526, measured up to

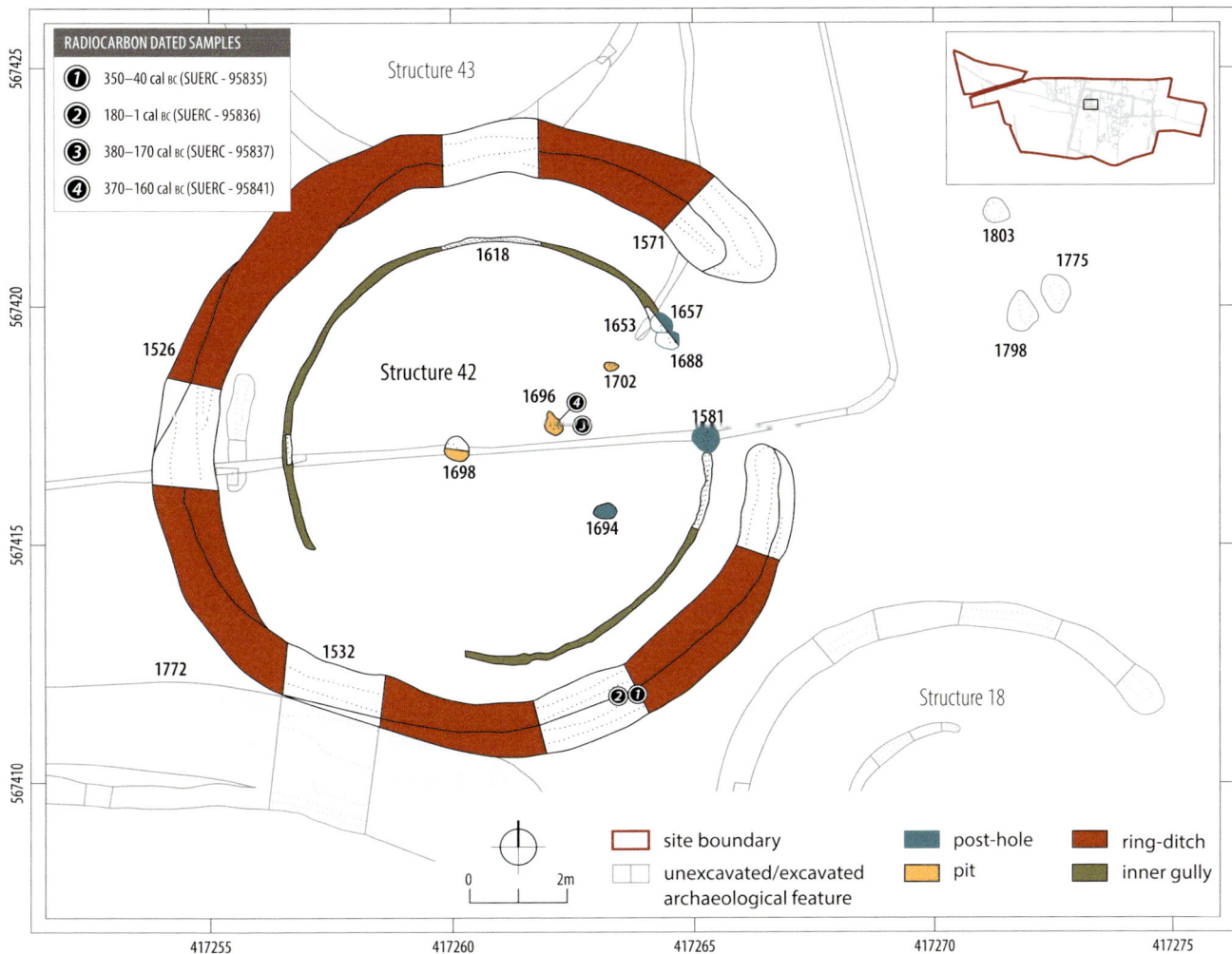

Figure 4.31 Plan of Structure 42

1.0 m in width, 0.3 m in depth and had regular sloping sides, a rounded base and contained a single deposit of dark brownish-grey fine sandy clay. This was cut by a final ring-ditch, 1532, which measured up to 1.02 m in width, 0.28 m in depth and had regular sloping edges, a rounded base and with a similar fill with rare charcoal. Two radiocarbon dates were retrieved from the fill of this ditch, dating to 350–40 cal BC (SUERC-95835) and 180–1 cal BC (SUERC-95836).

The inner gully measured up to 0.2 m in width and 0.12 m in depth and had irregular sides, a rounded irregular base and was filled by a naturally accumulated deposit of grey silty clay. The gully had two terminal ends which formed the east-facing entrance. The southern terminal end was clearly visible and had a post-hole at its end. Two post-holes and a pit were located at the northern terminus end of the inner gully, suggesting larger posts flanked the entrance into the interior space, and supported the structural walls.

Three pits and a post-hole were identified within the building, located within the interior of the inner gully. Post-hole 1694 was sub-circular and measured 0.52 ×

0.47 m in diameter and 0.39 m in depth with irregular edges, flat base, and a singular backfill with occasional small charcoal inclusions and rare very small bone fragments. The three pits were sub-circular in plan, with rounded breaks and signs of animal burrowing throughout. They contained natural silting deposits with rare small charcoal inclusions and showed no further indications of their functions. Charcoal retrieved from Pit 1696 returned two radiocarbon dates of 380–170 cal BC (SUERC-95837) and 370–160 cal BC (SUERC-95841).

STRUCTURE 45

Structure 45 was located to the north-east of structures 18 and 42, towards the northern edge of the main enclosure (Fig. 4.33). It comprised a heavily truncated curvilinear gully which was split into three segments. The structure had a projected diameter of *c.* 7 m and showed no obvious indication of an entrance due to extensive truncation. The three segments of gully measured 0.18–0.26 m in width and 0.04–0.06 m in depth and contained similar fills of naturally infilled silts. Internally a spread of material and a post-hole were present.

Post-hole 1789 measured 0.2 m in diameter and 0.14 m in depth, and had steep sides, a flat base and sharp breaks of slope. It contained a single deliberate backfill deposit containing moderate amounts of medium sub-rounded stones – possible packing material. Overlying the post-hole was a series of spreads (1788) *c.* 2 m in diameter comprising silts with medium burnt stone fragments, charcoal flecks and small fired clay fragments throughout. Samples of birch and alder charcoal from the spread were radiocarbon dated to 390–170 cal BC (SUERC-98239) and 200–40 cal BC (SUERC-98243). The spread across the centre of the structure may result from its demolition or collapse.

Phase 2 general

A large number of features have been assigned to the broader enclosure phase (Phase 2; see Fig. 4.11) likely representing continuous settlement development through-out this period. Several features were truncated by round-houses and enclosures belonging to Phase 2c but many displayed no stratigraphic relationship to surrounding features. As such, some of the features may relate to phases 2a and 2b with a more nuanced picture of development, organisation and intensity envisaged.

Structure 24

Structure 24 was located towards the eastern edge of the enclosure and showed signs of heavy truncation (Fig. 4.32). It comprised three concentric curvilinear gullies and four discrete features. The inner curvilinear gully had a projected diameter of 10.6 m and a possible east or south-east facing entrance. It measured up to 0.16 m in width, 0.07 m in depth, with gently sloping sides, rounded base and with a single deposit of silty clay. Immediately to the south-west was a secondary gully that curved around the inner gully with a *c.* 1 m gap. It measured up to 0.33 m in width, 0.15 m in depth, with gently sloping sides, a rounded base and with a single deposit also of silty clay. The gully straightened out towards the east, perhaps to respect the entrance to the roundhouse. An outer gully was located *c.* 0.35 m to the south-west of the secondary gully. It measured 2.2 m in length, 0.15 m in width, 0.04 m in depth and had gently sloping sides, a rounded base, with a single naturally infilled deposit of brownish-grey silty sand. It showed signs of particularly heavy truncation and may originally have extended much further. Its function with regards to the roundhouse was unclear.

Two pits, 0905 and 0907, and two post-holes, 0939 and 0944, were located towards the eastern side of the structure, possibly located within the entrance of the roundhouse. Pit 0905 measured 0.40 × 0.28 m in diameter, 0.05 m in depth and had gently sloping sides, a flat base and with a single natural infilling deposit. This was cut by Pit 0907 which measured 0.65 × 0.43 m in diameter, 0.10 m in depth with gently sloping sides, flat base and a single natural infilling deposit. Both pits likely related to the use of the structure, though no clear function was evident.

Post-hole 0939 was located 0.65 m to the east of pits 0905 and 0907 and measured 0.43 m in diameter, 0.28 m in depth with steep sides, a flat base and sharp breaks of slope. It contained two fills comprising a post-packing fill surrounding a post-pipe fill of mid-blueish-grey silty clay. Post-hole 0944 was located 1.3 m to the north of Post-hole 0939 and measured 0.6 × 0.4 m in diameter and 0.28 m in depth. It had steep sides, a flat base and sharp breaks of slope, and contained a post-packing fill with large sub-angular stones. Their relationship to the structure was unclear.

Structure 23

Structure 23 was located at the centre of the site truncated by Enclosure 2 (Phase 2b; see Fig. 4.25). It comprised an external curvilinear gully which survived in three segments, and an internal curvilinear gully, pit and four internal post-holes. The external gully had a diameter of 9.7 m and a probable east-facing entrance measuring 4.8 m in width. The three segments of the external gully were all similar in shape and size, measuring 0.22–0.27 m in width, 0.04–0.08 m in depth, with gently sloping sides and a flat base. They all contained natural infilling deposits comprising brownish-grey silts and clays. The inner gully, 0879, survived only in the south-west and measured 0.33 m in width and 0.11 m in depth, with gently sloping sides, flat base, and with a single natural infilling deposit. Its adjacency to the external gully was indicative of it forming a separate phase of construction, either being the original ditch or a recutting.

Four post-holes formed a rough arc along the northern side of the internal space. All four post-holes had moderately steeply sloping sides, rounded bases and gradual breaks of slope. Their fills were all dark brown silty clays with occasional small to large sub-rounded stones throughout. They appeared to follow a different alignment to inner gully suggesting a different function, perhaps as an internal division, or earlier phase of structure.

Structure 30

Structure 30 was located to the west of Structure 23 and was cut by a modern ditch (Fig. 4.25). The primary gully to the north measured 4.1 m in length with the terminus at the eastern end indicating the entranceway. It measured 0.37 m in width, 0.10 m in depth and had gently sloping sides, a rounded base and gradual breaks of slope. It contained a single fill of brown-grey silty clay. A small section of the gully was identified between the phases of Enclosure 2 to the south, suggesting a possible southern edge to this structure, which would give the roundhouse a diameter of 8.2 m. An associated post-hole and pit within the area of the structure provided no further clarity on the form or function of this heavily truncated roundhouse.

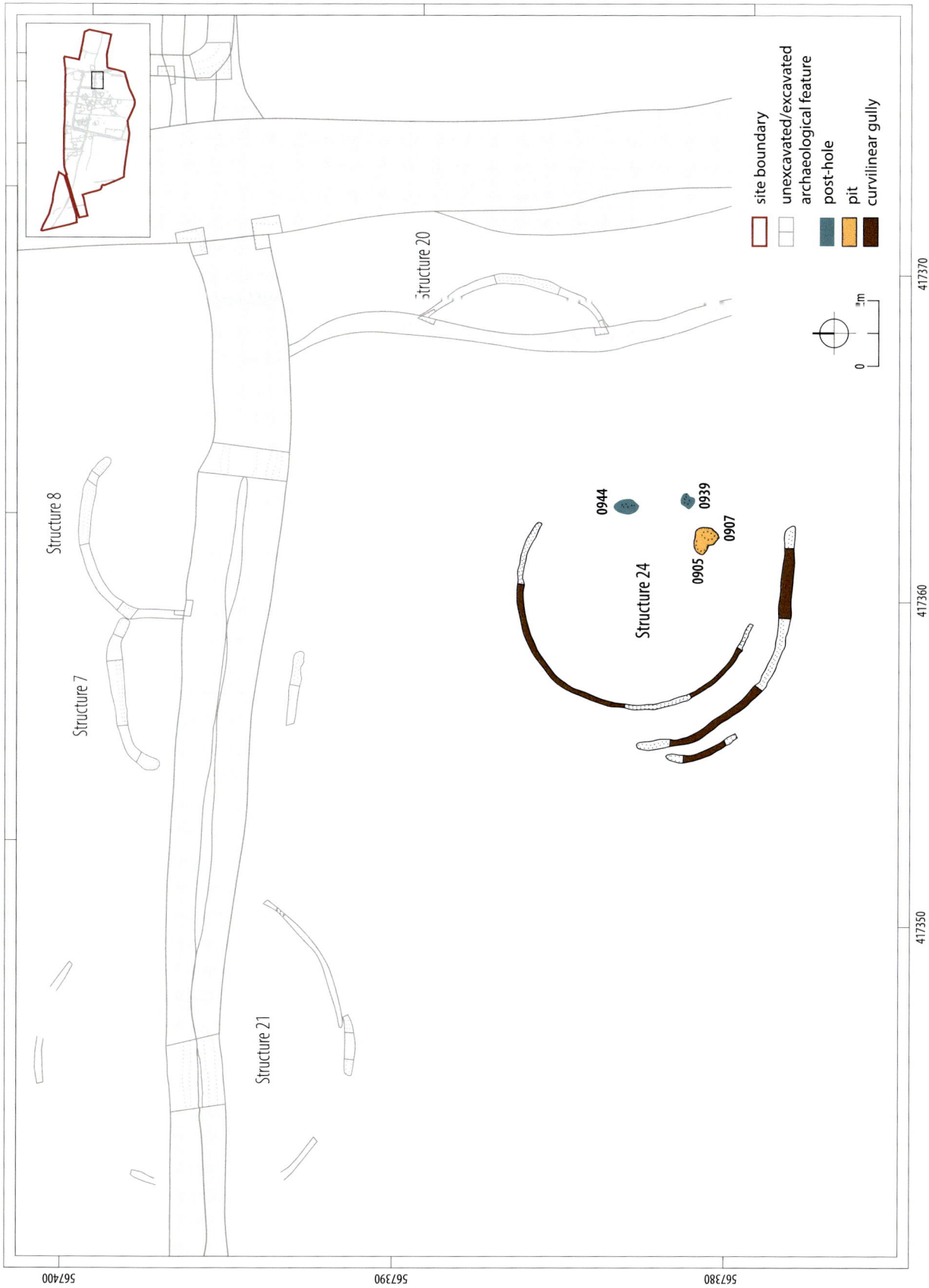

Figure 4.32 Plan of Structure 24 with structures 7, 8, 20 and 21 to the north

Structure 41

Structure 41 was located to the south-west of Structure 30 (Fig. 4.27). It comprised three lengths of a curvilinear gully and as a circular structure would have had a diameter of 11.6 m. It was truncated by the southern edge of Sub-Enclosure 2. Two short lengths of gully were identified to the west and to the south-east, whilst the main section of the ditch formed the northern edge of the structure. They measured 2.4 m, 2.5 m and 12.55 m respectively in length, measuring *c.* 0.35 m in width and 0.05–0.15 m in depth, with steep sides, flat bases, containing naturally infilled silting deposits. It had a probable east-facing entrance, though heavy truncation of the structure made this uncertain. Two radiocarbon dates were retrieved from the fills of the northern section of gully, dating to 360–60 cal BC (SUERC-95827) and 350–50 cal BC (SUERC-95831).

A post-hole, 1488, measuring 0.34 × 0.25 m in diameter and 0.31 m in depth, was located within the structure. It had vertical sides, a flat base and a sharp break of slope, and contained a single backfill with occasional medium sub-rounded stones and charcoal flecks, though no clear relationship with the structure was evident.

Structure 32

Structure 32 was located to the south of Structure 41 (Fig. 4.27). It consisted of a curvilinear gully with an estimated diameter of 6.6 m and an associated pit. The gully was formed of two segments measuring 5.5 m and 3.5 m in length, 0.28–0.35 m in width and 0.11–0.18 m in depth, with a flat base, steep sides and a single fill. Truncation was particularly prominent to the north-western side of the feature – it presumably originally formed a continuous gully at this side. Post-hole 1209 was located 0.1 m from the southern terminus of the main gully and measured 0.35 × 0.25 m in diameter and 0.18 m in depth. It had steep sides, a rounded base and gradual breaks of slope, and was in line with arc of the gullies, suggesting a likely connection to the structure.

Structure 31

Structure 31 was located towards the southern extent of the cluster of Phase 2 roundhouses (Fig. 4.28). It comprised a curvilinear gully, defining a space *c.* 7.5 m in diameter, which was truncated by a post-medieval ditch. The gully measured 11 m in length, 0.43 m in width and 0.08 m in depth with gently sloping sides, gradual breaks of slope and a flat base. It was filled by a single naturally infilled deposit of sandy clay. The surviving evidence suggest that if an entrance were present, it would have been roughly east or south-east facing. No other features were associated with this gully.

Structure 33

Structure 33 was located to the south-east of Structure 31 (Fig. 4.28). It was heavily truncated and comprised two

lengths of gully, 1307 and 1314, which measured 5 m and 3 m in length respectively defining an area 9.2 m in diameter. Gully 1307 measured 0.31 m in width, 0.10 m in depth, and contained a single natural infilling comprising mid-brownish-grey clayey silt. Gully 1314 measured 0.15 m in width, 0.05 m in depth and contained a similar natural infilling. Significant truncation precluded further interpretation of the structure.

Structure 39

Structure 39 was located south-west of structures 33, 31 and 32 (Fig. 4.11). It consisted of a single 3 m length of curvilinear gully. This gully measured 0.19 m in width and 0.05 m in depth, with a flat base, gently sloping sides and with a single natural infilling deposit. Assuming it had formed a ring-gully, it had a projected diameter of 5.3 m. Heavy truncation was evident, with no remains of the eastern or southern extents of the structure visible, and as such little was left to give a strong indication of the function of the structure, as was the case with Structure 36.

Structure 36

Structure 36 was located towards the western edge of the enclosure (Fig. 4.18). It consisted of a single 6 m length of curvilinear gully measuring 0.45 m in width and 0.08 m in depth, with a flat base, gently sloping sides and gradual breaks of slope. It had a projected diameter of 6.7 m and contained a single fill of dark grey silt with rare charcoal and stones throughout. Heavy truncation was evident, with no remains of the eastern extents of the structure visible.

Structure 56

Structure 56 was located immediately to the south of Structure 16 and overlaid the earlier Enclosure 0569 (Fig. 4.33). It comprised a short length of curvilinear gully which had been heavily truncated. On the eastern side, the gully ended in a rounded terminus suggesting that, if this gully did represent a ring-gully, the entrance may have been located on the east with the gully defining an area *c.* 9 m in diameter. The gully was up to 0.57 m in width, 0.21 m in depth, had steep sides, flat base, and contained a single naturally infilled deposit of grey silty sand.

Structure 16

Structure 16, located in the north-western corner of the main enclosure, comprised two overlapping curvilinear gullies (Fig. 4.33). It measured 8.9 m in diameter with an east-facing entrance measuring 3.5 m in width. The primary gully measured 7.6 m in length located on the south-west side of the structure, which had been truncated to the east by a gully recut. The gully measured 0.25 m in width and 0.05–0.08 m in depth, and had steep sides, an uneven base, with a single fill of brown clay.

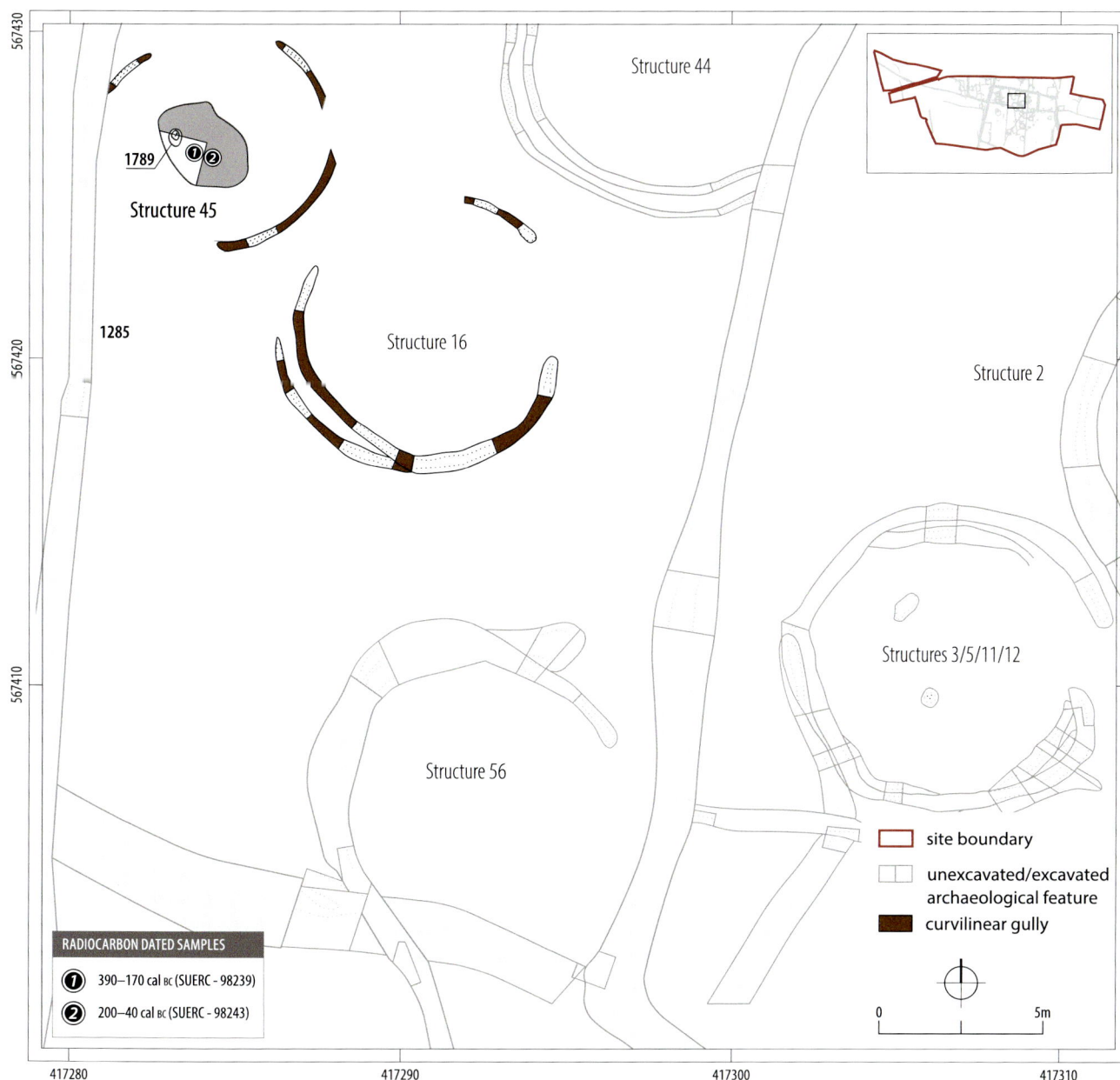

Figure 4.33 Plan of structures 45, 16 and 56

The secondary gully was C-shaped and constituted the southern and western sides of the structure, terminating in a rounded terminal to the east, forming the southern side of the entranceway. A short length of the gully was also identified along the northern side of the structure, with a rounded terminal forming the northern side of the entrance. The secondary gully measured 0.15–0.46 m in width, 0.05–0.12 m in depth and had steep sides, a rounded base and with a series of naturally infilled deposits of brown silty clay. An unfinished perforated weight was recovered from the southern section of the later gully, possibly for use as a fly weight for a bow drill (see stone tool discussion).

Post-built structures 13, 14 and 17

Three post-built structures were identified within the main enclosure to the east of structures 22 and 38, of which Structure 17 was assigned to sub-phase 2b – though will be discussed here with the other post-built structures (Fig. 4.34). The dimensions of the post-holes varied from 0.35–0.87 m in diameter, 0.1–0.36 m in depth, with many of the posts containing packing material. Structures 13 and 14 were sub-square four-post structures *c.* 2 m in length. A single date of 3010–2880 cal BC (SUERC-98237) was provided by the fill of Post-hole 634 of Structure 13, likely resulting from the dating of residual material. Post-hole 0597 of Structure 14 contained a sherd of green-glaze

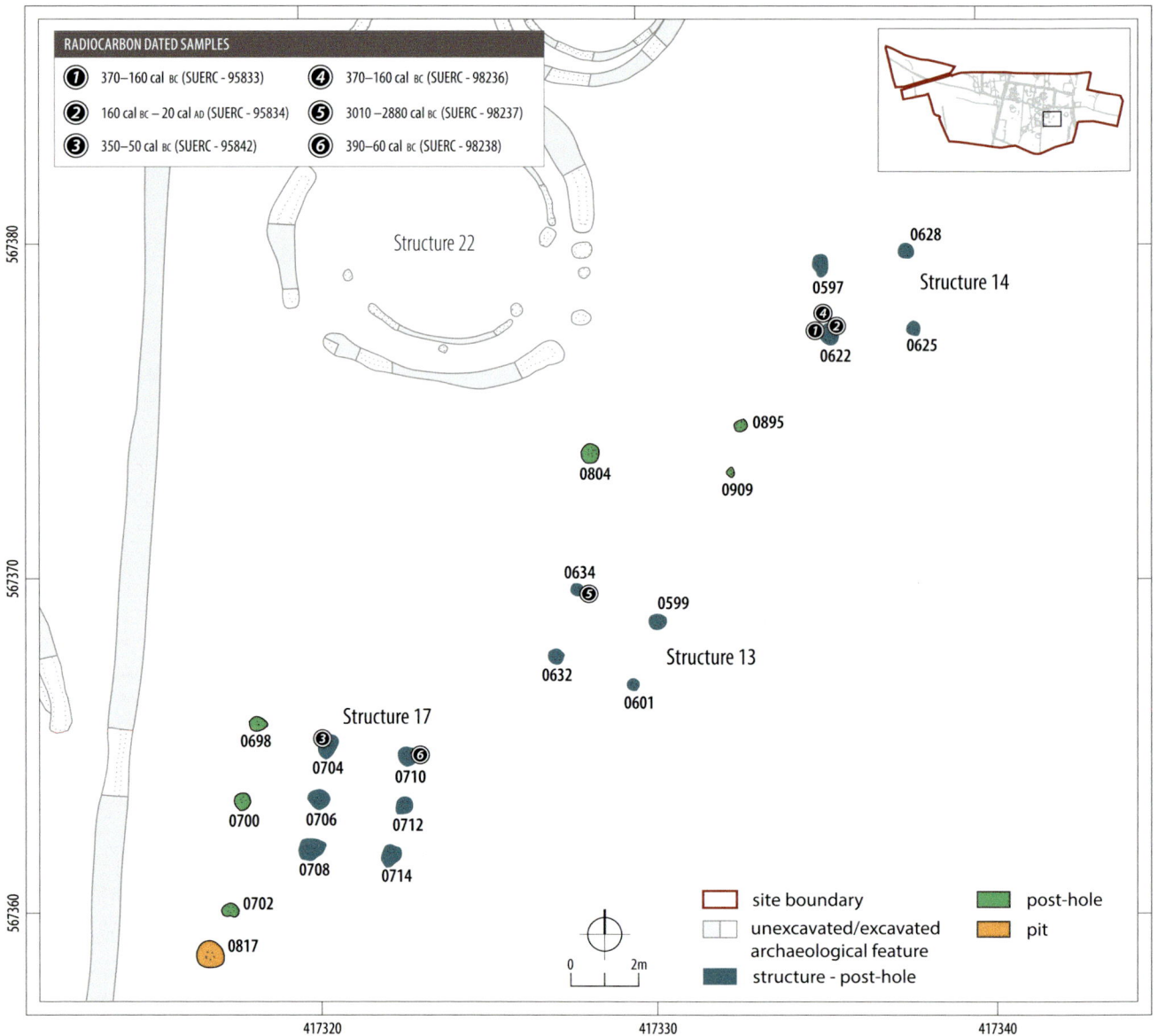

Figure 4.34 Plan of post-built structures

ceramic in its upper fill – likely an intrusive find resulting from modern ploughing. Three radiocarbon dates were obtained from charcoal and cereal grains from Post-hole 0622 of Structure 14. The sample provided dates of 370–160 cal BC (SUERC-95833), 160 cal BC–cal AD 20 (SUERC-95834) and 370–170 cal BC (SUERC-98236).

Structure 17 was a six-post structure of two rows of three posts aligned north–south. The structure measured 3.8 m in length and 3 m in width. Three associated post-holes, 0698, 0700 and 0702, and Pit 0817 formed a parallel line to the west of the main structure. Two comparable radiocarbon dates were received from samples from two post-holes of 350–50 cal BC (SUERC-95842) and 390–60 cal BC (SUERC-98238).

The five radiocarbon dates obtained from these post-built structures was indicative that they were contemporary with the main phase of activity within the enclosure, possibly forming raised storage platforms for grain or other perishable goods. It is possible that these structures all dated to Phase 2b, though it was not possible to ascertain if they were contemporary structures with each other.

Discrete features

Eight discrete pits and post-holes were also identified within the main enclosure and may have related to Phase 2. Three post-holes, 0804, 0895 and 0909, were located in close proximity to the post-built structures 13, 14 and 17 but didn't appear to directly relate to these structures (Fig. 4.34). A stone pounder was recovered from Post-hole 1409 located between structures 36 and 39 to the west (Fig. 4.18).

External enclosures

Two sub-square enclosures were located outside of the main enclosure, each built parallel to the main enclosure ditch (see Fig. 4.11). Enclosure 0205 was located 2 m from the outer eastern edge of the main enclosure and truncated the wider landscape boundary Ditch 0488. It formed a rectilinear enclosure measuring 11.2 × 9.9 m in plan with an east-facing entrance measuring 1.25 m in width. The ditch measured up to 1.10 m in width and 0.30 m in depth with gently sloping sides, a rounded base and with a fill of mid-orange-grey silty clay. Its southern terminus showed signs of recutting, suggesting a level of maintenance was undertaken to this open boundary that may have had its own corresponding inner bank and fence.

Enclosure 0514 was located 1.6 m to the north of the main enclosure ditch at its north-east corner. It formed a sub-square enclosure measuring 15.9 m north–south, and 18.9 m east–west, and had been truncated into three sections of gully, with much of the eastern edge truncated away. The gullies measured up to 1.10 m in width, 0.22 m in depth, with steep sides, rounded bases and with a series of grey silty and sandy clay fills. There were no signs of recutting of this enclosure, suggesting a single phase of use.

The enclosures likely acted as external stock enclosures, allowing for additional stock enclosure space outside the main enclosure, perhaps to keep certain groups of livestock separate.

Summary

The structures and enclosures that form Phase 2 have been grouped to allow for a discussion of site development. However, the broad sequence presented here does not represent the wholesale replacement of features following each sub-phase. The development of the site during this phase was likely more nuanced, representing the multifaceted construction, use, modification and abandonment of features as will be expanded upon in the discussion (see Chapter 5). The main enclosure appears to have been constructed early in this phase enclosing the majority of the structures. At some point the interior was divided through the creation of four sub-enclosures, with Sub-enclosure 4 in the south-west being positioned away from the structures, and only able to be assigned broad contemporaneity with the main enclosure. The three sub-enclosures to the north (1–3) were aligned upon the major pre-existing east-west boundary through the site, indicating a level of spatial continuity. The development of these enclosures appears later in the sequence with sub-enclosures 1 and 2 potentially changing access to the site through the creation of a narrow trackway to the north. While the enclosures have been broadly phased, their development is somewhat unclear as through the life of the settlement the boundaries appear to be established, modified, abandoned and then re-established.

Structures of this phase were centrally located, forming a rough north–south alignment, indicating a focus of human activity towards the centre of the enclosure, with some peripheral activity. The lack of structures to the south-east of the site may be indicative of increased truncation in these areas as the site sloped southwards. Alternatively, it may suggest that this lower-lying land with adjacent water sources was less suitable for domestic occupation and was used to contain animals or for other activities. Many of the structures are defined by single narrow curvilinear gullies with limited evidence of internal features. These features likely represent a variety of functions and potentially more ephemeral structures. Several of the structures also appeared to follow the style of roundhouse initially identified with Structure 2, and further seen in Structures 18, 22, 29 and 42. Structures 22 and 29 were of particular interest, with their inner gullies, outer ditches and multiple entrances (see discussion in Chapter 5).

Phase 3: additional enclosure

Phase 3 is characterised by the construction of a sub-square enclosure truncating the north-western edge of the earlier large enclosure (Fig. 4.35). Enclosure 0776 was defined by a ditch of comparable width and depth to the main enclosure with a distinct west-facing entrance. No structures within the enclosure were interpreted as contemporary, with Structure 47 and Structure 52, located in the entranceway, having been interpreted as belonging to Phase 1. It is unclear if there was a continuation or a break in activity between phases 2 and 3, but there was clear spatial continuity seen in the eastern and southern enclosure boundaries.

Enclosure 0776

Enclosure 0776 cut the north-eastern corner of Enclosure 0570 and encompassed an area of 1886 m² (Fig. 4.35). The excavation of six full sections across the ditch, and an additional nine relationship slots, revealed the ditch to measure 2.06–4.13 m in width and 1.05–1.9 m in depth, with steep sides and a rounded base with a gradual break of slope. A grey ware rim sherd of first–second-century AD date was recovered from the fill (1950) of the small section, 1949, excavated at the north-western corner. The northern terminus (1139) displayed the most complete sequence of deposits common to the enclosure ditch (Fig. 4.36). The basal fill of mid-blueish-grey clay (1140) was overlain by mottled orange-grey clayey silt within which rare small charcoal fragments were identified. The upper fills comprise similar mid-orange-brown sandy silts capped by a final top-soil rich fill that extended over an adjacent ditch. Ditch 1146 was identified next to the northern terminus and appeared to run parallel along the west side of the enclosure. It measured 1.05 m in width

AREA 2

0776
enclosure

FIG 4.36
(Left)

1146

FIG 4.36
(Right)

0652/0655

site boundary

Iron Age settlement Phase 3

other feature

0   25m

RADIOCARBON DATED SAMPLES

① 50 cal BC – 120 cal AD (SUERC - 92160)

② 150 cal BC – 209 cal AD (SUERC - 92160)

417200   417250   417300   417350

567350   567400   567450

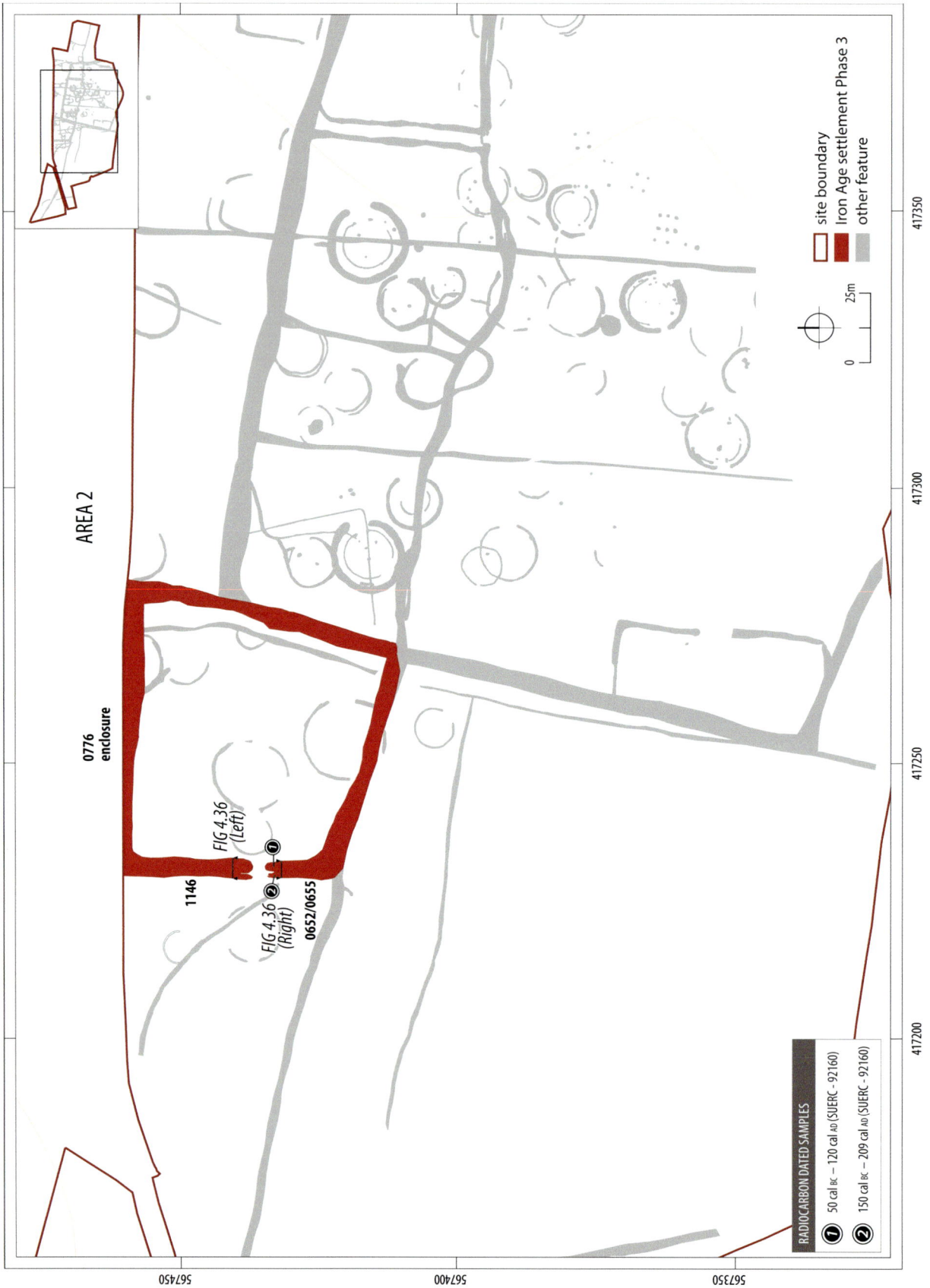

Figure 4.35 Lower Callerton Area 2 – Phase 3

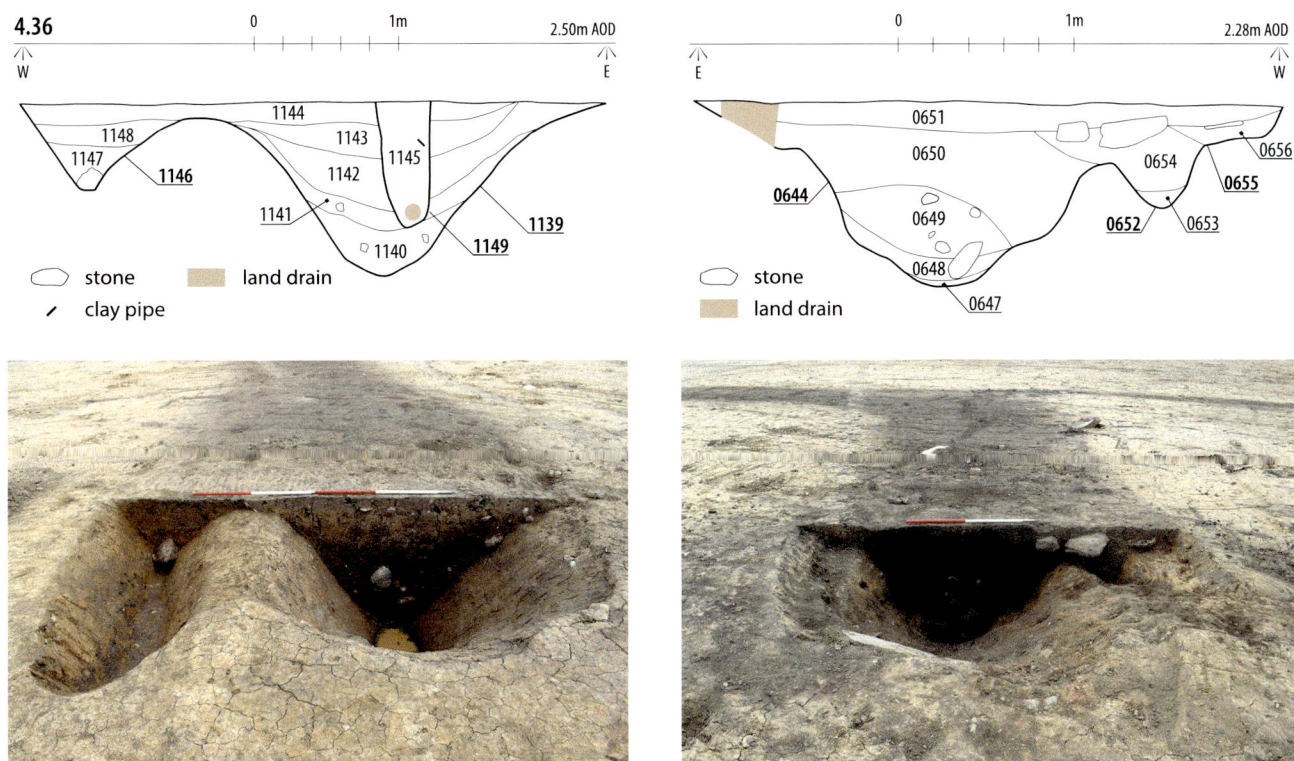

Figure 4.36 Photographs and sections of the northern (left) and southern (right) termini of Enclosure 0776

and 0.61 m in depth with steep sides, a rounded base and two silty clay fills.

A similar arrangement of ditches was identified during the excavation of the southern terminus. The terminus of the main ditch measured 2 m in width and 1.08 m deep with stepped edges (Fig. 4.36). The basal fills (0647 and 0648) of the terminus comprised dark grey silty clay with charcoal inclusions capped by a deposit of dumped material (0649). The deposit measured 0.30 m in thickness and comprised mottled orange-grey sandy clay with frequent small sub-angular stones, charcoal fragments and iron panning. Overlying this was a substantial natural silting deposit (0650) sealing the ditch. A body sherd from a Roman oxidised ware vessel was recovered from this deposit. Charcoal from the basal fill of the ditch (0647) was radiocarbon dated to 50 cal BC–cal AD 120 (SUERC-92160) while charcoal from the dumped deposit (0649) returned a date of between 150 cal BC–cal AD 20 (SUERC-92164). As with the northern terminus, further ditches cut the western edge of the ditch. Ditch 0652 measured 0.35 m in width, 0.51 m in depth and cut the southern terminus. This was then truncated by a smaller parallel ditch, 0655, that measured 0.04 m in width, 0.20 m in depth. The arrangement of ditches suggests that the west-facing portion of the enclosure was potentially later elaborated or redefined. No structures or internal features were definitively associated with this enclosure, so it was not possible to attribute the function of this enclosure to either domestic or livestock activities (Fig 4.36).

Unphased features

Due to the lack of stratigraphic or spatial relationships, two structures and several ditches and pits were not attributed to one of the previously described phases (Fig. 4.37). These structures and features were located to the north and west of the main enclosure and each may belong to any of the phases of occupation outlined above, to earlier pre-Iron Age activity, or to later activity post-abandonment of the enclosure settlement.

Structures

Structure 10 was located immediately north of Enclosure 0514 and beyond the north-eastern corner of the main enclosure. It comprised a sub-circular gully with a diameter of *c.* 6 m which had been truncated away along its eastern side. It measured 0.37–0.5 m in width and 0.06–0.11 m in depth and contained a single natural infilling deposit with moderate amounts of small charcoal flecks. A circular, shallow pit was located within the bounds of the gully and contained a single fill of mid-grey silty clay. The sub-circular plan of the gully indicated this was unlikely to have been a roundhouse, though no further indication of function was evident.

Table 4.1 Pottery assemblage by feature

Feature	Fill	Cat. No.	Fabric	Wt (kg)	No.
Area 2					
Pit 1722	1763	17	Grass-tempered	0.000	1
Enclosure 0776	0650	18	Oxidised ware	0.003	1
Enclosure 0776	1950	19	Grey ware	0.010	1

Structure 25 was located to the north of the main enclosure and comprised three curvilinear gully segments. The outer was formed of a single gully that measured 6 m in length, up to 0.40 m in width, 0.12 m in depth and had gently sloping sides, rounded base, with a single fill of brownish-orange silty clay. The inner gully, formed of two lengths, formed a rough U-shape, widening to the south. It measured up to 0.45 m in width, 0.16 m in depth, and formed a possible north-facing entrance to the enclosed space to the south, measuring 3.2 m in width. Again, no clear function was evident for this structure due to significant truncation of the southern section. It is likely it formed a wind-break or fence line for an open area of activity. A further short length of gully (0949) was located immediately to the south-east.

Ditches

Three ditches, 0595, 2005 and 2036, were identified across the site and probably dated to the Iron Age. Ditch 0595 was located immediately to the east of Enclosure 0514 and may have originally formed a fence line delineating the space directly north of the main enclosure during Phase 2. The ditch measured 45 m in length, 0.6 m in width and 0.16 m in depth with gently sloping sides, a rounded base and with a single silty clay fill.

Ditch 2005 was located to the west of Enclosure 0776 and was aligned north-west to south-east, terminating to the south-east, in close proximity to the southern terminal of Enclosure 0776. The ditch measured 0.46 m in width, 0.10 m in depth, with gently sloping sides, a rounded base and with a single fill of mid-orange to brownish-grey silty clay.

Ditch 2036 was a north to south aligned ditch *c.* 75 m in length, in two parts, which turned west at its northern end. It was located in the far west of site and may have originally formed an enclosure or boundary. It measured up to 0.67 m in width and 0.22 m in depth, containing a single fill similar in composition to Ditch 2005.

All three ditches likely formed wider boundaries. However, a lack of association with other features and the absence of chronological diagnostic features or finds precluded a more definitive understanding of their phasing.

The finds assemblage

The finds assemblage from Lower Callerton was limited with a small quantity of pottery, stone tools, fired clay and industrial waste recovered from the site.

Pottery
Alex Croom

A small assemblage of later prehistoric and Roman pottery was recovered from Lower Callerton consisting of a very small fragment of grass-tempered potentially Iron Age pottery and two sherds of Roman pottery, representing two vessels, weighing 0.013 kg. The pottery was quantified in its fabric categories by weight, sherd count and estimated vessel equivalents (EVEs, *i.e.* percentages of surviving rim diameters). The catalogue numbers refer to the entire Lower Callerton assemblage with the later prehistoric and Roman vessels included as catalogue numbers 17–19.

Location and distribution

A minute scrap of grass-tempered ware (Catalogue No. 17) was recovered from Pit 1722 within Structure 43. This is the only fabric which may date to the Iron Age (Table 4.1). A single body sherd of Roman oxidised ware (Catalogue No. 18) was recovered from deposit (0650) sealing Enclosure 0776. A rim sherd of Roman grey ware (Catalogue No. 19) was also found in fill (1950) of section 1949 of Enclosure 0776.

Iron Age Fabrics

There are no sherds in fabrics with the extremely large (*c.*12 mm) crushed rock temper that is typical of the region.

Grass-tempered

A mid-grey fabric with circular and fine, short impressions from grass or similar within the fabric; possibly dung-tempered (Millson 2013, 38). It has one surviving curved outer surface, but it is unclear if this came from a pot, briquetage or a fired clay object, although by the Iron Age organic-tempering, usually in oxidised fabrics, was generally restricted to briquetage.

Catalogue No. 17. Minute scrap (1763). Wt: <1 g.

Roman Fabrics

Oxidised Ware

Catalogue No. 18. Body sherd in an orange sandy fabric, slightly paler on the exterior, from a closed form such as a flagon or jar. The sherd is likely to be first or second century AD in date (0650). Wt: 3 g.

AREA 2

0595
ST10
0949
ST25
2005
2010
2036
2036

site boundary
unphased
other feature

0   25m

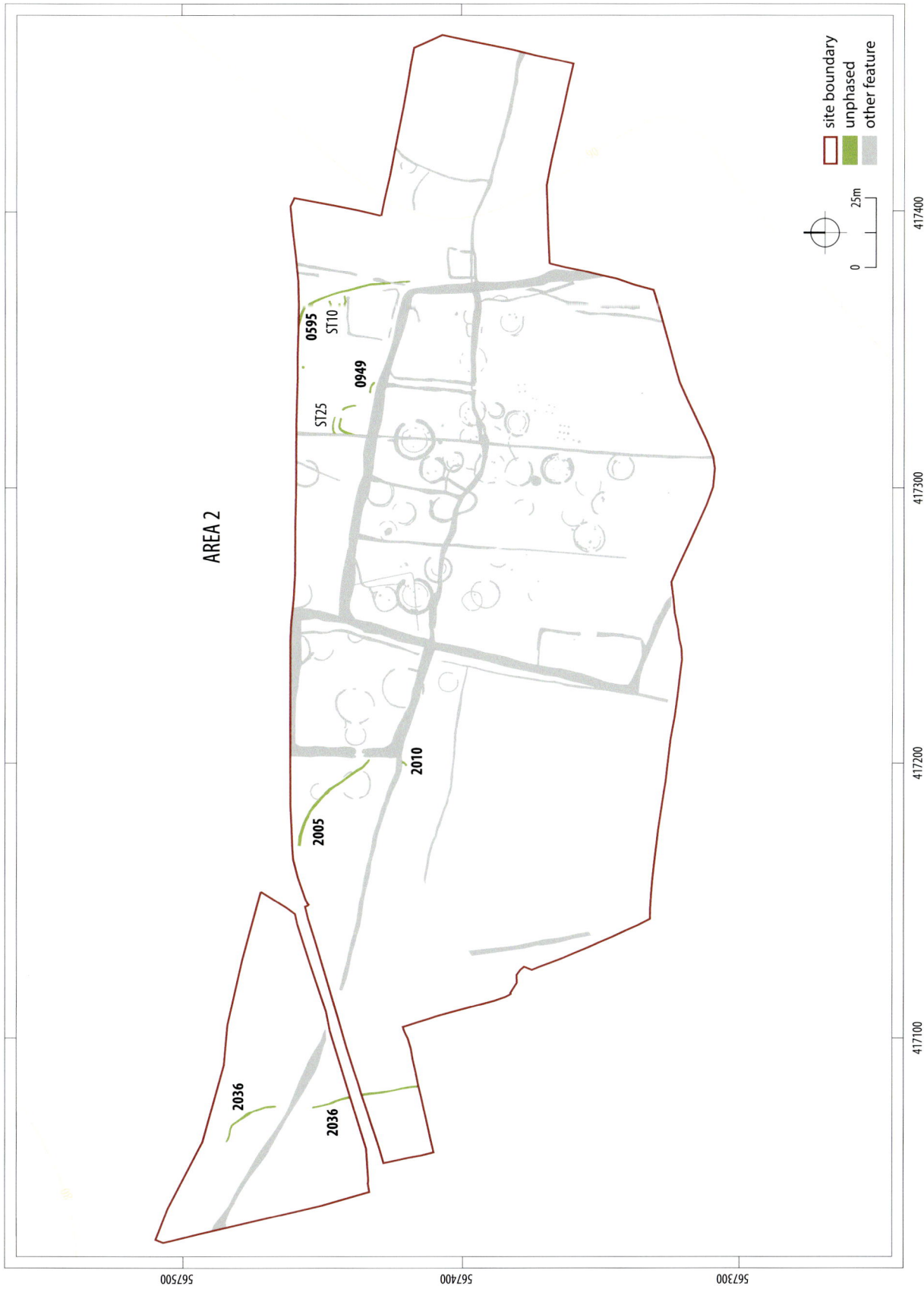

Figure 4.37 Lower Callerton Area 2 – unphased features

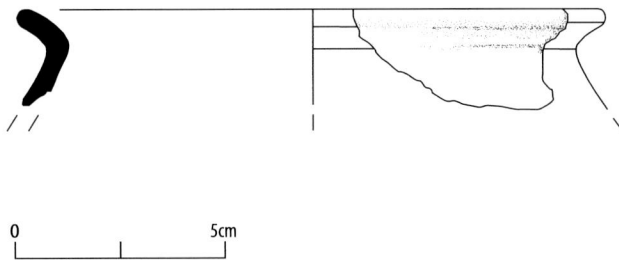

L_____I_____I

Figure 4.38 Sherd of a short everted-rimmed cooking pot (Cat. No. 19)

REDUCED WARE

> *Catalogue No. 19.* Sherd from a short everted-rimmed cooking pot in a hard, mid-grey fabric with buff core. Late first to second century AD in date (1950; Fig. 4.38). Wt: 10 g.

Discussion

There are no examples of the thick-walled vessels with large rock temper that are typical for late Bronze Age and later sites in the area, with just a small scrap of possible Iron Age briquetage. No briquetage was found at the nearby sites of East and West Brunton but is known from other nearby sites such as Dissington (Palyvos *et al.* 2017), West Shiremoor (ASDU 2017b) and Brenkley (van Wessel and Wilson 2020).

The sherd of Roman pottery from deposit 0650 capping Enclosure 0776 (Phase 3) is a body sherd and cannot be dated closely. The sherd from a cooking pot, found in fill 1950 of Enclosure 0776, is late first or second century AD in date. The presence of two Roman sherds makes the lack of obvious Iron Age pottery in this phase more noticeable. It is unusual for native sites in the region to produce more Roman pottery than local traditional ware, and even more unusual for them to have Roman pottery but no local traditional ware. Two other examples of such sites are known, the native settlements at Apperley Dene, County Durham, and Milking Gap, Northumberland, which are both dated to the second century by their pottery (Greene 1978, 31; Kilbride-Jones 1938, 341).

Stone tools
Fraser Hunter

The small assemblage of stone tools from Lower Callerton consists of six items, five from Phase 2 (broadly fourth to second century BC) and one unstratified. Most are domestic, but two relate to craft processes. The small size of the assemblage reflects in part the truncation of the site and the percentage of negative features which were investigated, but Iron Age sites in Northumberland rarely produce rich stone assemblages, as discussed below.

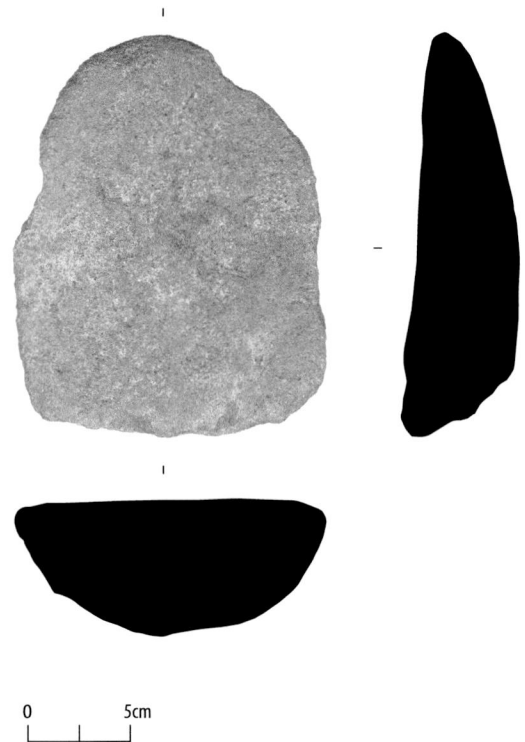

L___I___I

Figure 4.39 Lower Callerton broken saddle quern from Ditch 1772

Two items are parts of saddle querns, a base stone from Ditch 1772 (Sub-Enclosure 3, context 1726; Fig. 4.39) and a broken rubber from the gully of Structure 3 (context 0581; Fig. 4.40). This assemblage is too small to support any wide-ranging conclusions over the absence of rotary querns, which appeared over the course of the fourth–second centuries BC, but saddle querns did continue in use at this time (see below). Both items saw secondary use, the rubber as a fine hammer, the lower stone as an anvil. It also shows an area of iron staining, a feature noted regularly on both saddle and rotary querns which suggests a role in crushing iron ore or iron-rich pigments (Heslop 2008, 65).

The reuse of the rubber as a hammer links it to other cobble tools, of which one other is present: a pounder from Post-hole 1409 located between Structure 36 and Structure 39 (context 1410; Fig. 4.41). Cobble tools show no modification for their task, the form being affected by use-wear. Similar exploitation of an expedient stone is seen in the disc from the outer gully of Structure 29 (1185), its form entirely natural but with traces of use-polish around the edges of one face, which suggest it functioned as a pot lid.

Craft processes are also attested in the assemblage. The perforated disc from the gully of Structure 16 (0728) is unfinished, showing the manufacturing of stone items on site (Fig. 4.42). At first sight it looks like a spindle whorl, but its size, the way the perforation was made (by

Figure 4.40 Lower Callerton broken rubber from the gully of Structure 3 (0581)

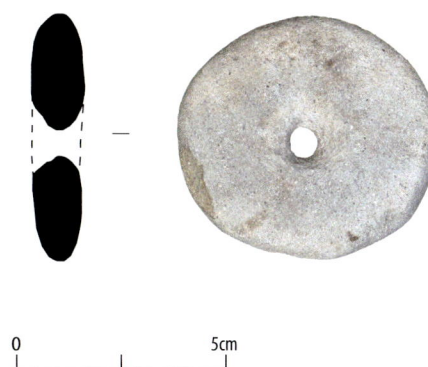

Figure 4.42 Lower Callerton unfinished weight

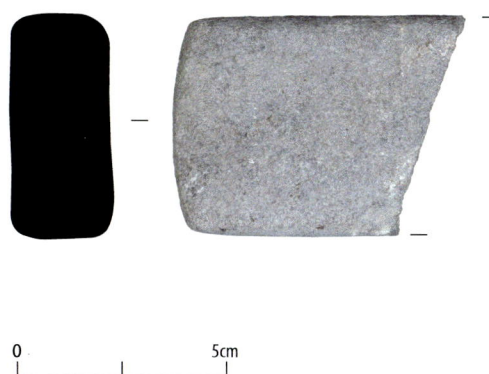

Figure 4.43 Lower Callerton metalworker's burnisher/cushion stone

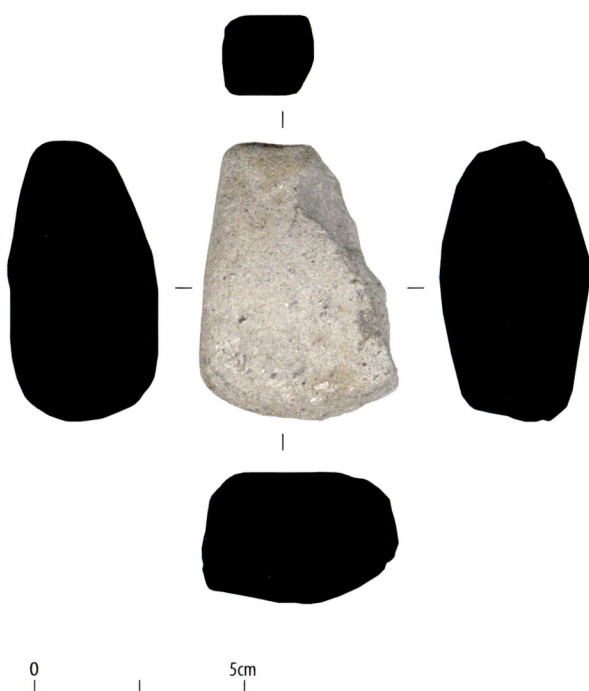

Figure 4.41 Lower Callerton stone pounder (1410)

bifacial pecking rather than drilling), and the size of the perforation if it had been completed argue against this. It is better seen as a weight; the relative care in its manufacture and its flatness suggest it may have been intended as a fly weight for a version of a bow drill known as a pump drill, to add momentum (*e.g.* Mercer 1975, 212, fig. 185; Salaman 1975, 190–1). Such a drill could be used for making holes in hard wood or stone.

The final craft process represented is intriguing, but frustratingly unstratified and broken. Nonetheless, the carefully-shaped 'cushion stone' or burnisher was a specialist tool (Fig. 4.43). In the post-medieval period, similar tools were used for smoothing cloth during weaving (Mitchell 1880, 130–2, figs 98, 100–3), but this creates a polish from the cloth which is little in evidence on this example. Such tools were used in other specialist tasks. In the Bronze Age, for instance, closely similar 'cushion stones' were used as sheet met-al-workers' tools, functioning as hammers and/or anvils (Boutoille 2019). Indeed, a Bronze Age date cannot be ruled out here, but similar tools are also found in the Iron Age, albeit infrequently (*e.g.* Curle and Cree 1916, 122, fig. 35.10; Cruickshanks 2020). They could have

Table 4.2 Stone artefacts from Iron Age and Romano-British sites in Northumberland. This list includes four sites in County Durham (Coxhoe, South Shields, Thorpe Thewles, West Brandon), and three roundhouse sites of Bronze Age / Iron Age date (see text). With Gowanburn River, publication seems to be selective; with West Whelpington, an overlying later settlement makes it hard to disentangle which finds are later prehistoric

Site	rot q	saddle q	cobble tool	whetstone	whorl	mortar	ball	weight	mould	disc	shale	other	Other detail	n	Ref	Site type
Belling Law	3		1						2			2	axehead; cup mark stone	8	Jobey 1977	rectilin
Blagdon Park						4							mortars may be cup-marked stones	4	Hodgson et al 2012	rectilin
Bridge House	2													2	Jobey 1960	rectilin
Brough Law			1											1	Jobey 1971	curvilin
Burradon	1	2	12									1	Neolithic axe	16	Jobey 1970	rectilin
Carry House Camp	5		x			2							mortar is a fossil	7	Rome Hall 1880	sub-rectangular
Chester House														0	Holbrook 1988	rectilin
Coxhoe	1	2		x				1	1	2	2		grooved stone; worked block	9	Haselgrove & Allon 1982	rectilin
Doubstead	1		7							1				9	Jobey 1982	rectilin
Fawdon Dene	1		2	1						1		1	knocking stone	6	Frodsham 2004, 184-7	curvilin & rectilin
Fox Covert								1	1					2	Hodgson et al 2012	pit alignment
Gowanburn River	6								2					8	Jobey & Jobey 1988	sub-rectangular
Halls Hill, East Woodburn		1	2	1								15	2 faceted stones/polissoirs and 13 polished frags of quern or cobble tools	19	Gates 2009	roundhouse, LBA/EIA
Harehaugh				4							1	1	drill bearing?	6	Carlton 2011	curvilin hillfort
Hartburn	5	4	6	2				1	1		1	1	pivot	21	Jobey 1973a	rectilin
High Knowes A														0	Jobey & Tait 1966	curvilin palisade
High Knowes B														0	Jobey & Tait 1966	curvilin
Huckhoe	45	3	3	2	3					1		2	grindstone; grooved stone	59	Jobey 1959	curvilin
Ingram Hill														0	Hogg & Richmond 1942; Hogg 1956	curvilin
Ingram South	1													1	Frodsham 2004, 182-4	rectilin
Kennel Hall Knowe	3		3	2	1									9	Jobey 1978	rectilin
Little Haystacks		2	4											6	Frodsham 2004, 177-8	curvilin
Lookout Plantation												1	Neolithic axe	1	Monaghan 1994	roundhouse, BA
Lower Callerton		2	1					1	1			1	burnisher	6	this volume	rectilin

(Continued)

Table 4.2 (Continued)

Site	rot q	saddle q	cobble tool	whetstone	whorl	mortar	ball	weight	mould	disc	shale	other	Other detail	n	Ref	Site type
Marden	2													2	Jobey 1963	rectilin
Middle Gunnar Peak	4		2	1								1	pivot	8	I Jobey 1981	rectilin
Milking Gap														0	Kilbride-Jones 1938	sub-rectangular
Murton High Crags W	17	3		5	1				1	1	7	3	counter; 2 cupmarks	38	Jobey & Jobey 1987	curvilin
Needle's Eye	6	6	1		2		1				1			17	Proctor 2012	curvilin
Pegswood	4	6	2	2	2	3	1					1	worked frag	21	Proctor 2009	rectilin
Riding Wood	4			1	1									6	Jobey 1960	rectilin
Shotton NE			2											2	Hodgson et al 2012	pit alignment
South Shields		2									3			5	Hodgson et al 2001	roundhouse
Standrop Rigg		2	4											6	Jobey 1983	roundhouse, BA
Thorpe Thewles	15	4	5	1	2			2		1		1	amber	31	Heslop 1987	rectilin
Tower Knowe	16		6	5	1	1		1				3	pivot; 2 cupmarks	33	Jobey 1973b	rectilin
West Brandon		7	2						1			1	cup-marked stone	11	Jobey 1962	rectilin
West Brunton		1	1	1					1					4	Hodgson et al 2012	rectilin
West Gunnar Peak	2		2	x		?				5		4	cup-marked stone, knocking stone, counter, sharpener	15	Rome Hall 1885; Hogg 1942	sub-rectangular
West Longlee	3				1							1	haematite	5	Jobey 1960	rectilin
West Whelpington	10	1		x		x			x					11	Evans & Jarrett 1987	curvilin palisade
Witchy Neuk		1												1	Wake 1939	curvilin

been used as hammers but could equally be burnishers for finishing off sheetwork; their very rarity supports a specialist function, although a detailed review and use-wear study of the type is needed to clarify their function. Nonetheless, from the Bronze Age parallels, the interpretation as a metal-working tool is plausible. Sheet-working is a rarely attested skill since it is a much less messy process than casting, but the products (most likely of bronze) can include spectacular pieces such as cauldrons.

The Lower Callerton stones in context: stone use in Iron Age and Romano-British Northumberland and Durham

The very sparsity of the assemblage led the writer to see how typical or atypical this was of the area. *Archaeologia Aeliana* was checked for relevant reports over the period 1925–2018; to this were added a few sites published in other journals or monographs, and a series of unpublished sites in the Ingram Valley which the writer worked on. This gave a dataset of 42 sites (38 from Northumberland, four from Co. Durham), and a total of 417 stone items. Most are Iron Age enclosure sites, though some Bronze Age and Iron Age isolated roundhouses were included for comparison (Jobey 1983; Monaghan 1994; Hodgson *et al.* 2001; Gates 2009). Given the reliance on published accounts, no attempt was made to study cobble tools in detail, and some identifications could undoubtedly be disputed (for instance, differentiating between mortars, cup-marked stones, and pivots). Nonetheless, at a broad level the comparison is useful. Table 4.2 summarises the data and provides references for individual sites. Broad site type was noted but as many are long-lived, often with a Romano-British phase, and stratification is poor, no attempt was made to study chronological change in any detail.

It is clear that the sparsity of the Lower Callerton assemblage is typical (Table 4.3); 25 of the 42 sites (60%) have between one and ten finds, and a further five have none at all. Table 4.4 indicates the types of finds, ranked by frequency in terms of the number of sites where they occur, not absolute numbers. Querns are by far the most

abundant, appearing on 74% of sites; cobble tools appear on 52% of sites, whetstones on 36%, but no other find category appears on more than 25% of sites, and then always in small numbers. This includes items that were presumably commonplace such as whorls (21% of sites, usually as single examples).

These relatively frequent finds represent the use of stone tools for everyday tasks: grinding grain in the case of querns, a range of domestic activities such as

Table 4.3 Size of stone tool assemblages in a sample of 42 later prehistoric/Romano-British sites in Northumberland and Co. Durham, with comparative data from 33 sites in East Lothian

No. of finds	No. of sites	E Lothian
0	5	8
1–5	12	14
6–10	13	1
11–15	3	5
16–20	3	2
>20	6	3

Table 4.4 Stone tools found on later prehistoric sites in Northumberland (and four sites in Durham), ranked by frequency. Querns consist of 157 rotary querns from 23 sites, and 49 saddle querns from 17 sites. 'Other' comprises cup-marked stones (7), pivot stones (3), Neolithic axeheads (2), polissoirs(?) (2), knocking stones (2), counters (2), amber, burnisher, drill bearing, 'grindstone', haematite, sharpening stone, unidentified (19). The two columns to the right give comparable data from East Lothian (querns: 69 rotary from 14 sites; 68 saddle from six sites)

	NORTHUMBERLAND		E LOTHIAN	
	n sites	n finds	n sites	n finds
quern	31	206	17	137
cobble tool	22	71	17	98
whetstone	15	26	13	53
disc	10	14	2	5
whorl	9	13	7	17
shale jewellery	8	17	11	48
mould	6	9	1	1
weight	5	5	0	0
mortar	4	9	7	64
ball	4	5	9	111
other	18	42	12	25
n	42	417	33	559

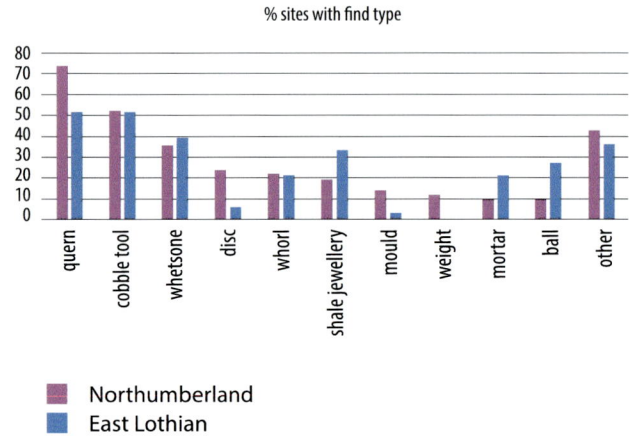

Figure 4.44 Comparison of stone tool assemblages in Northumberland/Durham and East Lothian, with types expressed as a percentage of excavated sites on which they occur

Table 4.5 Percentage of rotary quern fragments on sites with five or more examples

Site	No. of quern fragments	% Rotary querns
West Brandon	7	0
Pegswood	10	40
Needle's Eye	12	50
Hartburn	9	56
Thorpe Thewles	19	79
Murton High Crags West	20	85
West Whelpington	11	91
Huckhoe	48	94
Carry House Camp	5	100
Gowanburn River	6	100
Tower Knowe	16	100

Table 4.6 Quantification of the fired clay assemblage by feature

Feature	Cut	Quantity	Weight (g)	Description
Ditch 0257 (post-medieval)	Section cuts the outer ditch of Structure 2.	1	90	Withy impression
Structure 26	Hollow 1324	7	35	Burnt, abraded
Structure 27	Gully 0995	1	3	Abraded
Structure 47	Gully 1877	1	5	Possible surface

pounding and dehusking grain, preparing hides or grinding foodstuffs in the case of cobble tools, or sharpening iron blades in the case of whetstones. Table 4.5 considers sites with five or more querns; of the 11, one shows only saddle querns, three only rotary querns, and the majority a mixture of the two. Some of this reflects the continuing use of older querns as handy building material, but it also indicates a gradual transition from saddle to rotary quern. Saddle querns were less efficient but easier to make, and may also have continued to be better for grinding material other than grain, as Heslop (2008, 65) has argued and as the iron-staining on the Lower Callerton example might suggest.

Discs like the Lower Callerton example are paralleled on nine other sites; weights are recorded in four other instances, but none as regular as the one studied here. However, a pebble with central hollows on each face from Harehaugh hillfort looks from the illustration like a bearing for a bow drill (Carlton 2011, fig. 19a); the Callerton weight is plausibly seen as a fly-weight for such a tool.

The burnisher is not paralleled in other assemblages, but its suggested role is implied by other finds. Non-ferrous metalworking is attested on six sites by moulds intended for the casting of bars or discs. Bar ingots may have been handy units of metal, but discs were intended for hammering into sheet-work; the shaping and finishing of such items could involve cushion stones/burnishers like the Lower Callerton one.

Craft activities are otherwise not well represented in stone finds from the area. The spinning of yarn is attested occasionally by whorls, while the presence of disc roughouts and what seem to be unfinished items indicate shale-working at Doubstead and Murton High Crags (as a minimum).

The data may be compared with that for East Lothian, which was compiled some years ago (Hunter 2009) and has been recalculated to allow direct comparison (33 sites, 559 finds; the massive hillfort of Traprain Law was excluded as nothing similar has been excavated in north-east England). Table 4.3 shows that assemblage sizes are similar, with 70% having ten or fewer finds. Table 4.4 shows that the spectrum of finds is also similar; this is visualised in Figure 4.44, where percentage data are compared. In general the similarities are striking. One should not make too much of small differences with this size of data set, but some seem significant. Querns are more common finds in north-east England, while shale jewellery is notably more common in East Lothian even though raw material sources were also available in north-east England (Table 4.4). The prevalence of stone balls in East Lothian represents a distinctive regional type. Discs may appear more common in north-east England, but several further examples in East Lothian were classed specifically as palettes and appear in 'other', so this comparison is invalid; likewise, 'mortars' are a problematic class without inspection, as noted above. Moulds are notably more prevalent on Northumberland sites, occurring in ones and twos: their rarity in East Lothian is balanced by the multiple examples from Traprain Law (not included in this data; Burley 1956, 221), which suggests more centralised control of this aspect of bronzeworking.

In general, this brief comparison points to closely similar uses of stone tools in the two areas, with some intriguing differences, and similar careful approaches to their discard. More detailed work in East Lothian indicated a decline in cobble tools and an increase in whetstones towards the end of the Iron Age (Hunter 2009, 148), but the Northumberland data do not yet allow this to be evaluated. The Lower Callerton finds are a characteristically small assemblage, but add to the wider picture of stone tool use in the area's Iron Age; and in the cushion stone/burnisher they include an example of an unusual find category that will benefit from broader study.

Catalogue

QUERNS

c.0581 Rubber from a small saddle quern, ovoid in plan, shallow plano-convex in section. The grinding face is gently convex in two directions, showing extensive polish, dark staining and wear-scratching aligned on its short axis. Created by splitting a cobble; flaking around the edges probably arises from later use as a fine hammer. The freshness of a series of short blade cuts on the grinding surface indicates these are recent. Grey fine-grained sedimentary stone. L 141 mm, W 72 mm, T 27.5 mm, m 423.4 g. Fill of 0580, part of gully 0303 of Structure 3 (sf.1); phase 2a (Fig. 4.40).

c.1726 Broken saddle quern lower stone in coarse-grained buff sandstone. Created by splitting a boulder of the correct form, with minimal shaping beyond rounding the edges. Broad oval in plan, plano-convex in section; tapers in thickness to the surviving rounded end. Concave from use, with use-polish. There is a concentrated area of pecking towards one end from secondary use as an anvil, with a reddish-brown iron-stained area extending beyond this. Ancient break at other end. L 225 mm, W 165 mm, T 65 mm; m 2955.9 g. From slot 1725 through sub-enclosure 1772 in NW corner of main enclosure; phase 2 (Fig. 4.39).

COBBLE TOOL

c.1410 Pounder. Small, rather irregular cuboidal pebble, broken and spalled from use as a pot-boiler, but preserving wear at both ends from use as a pounder. Pale buff sandstone. 62 × 42.5 × 30.5 mm; m 106.5 g. Fill of isolated Post-hole 1409 between Structure 36 and Structure 39; possibly phase 2. <172> retent (Fig. 4.41).

OTHER

c.0728 Unfinished weight. Flat discoidal stone with unworn central biconical perforation (D min 7 mm, max 17 mm). The convex edge is irregular, with multiple abraded facets; in one area the natural edge survives. The irregular edge and unworn perforation indicate it is unfinished. It is rather large for a spindle whorl in both overall diameter and intended perforation diameter. More likely it was intended as a weight, the care in manufacture suggesting it was most likely a fly weight for a bow drill. Buff sandstone. D 61 × 65 mm, T 12.5–13.5 mm; m 81.8 g. Fill of 0727, gully associated with Structure 16 (sf.2); phase 2 (Fig. 4.42). *c.1185* Pot lid? Flat sub-circular stone with rounded edges. The form is entirely natural and unmodified, but both surfaces show slight smoothing around the margins. This excludes use as a palette or grinder, but would be consistent with use as a lid. Fine-grained sedimentary (?) stone. D 75.5 × 80 mm; T 9.5 mm; m 102.2 g. Fill of 1184, part of outer gully 1122 of Structure 29; phase 2b.

Unstratified Burnisher/cushion stone, recently broken. Carefully shaped from a flat cuboidal stone, the long edges rounded off and the surviving end gently convex in plan and section with chamfers on its longer edges. It does not preserve extensive use-wear, but one edge is slightly smoothed, as is one face, and one chamfer shows slight polish. There is a hint of a dark stain on one edge and a faint iron stain on the smoothed face, but much less than would be expected if it had been used for hide-preparation. This and the careful finish suggest it is a metalworker's tool, used in non-ferrous sheet metalworking to burnish and hammer metal, and as an anvil for working. L 77 mm, W 59 mm, T 28mm; m 221.1 g (Fig. 4.43).

Fired clay
Julie Franklin

A small assemblage of fired clay was recovered from Iron Age features totalling 133 g (Table 4.6). The fragments are generally small and formless, with a few burnt surfaces, and likely relate to structures and hearths. A sherd recovered from the section of post-medieval ditch (0257) which cut the outer ditch of Structure 2 had a withy impression. A possible surface was also identified on a sherd from Structure 47 (Area 2; Phase 1).

Industrial waste
Julie Franklin

Slag recovered from features across Area 2 totalled 469 g and mostly comprises lightweight and vesicular fragments characteristic of fuel ash slag (Table 4.7). Fuel ash slags are created by burning in the presence of

silicaceous material and can be created in domestic hearths or ovens or they can also occur naturally. Fragments of slag which appear denser may be related to metalworking and were found in a number of features in Phase 2, though in no case was more than 20 g of material found in any particular group thus there is no clear indication of on-site metalworking in any particular area. Magnetic residues recovered during sample processing contained a small amount of possible hammerscale and slag spheres. Hammerscale and slag spheres are created during iron smithing or smelting. However, they were found in such low concentrations that they are also not indicative of such activity in the immediate vicinity.

The palaeoenvironmental evidence
Michael Wallace

The palaeoenvironmental assemblage from Lower Calleron derived from 185 assessed samples and hand collected remains. A total of 124 cereal grains were recovered from these samples. Barley (*Hordeum vulgare*), glume wheats emmer (*Trtitcum dicoccum*) and spelt (*T.* cf. *spelta*), free threshing wheat (*T. aestivum*) and oat (*Avena* sp.) were present. Barley was seemingly the dominant crop, it being the only cereal to be represented by more than ten grains (53 grains). Relative proportions of cereals is difficult to judge because the next largest groups (50 grains) was cereal indeterminates. The only chaff evident was a single culm node. The wild seed assemblage comprised 78 seeds, of which the arable weed of brome grasses (*Bromus* spp.) and plants of wet environments (sedges, *Carex* spp., bristle club-rush, *Isplepsis selacea*, and club-rush, *Bolboschenus maritimus*) were predominant. Hazel (*Corylus avellena*) was recovered from 16 contexts. Sparse amounts of animal bone were recovered from just seven contexts, and two contexts contained marine shell.

The charcoal assemblage from Lower Callerton was substantial, with charcoal identified in 74% of Area 2 samples. Oak (*Quercus* spp.) was the dominant wood taxon, present in 56% of samples. Also present were alder (*Alnus* cf. *glutinosa*), hazel (*Corylus* cf. *avellana*) and birch (*Betula* spp.). Particularly common was charcoal of heather-type (Ericales) stems, being present in 41% of samples, and which was further evidenced by heather (*Calluna vulgaris*) seed capsules. The abundance of heather is particularly notable in Phase 2 and may be an indication of its use as roofing or bedding. The predominance of oak may be accounted for due to its strength and versatility, its beauty or long-life, and may have been used architecturally or as fuel, for example, in pyres or smelting (Dickson and Dickson 2000, 273–4).

The palaeoenvironmental assemblages have been presented in detail elsewhere for both Lower Callerton

Table 4.7 Quantification of industrial residues by feature and phase

Structure	Feature	Phase	Weight (g)	Description
Structure 21	Gully 0791	1	1	vitrified, denser
Structure 47	Gully 1875	1	1	denser, vitrified
Structure 43	Post-hole 1773	2a	2	denser, vitrified
Structure 34/ Structure 35	Pit 1397	2a/2b	9	large bubbles, possible fired clay attached to it
Structure 16	Gully 0733	2	1	vitrified, denser
Structure 33	Gully 1305 and 1312	2	5	dense, vitrified
Structure 38	Pit 1520	2b	18	denser, vitrified
Structure 2	Post-hole 0448	2b	6	lightweight and vesicular, two pieces denser, vitrified
Structure 2	Pit 0458	2b	15	dense, undiagnostic
Structure 17	Post-hole 0708	2b	14	vitrified, denser
Structure 26	Hollow 1324	2b	9	dense, vitrified
Structure 28	Post-hole 1161	2b	1	dense, vitrified
Structure 29	Inner gully 1275	2b	6	dense, vitrified
Structure 29	Pit 1282	2b	2	dense, vitrified
Structure 42	Gully 1649	2b	5	denser, vitrified

(Headland Archaeology 2020) and Morley Hill (Headland Archaeology 2019).

A scarcity of evidence

Palaeoenvironmental evidence from sites in north-east England are very variable (NERRF2: The Late Bronze Age and Iron Age), and assemblages as small as those from Morley Hill and Lower Callerton are not uncommon amongst prehistoric Northumberland sites. In the case of faunal remains this is largely due to the inhospitable burial conditions of acidic clays and sands that are detrimental to the preservation of bone (English Heritage 2011; Caffell *et al.* 2012). Little interpretative weight should be afforded to absence of faunal remains on these sites; the inhabitants of both settlements may well have utilised animal resources extensively with little evidence surviving in the archaeological record. Some significance may, however, be ascribed to the proportion of the main animal domesticates at Morley Hill. Taphonomic biases would be expected to over-represent larger, more robust bone. The predominance of sheep/goat over cattle may, therefore, be a genuine trend – albeit one to be accepted only cautiously given the small sample size.

Though the depositional conditions are not ideal for the preservation of charred plant remains, they do fair better than bone (Caffell *et al.* 2012). Despite this, the scarcity of charred plant remains at sites of dense Iron Age occupation is striking. The Lower Callerton cereal assemblage is too small to reliably infer trends in crop choice, but the seeming predominance of barley is

consistent with the surrounding sites of Blagdon Park 1 and 2 and East and West Brunton (*ibid.*). At these sites, whilst barley is a main crop, it is co-dominant with spelt. Given the prevalence of indeterminate cereals, it is not clear whether the comparative lack of spelt is a genuine trend at Lower Callerton.

Lower Callerton yielded very few archaeobotanical remains (averaging *c.* 0.04 charred seeds/litre ≡ 23 litres of sediment per seed) indicating that the potential for preservation by charring was minimal. Such rarity provides some implicit evidence on the use of the site. Certain human activities lead to large concentrations of plant matter on site, most notably crop processing and storage. Neither of these actually necessitates exposure to fire, a prerequisite of preservation by charring. Nevertheless, during daily activities and occasional mishaps plant remains on site get charred, and the occurrence of 'plant-rich' activities increases the chance of preserved remains. Whilst it is possible that the importance of taphonomy has been underestimated, a plausible explanation for meagre assemblage is that there was little opportunity for plant remains to be charred on site. This may be because crop processing and storage happened elsewhere, but it may also be a testament to the short duration of occupation on these sites.

Expanding interpretative value through stable isotope analysis

Given the diminutive nature of the Lower Callerton palaeoenvironmental assemblage, combined radiocarbon dating and stable isotope analysis of subset of grains was

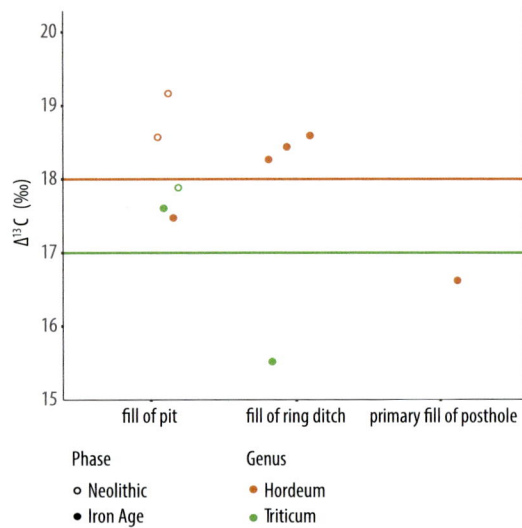

Figure 4.45 Δ¹³C results for cereal grain samples from Lower Callerton. Samples are grouped horizontally by feature type (horizontal position within group has no significance and is to improve legibility only). Lines indicate indicative thresholds for interpreting crop status (see text for explanation): above green line indicates well-watered wheat crops, and above orange line indicates well-watered barley crops

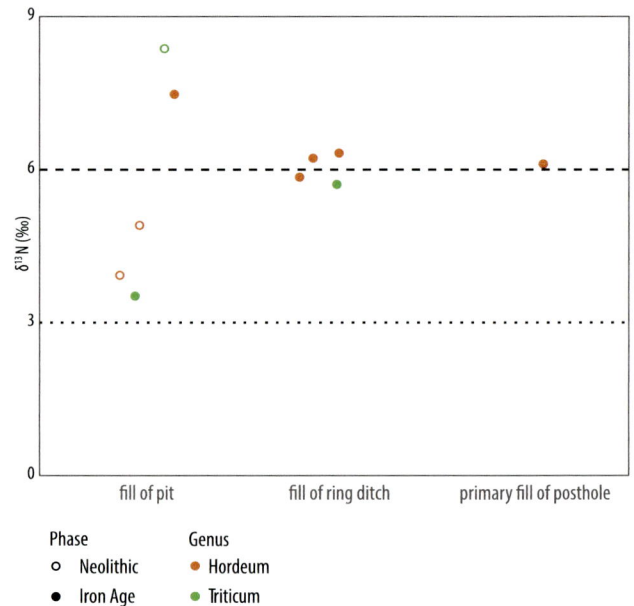

Figure 4.46 δ¹⁵N results for cereal grain samples from Lower Callerton. Samples are grouped horizontally by feature type (horizontal position within group has no significance and is to improve legibility only). Lines indicate indicative thresholds for interpreting crop status (see text for explanation): dotted line indicates transition from low to medium intensity manuring, and dashed line indicates transition from medium to high intensity manuring

undertaken to add further information regarding crop management practices in the past. Stable isotope analysis was applied to the Iron Age material in a similar manner to that of the Neolithic (see Chapter 2 for an introduction to this technique). Stable carbon isotope results are presented in Figure 4.45, and stable nitrogen isotope results in Figure 4.46.

Stable carbon isotope values were acquired from wheat grain taken from the ring-gully of phase 2b Structure 22 and a pit associated with phase 2b Structure 42. The pit sample has an isotopic value indicating a lack of water stress, and one that is comparable to wheat from Neolithic Pit 0195. The ring-ditch wheat, in contrast, has a very low Δ¹³C indicating the crop may have experienced water stress. With just two samples it is difficult to assign much significance to these varied results. For barley, albeit based on just five samples from structures 14, 29, 38 and 41, there is an apparent context-related trend in higher values for ring-gully grains, moderate for the pit fill and low for post-hole fill. The sample sizes make any interpretation of these trends risky, but taken as a whole the level of variability is noteworthy, with a range of 3‰. The management of crop watering was likely not a key concern in Iron Age Northumberland, and so variation in water availability was likely determined by the natural soil moisture levels in different locations. Further as water was a non-limiting factor on growth, other environmental factors (*e.g.* day-light, temperature) likely play a greater role in determining Δ¹³C. Again, this would point towards

stable carbon isotopes reflecting variation in growing conditions. The stable carbon isotope results, therefore, point towards generally good but highly varied growing conditions.

Stable nitrogen isotope analysis was applied to the same suite of samples as carbon. The seven samples (five of barley, two of wheat) from ring-gullies and post-holes show very consistent δ¹⁵N values around 6‰, which places the crops between the moderate and high intensity manuring ranges. Results from the pits are far more varied, with the wheat sample much lower and the barley sample somewhat higher. Unlike for water availability, manuring was determined by farmers in Iron Age Northumberland. We might, therefore, consider the δ¹⁵N results are a more 'anthropogenic signal'. In which case, the results indicate that the incidental deposits in ring-gullies and post-holes indicate a fairly standardised approach to soil management. In contrast, however, the two samples from pits – which may be incidental or purposeful depositions – are far more varied. As for the stable carbon isotope results there is testament to variation in agricultural practices, but unlike those results the stable nitrogen isotope values have an overall sense of consistency. Equating stable nitrogen isotope results to manuring intensity is simplistic, taking no account of natural soil conditions or other potential influences on results. One such possibility is the crop grew in heavy, waterlogged soils, which tends to increase $\delta^{15}N$. These soils prevail in the region, and as will be seen below, may be of importance to this interpretation.

The Iron Age economy of Northumberland: a contribution from Morley Hill and Lower Callerton

In her pioneering study of the agricultural economy of Iron Age Northumberland, Marijke van der Veen (1992) proposed that two agricultural economies existed in the region. At group A sites the crops emmer and barley predominated, and the ecology of the weed assemblage indicated good, fertile and heavily disturbed soils. At group B sites barley and spelt were the preferred crops, and the weeds indicated poor quality, undisturbed soils. Thus, group A implies intensive, small-scale agriculture, whereas group B implies extensive, large-scale agriculture.

The dichotomy between intensive and extensive modes of crop production (though others exist) has become a core element of studies of past agriculture (van der Veen and O'Connor 1998). Intensive agriculture is a system in which crops benefit from large amounts of tending, weeding, watering and manuring – what can be considered 'attentive farming' or 'garden agriculture' (though 'allotment agriculture' might conjure a more accurate mental image). Intensive regimes allow large yields to be extracted from relatively small areas of land, and so productivity is tied to access to resources (*e.g.* manure) and, most importantly, access to human labour. Extensive agriculture contrasts by lessening the need for human labour, by replacing tillage labour with traction animals and typically involving less tending, watering and manuring. In extensive agriculture, therefore, the yield per unit of land will typically be less than under an intensive system, but the losses can be offset by cultivating larger areas. Productivity is thus dependant on access to land and the animals to till it. Neither approach is *better* than the other, but it is important to note that intensive agriculture is more difficult to scale-up because increases in productivity require a proportional increase in human effort. For extensive agriculture, production can be increased with more land and more animals, with little increase in human labour required.

The Group A – Group B model of van der Veen (1992) presents an intriguing picture for Iron Age Northumberland as it supposes that both agricultural systems existed contemporaneously in close proximity. The differences in agricultural systems would have meant that neighbouring settlements would have recognisable differences in their daily and seasonal routines, and the relative importance of land, human labour, animal labour and manure would have varied.

Van der Veen uses the River Tyne to differentiate sites to the north that tend to fall into Group A, and sites to the south that are attributed to Group B (1992, 155). She highlights that neither soil nor climate explain this north-south divide, and instead suggests that settlement type and location – especially the link between intensive Group A sites with small, fortified hilltop settlements – provides a stronger correlation.

Situated immediately north of the River Tyne, Lower Callerton does not fall into either category seamlessly. Though technically north of the Tyne, it is a large lowland site with little or no evidence of fortification. The site differs markedly from the small hillforts to the north that are associated with Group A. The only sites in a similar location from van der Veen's study were the two Roman 'control' sites, both of which had assemblages broadly consistent with Group B sites to the south (van der Veen 1992, 143).

The Iron Age archaeobotanical assemblage from Lower Callerton is difficult to assign to either Group A or B. The main identifiable crop at Lower Callerton, barley, occurs at both types of sites. The relative abundance of emmer and spelt wheats is diagnostic, but there are too few remains of these from Lower Callerton to attempt an analysis of their ratios. Of the species identified as being the strongest indicators of Group A (van der Veen 1992), only *Chenopodium album* and *Stellaria* are present, in very small quantities. *Carex* spp. is the most dominant charred wild seed, but this genus is non-diagnostic for differentiating Groups A and B (van der Veen 1992, 121). The next most common charred wild seed is *Bromus* spp, which is an indicator for Group B (*ibid.*).

Given Lower Callerton's lowland location, large size, lack of fortification and weed assemblage, such as it is, a tentative attribution to Group B can be proposed. In turn, this implies an extensive mode of agricultural production with crops grown over a large area with low levels of resource input and human attention. The high $\Delta^{13}C$ values are to be expected given the temperate climate in which a lack of water was unlikely to have afflicted crops. High levels of variation in these values may, however, be anticipated in an extensive regime. Local water availability, shade and temperature likely varied according to the topographic situation of different crops. Despite the small sample size for Lower Callerton, the range of $\Delta^{13}C$ values is high – spanning 2‰ for wheat. The similarity of the three samples from ring gullies is, however, intriguing as to whether context of deposition has any bearing on results (this should be considered in similar, future work). In the case of $\delta^{15}N$, the results are somewhat different, with five of the seven samples having values falling in a narrow range between 5.73‰ and 6.32‰. Again, context provides interesting results, with the two samples bucking this trend for consistency being the two samples from pits. Taken as a whole the Iron Age cereals appear to be consistently well manured and to have been grown in varied locations.

The corpus of comparative stable isotope data for Britain is sparse but data are available from Danebury hillfort, Hampshire (Lightfoot and Stevens 2012), and Stanwick, Northamptonshire (Lodwick *et al.* 2021). In both cases, interpretations of extensive crop regimes have been reached. High levels of variation in $\Delta^{13}C$ values are apparent, which are also inferred to indicate varied sources of crops. The $\delta^{15}N$ results vary, with Danebury, furthest south, producing values in the region of 3–4‰, whilst at Stanwick the results for the Iron Age phase are also around 6‰. Both the Lightfoot and Stevens (2012) and Lodwick *et al.* (2021) studies have much larger sample sizes than that from Lower Callerton and accordingly their interpretations carry much greater weight. Indeed, whilst informative, the sample sizes presented are so small as to preclude any further statistical analysis. It is hoped, however, that the Lower Callerton isotope dataset goes some way to demonstrating the potential of stable isotope analysis for small assemblages. This potential will be of yet more importance when sufficient numbers of sites are analysed as to warrant inter-site studies.

Conclusion: crop agriculture at Lower Callerton

The model of extensive agriculture suits the sprawling nature of the Lower Callerton settlement. The lack of a tight, organised settlement plan appears to have extended to the fields and husbandry of crops. As a whole, the results seem to identify the site as practising Group B extensive agriculture (van der Veen 1992), further highlighting the distribution of this type of regime northwards (Hodgson *et al.* 2012, 203; pers. comm.). Yet the high $\delta^{15}N$ values point towards quite substantial levels of manuring, and whilst soil base-levels are unknown and other factors may be in play, the low input that might be assumed to be part of an extensive agriculture model is not apparent in the data. It may be that Iron Age farmers were able to maintain good levels of manuring despite operating extensively. A downside of large-scale extensive agriculture is soil exhaustion and, whilst this problem may have set in during the Roman period (Lodwick *et al.* 2021, 22), it seems to have been successfully avoided in the Iron Age. This apparent proficiency for the management of manuring brings to mind a quote highlighted by Hodgson *et al.* (2012, 1–2) at the start of *The Iron Age on the Northumberland Coastal Plain*: "every field appears by culture like a garden, plentifully manured with dungs" (Wallis 1769, 36); perhaps this observation is one that has roots extending into prehistory?

Radiocarbon dating and chronological modelling

Derek Hamilton

A total of 70 samples of charcoal (54), charred cereal grains (14), and carbonised nutshell (2) were radiocarbon dated from 47 individual contexts associated with the fills of enclosure ditches (3), pits (14 total, 5 of which were associated with structures), and features considered to form the remains of 20 structures – post-holes, internal spreads, ring-ditches, gullies, etc. – at the site of Lower Callerton. All the samples were single entities (Ashmore 1999) and were processed at the Scottish Universities Environmental Research Centre (SUERC) for radiocarbon dating by accelerator mass spectrometry (AMS) following the methods of Dunbar *et al.* (2016).

The SUERC lab maintains rigorous internal quality assurance procedures, and participation in international inter-comparisons (Scott 2003; Scott *et al.* 2010) indicate no laboratory offsets; thus, validating the measurement precision quoted for the radiocarbon ages.

The results are presented (Table 4.8) as conventional radiocarbon ages (Stuiver and Polach 1977). They have been calibrated using the internationally agreed terrestrial calibration curve (IntCal20) of Reimer *et al.* (2020) and the OxCal v4.4 computer program (Bronk Ramsey 2009). Simple calibrated results using the maximum intercept method are presented at single 95% confidence intervals in plain text and rounded outward to ten years. The probability distributions shown in Figures 4.47, 4.48 and 4.51 were made using the probability method (Stuiver and Reimer 1993), as implemented in OxCal.

Methodological approach

A Bayesian approach (Buck *et al.* 1996) has been applied to the interpretation of the chronology of the archaeological activity that was revealed through excavation at Lower Callerton. Although simple calibrated dates are accurate estimates of the radiocarbon age of samples, this is not, usually, what archaeologists really wish to know. It is the dates of the archaeological events represented by those samples, such as the start and end of activity, that is of particular interest. The chronology of this activity can be estimated not only by using the absolute dating derived from the radiocarbon measurements, but also by using stratigraphic relationships between samples and the relative dating information provided by the archaeological phasing.

The methodology used here allows the combination of these different types of information explicitly, to produce realistic estimates of the dates of archaeological interest. The posterior density estimates produced by this modelling are not absolute, rather they are interpretative estimates, which can and will change as further data become available and as other researchers choose to model the existing data from different perspectives.

Table 4.8 Calibrated radiocarbon dates from Lower Callerton

Lab ID	Feature	Context description	Material dated	$\delta^{13}C$ (‰)	Radiocarbon age (BP)	Calibrated date (95% confidence)
SUERC-95776	ENCLOSURE 182	Fill (0104) of Ditch 0182	Charcoal: Prunoideae sp.	−26.0	3162±26	1430–1260 cal BC
SUERC-95775	ENCLOSURE 182	*as SUERC-95775*	Charcoal: cf. *Corylus avellana*	−25.4	3081±26	1500–1400 cal BC
SUERC-92160	ENCLOSURE 776	Basal fill (0647) of southern terminus of Ditch 0644	Charcoal: *Calluna vulgaris*	−26.9	1988±25	50 cal BC–cal AD 120
SUERC-92164	ENCLOSURE 776	Middle fill (0649) representing a dump of material in southern terminus of Ditch 0644	Charcoal: *Calluna vulgaris*	−25.7	2055±23	150 cal BC–cal AD 20
SUERC-95832	ENCLOSURE 1422	Second fill (1452) of Ditch 1450	Charcoal: *Quercus* sp.; roundwood	−24.8	2068±26	170 cal BC–cal AD 10
SUERC-98225	PIT 1002	Single fill (1003) of pit located in the entranceway of Roundhouse 22	Charcoal: *Alnus glutinosa*	−25.7	4784±27	3640–3520 cal BC
SUERC-98226	PIT 1002	*as SUERC-98225*	Charred nutshell: *Corylus avellana*	−22.9	4704±25	3630–3370 cal BC
SUERC-95781	PIT 189	Single fill (0190) in Pit 0189. Fill contained numerous cereal grains	Charred cereal grain: *Hordeum vulgare*	−23.1	4908±26	3760–3640 cal BC
SUERC-95782	PIT 191	Single fill (0192) of Pit 0191	Charred cereal grain: *Hordeum vulgare*	−24.7	3524±26	1940–1740 cal BC
SUERC-95783	PIT 195	Fill (0187) of Pit 0195	Charred cereal grain: *Triticum dicoccum*	−24.7	4866±26	3700–3630 cal BC
SUERC-95792	PIT 693	Single fill (0694) of Pit 0693	Charcoal: *Ericales* sp.	−26.8	2162±26	360–100 cal BC
SUERC-98227	PIT 999	Fill (0997) of large Pit 0999. Possible *in situ* burning	Charcoal: *Corylus avellana*	−25.6	4133±23	2880–2580 cal BC
SUERC-98228	PIT 999	*as SUERC-98227*	Charred nutshell: *Corylus avellana*	−24.2	4102±27	2870–2500 cal BC
SUERC-95784	PIT 1775	Single fill (1776) in Pit 1775	Charcoal: *Alnus glutinosa*	−25.0	4770±26	3640–3510 cal BC
SUERC-95785	PIT 1803	Lower charcoal-rich fill (1804) in Pit 1803	Charcoal: *Maloideae* sp.	−25.2	4866±26	3700–3630 cal BC
SUERC-95777	SPREAD 175	This is a spread (175) of burnt material next to Pit 0167. The area is sub-circular and represents *in situ* burning	Charcoal: *Corylus* cf. *avellana*	−26.9	4777±26	3640–3520 cal BC
SUERC-92157	STRUCTURE 2	Initial silting (0237) of the northern terminus [0235] of the outer ring-ditch of large complex roundhouse Structure 2	Charcoal: *Calluna vulgaris*	−26.5	2202±25	380–170 cal BC
SUERC-92158	STRUCTURE 2	The fourth and upper fill (0245) of the southern terminus [0241] of the outer ring-ditch of Structure 2	Charcoal: *Calluna vulgaris*	−25.8	2158±24	360–100 cal BC
SUERC-95795	STRUCTURE 3	Single fill (0305) of the ring-gully [0304] of Structure 3	Charcoal: *Ericales* sp.	−27.3	2170±26	360–110 cal BC
SUERC-95796	STRUCTURE 3	*as SUERC-95795*	Charcoal: *Corylus avellana*	−27.0	2186±26	370–160 cal BC

(Continued)

Table 4.8 Calibrated radiocarbon dates from Lower Callerton (Continued)

Lab ID	Feature	Context description	Material dated	$\delta^{13}C$ (‰)	Radiocarbon age (BP)	Calibrated date (95% confidence)
SUERC-92159	STRUCTURE 5	Fill (0360) of the terminus of the outer ring-gully [0359] of Structure 5	Charcoal: *Calluna vulgaris*	−26.1	2175±25	360–150 cal BC
SUERC-95793	STRUCTURE 5	*as SUERC-92159*	Charcoal: *Ericales* sp.	−26.9	2206±26	380–170 cal BC
SUERC-95794	STRUCTURE 5	*as SUERC-92159*	Charred cereal grain: *Hordeum vulgare*	−24.0	2175±26	360–150 cal BC
SUERC-98237	STRUCTURE 13	Fill (0635) of Post-hole 0634	Charcoal: *Corylus avellana*	−26.1	4308±27	3010–2880 cal BC
SUERC-95833	STRUCTURE 14	Primary fill (0623) of Post-hole 0622 in 4-post Structure 14, east of Structure 22	Charcoal: *Alnus glutinosa*	−26.8	2192±26	370–160 cal BC
SUERC-95834	STRUCTURE 14	*as SUERC-95833*	Charred cereal grain: *Hordeum vulgare*	−25.2	2059±26	160 cal BC–cal AD 20
SUERC-98236	STRUCTURE 14	*as SUERC-95833*	Charcoal: *Ericales* sp.	−26.0	2196±26	370–170 cal BC
SUERC-95801	STRUCTURE 15	Fill (0696) of the outer ring-gully [0695] of Structure 15	Charcoal: *Ericales* sp.	−25.1	2153±26	360–50 cal BC
SUERC-95802	STRUCTURE 15	*as SUERC-95801*	Charred cereal grain: *Hordeum vulgare*	−23.4	2123±26	350–50 cal BC
SUERC-95842	STRUCTURE 17	Fill (0705) in Post-hole 0706 of the 6-post Structure 17, east of Structure 38	Charcoal: *Ericales* sp.	−26.7	2138±26	350–50 cal BC
SUERC-98238	STRUCTURE 17	Fill (709) in Post-hole 0710 of the 6-post Structure 17, east of Structure 38	Charcoal: *Betula* sp.	−24.9	2187±42	390–60 cal BC
SUERC-95797	STRUCTURE 18	Single fill (0476) of outer ring-ditch terminus [0475] of Structure 18	Charcoal: *Alnus glutinosa*	−25.9	2130±26	350–50 cal BC
SUERC-95786	STRUCTURE 18	Single fill (0660) of a section [0659] of the outer ring-ditch of Structure 18	Charcoal: *Salix* sp.	−25.9	2157±26	360–60 cal BC
SUERC-95803	STRUCTURE 22	Fill (0846) in the southern segment of the outer ring-ditch [0844] of Structure 22	Charred cereal grain: *Hordeum vulgare*	−22.9	2120±26	350–40 cal BC
SUERC-95804	STRUCTURE 22	*as SUERC-95803*	Charcoal: *Ericales* sp.	−26.0	2153±26	360–50 cal BC
SUERC-98229	STRUCTURE 26	Charcoal-rich fill (1187) of the terminus of ring-gully [1046] for Structure 26	Charcoal: *Ericales* sp.	−25.6	2132±26	350–50 cal BC
SUERC-98233	STRUCTURE 26	Fill (1325) in Pit 1408 that is associated with Structure 26. The pit is external to and cuts the ring-ditch of Structure 26	Charcoal: *Ericales* sp.	−25.7	2168±26	360–110 cal BC
SUERC-98234	STRUCTURE 26	*as SUERC-98233*	Charcoal: *Betula* sp.	−25.5	2136±23	350–50 cal BC
SUERC-95805	STRUCTURE 28	Fill (1071) of the inner ring-gully [1070] of Structure 28	Charcoal: *Alnus glutinosa*	−25.6	3984±26	2580–2460 cal BC

(Continued)

Table 4.8 (Continued)

Lab ID	Feature	Context description	Material dated	$\delta^{13}C$ (‰)	Radiocarbon age (BP)	Calibrated date (95% confidence)
SUERC-95806	STRUCTURE 28	*as SUERC-95805*	Charcoal: *Ericales* sp.	−27.3	2157±26	360–60 cal BC
SUERC-98244	STRUCTURE 28	Fill (1107) of the outer ring-gully [1106] of Structure 28	Charcoal: cf. *Alnus glutinosa*	−28.8	2090±25	180–1 cal BC
SUERC-98245	STRUCTURE 28	*as SUERC-95805*	Charcoal: *Ericales* sp.	−25.7	2174±26	360–150 cal BC
SUERC-98246	STRUCTURE 28	Fill (1163) of Post-hole 1161 in Structure 28. The post-hole contained large amounts of birch charcoal	Charcoal: *Betula* sp.	−25.6	2059±26	160 cal BC–cal AD 20
SUERC-95807	STRUCTURE 29	Lower fill (1115) of the northern terminus of ring-gully 1114	Charcoal: *Alnus glutinosa*	−25.3	2105±26	340–40 cal BC
SUERC-95811	STRUCTURE 29	*as SUERC-95807*	Charcoal: *Betula* sp.	−24.6	2206±26	380–170 cal BC
SUERC-95812	STRUCTURE 29	Basal fill (1283) of Pit 1282 at the centre of Structure 29	Charred cereal grain: *Hordeum vulgare*	−22.9	2164±26	360–100 cal BC
SUERC-98235	STRUCTURE 29	Single fill (1105) of the southern terminus of the outer ring-gully 1104 of Structure 29	Charcoal: *Alnus glutinosa*	−24.7	2102±26	200–40 cal BC
SUERC-95813	STRUCTURE 35	Primary fill (1346) of the Ring-gully [1345] for Structure 35	Charcoal: *Alnus glutinosa*	−24.8	2196±26	370–170 cal BC
SUERC-95854	STRUCTURE 35	*as SUERC-95813*	Charcoal: *Corylus avellana*	−25.9	2209±28	390–170 cal BC
SUERC-95814	STRUCTURE 37	Fill (1372) of ring-gully [1371] of Structure 37	Charcoal: *Ericales* sp.	−27.7	2067±26	170 cal BC–cal AD 10
SUERC-95815	STRUCTURE 37	*as SUERC-95814*	Charcoal: *Quercus* sp.; roundwood	−25.1	2106±26	340–40 cal BC
SUERC-95816	STRUCTURE 37	Fill (1386) of Pit 1385 in Structure 37. The base of the pit was heat-affected, and the assemblage is likely the result of *in* situ burning.	Charcoal: *Ericales* sp.	−26.8	2081±26	180 cal BC–cal AD 10
SUERC-95817	STRUCTURE 37	*as SUERC-95816*	Charred cereal grain: *Hordeum vulgare*	−23.7	2096±26	200–40 cal BC
SUERC-95821	STRUCTURE 38	Fill (1449) of the terminus of the southern arc of outer ring-ditch [1447] of Structure 38	Charred cereal grain: *Hordeum vulgare*	−22.9	2025±26	100 cal BC–cal AD 70
SUERC-95822	STRUCTURE 38	*as SUERC-95821*	Charcoal: *Betula* sp.	−25.2	2031±26	100 cal BC–cal AD 60
SUERC-95823	STRUCTURE 38	Single fill (1514) of the northern arc of the outer ring-ditch [1513] of Structure 38	Charcoal: *Betula* sp.	−25.4	2135±26	350–50 cal BC
SUERC-95824	STRUCTURE 38	*as SUERC-95823*	Charred cereal grain: *Hordeum vulgare*	−23.3	2134±26	350–50 cal BC
SUERC-95827	STRUCTURE 41	Fill (1464) of the ring-gully [1463] of Structure 41	Charred cereal grain: *Hordeum vulgare*	−21.0	2158±26	360–60 cal BC

(Continued)

Table 4.8 Calibrated radiocarbon dates from Lower Callerton (Continued)

Lab ID	Feature	Context description	Material dated	$\delta^{13}C$ (‰)	Radiocarbon age (BP)	Calibrated date (95% confidence)
SUERC-95831	STRUCTURE 41	*as SUERC-95827*	Charcoal: *Betula* sp.	−26.0	2123±26	350–50 cal BC
SUERC-95835	STRUCTURE 42	Fill (1536) of ring-ditch [1535] of Structure 42	Charred cereal grain: *Hordeum vulgare*	−22.2	2118±26	350–40 cal BC
SUERC-95836	STRUCTURE 42	*as SUERC-95835*	Charcoal: *Alnus glutinosa*	−27.7	2091±26	180–1 cal BC
SUERC-95837	STRUCTURE 42	Fill (1697) of Pit 1696 within the area delineated by the ring-ditch to Structure 42	Charcoal: *Alnus glutinosa*	−27.7	2205±26	380–170 cal BC
SUERC-95841	STRUCTURE 42	*as SUERC-95837*	Charred cereal grain: *Triticum* sp.	−22.2	2192±26	370–160 cal BC
SUERC-95825	STRUCTURE 43	Fill (1763) of Pit 1722 within the interior of Structure 43	Charcoal: *Ericales* sp.	−25.2	2223±26	390–190 cal BC
SUERC-95826	STRUCTURE 43	*as SUERC-95825*	Charcoal: *Betula* sp.	−27.2	2161±26	360–100 cal BC
SUERC-98224	STRUCTURE 43	Fill (1570) of ring-gully [1569] of Structure 43. Sample only contained alder charcoal	Charcoal: *Alnus glutinosa*	−26.2	2212±23	380–170 cal BC
SUERC-98239	STRUCTURE 45	Spread (1788) that overlay a post-hole in Structure 45. Possibly represents *in situ* burning	Charcoal: *Betula* sp.	−26.1	2213±26	390–170 cal BC
SUERC-98243	STRUCTURE 45	*as SUERC-98239*	Charcoal: *Alnus glutinosa*	−27.2	2107±23	200–40 cal BC
SUERC-95791	STRUCTURE 46	Single fill (1826) of ring-gully [1813] of Structure 46	Charcoal: *Ericales* sp.	−24.9	2210±26	390–170 cal BC
SUERC-95787	STRUCTURE 46	Upper fill (1833) of ring-gully [1831] of Structure 46	Charcoal: *Alnus glutinosa*	−25.7	2245±26	400–200 cal BC

The technique used is a form of Markov Chain Monte Carlo sampling and has been applied using the program OxCal v4.4 (http://c14.arch.ox.ac.uk/). Details of the algorithms employed by this program are available in Bronk Ramsey (1995; 1998; 2001; 2009) or from the online manual. The algorithm used in the models can be derived from the OxCal keywords and bracket structure shown in Figures 4.47–9.

Samples and models

The following paragraphs describe the samples that were dated and their relationship to other dated samples, contexts, and features. Where more than one radiocarbon result is available from an individual context, a statistical test has been used to check for consistency between the measurements following the methods described by Ward and Wilson (1978). Where the test demonstrates consistency between two or more measurements, this provides stronger evidence for the security of the dated deposit. Where the results are not consistent, several

potentialities must be considered. The first is that one or more samples in a context are residual or intrusive. More often than not, material should be expected to be reworked and thus older than expected except where there is evidence that might suggest intrusive material (*i.e.* larger roots or animal burrows). The second potential issue is that the material is representative of a longer period of activity than initially considered – burnt spread composed of structural material that dates from the construction and activity material that dates from the potential long-use of a structure. Finally, it must be remembered that radiocarbon dating involves complex chemistry, physics, and statistics and that it is possible for dates to be not just statistical outliers, but simply incorrect. While there are a series of quality checks that laboratories put in place to minimise errors, they can occur from time-to-time. Nearly all of the statistical tests for paired results showed consistency, and only two samples from putative Iron Age contexts returned results that were Neolithic (*e.g.* non-Iron Age). This suggests

OxCal v4.4.2 Bronk Ramsey (2020); r:2 Atmospheric data from Reimer et al (2020)

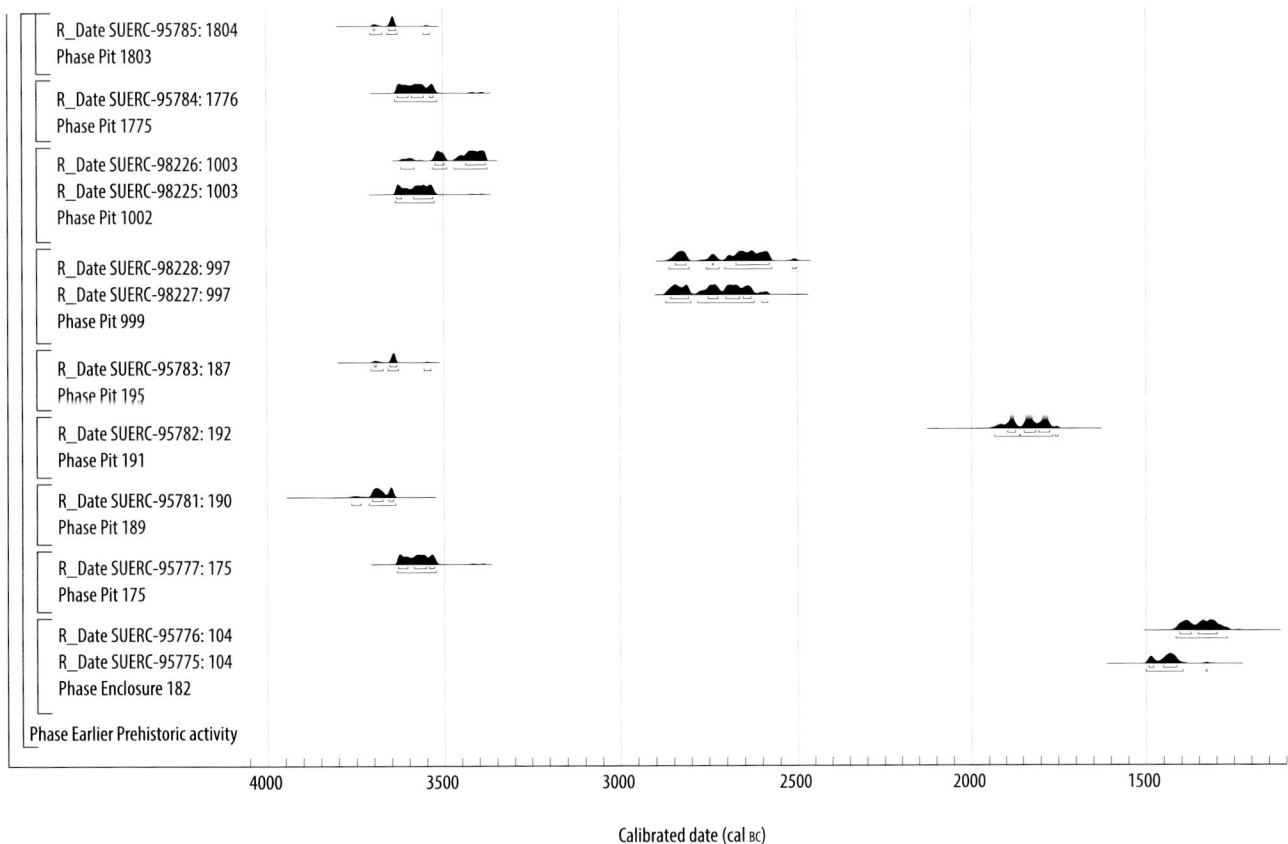

Figure 4.47 Calibrated results from the earlier prehistoric features at Lower Callerton

the programme of sampling and radiocarbon dating at Lower Callerton was extremely rigorous.

Earlier prehistoric features

Enclosure Ditch 0182 and eight pits (0175, 0189, 0191, 0195, 0999, 1002, 1775 and 1803) have radiocarbon dates that place the associated activity in the earlier prehistoric periods of the Neolithic and Bronze Ages. Pits 0175, 0189, 0195, 1002, 1775 and 1803 all date to the middle half of the fourth millennium cal BC. There are two results (SUERC-98225/6) on a fragment of alder charcoal and a hazel nutshell, respectively, from fill (1003) in Pit 1002 that are not statistically consistent (T'=4.7; df=1; T'(5%)=3.8). The later date (SUERC-98226) provides the more reliable date for this feature in 3630–3370 cal BC (95% probability; Fig. 4.47).

The two results (SUERC-98227/8) on single fragments of hazel charcoal and a hazel nutshell, respectively, from fill (0997) in Pit 999 are statistically consistent (T'=0.8; df=1; T'(5%)=3.8). The later date (SUERC-98228) dates the feature to 2870–2500 cal BC (95% probability; Fig. 4.47).

Both Pit 0191 and Enclosure 0182 date to the second millennium cal BC. There are two results (SUERC-95775/6)

on fragments of hazel and Prunoideae charcoal, respectively, in fill (0104) of Enclosure 0182 that are not statistically consistent (T'=4.9; df=1; T'(5%)=3.8). The later date (SUERC-98226) provides the best estimate for the date of the feature in 1420–1270 cal BC (95% probability; Fig. 4.47).

Iron Age features

The remainder of the dated features were thought to date to the later Iron Age, but the presence of earlier activity did result in a few fragments of residual material being dated. What follows is a brief description of the later prehistoric contexts and features that were dated, with particular reference made to any stratigraphic relationships made between features (intercutting ditches or pits) and to the statistical consistency of paired samples from the same context.

STRUCTURE 2

Heather charcoal was dated from two contexts in the outer ring-ditch of Structure 2, which had four fills. SUERC-92157 is from the primary fill (0237) of the ditch, while SUERC-92158 is from the upper fill (0245).

STRUCTURES 3 AND 5

The ring-gullies of Structures 3 and 5 are stratigraphically linked, with outer ring-gully [0359] of Structure 5 cut by the ring-gully [0304] of Structure 3. The three radiocarbon dates from (0360) in ring-gully [359] are statistically consistent (T'=1.0; df=2; T'(5%)=6.0), as are the two measurements from (305) in ring-gully [304] (T'=0.2; df=1; T'(5%)=3.8).

PIT 0693

There is a single radiocarbon result (SUERC-95792) on a fragment of *Ericales* sp. charcoal from the single fill (0694) if Pit 0693.

STRUCTURE 13

The radiocarbon date (SUERC-98237) from four-post Structure 13 is on a sample of hazel charcoal from within the fill (0635) of a post-hole. The result is Neolithic in date and likely to be from residual material. The result is excluded from any modelling that follows.

STRUCTURE 14

There are three radiocarbon results from alder and *Ericales* sp. charcoal, as well as a charred barley grain, from the single fill (0623) of Post-hole 0622 in four-post Structure 14. The three results are not statistically consistent (T'=17.9; df=2; T'(5%)=6.0) and represent material of similar but different ages. It is possible the charcoal samples are from residual material, or the grain is intrusive, but it is also equally plausible the material collected in the post-hole over an extended period of use of the structure.

STRUCTURE 15

There are two dating results on a fragment of *Ericales* sp. charcoal and grain of barley in the fill (0696) of outer ring-gully [0695]. The measurements are statistically consistent (T'=0.7; df=1; T'(5%)=3.8) and could be the same actual age.

STRUCTURE 17

Charcoal was dated from two post-holes in six-post Structure 17. SUERC-95842 is from fill (0705) of Post-hole 0706 and SUERC-98238 is from fill (0709) of Post-hole 0710.

STRUCTURE 18

There are two radiocarbon dates from charcoal recovered from two sections of the single fill in the outer ring-ditch of Structure 18. SUERC-95786 is from a fragment of willow charcoal in fill (0660) of [0659], and SUERC-95797 is from a fragment of alder charcoal in fill (0476) of [0475].

STRUCTURE 22

There are two dated samples from a fill (0846) in the outer ring-ditch [0844] of the complex Structure 22. The two measurements are statistically consistent (T'=0.8; df=1; T'(5%)=3.8) and so could be the same actual age.

STRUCTURE 26

There are three radiocarbon dates from the ring-gully terminus and a pit associated with Structure 26, which cuts the ring-gully. A fragment of *Ericales* sp. charcoal from the charcoal-rich fill (1187) provides a date for gully [1052]. There are two radiocarbon results from *Ericales* sp. and birch charcoal in fill (1325) of Pit 1408. The two measurements are statistically consistent (T'=0.9 ; df=1; T'(5%)=3.8) and could be the same actual age.

STRUCTURE 28

Five fragments of charcoal were dated from the inner and outer ring-gully and a post-hole associated with Structure 28. The inner ring-gully [1070] had fragments of alder and *Ericales* sp. dated from fill (1071) and the outer ring-gully [1106] had fragments of the same species dated from fill (1107). The alder in the inner ring-gully was dated (SUERC-96805) to the Neolithic and has been excluded from all further modelling below. The fill (1163) of Post-hole 1161 was dated from a fragment of birch charcoal, of which there was a considerable amount recorded in the fill. The two measurements from the outer ring-gully [1106] are not statistically consistent (T'=5.4; df=1; T'(5%)=3.8) and likely represent the deposition of material over an unknown period of time.

STRUCTURE 29

There are four radiocarbon results from three samples of charcoal and one barley grain from the ring-gully and a pit associated with Structure 29. The lower fill (1115) in the gully's [1114] northern terminus was dated with a fragment of alder and one of birch. The two measurements are not statistically consistent (T'=7.5; df=1; T'(5%)=3.8) and likely represent material of different ages within the deposit. The southern gully terminus [1104] was also dated with a sample of alder charcoal, while Pit 1282 was dated with a single charred barley grain.

STRUCTURE 35

Fragments of hazel and alder charcoal were dated from the primary fill (1346) of ring-gully [1345]. The two measurements are statistically consistent (T'=0.1; df=1; T(5%)=3.8) and could be the same actual age.

STRUCTURE 37

There are four radiocarbon results from the ring-gully and a pit associated with Structure 37. The measurements on fragments of *Ericales* sp. and oak roundwood charcoal from the fill (1372) of ring-gully [1371] are statistically consistent (T'=1.1; df=1; T'(5%)=3.8) and could be the same actual age. Similarly, the measurements on a fragment of *Ericales* sp. charcoal and a barley grain in the fill (1386) of Pit 1385, which showed evidence of *in situ* burning, are also statistically consistent (T'=0.2 ; df=1; T'(5%)=3.8) and could be the same actual age.

Structure 38

There are two dated samples each from the northern terminus of ditch [1447] and the southern arc [1513] of the ring-ditch for Structure 38. The measurements on a barley grain and fragment of birch charcoal in fill (1449) of [1447] are statistically consistent (T'=0.0; df=1; T'(5%)=3.8) and could be the same actual age. Similarly, the measurements on another paired barley grain and fragment of birch charcoal in fill (1514) of [1513] are statistically consistent (T'=0.0; df=1; T'(5%)=3.8) and could be the same actual age.

Structure 41

The measurements on a fragment of birch charcoal and a charred barley grain in the fill (1464) of ring-gully [1463] of Structure 41 are statistically consistent (T'=0.9; df=1; T'(5%)=3.8) and could be the same actual age.

Structure 42 and 43

The ring-ditch of Structure 42 cut Structure 43. There are three radiocarbon-dated samples from Structure 43. There is a single result (SUERC-98224) from a fragment of alder charcoal in the fill (1570) of ring-ditch [1569]. There are samples of *Ericales* sp. and birch charcoal from the fill (1763) of Pit 1722; the two measurements are statistically consistent (T'=2.8; df=1; T'(5%)=3.8) and could be the same actual age. From Structure 42 there are two dated samples each from the ring-ditch [1535] and Pit 1696. A fragment of alder charcoal and a charred barley grain in fill (1536) of ditch [1535] are statistically consistent (T'=0.5; df=1; T'(5%)=3.8), while a fragment of alder charcoal and a grain of wheat from the fill (1697) of Pit 1696 are also statistically consistent (T'=0.1; df=1; T'(5%)=3.8). In both cases, the measurements could be the same actual age.

Structure 45

There are two radiocarbon dates on alder and birch charcoal from a spread (1788) that appears to form *in situ* burning over a post-hole in Structure 45. The two measurements are not statistically consistent (T'=9.3; df=1; T'(5%)=3.8) and likely represent material of different ages, perhaps a combination of burnt structural debris and charcoal from the use of the structure.

Structure 46 and Enclosure 0776

There is one final set of stratigraphic sequences that were dated at Lower Callerton. From the ring-gully of Structure 46, a sample of *Ericales* sp. charcoal was dated (SUERC-95791) from fill (1826) of [1813], while a sample of alder charcoal was dated (SUERC-95787) from fill (1833) of [1831]. Structure 46 was cut by Enclosure ditch 0776, which was dated (SUERC-92160 & -92164) by fragments of heather charcoal in two fills in [644] – the basal fill (647) and the middle fill (649), respectively.

Ditch 1422 (Sub-enclosure 4)

There is one final radiocarbon result from Lower Callerton, a fragment of oak roundwood charcoal was dated (SUERC-95832) from the second fill (1452) of ditch [1422], which formed Sub-enclosure 4

Results

The initial chronological model for Lower Callerton aimed to estimate the start and end dates of the Iron Age activity, along with the overall span of the activity, by only following the general assumption that the material dated was from a single relatively continuous period of activity on the site (see Hamilton and Kenney 2015 for a broader discussion of the 'simple bounded phase' model in OxCal), and then incorporating the observed stratigraphic relationships between contexts or features and/or feature groups. This first model has good agreement between the radiocarbon dates, the observed stratigraphy, and the general grouping of the Iron Age activity into a single phase (Amodel=83). This initial model estimates the Iron Age activity at Lower Callerton began in either *375–320 cal BC (34% probability*; Fig. 4.48; *start: Iron Age Lower Callerton*) or *265–205 cal BC (61% probability*), and probably in either *360–340 cal BC (20% probability*) or *245–215 cal BC (48% probability*). The Iron Age activity ended in either *140–110 cal BC (6% probability*; Fig. 4.48; *end: Iron Age Lower Callerton*) or *100 cal BC–cal AD 15 (89% probability*), and probably in *90 cal BC–cal AD 5 (68% probability*). The overall span of the Iron Age activity was either *70–225 years (61% probability*; Fig. 4.49; *span: Iron Age Lower Callerton*) or *275–380 years (34% probability*), and probably either *130–190 years (43% probability*) or *300–360 years (25% probability*).

The bi-modal nature of the overall 'start' probability is largely driven by the strong 'wiggle' in the middle Iron Age period of the radiocarbon calibration curve (Fig. 4.50). It is possible to overcome this sometimes with the inclusion of further informative priors, archaeological phasing to complement the observed stratigraphic relationships. Therefore, a second model was created that incorporated the site phasing provided by the archaeologists. In OxCal this was accomplished by cross-referencing dates into their respective phases and including a 'Date' parameter to estimate when the Phase transitions occurred (Figs 4.51a and 4.51b). This model has good agreement between the radiocarbon dates, the observed stratigraphy,

OxCal v4.4.2 Bronk Ramsey (2020); r:2 Atmospheric data from Reimer et al (2020)

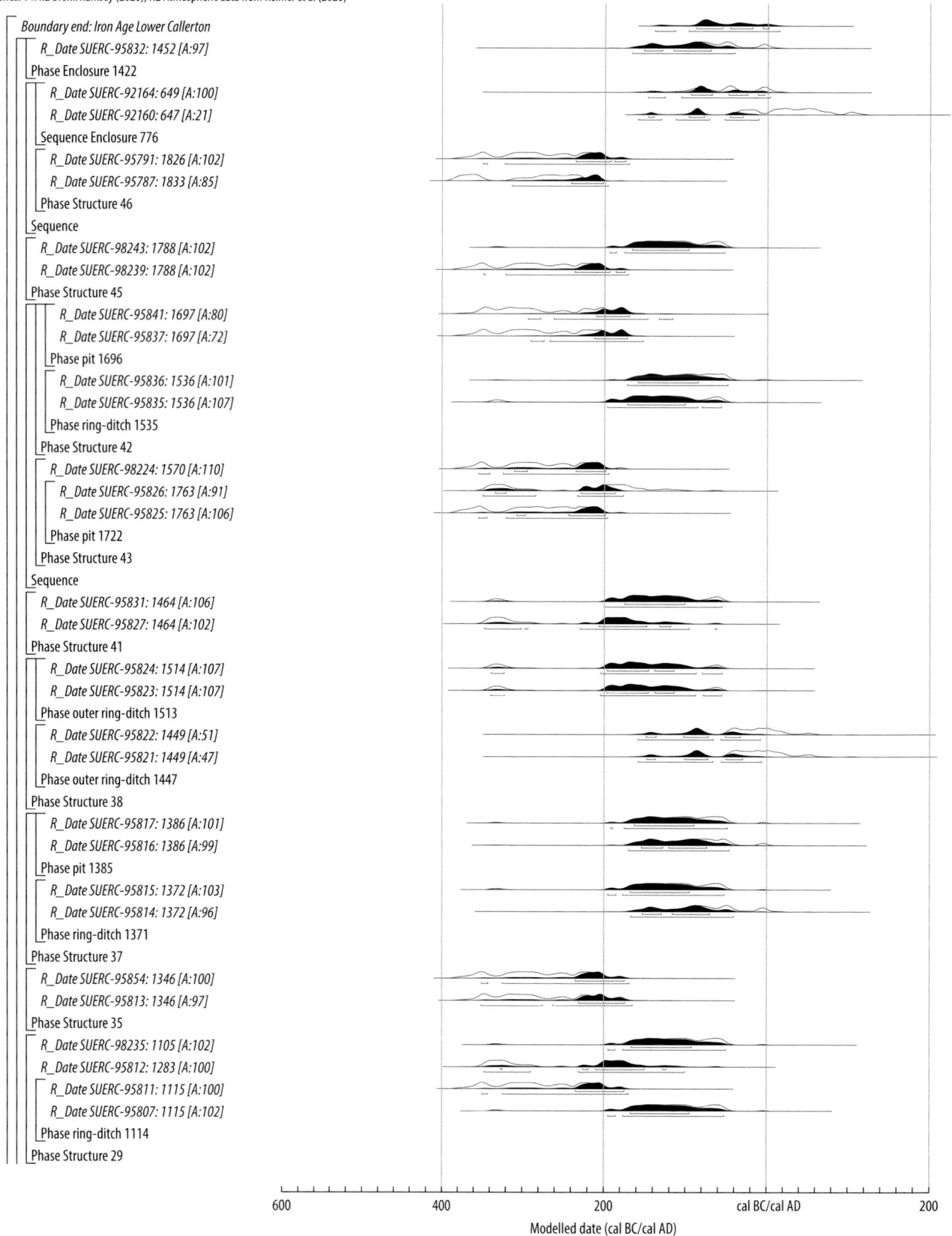

Boundary end: Iron Age Lower Callerton
R_Date SUERC-95832: 1452 [A:97]
Phase Enclosure 1422
R_Date SUERC-92164: 649 [A:100]
R_Date SUERC-92160: 647 [A:21]
Sequence Enclosure 776
R_Date SUERC-95791: 1826 [A:102]
R_Date SUERC-95787: 1833 [A:85]
Phase Structure 46
Sequence
R_Date SUERC-98243: 1788 [A:102]
R_Date SUERC-98239: 1788 [A:102]
Phase Structure 45
R_Date SUERC-95841: 1697 [A:80]
R_Date SUERC-95837: 1697 [A:72]
Phase pit 1696
R_Date SUERC-95836: 1536 [A:101]
R_Date SUERC-95835: 1536 [A:107]
Phase ring-ditch 1535
Phase Structure 42
R_Date SUERC-98224: 1570 [A:110]
R_Date SUERC-95826: 1763 [A:91]
R_Date SUERC-95825: 1763 [A:106]
Phase pit 1722
Phase Structure 43
Sequence
R_Date SUERC-95831: 1464 [A:106]
R_Date SUERC-95827: 1464 [A:102]
Phase Structure 41
R_Date SUERC-95824: 1514 [A:107]
R_Date SUERC-95823: 1514 [A:107]
Phase outer ring-ditch 1513
R_Date SUERC-95822: 1449 [A:51]
R_Date SUERC-95821: 1449 [A:47]
Phase outer ring-ditch 1447
Phase Structure 38
R_Date SUERC-95817: 1386 [A:101]
R_Date SUERC-95816: 1386 [A:99]
Phase pit 1385
R_Date SUERC-95815: 1372 [A:103]
R_Date SUERC-95814: 1372 [A:96]
Phase ring-ditch 1371
Phase Structure 37
R_Date SUERC-95854: 1346 [A:100]
R_Date SUERC-95813: 1346 [A:97]
Phase Structure 35
R_Date SUERC-98235: 1105 [A:102]
R_Date SUERC-95812: 1283 [A:100]
R_Date SUERC-95811: 1115 [A:100]
R_Date SUERC-95807: 1115 [A:102]
Phase ring-ditch 1114
Phase Structure 29

600   400   200   cal BC/cal AD   200

Modelled date (cal BC/cal AD)

Figure 4.48 (a&b) Initial chronological model for the Iron Age activity at Lower Callerton. Each distribution represents the relative probability that an event occurred at some particular time. For each of the radiocarbon measurements two distributions have been plotted, one in outline, which is the result of simple radiocarbon calibration, and a solid one, which is based on the chronological model use. The other distributions correspond to aspects of the model. For example, 'start: Iron Age Lower Callerton' is the estimated date that settlement activity began at the site, based on the radiocarbon dating results. The large square 'brackets' along with the OxCal keywords define the overall model exactly

OxCal v4.4.2 Bronk Ramsey (2020); r:2 Atmospheric data from Reimer et al (2020)

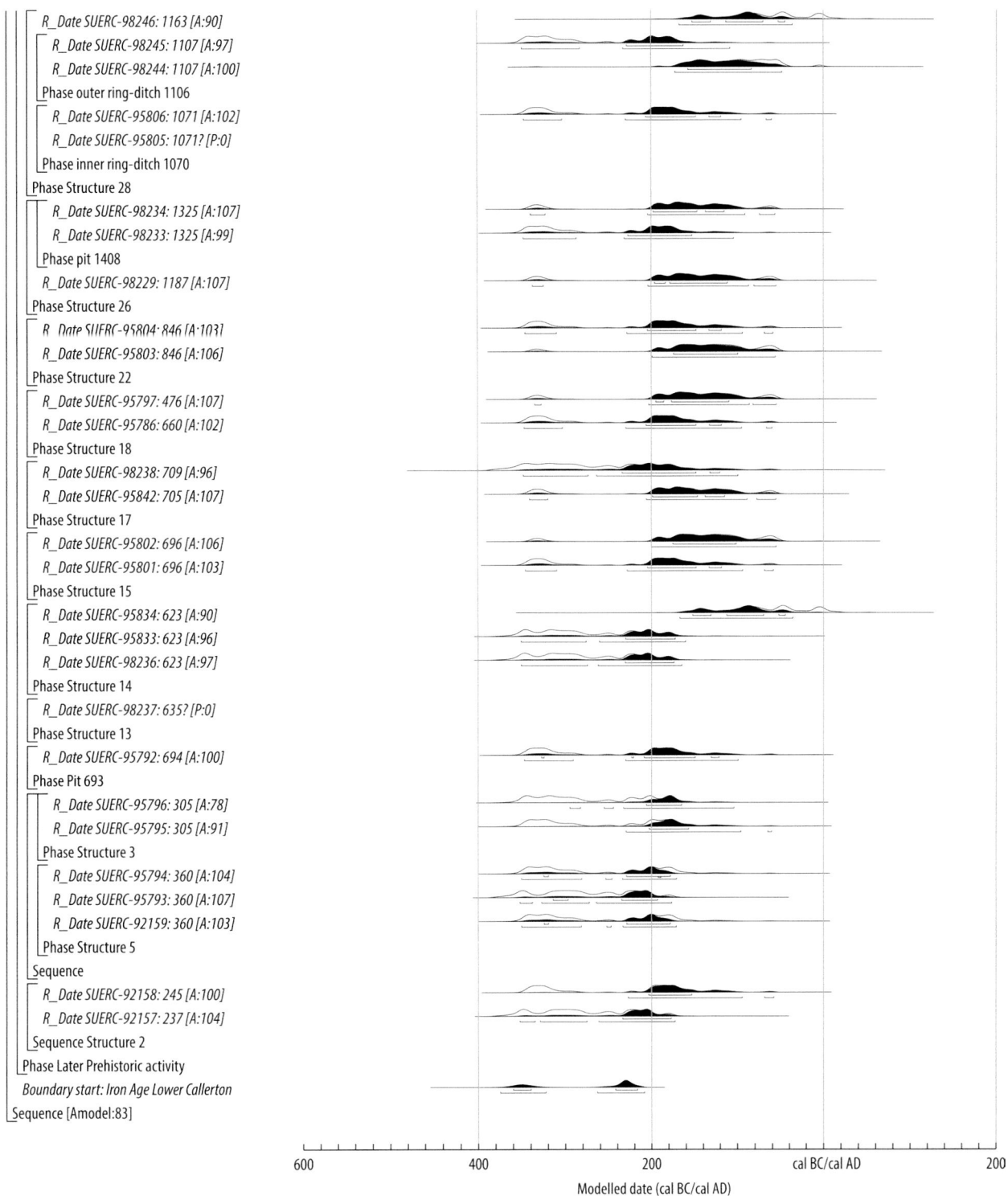

R_Date SUERC-98246: 1163 [A:90]
R_Date SUERC-98245: 1107 [A:97]
R_Date SUERC-98244: 1107 [A:100]
Phase outer ring-ditch 1106
R_Date SUERC-95806: 1071 [A:102]
R_Date SUERC-95805: 1071? [P:0]
Phase inner ring-ditch 1070
Phase Structure 28
R_Date SUERC-98234: 1325 [A:107]
R_Date SUERC-98233: 1325 [A:99]
Phase pit 1408
R_Date SUERC-98229: 1187 [A:107]
Phase Structure 26
R_Date SUERC-95804: 846 [A:103]
R_Date SUERC-95803: 846 [A:106]
Phase Structure 22
R_Date SUERC-95797: 476 [A:107]
R_Date SUERC-95786: 660 [A:102]
Phase Structure 18
R_Date SUERC-98238: 709 [A:96]
R_Date SUERC-95842: 705 [A:107]
Phase Structure 17
R_Date SUERC-95802: 696 [A:106]
R_Date SUERC-95801: 696 [A:103]
Phase Structure 15
R_Date SUERC-95834: 623 [A:90]
R_Date SUERC-95833: 623 [A:96]
R_Date SUERC-98236: 623 [A:97]
Phase Structure 14
R_Date SUERC-98237: 635? [P:0]
Phase Structure 13
R_Date SUERC-95792: 694 [A:100]
Phase Pit 693
R_Date SUERC-95796: 305 [A:78]
R_Date SUERC-95795: 305 [A:91]
Phase Structure 3
R_Date SUERC-95794: 360 [A:104]
R_Date SUERC-95793: 360 [A:107]
R_Date SUERC-92159: 360 [A:103]
Phase Structure 5
Sequence
R_Date SUERC-92158: 245 [A:100]
R_Date SUERC-92157: 237 [A:104]
Sequence Structure 2
Phase Later Prehistoric activity
Boundary start: Iron Age Lower Callerton
Sequence [Amodel:83]

600   400   cal BC/cal AD   200

Modelled date (cal BC/cal AD)

Figure 4.48 (a&b) Continued

OxCal v4.4.2 Bronk Ramsey (2020); r:2

span: Iron Age Lower Callerton

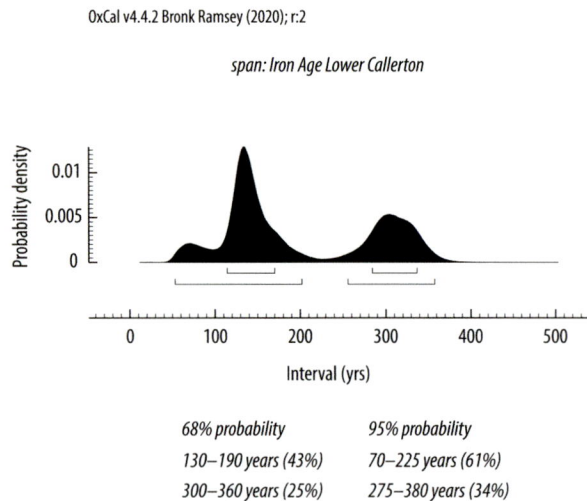

68% probability

130–190 years (43%)

300–360 years (25%)

95% probability

70–225 years (61%)

275–380 years (34%)

Figure 4.49 Span of the Iron Age settlement activity in the model shown in Figure 4.48

OxCal v4.4.2 Bronk Ramsey (2020); r:5 Atmospheric data from Reimer et al (2020)

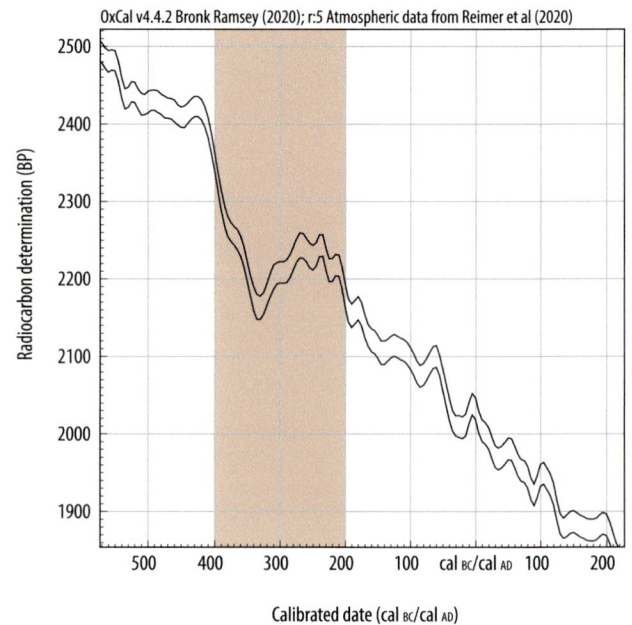

Calibrated date (cal BC/cal AD)

Figure 4.50 Section of the IntCal20 calibration curve (Reimer et al. 2020) that pertains to the middle Iron Age and shows the 'wiggle' in the period c. 400–200 cal BC (highlighted in red)

and the inferred phase relationships (Amodel=95). This revised model estimates:

- The dated Iron Age activity at Lower Callerton began in either *385–315 cal BC* (*77% probability*; Fig. 4.52; *start: Iron Age (Lower Callerton)*) or *265–215 cal BC* (*18% probability*), and probably either *370–330 cal BC* (*64% probability*) or *235–225 cal BC* (*4% probability*). Since there are no dated features that are in Phase 1, this date is the equivalent of the beginning of Phase 2.
- Phase 2 at Lower Callerton spanned either *115–210 years* (*17% probability*; Fig. 4.52; *span: IA Phase 2 (Lower Callerton)*) or *250–345 years* (*78% probability*), and probably *275–330 years* (*68% probability*).
- The transition to Phase 3 occurred in *105–25 cal BC* (*95% probability*; Fig. 4.52; *transition: IA Phase 2/3 (Lower Callerton)*), and probably in *60–35 cal BC* (*68% probability*).
- The third phase of activity at Lower Callerton spanned *5–70 years* (*95% probability*; Fig. 4.52; *span: IA Phase 3 (Lower Callerton)*), and it probably spanned *15–55 years* (*68% probability*).
- The Iron Age activity at Lower Callerton ended in either *90–70 cal BC* (*10% probability*; Fig. 4.52; *end: Iron Age Lower Callerton*) or *45 cal BC–cal AD 25* (*85% probability*), and probably in *35 cal BC–cal AD 10* (*68% probability*).
- Overall, this model estimates the dated Iron Age settlement activity at Lower Callerton spanned either *130–240 years* (*17% probability*; Fig. 4.53; *span: Iron Age Lower Callerton*) or *285–395 years* (*78% probability*), and probably *305–375 years* (*68% probability*).

While the large number of dates in Phase 2 appear to reduce the overall utility of the chronological modelling efforts, this modelling choice is most representative of the overall complexity of the settlement archaeology at Lower Callerton. A combination of visual inspection of the posterior probability density estimates for the dates and the 'Order' query in OxCal enables some exploration of the chronological relationships between roundhouses in Phase 2.

Phase 2 can be broken up into two broad periods of activity, but it is important to stress that the phases are not necessarily chronologically separate from one another. The chronology and associated archaeology should be considered as part of a continuously evolving settlement. The earlier period of activity is best represented by Structures 5, 35, and 43, and perhaps Structure 3. These represent settlement activity dating to the late fourth through the third centuries cal BC.

The second broad period of activity in Phase 2 is represented by activity dating to the second century cal BC. This is clearly demonstrated by the dating from structures 2, 15, 18, 22, 26, 37, 41, and 42. Additionally, structures 28, 29, and 45 and six-post Structure 17 are predominately dated to this period, but with the potential to either date between across the third/second century cal BC divide or to contain some residual material in the dating samples.

OxCal v4.4.2 Bronk Ramsey (2020); r:2 Atmospheric data from Reimer et al (2020)

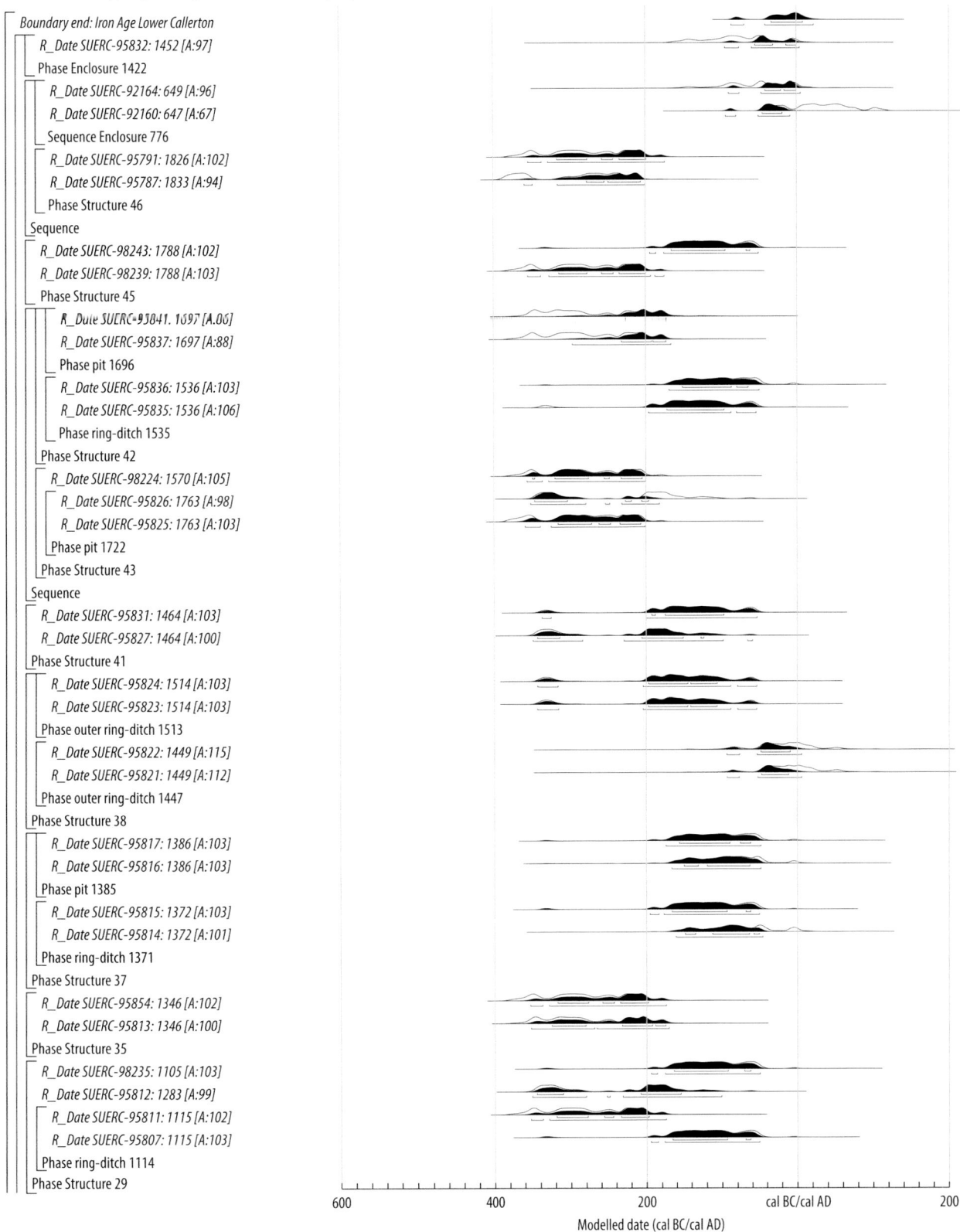

Boundary end: Iron Age Lower Callerton
R_Date SUERC-95832: 1452 [A:97]
Phase Enclosure 1422
R_Date SUERC-92164: 649 [A:96]
R_Date SUERC-92160: 647 [A:67]
Sequence Enclosure 776
R_Date SUERC-95791: 1826 [A:102]
R_Date SUERC-95787: 1833 [A:94]
Phase Structure 46
Sequence
R_Date SUERC-98243: 1788 [A:102]
R_Date SUERC-98239: 1788 [A:103]
Phase Structure 45
R_Date SUERC-95841: 1697 [A:86]
R_Date SUERC-95837: 1697 [A:88]
Phase pit 1696
R_Date SUERC-95836: 1536 [A:103]
R_Date SUERC-95835: 1536 [A:106]
Phase ring-ditch 1535
Phase Structure 42
R_Date SUERC-98224: 1570 [A:105]
R_Date SUERC-95826: 1763 [A:98]
R_Date SUERC-95825: 1763 [A:103]
Phase pit 1722
Phase Structure 43
Sequence
R_Date SUERC-95831: 1464 [A:103]
R_Date SUERC-95827: 1464 [A:100]
Phase Structure 41
R_Date SUERC-95824: 1514 [A:103]
R_Date SUERC-95823: 1514 [A:103]
Phase outer ring-ditch 1513
R_Date SUERC-95822: 1449 [A:115]
R_Date SUERC-95821: 1449 [A:112]
Phase outer ring-ditch 1447
Phase Structure 38
R_Date SUERC-95817: 1386 [A:103]
R_Date SUERC-95816: 1386 [A:103]
Phase pit 1385
R_Date SUERC-95815: 1372 [A:103]
R_Date SUERC-95814: 1372 [A:101]
Phase ring-ditch 1371
Phase Structure 37
R_Date SUERC-95854: 1346 [A:102]
R_Date SUERC-95813: 1346 [A:100]
Phase Structure 35
R_Date SUERC-98235: 1105 [A:103]
R_Date SUERC-95812: 1283 [A:99]
R_Date SUERC-95811: 1115 [A:102]
R_Date SUERC-95807: 1115 [A:103]
Phase ring-ditch 1114
Phase Structure 29

600   400   200   cal BC/cal AD   200

Modelled date (cal BC/cal AD)

Figure 4.51a The observed stratigraphic relationships portion of the alternate chronological model for Lower Callerton. The revised phasing with Structures 2 and 42 moved into Phase 2 is shown in Fig 4.51b

OxCal v4.4.2 Bronk Ramsey (2020); r:2 Atmospheric data from Reimer et al (2020)

Figure 4.51a Continued

OxCal v4.4.2 Bronk Ramsey (2020); r:2 Atmospheric data from Reimer et al (2020)

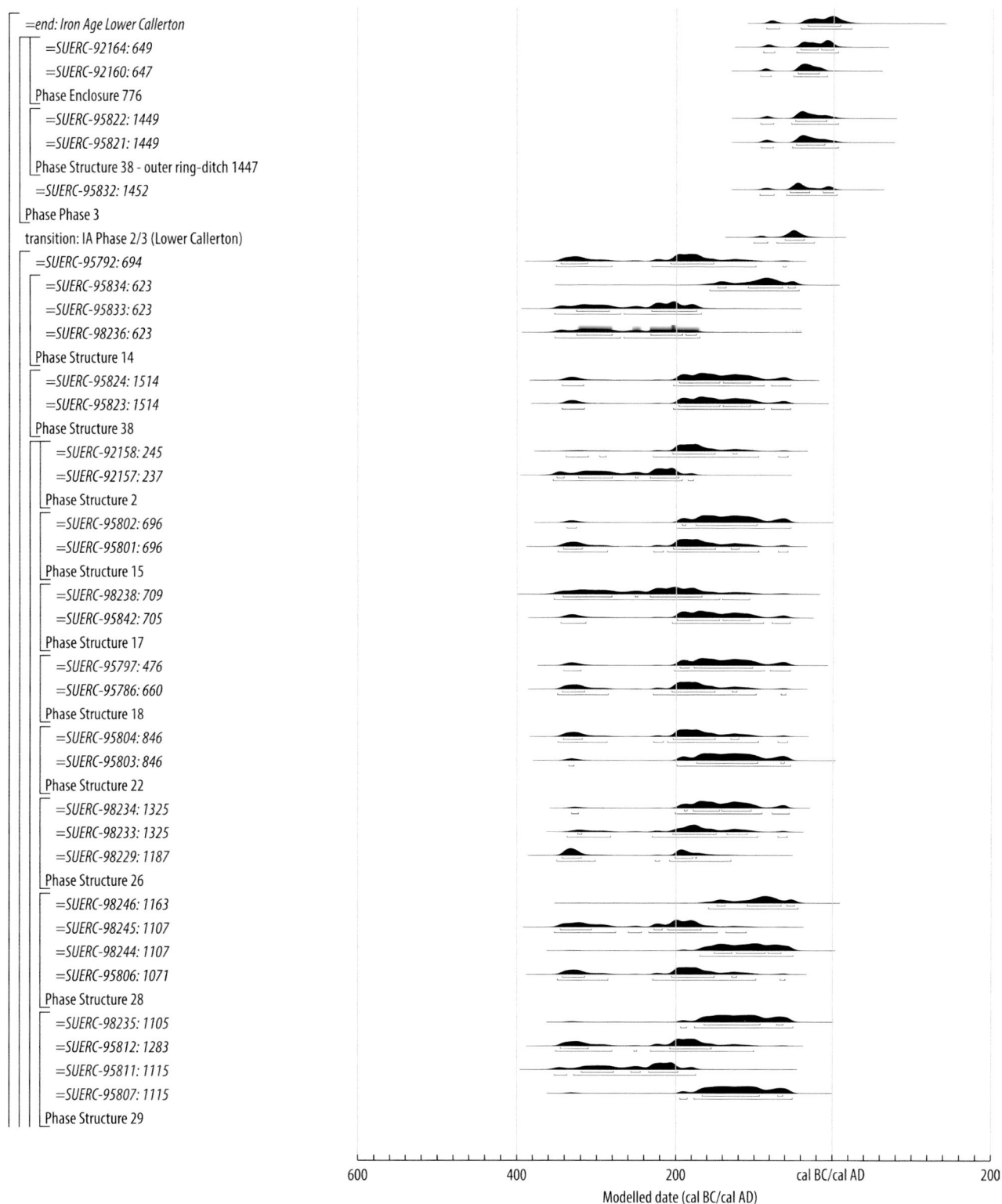

=end: Iron Age Lower Callerton
=SUERC-92164: 649
=SUERC-92160: 647
Phase Enclosure 776
=SUERC-95822: 1449
=SUERC-95821: 1449
Phase Structure 38 - outer ring-ditch 1447
=SUERC-95832: 1452
Phase Phase 3
transition: IA Phase 2/3 (Lower Callerton)
=SUERC-95792: 694
=SUERC-95834: 623
=SUERC-95833: 623
=SUERC-98236: 623
Phase Structure 14
=SUERC-95824: 1514
=SUERC-95823: 1514
Phase Structure 38
=SUERC-92158: 245
=SUERC-92157: 237
Phase Structure 2
=SUERC-95802: 696
=SUERC-95801: 696
Phase Structure 15
=SUERC-98238: 709
=SUERC-95842: 705
Phase Structure 17
=SUERC-95797: 476
=SUERC-95786: 660
Phase Structure 18
=SUERC-95804: 846
=SUERC-95803: 846
Phase Structure 22
=SUERC-98234: 1325
=SUERC-98233: 1325
=SUERC-98229: 1187
Phase Structure 26
=SUERC-98246: 1163
=SUERC-98245: 1107
=SUERC-98244: 1107
=SUERC-95806: 1071
Phase Structure 28
=SUERC-98235: 1105
=SUERC-95812: 1283
=SUERC-95811: 1115
=SUERC-95807: 1115
Phase Structure 29

600   400   200   cal BC/cal AD   200

Modelled date (cal BC/cal AD)

Figure 4.51b The cross-referenced phasing information that was used to provide further informative prior constraints on the radiocarbon dates in the main part of the revised chronological model shown in Fig. 4.51a

OxCal v4.4.2 Bronk Ramsey (2020); r:2 Atmospheric data from Reimer et al (2020)

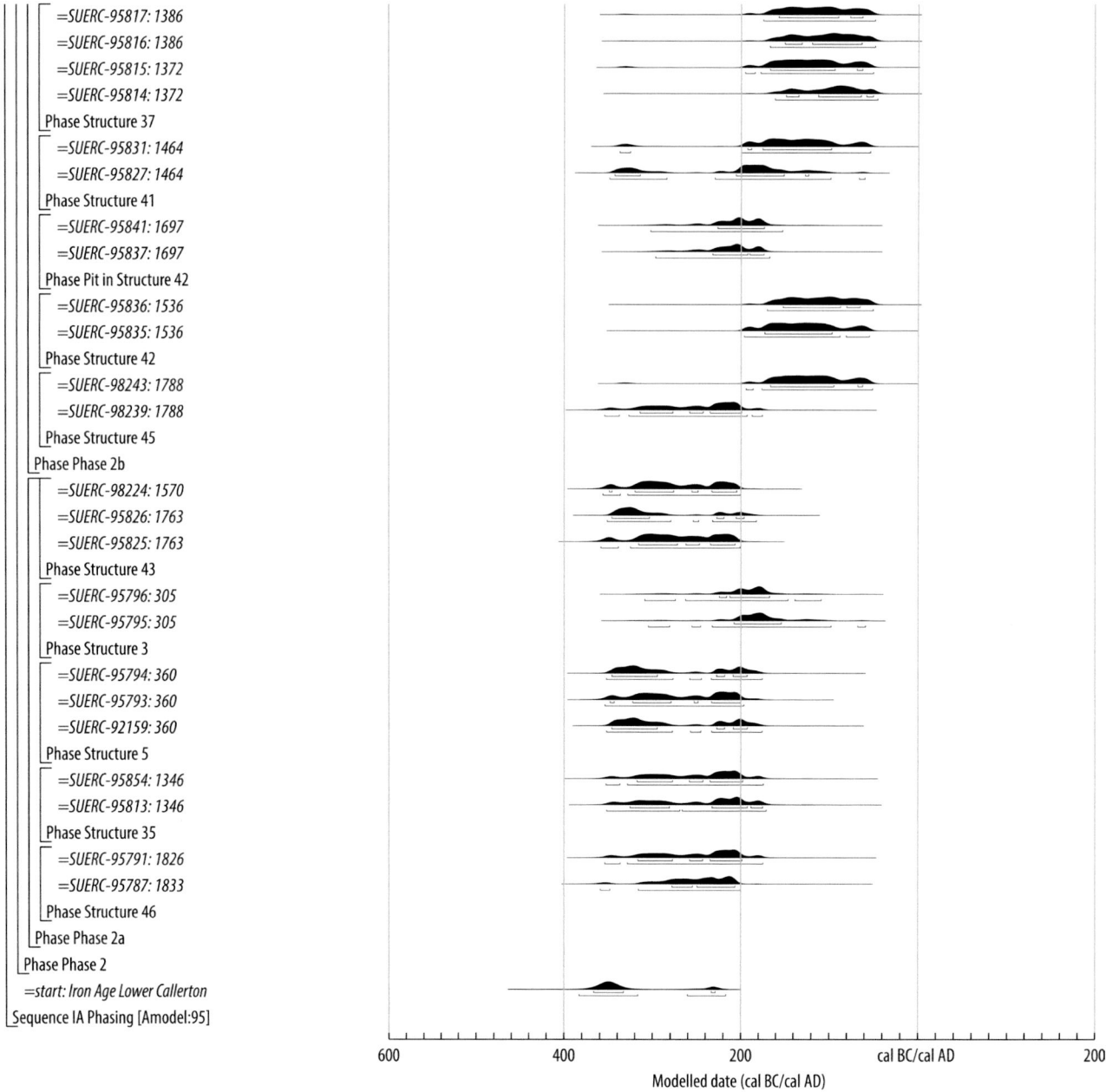

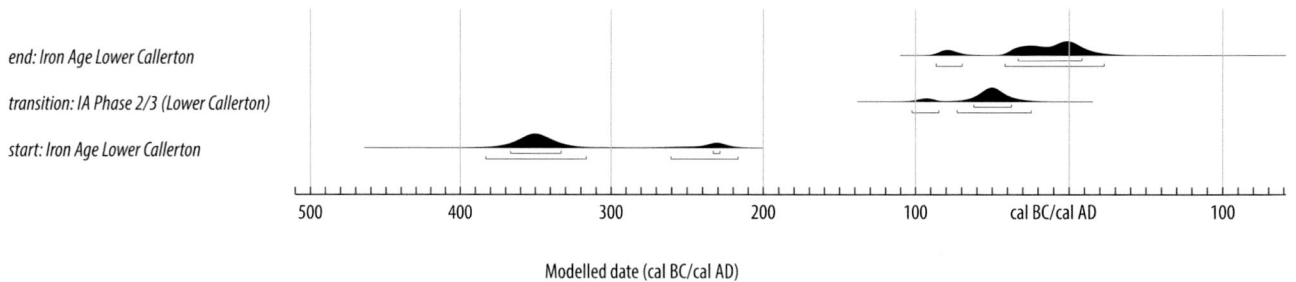

=SUERC-95817: 1386
=SUERC-95816: 1386
=SUERC-95815: 1372
=SUERC-95814: 1372
Phase Structure 37
=SUERC-95831: 1464
=SUERC-95827: 1464
Phase Structure 41
=SUERC-95841: 1697
=SUERC-95837: 1697
Phase Pit in Structure 42
=SUERC-95836: 1536
=SUERC-95835: 1536
Phase Structure 42
=SUERC-98243: 1788
=SUERC-98239: 1788
Phase Structure 45
Phase Phase 2b
=SUERC-98224: 1570
=SUERC-95826: 1763
=SUERC-95825: 1763
Phase Structure 43
=SUERC-95796: 305
=SUERC-95795: 305
Phase Structure 3
=SUERC-95794: 360
=SUERC-95793: 360
=SUERC-92159: 360
Phase Structure 5
=SUERC-95854: 1346
=SUERC-95813: 1346
Phase Structure 35
=SUERC-95791: 1826
=SUERC-95787: 1833
Phase Structure 46
Phase Phase 2a
Phase Phase 2
=start: Iron Age Lower Callerton
Sequence IA Phasing [Amodel:95]

600   400   200   cal BC/cal AD   200

Modelled date (cal BC/cal AD)

Figure 4.51b Continued

OxCal v4.4.2 Bronk Ramsey (2020); r:2 Atmospheric data from Reimer et al (2020)

end: Iron Age Lower Callerton
transition: IA Phase 2/3 (Lower Callerton)
start: Iron Age Lower Callerton

500   400   300   200   100   cal BC/cal AD   100

Modelled date (cal BC/cal AD)

Figure 4.52 Summary of the start, end, and transition dates for the Iron Age settlement activity at Lower Callerton that is shown in the model in Figs 4.51a and b

OxCal v4.4.2 Bronk Ramsey (2020); r:2 Atmospheric data from Reimer et al (2020)

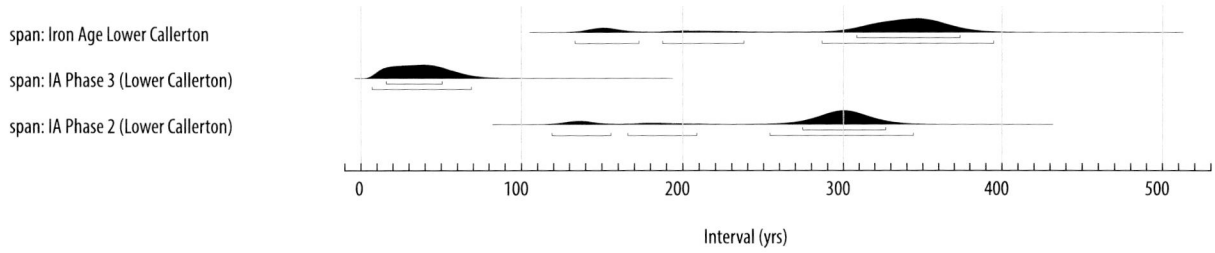

Figure 4.53 The spans of the phases of Iron Age activity at Lower Callerton as derived from the chronological model shown in Figs 4.51a and b

5

Discussion

The excavations at Lower Callerton and Morley Hill have revealed substantial Iron Age settlements. The sites contribute to the increasingly complex picture of Iron Age settlement emerging across a region that has witnessed a significant rise in archaeological investigation over the past 20 years. Iron Age settlement across the Northumberland coastal plain is often defined by the emergence of rectilinear enclosures in the later first millennium BC (Hodgson *et al.* 2012, 189). The work by Jobey at West Brandon (1962), High Knowes (1966), Burradon (1970) and Boggle Hill (1984) form the foundations of settlement classification and development (Fig. 5.1). It was proposed that a phase of unenclosed settlement may underlie many of the enclosures, and this has been borne out in subsequent work and defined as the standard pattern of development (Hodgson *et al.* 2012, 186). The predominance of rectilinear enclosures has raised questions about the connectivity and contemporaneity of the sites and the implications of this on settlement development and wider landscape organisation. This picture has become increasingly complex due to the identification of settlements, such as Blagdon Park 1 (NAA 2008; Hodgson *et al.* 2012), Pegswood Moor (Proctor 2009) and now Lower Callerton, which vary in extent, form and pattern of development. The new datasets from Morley Hill and Lower Callerton can be placed within this growing corpus of research to explore themes of settlement development, organisation and wider connections, the role of enclosure, architectural features and finally the decline in settlement and the impact of Roman contact.

Rectilinear enclosures: Morley Hill

The three settlements at Morley Hill are comparable in form with rectilinear enclosures identified and excavated across the region. The double-ditched enclosure of Morley Hill Enclosure 1 is comparable with Blagdon Park 2 (Hodgson *et al.* 2012), Brenkley (van Wessel and Wilson

2020) and Burradon (Jobey 1962) while the single enclosure of Morley Hill Enclosure 2 can be compared with enclosures at East and West Brunton (Hodgson *et al.* 2012) and West Shiremoor (ASDU 2017b; Fig. 5.2). The extent of the settlement visible at Morley Hill Enclosure 3 makes it difficult to directly compare, but shared characteristics with the other rectilinear enclosures can be recognised.

The distinctive double-ditched enclosure at Morley Hill Enclosure 1 survives as an earthwork providing indications of features, such as banks, alluded to at other sites. The results of the geophysical survey and limited excavations indicated the presence of substantial inner and outer ditches with an aligned entranceway (AD Archaeology 2013). The enclosures at Blagdon Park 2 are comparable where the final form of the settlement, the double-ditched enclosure, represents the main phase of activity developing after 350 BC (Hodgson *et al.* 2012, 37). The inner enclosure ditch at Blagdon Park 2 measured on average 4.70 m wide and 1.30 m deep with an east-facing entrance (*ibid.*, 25). Two large roundhouses, displaying evidence of having been rebuilt multiple times, were located within the inner enclosure. The outer enclosure ditch was narrower in width with evidence for a metalled surface across the entranceway as identified at Morley Hill Enclosure 1. The settlements at Morley Hill Enclosure 1 and Blagdon Park 2 are remarkably similar to the site excavated by Headland Archaeology in 2013 at Brenkley located only 600 m to the south of Blagdon Park 2 and 3.5 km north of Morley Hill Enclosure 1 (van Wessel and Wilson 2020). At Brenkley the inner and outer enclosure ditches were also interpreted, from the limited dating evidence, to be contemporary (*ibid.*).

At Brenkley a further large enclosure, Ditch C, surrounded the double-ditched enclosure. This is a feature more typically identified at extensive or multiple enclosure sites. A single radiocarbon date from the ditch, 180–1 cal BC (SUERC-26979), and the overall organisation of the site, suggested Ditch C was contemporary

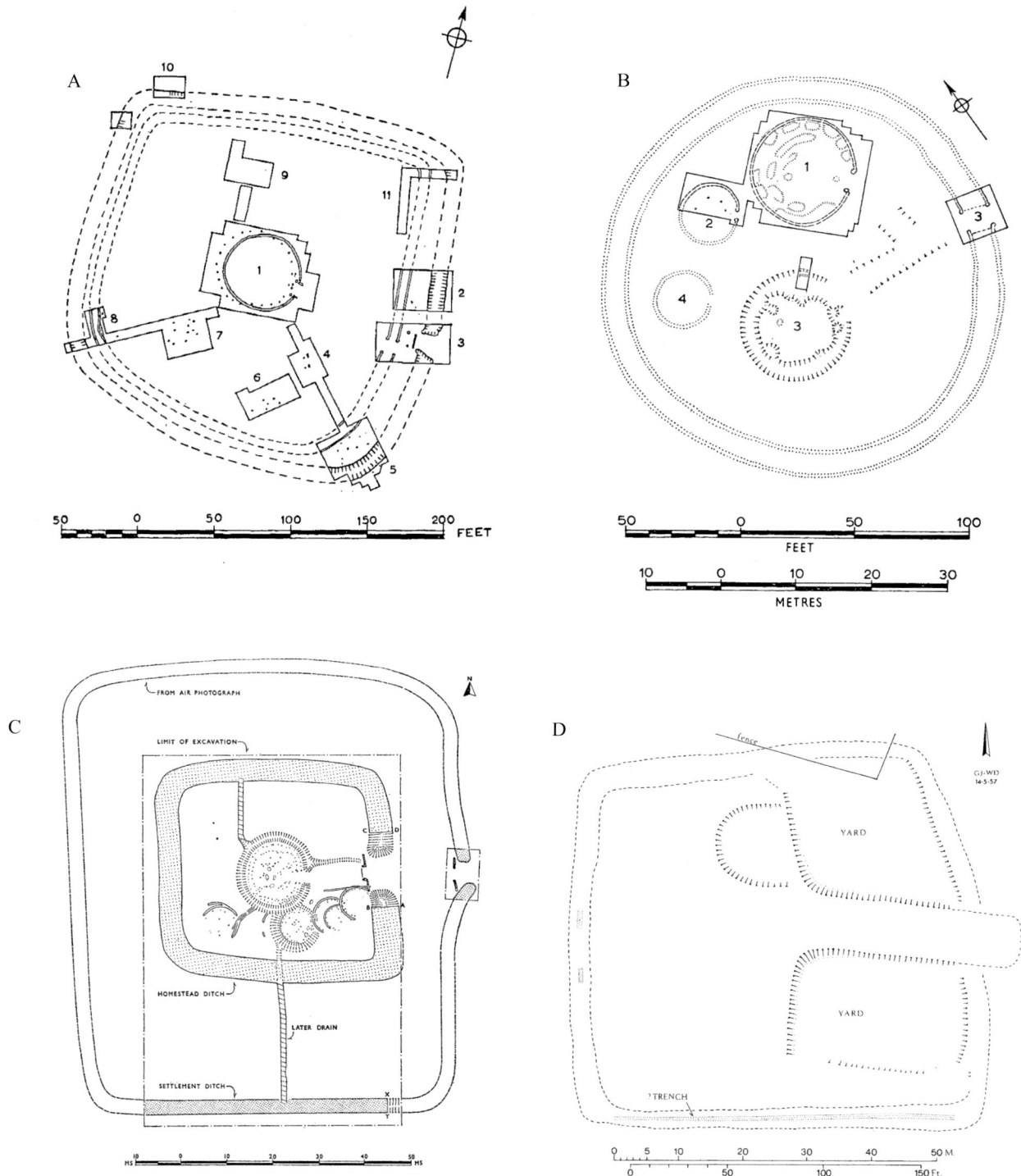

Figure 5.1 Excavations and surveys carried out by George Jobey: West Brandon (A) (1962); High Knowes (B) (1966); Burradon (C) (1970); Boggle Hill (D) (1984)

with the double-ditched enclosure (van Wessel and Wilson 2020). A similar enclosure ditch was identified at West Brunton surrounding two rectilinear enclosures, Enclosure A and B, and a series of intercutting structures (Hodgson *et al.* 2012, 67). Enclosure A measured 43 m by 34 m and was defined by a 5–8 m wide ditch surrounding a large central roundhouse with an east facing entrance

(*ibid.*, 73). To the north, Enclosure B was defined by a ditch *c.* 4.50 m wide surrounding an area 45 m by 56–62 m again with a central roundhouse (*ibid.*, 73). The northern edge of Enclosure B was aligned to the large surrounding enclosure with the arrangement of features reminiscent of Morley Hill Enclosure 2. The presence of a rectilinear enclosure which appears to 'hang' from

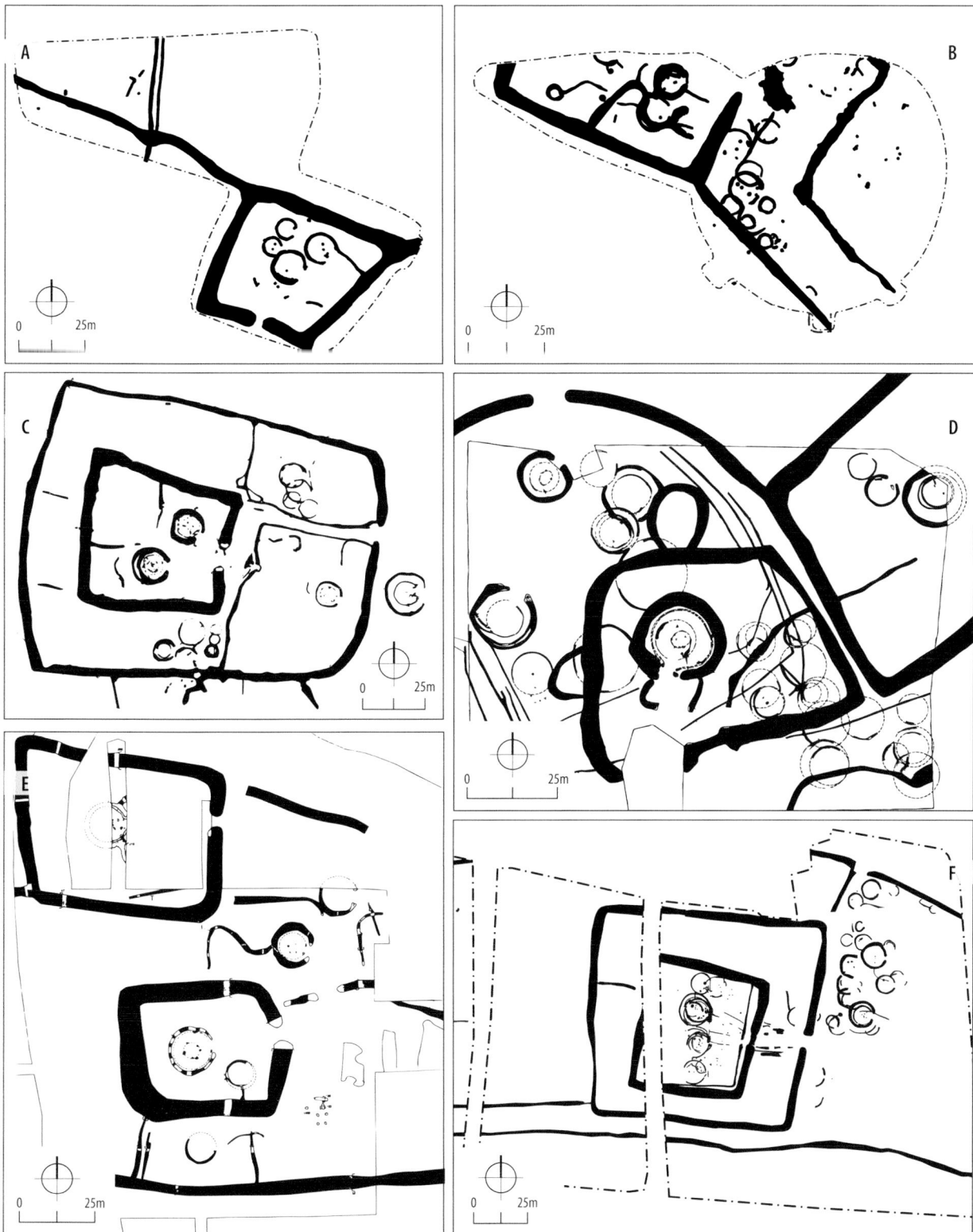

Figure 5.2 Morley Hill Enclosure 2 (A) and Morley Hill Enclosure 3 (B) compared to Blagdon Park 2 (C) (Hodgson et al. *2012), West Brunton (D) (*ibid.*), East Brunton (E) (*ibid.*) and Brenkley (F) (van Wessel and Wilson 2020)*

a larger enclosure or linear boundary was also witnessed at West Shiremoor. At West Shiremoor, located 6.5 km east of Morley Hill Enclosure 2, a rectangular enclosure defined by a 2.90 m wide and 1.70 m deep ditch with a

further boundary extending to the west was excavated by ASDU in 2017 (2017b, 6).

The more complex arrangement of enclosures, adjoining boundaries and groups of structures witnessed at

Morley Hill Enclosure 3 is also seen at East Brunton. At East Brunton, located 1.9 km to the south of Morley Hill Enclosure 3, an earlier unenclosed settlement was followed by two later Iron Age enclosures (Hodgson *et al.* 2012, 54). Enclosure 1 was defined by a 5 m wide ditch that surrounded a large roundhouse with a gully that potentially drained into the enclosure ditch (*ibid.*, 57). Enclosure 2 was of similar dimensions with a ditch measuring 5.82 m wide surrounding a group of roundhouses with the curvilinear ditch extending from the eastern corner (*ibid.*, 59). The arrangement of ditches with structures between the enclosures is comparable to the partial enclosure and ditches at Morley Hill Enclosure 3. The concentration of intercutting structures, with possible drainage features, within the enclosure at Morley Hill Enclosure 3 is unusual but not unique. A similar arrangement was excavated at East Wideopen, located only 1.5 km to the east of Morley Hill Enclosure 3 (ASDU 2014b). The enclosures uncovered at Morley Hill are all comparable with those across the region, displaying a similar arrangement of features and pattern of development.

The beginnings of enclosed settlement

The earliest Iron Age activity at many sites is defined by an unenclosed phase of settlement. Sites such as East Brunton, West Brunton, Blagdon Park 2 (Hodgson *et al.* 2012) and St. George's Hospital (ARS Ltd 2016) all showed evidence for unenclosed settlement pre-dating the enclosures. Due to the limited number of direct stratigraphic relationships on many sites, it is often difficult to determine whether structures belong to unenclosed settlement or later phases, a problem identified early by Jobey (1987, 167). This was the case at Morley Hill Enclosure 3 where, despite a high number of structures, the lack of stratigraphic relationships, poor preservation, and dearth of distinctive artefacts provided limited chronological resolution for earlier phases. Structures 5 and 12 located outside the main enclosure may have belonged to an earlier unenclosed phase if the presence of an external bank is accepted. These structures would have been located under the bank, perhaps owing their preservation to this, with the later structures appearing to be aligned along it.

At many sites, palisade enclosures appeared to form an integral part of earlier settlement. The palisades were identified in the archaeological record as narrow, steep-sided rectilinear ditches, often comparable in overall size to the later enclosures. A series of rectilinear palisade ditches were uncovered at East Brunton with earlier ditches identified underlying Enclosure A at West Brunton (Hodgson *et al.* 2012). Several recent excavations have also shown evidence for palisaded enclosures including at Hoodsclose (Muncaster 2011), St George's Hospital (ARS Ltd 2016), East Wideopen (ASDU 2014b) and West Shiremoor, where an earlier palisade was almost entirely truncated by the later rectilinear enclosure (ASDU 2017b).

The presence of a palisade enclosure underlying the later enclosure, seen at West Brunton and West Shiremoor, was also identified at Brenkley Lane (van Wessel and Wilson 2020). The entrance of the palisade at Brenkley aligned with that of the later inner enclosure ditch, suggesting a continuity of settlement between phases. In this case, the later enclosure appears to directly replace the palisade. Palisade enclosures, whilst common, are not a prerequisite for rectilinear enclosures as no evidence for earlier palisades was uncovered at Morley Hill. It should be noted that not all palisades developed into ditched enclosures, for example, no evidence of later enclosures was found during the excavations of Arcot Phase 1, where a rectilinear palisade surrounded three structures (ASDU 2019).

While no radiocarbon dates were obtained from material associated with structures confidently assigned to this phase at Morley Hill, where sites have been dated the earlier phases consistently belong to the early to middle Iron Age. The Bayesian modelling of the dates from Blagdon Park 2 estimated that settlement began 1405–430 cal BC (95% probability) and 885–565 cal BC (68% probability; Hamilton 2012, 124). At East Brunton a *terminus post quem* of 770–400 cal BC (UBA-7820) was indicated for the palisade enclosure followed by unenclosed settlement centred around 400 cal BC (Hamilton 2012, 120). A similar range of dates was recovered from West Brunton with open settlement beginning before 400 BC until 200 BC (Hamilton 2012, 121). The palisade at East Wideopen was radiocarbon dated to 780–425 cal BC (SUERC-49653; ASDU 2014b) as was the earliest activity at Arcot ranging from 760–400 cal BC (ASDU 2019, 9). The basal fill of the palisade at Brenkley indicated a later date of 370–200 cal BC (SUERC-53146, van Wessel and Wilson 2020). A single small pit, Pit 5455, at Morley Hill Enclosure 3 was dated to 774–482 cal BC (SUERC-83346) at least suggesting the presence of activity during this period. The development of rectilinear enclosures appears to represent a dramatic shift in settlement organisation moving into the later Iron Age.

Enclosure development

The development of the distinctive enclosed settlements in most cases represents a significant reorganisation of the settlement. At smaller scale sites structures appear to have become concentrated within a single enclosure, while at larger sites multiple contemporary substantial enclosures defined the settlement.

At all excavated examples, the rectilinear enclosures represent the primary phase of settlement activity. The re-analysis of the radiocarbon dates from Blagdon Park 2, East and West Brunton and the subsequent Bayesian modelling provide detailed considerations of settlement development which can be compared with subsequent excavations (Hodgson *et al.* 2012; Hamilton 2012; 2010).

The radiocarbon dating of Blagdon Park 2 indicated enclosed activity dating from around 350 BC to AD 90 (Hodgson *et al.* 2012, 119) with the modelling of 16 samples suggesting that initial enclosure took place 395–60 cal BC (95% probability) with the site remaining enclosed for 25–540 years (95% probability; Hamilton 2012, 124). A similar picture was proposed for East Brunton with a smaller number of dates indicating enclosed activity beginning in 335–115 cal BC (95% probability) and lasting 1–190 years (95% probability; *ibid.*, 126). This was mirrored at West Brunton with enclosure beginning in 320–170 cal BC (95% probability) and continuing for 285–500 years (95% probability; *ibid.*, 130). The modelling concluded that the sites became enclosed as part of a wider shift towards enclosure in the first millennium BC, with this change witnessed across the coastal plain at *c.*200 cal BC (Hamilton 2010; 2012, 131).

The single radiocarbon date from Morley Hill Enclosure 2 fits within this broader pattern, appearing to suggest activity within the enclosure dating to 360–60 cal BC (SUERC-83347). The dates from structures within Morley Hill Enclosure 3 and the enclosure ditch terminus fall later, from 100 cal BC–cal AD 110. The radiocarbon dates from the enclosure ditches at Brenkley Lane are comparable indicating activity 172 cal BC–cal AD 8 (Ditch C, SUERC-26979) and 97 cal BC–cal AD 77 (Ditch A, SUERC-53139; van Wessel and Wilson 2020). The range of dates recovered from East Wideopen again present a similar picture with structures grouped within the primary phase of enclosure dated to 360 cal BC–cal AD 10 (ASDU 2014b, 85). The overall phasing at East Wideopen was concluded to represent multiple phases of development with the enclosed settlement dating from *c.* 200–100BC with abandonment in *c.* AD 100 (*ibid.*, 48).

Final activity

The abandonment or post-enclosure phases of settlement are difficult to define. Many settlements appear to fall out of use in the early first millennium AD, prior to the Roman conquest, or early in the Roman period (see later discussion). The collative assessment of the dated sites in the region presented a stark picture of widespread abandonment (Hodgson *et al.* 2012, 214). At Blagdon Park 2, the Bayesian modelling estimated that the settlement fell out of use 50 cal BC–cal AD 225 (95% probability) and probably in 30 cal BC–cal AD 80 (68% probability; Hamilton 2012, 124). The model presents the end of the dated structural sequence with no later modifications to the enclosures noted. At West Brunton the radiocarbon dates from the ditch infills along with the Bayesian modelling estimates that the settlement went out of use in cal AD 85–240 (95% probability) and in cal AD 100–175 (68% probability; Hamilton 2012, 130). It should be noted that no Roman material was recovered from either site. There is no evidence for the later reorganisation of the

settlements to match the investment in the construction of the enclosures. Certainly the upstanding remains from Morley Hill Enclosure 1 today highlight the longevity and lasting impact of the ditches and possible banks. Identifying evidence of final settlement is difficult but in some cases insights can be teased out as to the complex and variable nature of declining activity.

At East Wideopen, a sub-enclosure was backfilled before the final phase of activity defined by two roundhouses, 7a/b and 11b, dated to 92 cal BC–cal AD 65 (SUERC-49651) and 60 cal BC–cal AD 65 (SUERC-49654; ASDU 2014b, 47). The reworking of the enclosure ditch was also noted at Brenkley where backfilled deposits within the rectilinear enclosure ditch were dated to 100 cal BC–cal AD 80 (SUERC-53139; van Wessel and Wilson 2020). The inner ditch at Brenkley appeared to be capped by a layer of poorly sorted sub-angular stones with a small assemblage of Roman pottery recovered predominately from pits within the central area (van Wessel and Wilson 2020). A fragment of a Roman wine cooler and a glass armlet were also recovered from the site (*ibid.*). Roman material was also found at East Brunton where the Bayesian modelling suggested the dated settlement ended in 170 cal BC–cal AD 5 (95% probability) and in 145–50 cal BC (68% probability; Hamilton 2012, 128). Traces of Roman ceramics were recovered from a gully to the south of the enclosures and a melted glass object, possibly a glass bangle of Roman date, was recovered from Roundhouse A located to the north of Enclosure 1 (Hodgson *et al.* 2012, 59–60). A similar shift in settlement focus has been proposed at Morley Hill Enclosure 3, where several structures to the east of the enclosure represent a later phase of unenclosed settlement. The evidence from the excavated sites tentatively indicates limited activity, influenced by the enclosures, but crucially appearing to post-date the height of the settlement.

Extensive enclosed settlements: Lower Callerton

The extensive settlement uncovered at Lower Callerton differs in form from the rectilinear enclosures identified across the region. Lower Callerton is defined by a large enclosure with internal enclosed areas with multiple phases of structures. The site contained features in some respects comparable to larger rectilinear enclosure sites such as Blagdon Park 2, but far more so to sites such as Pegswood Moor, Morpeth (Fig. 5.3). Extensive excavations at Pegswood Moor in 2000 by Pre-Construct Archaeology Limited revealed a network of enclosures, trackways, dwellings and activity areas markedly different in character to the rectilinear enclosure settlements (Proctor 2009). The site appears to follow the broad pattern of development established across the region with unenclosed settlement succeeded by an extensive enclosure in the later Iron Age (*ibid.*, 6). The identification and

Figure 5.3 Lower Callerton (right) in overall plan compared to Pegswood Moor (left) (Proctor 2009)

analysis of extensive settlements at Lower Callerton and Pegswood Moor paint an increasingly complex picture of Iron Age settlement across the region.

At Lower Callerton the unenclosed settlement comprised structures of varying sizes, often defined by single curvilinear ditches, located to the north of the linear boundary which extended east to west across the site. A limited number of features, structures 7 and 8 and 21, may predate the boundary but the stratigraphic relationship was not clear due to the truncation by later enclosures. The development of settlements along contemporary or pre-existing boundaries is an established trend in the Iron Age and can be witnessed across the region. In some cases these boundaries are defined by pit alignments such as those noted at Blagdon Park 1, Shotton North East, Shotton Anglo Saxon Site, and at Fox Covert, principally dating from the late Bronze Age to the early Iron Age (Hodgson *et al.* 2012). Iron Age activity at Shotton North East and Blagdon Park 1 was clearly positioned along the earlier boundaries (Hodgson *et al.* 2012). Pit alignments and boundaries may have formed the basis for travel between settlements or areas, effectively acting as a continuous trail marker or as an analogue to trackways. Acting to both define and link areas the boundaries would have influenced movement across the landscape and perhaps mirrored social relations and connections between settlements. At Shotton North East, the structures were accompanied by a palisade or stock enclosure aligned upon the earlier boundary (Hodgson *et al.*

2012). A series of structures to the west at Lower Callerton may also relate to the remains of a palisade mirroring the earlier phases of the rectilinear enclosures. The unenclosed settlement at Lower Callerton predates the main phase of enclosure beginning in 385–315 cal BC (77% probability) with the comparative dating of palisades indicating this may have begun as early as 700–400 BC. The dates from Brenkley and Pegswood do indicate the possibility of later unenclosed settlement more immediately predating enclosure (Proctor 2009, 66).

The robust program of radiocarbon dating and subsequent Bayesian modelling at Lower Callerton indicates that while distinct phases can be identified within the enclosed settlement there is strong evidence for overall continuity of occupation and continual development. The Bayesian modelling indicated initial enclosure at 385–315 cal BC (77% probability) with activity lasting over 200 years. The development of enclosure at Lower Callerton can be compared with that at Pegswood Moor where the artefactual evidence and radiocarbon dates offer two models. The artefactual evidence along with the initial suite of radiocarbon dates, obtained from charred organic residues adhering to pottery sherds, indicated that enclosed activity was established in the latter two centuries BC and lasted for around 200 years (Proctor 2009, 67). The later reassessment of the carbonised residues highlighted the potential for contamination by old carbon with an additional set of radiocarbon dates, obtained from plant macrofossils, subject to Bayesian modelling (Hamilton 2010, 158). The modelling indicated that enclosure began later in 25 cal BC–cal AD 55 (95% probability) and was potentially short-lived lasting 1–85 years (*ibid.*, 162). The results are caveated as the inclusion of some of the dates from the carbonised residues would introduce the possibility that the site was enclosed earlier around the third century cal BC (*ibid.*, 162). Crucially, the complication of the dates and a recognition of the nuances indicate that, despite the difference in settlement form, the enclosures at Lower Callerton and Pegswood are broadly contemporary with the rectilinear enclosures.

The enclosed phase of settlement at Lower Callerton, Phase 2, is defined by the construction of a large enclosure surrounding a *c.* 1.5 ha area. The rectangular enclosure defines the settlement foci with structures concentrated in the northern half. The southern extent of the enclosure may have been defined by a watercourse; a stream presently runs to the south of the site, with this area falling beyond the scope of the excavation. The scale of the enclosure is comparable to Blagdon Park 2 which covered an overall area of 1.5 ha. No clear entrance to the enclosure was identified, raising the possibility that this was located to the south, or – given the extent of later modifications – that the earlier entrance has been obscured. The structures associated with the initial phase of enclosure were defined by single ring-gullies which, in the case of structures 3, 11 and 12, indicated the maintenance and replacement of structure at the same location. Structure 43 to the north-west was also defined by a single ring-gully with a further gully that extended to the main enclosure. Unlike at Morley Hill, this is the only structure with evidence for such a drainage channel. Activity appears to have extended beyond the enclosure with the radiocarbon dates from Structure 46, 400–200 cal BC (SUERC-95787) and 390–170 cal BC (SUERC-95791), suggesting it also belonged to this phase. Several of the single ring-gully defined structures within Phase 2 may have related to the initial enclosure of the site suggesting a wide spread of activity.

The settlement appears to evolve in complexity with construction of sub-enclosures dividing the interior space, large roundhouses, ancillary structures, and small enclosures or pens extending activity into the wider area. Sub-enclosure 1 was aligned to the north-eastern corner of the main enclosure, defined by a relatively shallow 0.33 m deep ditch. No features were uncovered within the enclosure suggesting it did not define a domestic space. The fills of the ditches provided no indication of function but a variety of uses could be envisaged including cultivation and for livestock perhaps on a seasonal basis. The ditches alone would not have been substantial enough to constrain livestock but may have been supported by fences, hurdles, tethering or simply supervision. In contrast to Sub-enclosure 1, a large complex roundhouse, Structure 2, was located within Sub-enclosure 2. The enclosure

appeared to define the space or working area surrounding the roundhouse. A similar roundhouse, Structure 42, was located to the west within the third possible sub-enclosure defined by Ditch 1772. This ditch was recut multiple times with a post-hole identified at the base of the easternmost section. The post-hole at the base of the ditch may tentatively indicate the presence of structures bridging the ditches offering a solution to the lack of entranceways identified across the site, traditionally defined by breaks in the ditches.

A narrow, *c.* 2.5 m wide, race or trackway ran between sub-enclosures 1 and 2 with a series of pits and a short ditch suggesting the presence of a gate feature at its southern end. The passage controls access to the interior of the enclosure from the north and is the only clearly defined entranceway. The multiple narrow trackways at Pegswood Moor were interpreted as stock herding features primarily for sheep as explored at other fenland field systems (Pryor 1996; 2006; Proctor 2009, 67). The trackway at Blagdon Park 2, like at Lower Callerton, defines the only entranceway into the enclosure. At Blagdon Park 2 the role of the trackway in directing the movement of livestock was also highlighted with animals potentially being brought into the enclosure overnight, seasonally or for significant occasions (Hodgson *et al.* 2012, 197). The trackway at Lower Callerton may also have served to direct movement towards the series of post-defined structures and past the row of roundhouses with multiple entrances. Structure 22, immediately north of the trackway, was defined by three sections of an outer ditch with post-holes flanking two of the three possible entrances. To the south, Structure 38 was a similarly complex structure with a dual aperture to the east and west. Structure 29, further to the south-west, was again comparable in form with two entrances. These roundhouses were surrounded by potentially contemporary structures and may have served a specific function as discussed in the proceeding sections.

The final phase of enclosure at Lower Callerton occurred in 105–25 cal BC (*95% probability*) and spanned 5–70 years (*95% probability*) marked by the construction of Enclosure 0776. Enclosure 0776 cut the northeastern corner of the main enclosure with no contemporary structures identified within. The final phase at Pegswood Moor also comprised a single enclosure, Enclosure 11, defined by the cut for a timber post and plank built fence (Proctor 2009, 36). The limited number of internal features, the presence of multiple entrances and the possible trackway informed the interpretation as a stock enclosure rather than for habitation (*ibid.*, 39). The enclosure at Pegswood Moor was potentially associated with further boundaries interpreted as forming part of the Romano-British phase of activity. The dating of this phase is predicated on the recovery of glass armlet fragments from backfilled deposits and Enclosure 11, which date from the late first to early second century AD (*ibid.*, 83). The enclosure at Lower Callerton appears more substantial and at first glance is reminiscent of the rectilinear enclosures which define much of the region. However, the width of the planned ditch may be slightly misleading with the excavation of the termini indicating the recutting of parallel narrow ditches. The radiocarbon dates and stratigraphic relationships support the interpretation of this as the final enclosure on site. A body sherd from a Roman oxidised ware vessel was recovered from the ditch mirroring the limited Roman material recovered from many sites. The dated evidence suggests that activity at Lower Callerton ended early in the first millennium, likely 45 cal BC–cal AD 25 (*85% probability*). This is comparable to the pattern emerging for enclosed Iron Age sites with declining or final activity in the early first millennium AD.

Settlement scale, distribution and wider connections

The primary phase of enclosure at both Morley Hill and Lower Callerton followed the expected pattern for the region falling between 400BC–AD100. The detailed program of radiocarbon dating and Bayesian modelling at Lower Callerton helped to refine and bound the chronologies of the site, whereas Morley Hill faced significant problems of preservation and suitability of material for dating. Sites such as Lower Callerton, Pegswood Moor (Proctor 2009) and West Brunton (Hodgson *et al.* 2012) presented evidence for almost continuous activity within this timeframe. Morley Hill, based on somewhat limited radiocarbon dating, indicated a series of adjacent enclosures forming a sequence of consecutive but discrete settlement activities spanning the period. The broadly contemporaneous date and seemingly close distribution of Iron Age settlements raises a key set of inter- and intra-site questions such as how long were these settlements actively used; were the sites contemporary with one another; and was there continuity of settlement activity or did it occur in discrete phases? Sites of varying forms across the region could be tentatively presumed to form a contemporary landscape of communities connected throughout the peak of the later Iron Age in the first centuries BC and AD.

The density of identified settlements within the immediate vicinity of Morley Hill is high with the sites East Wideopen, East Brunton, West Brunton, and the two cropmarks comprising Hazlerigg South located within 2 km. Within 4 km of Morley Hill further sites include Burradon; the southern edge of another cluster of settlements extending northwards from Brenkley (van Wessel and Wilson 2021); and Gardener's Houses (Biggins *et al.* 1997) (Fig. 5.4). There is a high probability that many more undiscovered sites are located in the intervening agricultural land and many more may once have existed to the south within the footprint of the City of Newcastle. The best estimate of the spacing of settlements on the coastal plain appears to have been every 1 km (Hodgson *et al.* 2012, 191). Clusters of settlements can be identified, which most likely relate to the modern focus of

development, such as those surrounding Morley Hill and the cluster of settlements towards Morpeth, including Pegswood Moor (Proctor 2009).

Broadly contemporary Iron Age settlements of varying scales from small farmsteads to larger settlements have now been identified across the region. Many of the smaller scale rectilinear enclosures, such as Morley Hill Enclosure 2, have been understood as farmsteads comprising small clusters or individual structures often rebuilt several times in similar locations, and with a smaller footprint of habitation area (Fig. 5.5). Larger sites, such as Brenkley, Blagdon Park 2 and including Lower Callerton and Pegswood Moor, share similarities in form with complex arrangements of space and a greater variety of features including for livestock, working areas and seemingly specialist structures. It is proposed that the larger, more populated settlements may have served as focal points within the wider community for social interaction and the trade of both material goods and of cultural and technological knowledge.

Very large settlements with increased structural and perhaps social complexity, known elsewhere as 'oppida', have yet to be identified on the Northumberland Coastal Plain (Harding 2017, 356). An example of such a site, Stanwick, situated at the southern extent of the wider coastal plain, covered an area of 270 ha and has been identified as a significant, possibly 'royal' site, with connections to the regional elite Queen Cartimandua, with whom significant Roman contact was made (Haselgrove 2016; Harding 2017, 342). Iron Age settlement on the coastal plain appears to have been focused primarily on farmsteads, with occasional larger settlements. However, to correlate settlement size and complexity with social stratification and hierarchy would be an oversimplification. Armit (2019, 105–6) and Hill (2006; 2011, 251) have both suggested that across much of Britain there is a significant lack of evidence (*e.g.* rich burials, wealthy dwellings, etc.) for obvious social stratification, including at more complex 'hillfort' sites such as Broxburn. The nature of social organisation in the Iron Age has been the subject of intense and complex debate as interpretations have moved away from hierarchical models (Moore and Gonzalez-Alvarez 2021, 129). The model presented for the Northumberland Coastal Plain by Hodgson explores the role of the rectilinear enclosures as representing the widespread upper portion of Iron Age society as opposed to a narrow elite (Hodgson *et al.* 2012, 209). Within this model, a key observation is that the rectilinear enclosures cannot be representative of the entire population with the argument made that perhaps the contemporary more open or unenclosed settlements were subordinate but not socially immobile (*ibid.*, 209–10). The excavations at Lower Callerton add further complexity to this with the site displaying elements comparable with rectilinear enclosures and unusual structures. The enclosure ditches at Lower Callerton and Morley Hill Enclosure 2 were arguably equally grand, involving the removal of roughly

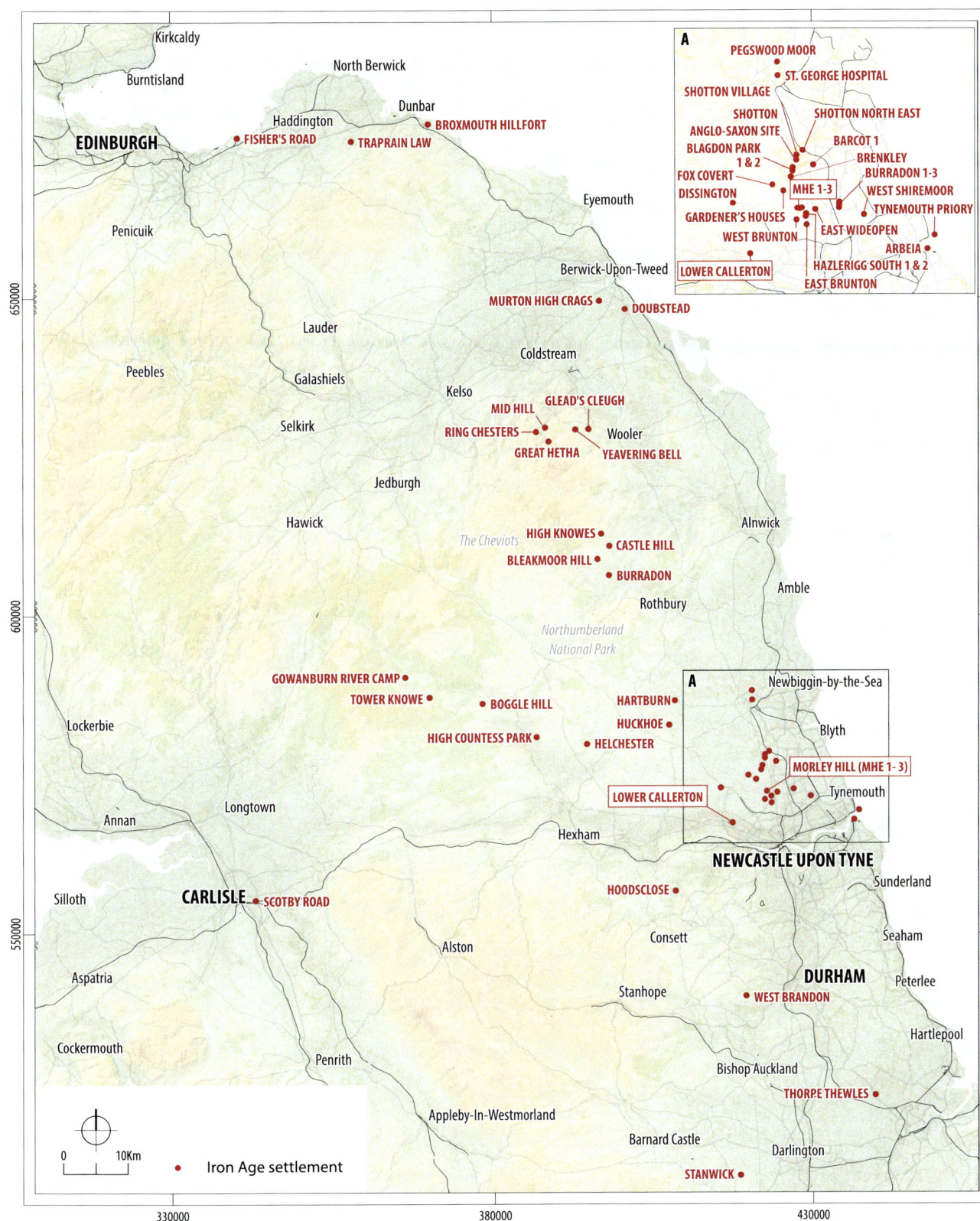

Figure 5.4 Location of key Iron Age settlement sites across the north-east with Morley Hill and Lower Callerton noted within a dense cluster to the north of Newcastle

the same amount of material – both massive undertakings that would have required a significant amount of person hours to complete. It is proposed that social connection and reciprocity could have provided the motivation to cooperate on such projects, even when these ditches were excavated for fewer settlement inhabitants. Armit has suggested that beyond the northern boundary of Northumberland, in East Lothian, Iron Age communities may have

formed societies with 'strongly embedded social values that stress equality and reciprocity' (2019, 107). Models such as this often place the emphases on the community as opposed to the individual as the foci for wider social organisation with connections and cooperation expressed through a range of actions potentially including enclosure construction, agriculture, feasting and gathering (van der Veen and Jones 2006; Moore 2007; Hill 2011; Garland 2017). The role of gathering or special spaces within more extensive enclosed settlements can now be identified such as the potential communal nature of the roundhouses with multiple entrances at Lower Callerton or the feasting areas identified at Pegswood Moor (Proctor 2009, 73). At Pegswood Moor it is proposed that the site served as a gathering place for wider communities for the exchange of knowledge and goods, seasonal agricultural activities and feasting at key times of the year (*ibid.*). Sites such as Pegswood Moor and Lower Callerton arguably performed a key role within wider networks of often closely spaced settlements.

Settlements on the Northumberland Coastal Plain cannot be viewed in isolation with sites likely having wider connections to the north, south and in the neighbouring upland regions. The reliance on modern boundaries to define areas tends to lead towards preconceived notions of identity, culture and separation (Crellin *et al.* 2016). Whilst a study must be bounded to some extent to maintain its focus, it is worth noting that there are many similarities in settlement activity across southern Scotland and northern England. Looking northwards from the Northumberland Coastal Plain, settlements such as Murton High Crags (Jobey and Jobey 1987) and Doubstead near Alnwick (Jobey 1982) show signs of similarity in enclosure style and internal structure forms. Further north the site at Fisher's Road West, Port Seton, showed many features that are comparable with activity in Northumberland (Haselgrove and McCullagh 2000). The site was dated to 400 BC–AD 200 with a pre-enclosure palisaded settlement followed by a rectilinear enclosure settlement. The density of rectilinear enclosures throughout the lowlands and into the higher elevations was comparable in East Lothian to that in Northumberland (*ibid.*, 2).

To the west, geographical boundaries such as the upland areas of the Pennines and Northumberland National Park create divisions that may have been less divisive during the Iron Age than are presumed. The delineation between upland and lowland can be roughly given at the elevation of around 175 m OD, which was to some extent physically delineated during the Roman Iron Age by the Roman road The Devil's Causeway heading from Corbridge in the south up to Berwick upon Tweed at its northern end (Hodgson *et al.* 2012, 212). Within upland areas the spread of settlements mirrored the lowland areas, with a spacing of roughly 1 km, for example the six settlements identified around High Countess Park (Jobey 1963; Fig. 5.4). Further upstream along the River North Tyne from High Countess

Park a large number of Iron Age settlement sites, of which several have been excavated, continued along the length of the river (Fig. 5.6). Ultimately, many of the perceived differences between upland and lowland settlements may relate more closely to resource and pasture access, and the preferential preservation of upland sites.

Iron Age settlement on the North Cumberland Plain further to the west include unenclosed sites and settlements surrounded by single or multiple ditched enclosures of varying form including rectangular (McCarthy 2000, 136). Several sites follow a similar pattern of development as seen at The Lanes, Carlisle, where unenclosed and palisaded phases of settlement formed similar patterns to settlements found east of the Pennines (*ibid.*). Somewhat coincidentally, the discovery of a Bronze Age arrowhead was also found at The Lanes, again showing the longevity of human activity at these sites. Two other sites, Burgh-by-Sands and Scotby Road, also showed signs of palisaded Iron Age enclosures underlying Roman activity, with an all-too-familiar lack of ceramic finds, another feature shared with Northumberland Iron Age communities (*ibid.*).

Settlement in the age of enclosure

The Iron Age witnessed a marked increase in the construction of boundaries and enclosures leading to Haselgrove defining the period as 'the age of enclosure' (2007; Romankiewicz *et al.* 2019, 1). As already noted, a defining aspect of Iron Age Northumberland settlement is the construction of substantial enclosure settlements of varying scales and complexity. Rectilinear enclosure sites have been demonstrated to range from a single enclosure surrounding a group of roundhouses, such as Morley Hill Enclosure 2, to complex double-ditched enclosures with subdivisions such as Brenkley and Blagdon Park. The excavation of extensive sites such as Lower Callerton and Pegswood Moor have added complexity to this picture, offering new settlement form with unique elements and features comparable with the more widely recognised rectilinear enclosures. The possible contemporaneity of these sites indicates a wide range of settlement patterns, scales, activities, relationships and wider connections.

The role of enclosure

The ditched enclosures can be described as monumental in scale with their construction, whether at sites like Morley Hill or Lower Callerton, representing a significant investment in time and resources. The widespread development of enclosure in the middle to later Iron Age points to their integral role within these societies. The function of Iron Age settlement enclosures in Northumberland has long been debated with traditional arguments focusing on themes such as defence. A more nuanced discussion of boundaries and enclosures has developed in recent

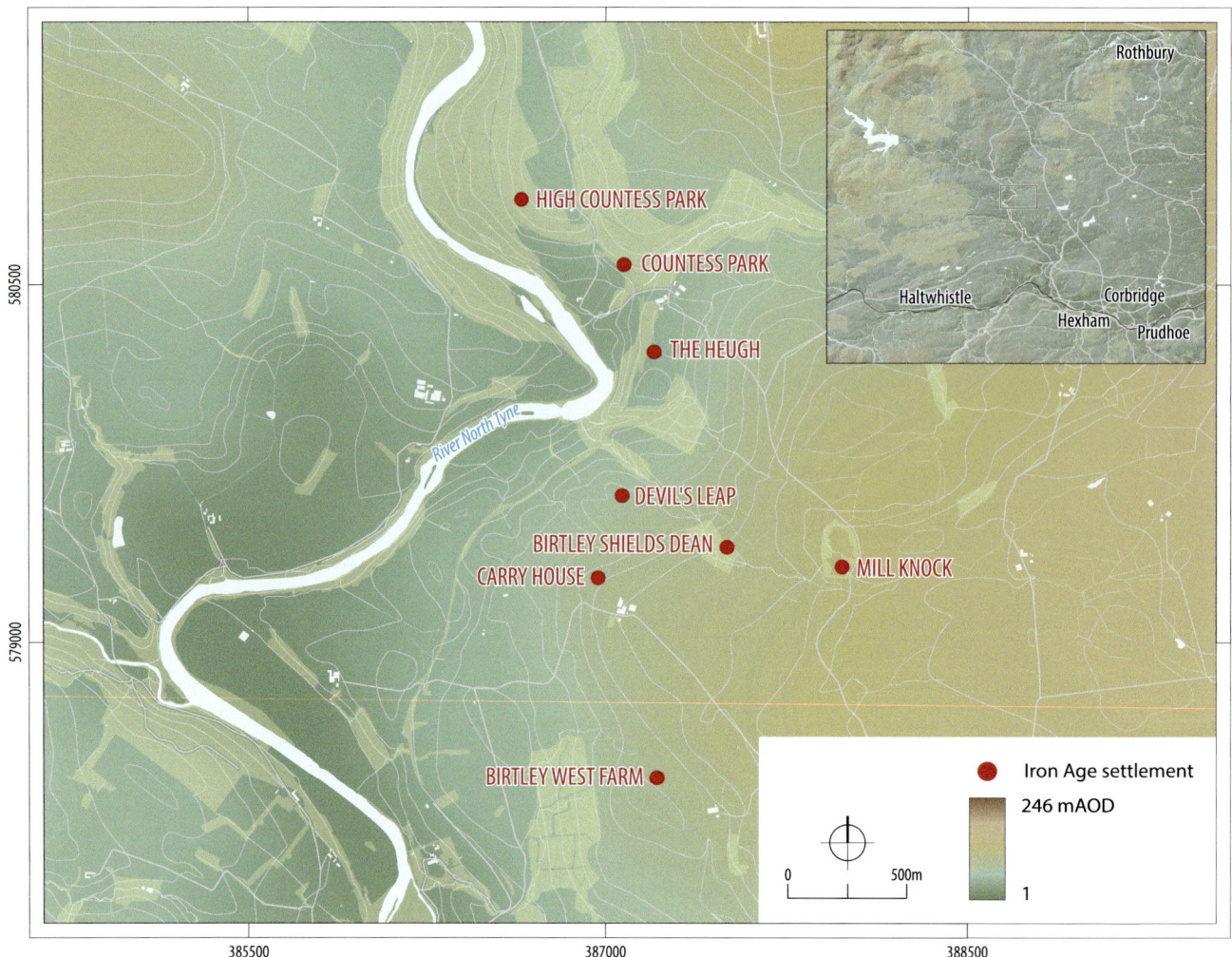

Figure 5.6 Distribution of upland settlements mentioned in the text along the River North Tyne

years to consider the practical division of space and the societal impact of this (Fell 2009, 17). A key feature of the enclosures which impacts our understanding of their function is the debatable presence of associated banks.

It has been proposed in many cases that a corresponding bank, formed from the upcast material created during excavation of the ditch, accompanied the ditches. Evidence for the presence of external banks was identified in the upstanding remains and geophysical survey at Morley Hill Enclosure 1 (AD Archaeology 2013; 2015). External and internal banks were proposed at West Brunton along with the possibility of banks accompanying inner boundaries as at South Shields (Hodgson *et al.* 2001, 97; Hodgson *et al.* 2012, 95). At Blagdon Park 2, layers of clean sand within the interior ditch fill were interpreted as material resulting from the slumping of an external and internal bank (Hodgson *et al.* 2012, 25). The fill of the outer enclosure also contained material interpreted as deriving from the erosion of a clay bank (*ibid.*). The presence of internal banks is favoured at Blagdon Park 2 to better allow for movement around the site and the overall settlement organisation (*ibid.*, 39). At Burradon,

patches of leached turf identified along the inside edge of the ditch were interpreted as evidence of an internal bank (Jobey 1970, 64). At Morley Hill 2 and 3 the presence of an external bank is favoured due to the limited space within the enclosure and the presence of drainage features. At Morley Hill several of the structures were defined by ditches with accompanying gullies that appear to drain into the enclosure ditch. The presence of an internal bank would potentially create a basin within the interior of the enclosure and would have needed to include gaps to allow the gullies to reach the ditch. At Morley Hill Enclosure 3 the linear alignment of structures 4, 6 and 7 and the gap between the enclosure and the structures may also indicate that they were constructed in relation to an external bank. The presence of an accompanying bank to the main enclosure at Lower Callerton is less certain although low upcast banks, to aid in livestock management, were proposed at Pegswood Moor (Proctor 2009, 68).

The role of enclosure in livestock management has been proposed at several sites with animal husbandry being a crucial element of Iron Age subsistence strategies. The well-preserved animal bone assemblage from Thorpe

Thewles provides the core resource for a wider regional understanding (Heslop 1987). The less well-preserved animal bone assemblages across Northumberland, including from Lower Callerton and Morley Hill, indicate the presence of cattle, sheep, pig and horse (Hodgson *et al.* 2012, 203). Many of the enclosures showed distinct areas with minimal structural remains and/or a lack of evidence for a domestic function, and sub-enclosures that may have contained and separated animals from living spaces within settlements. Double-ditched settlements like Brenkley, Burradon, Blagdon Park 2 and possibly Morley Hill Enclosure 1 may have had an inner domestic space within the central enclosure, with a separate livestock zone between the two ditches (Hodgson *et al.* 2012, 205; van Wessel and Wilson 2020). At Lower Callerton, sub-enclosures 1 and perhaps 4 may have functioned as seasonal stock enclosures, with numerous stock enclosures and pens identified at Pegswood Moor (Proctor 2009, 70). The enclosures, as part of a wider network of settlements, may have had a key role in the movement of people and livestock between upland, lowland and coastal areas.

The relatively flat and agriculturally viable land of the Northumberland coastal plain isn't without its challenges for settlement, especially considering the underlying clay-heavy superficial deposits into which structures would have been constructed, land grazed, and crops grown. Evidence for the ditches being used intentionally as land drainage has until now been limited and somewhat speculative; however, the excavations at Morley Hill show clear signs of water management on site. At Morley Hill Enclosure 2 a gully led from Structure 17 to the surrounding enclosure ditch, likely diverting water away from the working area. At Morley Hill Enclosure 3, the S-shaped ditches truncating the edge of Structure 18 (ditches 5638, 5369 and 5370) indicated that some internal features were connected to the outer enclosure ditch likely to facilitate drainage. Further evidence of the wet conditions at Morley Hill Enclosure 3 was suggested by the presence of a metalled trackway leading into the main enclosure. A large spread of poaching (animal-based disturbance through trampling of wet ground) was present just outside the main enclosure entrance, indicating that the frequent use of this entranceway and the wet conditions were causing issues with the ground stability. In an effort to address this, a 2.5 m-wide corridor of stones was placed through the area of poaching, leading directly into the enclosure entrance. A similar area of poaching, fixed through the placement of loose stone, was identified during the trenching undertaken at Morley Hill Enclosure 1 (AD Archaeology 2015). The cutting of the ditches through primarily clay-based ground would have led to the retention of water, indicating that regardless of the function of the enclosure, they would have likely been filled with water to some level at most sites. The washing of material into these ditches may have been commonplace, particularly around entrances of enclosures and would likely have required repeated, possibly seasonal maintenance to keep them free from excessive silting. Evidence of this redigging of the ditch of the enclosure from the final phase of Lower Callerton was clear at its entranceway, with five distinct phases visible.

The function of many boundaries and the meaning behind the division can at times be difficult to distinguish, although a key component of enclosure is the clear divide between inside and outside. The function of the inside vs. outside divide was inherently intentional, and a significant amount of labour would have to be put into creating and maintaining these boundaries. Archaeological evidence and modern reconstruction efforts have shown that a roundhouse could be effectively constructed by a small group of 2–4 adults – the minimum number of occupants likely to inhabit such a structure and requiring no external assistance (Pope 2003, 181). However, enclosure ditches reveal a different story altogether with a significant investment of time and effort required to excavate settlement boundaries. The main enclosure ditch at Lower Callerton measured *c.* 480 m in length with an average cross-section area of 3 m in width and 0.90 m in depth. If an additional 0.30 m is added to account for truncation, based on the depth of topsoil, this equates to a cubic volume of 1,900 m^3. Given that 1 m^3 of dry glacial clay weighs roughly 1.7 tonnes (Aqua-calc 2021) the cutting of the ditch may have involved the removal of around 3,200 tonnes – a serious undertaking to excavate. The enclosure ditch at Morley Hill Enclosure 2 measured 200 m in length with an average width of 4 m and an average depth of 1.70 m. Again adding an additional 0.30 m to account for truncation this equated to a volume of 1,720 m^3 or the removal of 3,000 tonnes of material – very similar to the much longer boundary at Lower Callerton. This raises the question of how this was achieved, particularly at sites such as Morley Hill, which appear to have had only one or two structures in use at once, possibly representing a single family unit. The wider community may have played a part in supporting the construction of the ditch, either through providing labour, or through reciprocal ditch-digging for newly establishing settlements (as explored by Hamilton 2010, 262). Sharples (2007, 180) has explored the construction of hillfort ramparts and other boundaries with their construction viewed as conspicuous consumption of resources, including labour, in a form of potlatch. It is likely that this system of repeated and seasonal cooperation would have formed a strong social element between neighbouring settlements, perhaps forming a central aspect of their shared cultural values and social identity. It can be purported that the presence of the ditch in itself may have acted as a socially cohesive boundary for a settlement, affecting the layout and function of 'internal' and 'external' spaces. Enclosures, both palisaded and ditch-and-bank, define the boundaries of many settlement activities, primarily domestic and industry/craft areas. By delineating a space, this would inherently form a connection between those dwelling within the space. For the smaller farmstead settlements such as Morley Hill Enclosure 2 or Burradon this may have established the limits of the direct family unit; whilst for larger type settlements it would have established a connection between multiple small groups or individuals.

Structures, spaces and roundhouses

The enclosures surround a variety of structures with the form and function of roundhouses somewhat difficult to ascertain, particularly on the Northumberland Coastal Plain, due to the lack of upstanding remains and lack of post-holes used in their construction. The commonly held image of an Iron Age roundhouse is that of a large, post-built structure, formed from cylindrical walls with a conical thatched roof above. The walls are usually depicted with thick wooden roof supports, interwoven with wattle and daub, with a grand entrance, usually with porch. Examples of reconstructions of roundhouses can be seen in Reynolds' (1982) artist's impression of a multi-post-ringed structure with thatched roof and cross-beam architecture; Harding's (2017, 141, fig. 4.16) artist's impression of the post-and-ditch structures at Culduthel; and modern experimental reconstructions of roundhouses at Butser Farm, Hampshire (Reynolds 2003), the Ancient Technology Centre in Dorset (ATC 2021) and Castell Henllys, Wales (Mytum and Meek 2020). These examples are a useful starting point and have been extensively researched from many angles, including ethnographic study, architectural and materials science, and practical experimentation, as well as the well-preserved structure discovered during archaeological excavation such as the Bronze Age structural remains uncovered at Must Farm in eastern England (Malim *et al.* 2015). At Lower Callerton and Morley Hill a range of potential architectural styles were identified including structures defined by ring-gullies with and without post-holes, structures with inner and outer ditches and large more complex structures with a range of features. At Lower Callerton, post-built structures were also identified alongside roundhouses with multiple entrances.

Ring-gully defined structures and spaces

The most common feature remaining in the archaeological record for roundhouses in the Northumberland Coastal Plain is a curvilinear ditch or gully, usually with an east to south-east-facing entrance. The majority of the structures at both Lower Callerton and Morley Hill were single ditches that often showed evidence for intentional construction as opposed to being formed due to water-erosion as a 'drip-gully'. At Morley Hill Enclosure 2 the curvilinear ditch that surrounded Structure 14 appears to have been recut and maintained. A roundhouse, of which no structural evidence remains, may have sat within the enclosed space as is traditionally presented. At Morley Hill Enclosure 3, the majority of structures were defined by single curvilinear gullies with limited evidence of internal features. Structure 7 provides rare evidence of

structural features with a pair of post-holes flanking the entrance. In some instance, the single curvilinear gullies were comparable to the inner gullies of the more complex structures indicative of a similar structural function perhaps as wall slots. However, often the gullies were not accompanied by internal features such as post-holes to support a roof. A similar lack of post-holes was noted at Pegswood Moor (Proctor 2009), East Brunton (Hodgson *et al.* 2012) and Brenkley (van Wessel and Wilson 2021) amongst others. The lack of post-holes or clear structural features within many of the curvilinear gullies makes an interpretation of the structures highly problematic. The more substantial roundhouses offer far more clues as to their construction and the activities within. However, they are far from the most common structures with many sites dominated by structures defined by single gullies. This raises the question as to whether the missing elements are a result of truncation, differing construction styles or potentially the type of occupation.

At Morley Hill Enclosure 2, Structure 17 offers an alternative interpretation for some of the spaces defined by the single gullies. Structure 17 was formed of a curvilinear gully, bounding an internal area of 10.2 m in diameter, with its northern edge continuing downslope eastward to allow drainage directly into the main enclosure ditch. This implies that this specific curvilinear gully was indeed used for managing water. While evidence of a potential structure may have been removed by later truncation, it is possible that it defined an external working space (as shown in the reconstruction Fig. 5.5). Given the variety of activities and visitations to the site it is also worth considering that the structure itself may have been temporary such as a tent or other archaeologically invisible structure (*e.g.* turf walls) that would have required water-management to keep dry. As was the case with the settlement enclosure ditches, the curvilinear gullies may have acted to delineate the bounds of the dwelling or activity which may not have necessarily been domestic.

The variety of structure and working areas was highlighted by the presence of possible ancillary structures at Morley Hill Enclosure 3. Structures 8–11 were defined by single ditches with unusually narrow entrances. Similar structures were also noted at Blagdon Park 2 where structures 5, 7 and 12 were grouped as representing a specialist production zone. Burnt material, including fired clay, was recovered from associated pits and a smithing hearth base was found 40 m away (Hodgson *et al.* 2012, 31). Very little material was recovered from the structures at Morley Hill suggesting a different specialist function. At Lower Callerton, Structure 15 with its wide north-east-facing entrance was also interpreted as potentially having a specific function and may have been paired with Structure 22. At Pegswood Moor, small structures defined by single curvilinear gullies were also considered to have a variety of functions including for specialist craft activities and storage (Proctor 2009).

Figure 5.7 North-facing photograph of the smaller double-ringed roundhouse, Structure 15, at Lower Callerton

Ring-ditches, ring-gullies and post-holes

There are numerous examples of structure with more complex architectural features such as outer ring-ditches, inner and outer ring-gullies and arrangements of post-holes. Examples with inner and outer ring-gullies included Structure A at East Brunton, and R50 at Blagdon Park (Hodgson *et al.* 2012). At Lower Callerton several round-houses, such as structures 18, 28, 29, 24 and 23, were similar in form with an inner and outer ring-gully or ditch (Fig. 5.7). Structure 18 provides the clearest example of this with a 0.65 m wide outer ditch and a narrower 0.20 m wide inner gully. Structure 24 was comparable in form with Structure 23 displaying evidence for additional post-holes. The presence of post-holes within the structures was more commonly identified at the larger roundhouses. At Lower Callerton, structures 2 and 42 were surrounded by continuous wide ring-ditches and inner wall slots both with post-holes at the termini (Fig. 5.8). A piece of fired clay with withy impressions was recovered from the ring-ditch of Structure 2 hinting at the presence of wattle walls. These roundhouses represent the largest on site and appeared to be situated within sub-enclosures. Pits within the structures, particularly Structure 2, contained diverse charcoal assemblages indicative of domestic hearth waste. A feature of many roundhouses at Lower Callerton, including structures 2, 22, 29, 28 and 42, was

the presence of large posts at the termini of numerous inner ring-gullies. Large, distinct post-settings at the terminals of ring-gullies are a feature identified at other sites including High Knowes Structures 1 and 2 (Jobey 1966), Doubstead (Jobey 1982), West Brunton house 1A (Hodgson *et al.* 2012), and potentially structures 44 and 50 at Blagdon Park 1 (*ibid.*). The presence of a more limited number of post-holes again raises questions surrounding roundhouse construction techniques with a range of possible options including the use of post-pads, wall slots and cob or earth walls.

The inner ring-gullies in some instances may have functioned as wall slots. An example of this was uncovered at South Shields where a roundhouse dating to the middle Iron Age, was defined by an outer ditch and an inner ring groove with post-holes at its entrance (Hodgson *et al.* 2001, 96). The shape of the ring-groove was indicative of its construction using 1–2 m stretches of straight rows or panels of posts, with some post-settings apparent within the slots (*ibid.*). A similar arrangement was seen at Melsonby (Fitts *et al.* 1999) with an outer curvilinear ditch, an inner structural ring-gully, with a further inner stake-hole ring set just inside the ring-gully. The possibility of cob or earth walls can also be explored with the inner wall slot defining the retaining wall to support a cob (subsoil-based) wall (Romankiewicz pers. comm.). The 0.2 m wide ring-gullies,

Figure 5.8 South-east-facing photograph of Post-hole 1581 at the terminus of the inner gully of Structure 42, Lower Callerton

especially if combined with cob wall structure, would have provided adequate support for a thatched roof structure. Examples of cob walls can be found further afield such as the indications of a turf wall bounded by stone lining at Traprain Law (Cree 1923, 188) and the decayed turf structural elements identified at Ironshill in Angus (Pollock 1997, 348). The role of turf in roundhouse construction can be difficult to identify but may provide an avenue to explain the limited number of interior post-holes which may have been needed to support wide roofed structures (Romankiewicz 2019). The environmental assemblages provide some indication of the construction material with evidence for oak being the primary wood used in construction. Smaller quantities of hazel wood were identified at Lower Callerton, possibly relating to wattle and daub structural elements. The wide distribution of burnt heather across Lower Callerton and its presence in association with most structures indicated its potential use as thatch for roofing. Heather was a common material used for fodder, fuel, bedding, and thatch on Iron Age sites (Frodsham 2004, 44; Hodgson *et al.* 2012, 176).

The architectural features displayed by the larger roundhouses at Lower Callerton were mirrored in the group of three structures with multiple entrances. Structure 22 was defined by an outer ditch divided into three segments with an inner wall slot with breaks mirroring

the ring-ditch. A set of four post-holes, aligned to the ring-ditch and wall slot, at the east-facing entrance may indicate the presence of a more elaborate porch or entranceway than seen at other structures. A post-hole was also uncovered at the south-western break in the ditches indicating that this too was perhaps a more formalised entrance. Structure 22 is unique on site with the presence of three possible entrances and a porch feature. The larger Structure 38 to the south appeared to have two entrances with a spread of post-holes potentially forming a post-ring but the alignment is far from clear (Fig. 5.9). This roundhouse may have undergone several phases of construction and modification leading to the complex arrangement of features in plan. Structure 29 was similar in form with a narrow inner gully and post-holes potentially flanking both the east- and west-facing entrances. The presence of post-holes at the entrance may not have been strictly structural with a totemic function suggested for similar features found at roundhouses in Northamptonshire (Chapman 2020, 127). The structures with multiple entrances are explored further in the proceeding sections as rare but not unique examples.

Roundhouse dimensions

Traditional studies of Iron Age roundhouses have tended to associate size with status, although some have argued

Figure 5.9 West-facing photograph of the double entrance at Structure 38

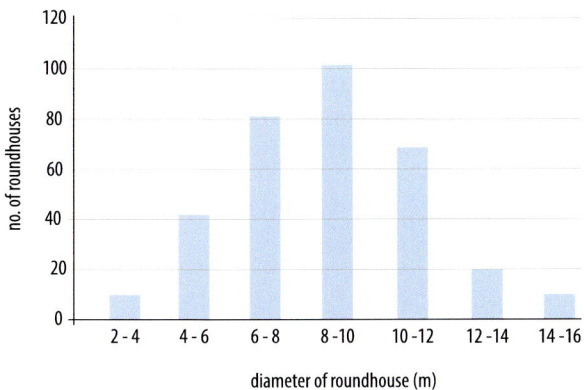

Figure 5.10 Graph showing the number of roundhouses from 14 Iron Age sites grouped by diameter at 2 m intervals

that this theory is more likely tied to modern ideas of status and wealth rather than being applicable to Iron Age societies (Pope 2003, 107). A comparative assessment of roundhouse diameter from sites across the region (comprising Arcot Phase 1, Blagdon Park 1 and 2, Brenkley, East Brunton, West Brunton, Burradon, Lower Callerton, Hartburn, Morley Hill Enclosure 2 and 3, Pegswood Moor, Saint George's Hospital, West Shiremoor, Shotton North-East and East Wideopen) indicated an average of 8.52 m (Fig. 5.10) This is consistent with the data gathered by Pope (2003, 136) which indicated an 8.80 m average

diameter for wall-slot structures within Britain. Across the analysed sites there is a general peak in structure size of 8–10 m in diameter.

There is very little evidence for correlation between the size of structures and any specific function on sites in the Northumberland Coastal Plain. However, it seems unlikely that any of the smaller structures (<5 m diameter) were dwellings for a family unit, rather that they may have served as storage structures or for activities that required minimal space and a level of shelter. However, there does appear to be a positive correlation between the more complex, multi-structure and multi-enclosure settlements and a greater range in structure sizes (Fig. 5.11).The sites of Brenkley, East Brunton, Lower Callerton, West Brunton and Hartburn all fit into this model, with large settlement boundaries, multiple roundhouses, and the greatest range of structure sizes, often with a high number of structures of above average size (they include many of the largest structures measured). The greater range of structure sizes potentially correlates to, not a wider variety of activities necessarily, but the advent of specialist structures such as for working areas, community spaces and storage.

Entrances and orientation

The meaning and purpose of entrance orientation has long been a focal point for discussions on roundhouse significance and use. The first and most discussed factor

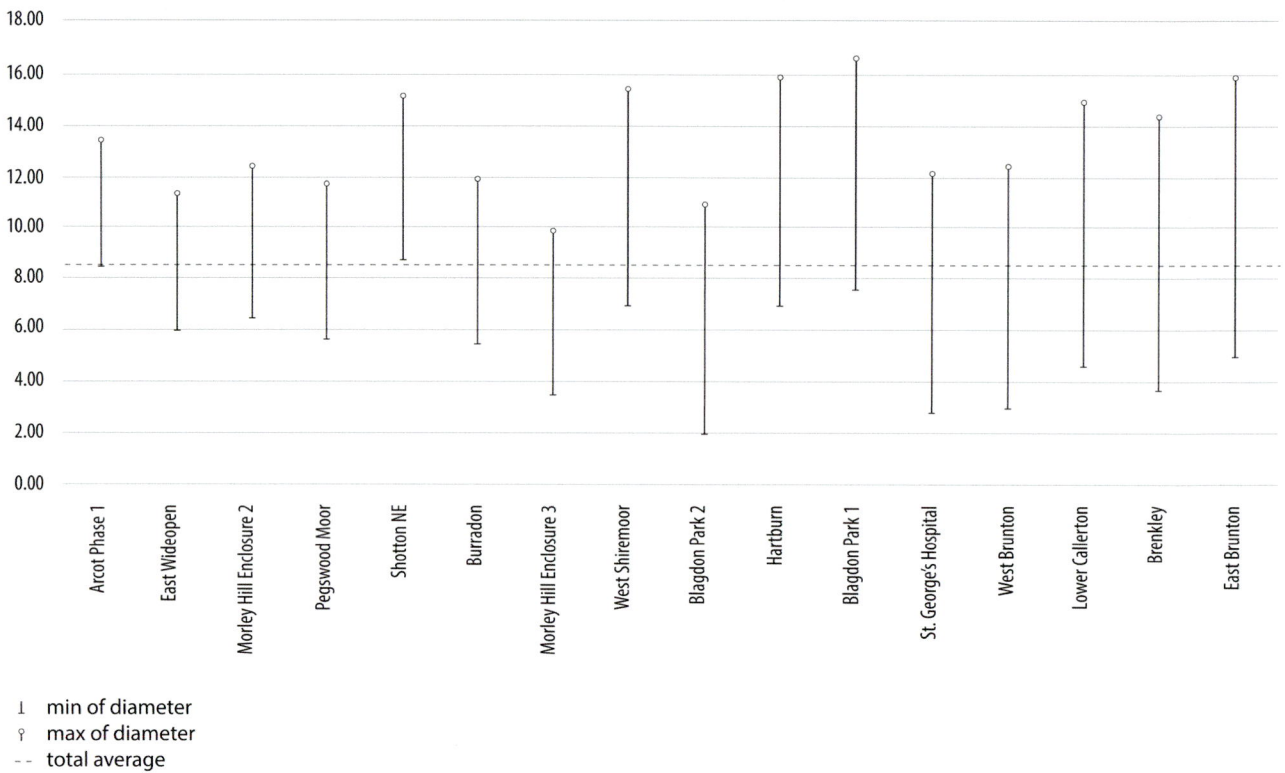

l min of diameter
? max of diameter
- - total average

Figure 5.11 Graph showing the range of roundhouse diameters against the total average with sites ordered from smallest to largest range

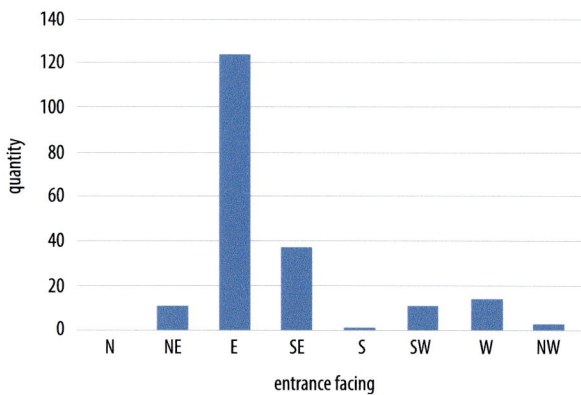

Figure 5.12 Graph showing the overall distribution of entrance alignments

for orientation of entrances is the function of light within a dwelling (Pope 2007, 206). It is generally considered that the only method for getting light into a roundhouse is through its entrance – it would therefore have been beneficial to maximise the light entering the structure. In Britain it has been well established that an east-/south-east-facing entrance will generally maximise the morning light entering a structure (though to varying degrees of success seasonally). A comparative analysis of the entrance directions of structures from several sites on the Northumberland Coastal Plain (comprising Arcot Phase 1, Blagdon Park, Brenkley,

East Brunton, West Brunton. Burradon, Lower Callerton, Hartburn, Morley Hill, Pegswood Moor, St. George's Hospital, West Shiremoor, Shotton North-East and East Wideopen) has revealed a distinct peak of entrance direction in an easterly direction (Fig. 5.12). A second peak (12%) of W/SW facing entrances can be seen, which would correspond to maximising sunlight in the evening. It is worth noting that these effects would be somewhat exaggerated in the winter, with much less sunlight being available each day, regardless of orientation.

At several sites where defined entrances could be identified the majority faced in the same direction, for example at West Brunton and Burradon. Structures generally had their entrances aligned with the main enclosure entrance, as at East Brunton. In contrast, at Morley Hill Enclosure 2 the structures were oriented eastwards while the enclosure entrance was oriented southwards. There are many other factors that may have strongly influenced the alignment of the entrances, including drainage, as it may have been beneficial to have structures facing downslope to prevent water running into the dwelling. The effects of weather and prevailing winds may have had a similar impact, with structures built in the most efficient orientation to avoid wind and rain from entering their interior. This is much more difficult to assess, as both climatic variation and landscape (including modern and historic tree coverage, and modern buildings) may have changed significantly. Another complication in the understanding of structure entrances, exemplified at Lower Callerton, is the presence of multi-entranced structures.

Multiple entrance structures

At Lower Callerton, three roundhouses with multiple entrances were identified, with a further two tentative examples also present. Structures 29, 38 and 22 represent the clearest examples with structures 47 and 53 being heavily truncated. Structures 29 and 38 both had east-south-east- and west-south-west-facing entrances. The breaks in the inner ring-gullies, interpreted as wall slots, were matched by breaks in the outer ring-ditch to create well defined intentional entrances. The alignment of the entrances would allow light to be maximised within the structures in the morning and evening – the two times of day members of an agrarian community would potentially be inside rather than working the land or tending to livestock. Structure 22 followed a similar pattern of entrances with a third smaller north-western facing entrance of unclear function. The roundhouses with multiple entrances at Lower Callerton were some of the most architecturally complex on site with possible evidence for porches or large posts flanking the entrances. As discussed previously the elaboration of the entranceways may have had a structural and symbolic purpose.

Multi-entrance structures, although less well defined, were uncovered at Pegswood Moor where structures 1 and 7 both had west- and east-facing entrances within their inner wall slot, although these were not matched by their single-entranced outer ditches (Proctor 2009, 77). At St. George's Hospital Roundhouse 3 comprised a single, slightly irregular ring-gully with opposed north-east- and south-west-facing entrances (ARS Ltd 2016). At West Shiremoor roundhouse F206/F293 had opposing entrances facing east-south-east and west-north-west although truncation from multiple phases of later structure made this less than definitive. Structures 2 and 4 at Blagdon Park 1 both had opposed north-east- and south-west-facing entrances. Structure 2 at Blagdon Park 2 had both an inner wall slot and outer ditch, both with entrances at their eastern and western sides, with an additional shallow scoop connecting the terminal ends of the western entrance to the outer ditch (Hodgson *et al.* 2012). The majority of sites in the region including Morley Hill, Brenkley and East Brunton, had no examples of multi-entranced structures, and those that did generally only had one or two examples, indicating that they were never a dominant structure type. Although not centred around a structure, the presence of feasting areas at Pegswood Moor brings the role of communal spaces and activities to the fore (Proctor 2019, 68). The structures at Lower Callerton may have functioned as gathering or communal spaces, thus differentiating them from 'typical' domestic roundhouses. Lower Callerton appears to be a dynamic site with large roundhouses,

four-post storage structures, and working areas that may have acted as a hub for a wider community (Fig. 5.13).

Post-built structures

Four-post structures, comprising a series of four post-holes in a square or sub-square configuration, usually with a spacing of around 2 m between posts, have been found at sites across the Northumberland Coastal Plain. At Lower Callerton structures 13, 14 and 17 fell into this category (although Structure 17 comprised a series of six post-holes in a 2 × 3 arrangement), all located to the south-east of the main cluster of structures within the enclosure (Fig. 5.10). At Morley Hill, Structure 12 comprised four pits, each recut, which may also have formed another example of a four-post structure. Such four-post structures have been revealed at Iron Age and Romano-British sites across Britain, and although no definitive evidence for their function has been established, they are traditionally interpreted as granaries, with raised floors for keeping grain (or other goods) away from pests and damp (Reynolds 1974; Cunliffe 2005, 394; Van der Veen 2007; Hodgson *et al.* 2012, 47). Other four-post structures have been identified at Iron Age sites in Northumberland, such as Hoodsclose (Muncaster 2011) and Burradon (Jobey 1970).

Agriculture and activities

The activities taking place within the roundhouses, structures and enclosures are suggested by the often limited environmental and artefactual assemblages. An agrarian focus comes to the fore with the isotopic analysis of cereal remains from Lower Callerton indicating extensive agricultural activity in the surrounding area. The cultivation of the wider landscape surrounding the settlements adds to the idea of the enclosures acting as focal points within a dynamic and productive landscape. The role of livestock within this has been demonstrated to be key, with cereals grown in well manured locations and a range of domesticates identified at both sites. The archaeobotanical and animal bone assemblages from Morley Hill Enclosure 2 and 3 are comparable to sites across the region offering limited insights into the site-specific economy and agricultural practices. The small cereal grain assemblage in terms of taxa is comparable to sites such as Blagdon Park 2, Shotton North-East, West Brunton and East Brunton (Hodgson *et al.* 2012). However, unlike at East and West Brunton, there is no evidence at Morley Hill for extensive crop production and processing with a lack of diagnostic weed seeds and associated chaff. The preservation conditions across Morley Hill were extremely poor which offers a partial explanation for the lack of evidence. Yet, it is also worth considering whether this is due to specific processes being undertaken on-site such as limited or more piecemeal processing of grain. The animal bone assemblage is also typical with the major

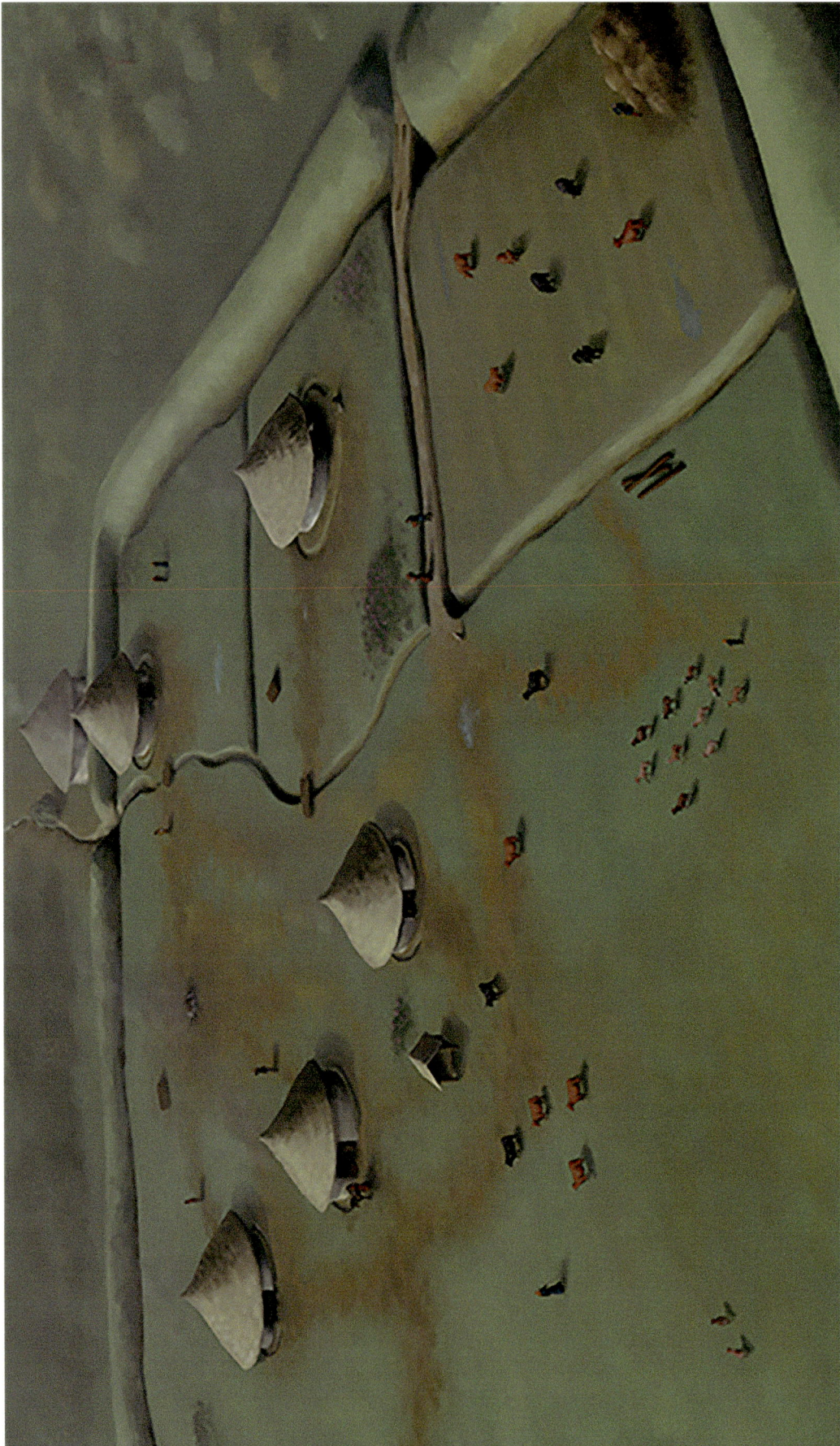

Figure 5.13 Artist's reconstruction of Lower Callerton by Eleanor Winter

Figure 5.14 East-facing photograph of post-built Structure 14 at Lower Callerton

domesticates, cattle, sheep/goat and horse, all present. The identifiable bones were largely middle and low utility bones and likely represent the less desirable elements discarded during the butchery process. The fragmentary nature of the bones precludes any detailed analysis of dietary preferences and butchery techniques. Again the assemblage is comparable with those from sites across the region with the assemblage from East and West Brunton indicating that both cattle and sheep/goat were central to the livestock strategies (Gidney 2012, 163). The single horse tooth from the enclosure ditch of Morley Hill Enclosure 2 provides very limited evidence for the presence of potentially higher status animals (Cross 2011; Gidney 2012). The model of extensive agriculture indicated by the isotopic analysis at Lower Callerton suits the extensive nature of the settlement. Within the settlement areas may have been given over to crop processing, livestock husbandry and the collection of manure. As noted above, the four-post structures have been traditionally seen as grain stores, with those at Lower Callerton perhaps being used to store grain from the surrounding landscape. The animal bone assemblage was scarce due to poor preservation conditions offering few insights although it can be reasonably assumed a similar range of domesticates were present.

The distribution and nature of other activities across the site was unclear due to the paucity of finds. At both sites the limited material potentially indicated very limited metalworking but no foci for this activity was found. The stone tool assemblage from Lower Callerton included the base of a saddle quern and craft working tools such as a possible fly weight for a bow drill used in wood and stone working. A cushion stone or burnisher was also recovered, potentially used in metal sheet working. The small assemblage gives a limited insight into the wide range activities taking place on site. The lack of finds, particularly ceramic, is interesting with assemblages from sites across the region being highly variable in quantity. For the early Iron Age, it has been asserted that Iron Age communities in this region were effectively and intentionally aceramic (Harding 2017, 27). Pottery was retrieved from Lower Callerton and Morley Hill, however, the vast majority of pottery was either earlier prehistoric or Roman. The causes of this reduced ceramic consumption may be multi-faceted, perhaps due to a decline in specialist skill; poorer quality pottery that does not survive well in the archaeological record; or perhaps a higher value placed on pottery, with even broken sherds not being discarded so readily. A heavier reliance on other materials such as wood, leather, textiles or metalwork may have supplanted

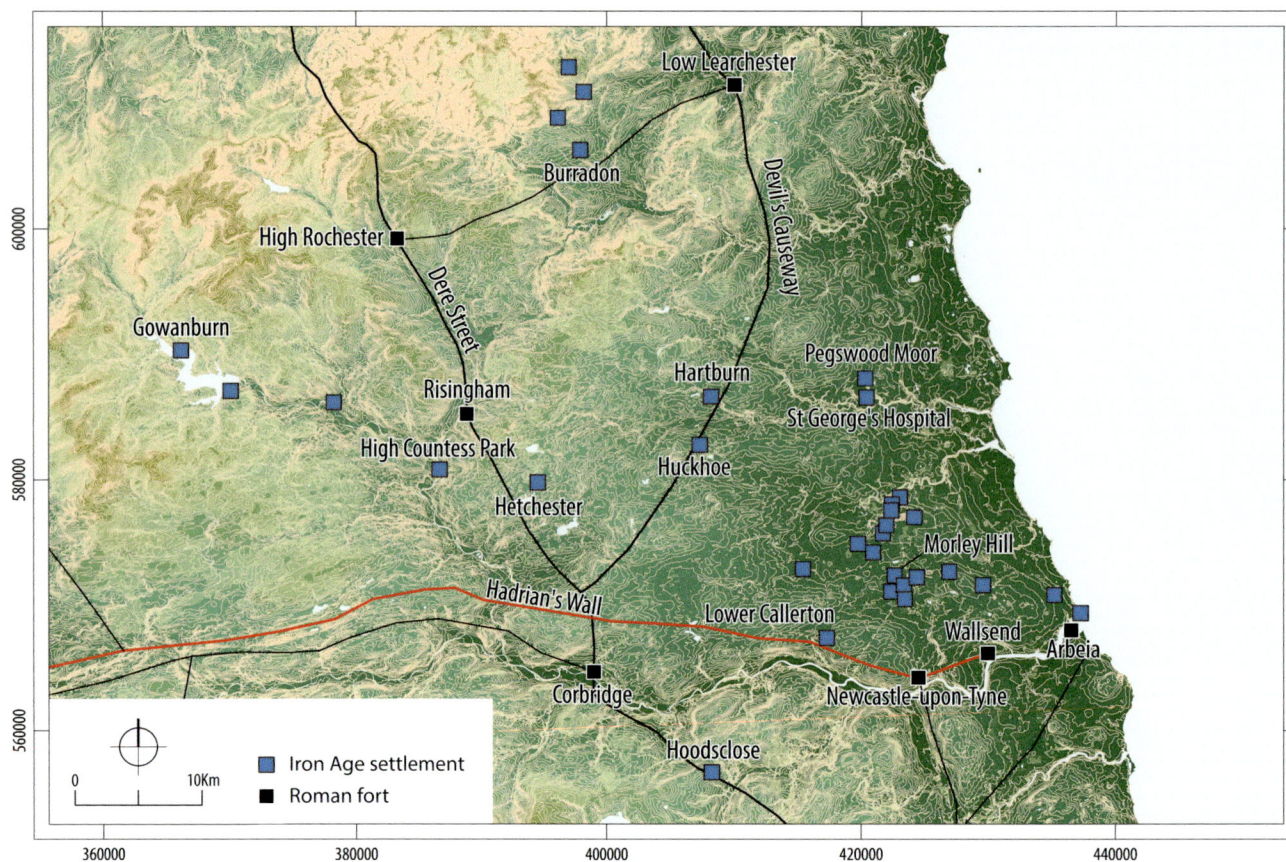

Figure 5.15 Distribution of Iron Age settlements in relation to Hadrian's Wall

the requirement for pottery. If a more mobile portion of the community were envisaged, perhaps practising transhumance, other materials could be seen as far more transportable than heavy ceramic vessels.

Contact with the Roman world

The Roman conquest of Britain began in AD 43 with expansion northwards up to parts of Scotland over the course of the following 40 years. The Roman military first appeared in any numbers in the far north of England as part of Agricola's northern campaigns from the late AD 70s, and by the latter part of the first century there were a series of large forts along the Tyne-Solway (the Stanegate), possibly forming a 'proto-frontier' (Hodgson 2000, 19). In AD 122 construction began on Hadrian's Wall just to the north of the Stanegate, which formed the northernmost frontier of the Roman Empire (Fig. 5.15); this was subsequently followed by the construction of the Antonine Wall from AD 142 between the Firth of Forth and the Clyde estuary at Old Kilpatrick. Numerous Roman Forts were constructed along the length of these walls, typically associated with military communities or 'vici', and such a huge military presence inserted into the landscape would certainly have had a pronounced impact on the local populations.

The settlements at Lower Callerton and Morley Hill both lie very close to the line of the Tyne-Solway military zone (Fig. 5.15), and both had some evidence for activity during the later first century AD. However, in the case of Lower Callerton, which lies less than 1 km to the north of Hadrian's Wall, Bayesian modelling has suggested occupation had ceased by *c.* AD 20 at the latest, with abandonment potentially resulting from a variety of factors and not solely as a response to direct Roman influence. The two sherds of late first- to second-century pottery recovered from this site do not clearly indicate any sustained occupation or reoccupation at this time, though they do suggest the settlement was still at least visible in the landscape. The rigorous programme of radiocarbon dating at Lower Callerton is not free from critique with poor preservation and lack of event features presenting interpretational challenges. However, a broad range of features were sampled with multiple dates from charcoal and cereal grains obtained from single features and individual contexts to test issues of residuality and intrusion. The dates and resulting model allow for the development of the Iron Age settlement to be explored including its decline, as discussed more fully below. The limited artefactual evidence for Roman interaction is matched by the lack of material dated to this period. Given the number of dates and features sampled, if a later phase of equally intensive Roman occupation were present it is likely, even accounting for truncation, that this would have been detected.

The settlement at Morley Hill further to the north-east does have somewhat more evidence for occupation contemporary with the early Roman military presence, and possibly into the second century AD, though the problems of precise dating in this region have been highlighted above and elsewhere (*e.g.* Brindle 2016, 313). The 59 sherds of Roman pottery from this site possibly came from a single grey ware cooking pot associated with one of the structures, while two radiocarbon dates (SUERC-83345; SUERC-61970) presented the possibility of activity into the early second century AD. A further radiocarbon date of cal AD 85–240 (95% confidence; SUERC-83350) obtained from a fragment of burnt animal bone within a post-hole is the best indication of second-century activity, though it does not provide any firm conclusions as to whether any final abandonment was pre- or post-construction of Hadrian's Wall.

The varied chronological trajectories of Morley Hill, Lower Callerton and other sites in the region suggest that the reasons for their apparent ending would have been multifarious, and not totally as a direct result of contact with the Roman world. The overall decline and abandonment of settlements in this region will now be considered in the context of longer-term social processes, Roman influence, and environmental factors.

The decline of Iron Age settlement

Iron Age communities in Northumberland had undergone significant change over hundreds of years, including the development of large enclosure settlements and increasing variety and complexity in structural forms, as well as a multitude of technological and social developments. Despite all of this it is apparent that these settlements were abandoned in large numbers during the early first millennium AD – both farmsteads and village-sized settlements. Is there a simple answer to why such strongly interconnected, supportive communities declined in such a marked way, abandoning well-established, productive land? Can we attribute these changes purely to Roman influence, as many have previously proposed? Or is it possible that this decline was already beginning to take hold prior to the Roman military occupation of the region in the AD 70s (Hodgson *et al.* 2012, 213) and the later construction of Hadrian's Wall from AD 122, which so completely drove a barrier through the heart of the coastal plain?

As has just been alluded to, there was a significant decline in the number of Iron Age settlements on and around the Northumberland coastal plain within the first and particularly second centuries AD, with the majority of coastal plain enclosure settlements apparently being abandoned during this period. However, it is possible that levels of truncation may in some instances have removed

evidence for later activity, and in many cases precise dating is difficult to ascertain, in part due to many sites being dated purely from local ceramic evidence, which is notoriously long-lived within the region when it manages to make it into the archaeological record (Brindle 2016, 313). There has also often been an assumption that the presence of minimal Roman pottery implied direct Roman activity in the vicinity on a large scale (*e.g.* Hartburn: Jobey 1973), thereby perhaps suggesting a later date for occupation than may have been the case. More recent excavations and the general adoption of Bayesian modelling where possible has helped in our understanding of the chronology of the region, however, we are a long way short of having a strong dataset to firmly conclude this debate. Several of the more recent sites, such as Lower Callerton, Morley Hill Enclosure 3, East Brunton and potentially Brenkley, may have fallen out of use in the first century AD, though in the case of Brenkley at least there is evidence for this final 'abandonment' phase falling into the late first century AD (or later) and therefore perhaps associated with Roman occupation. The others were probably abandoned prior to any direct Roman contact in the area and may thus be part of a longer period of settlement flux alongside sites such as Arcot and Morley Hill Enclosure 2, abandoned during third and second centuries BC.

It is worth at this point highlighting the rise and subsequent decline of occupation at Lower Callerton. As with many of the larger sites throughout the Coastal Plain, it reached its peak of complexity, and probably population density, in its enclosure phase (Phase 2; *c.* late second to mid-first century BC), with the largest and most complex structures relating to this substantial ditch-and-bank phase of settlement. The more limited size and scale of enclosure within the subsequent phase of occupation (Phase 3; *c.* first century BC to early first century AD) suggested a significant decline in activity. The enclosed space shifted from the 1.5 ha main enclosure to the north-western enclosure that measured 0.17 ha in area. Further from this decline, the later enclosure at Lower Callerton shows evidence of reduced effort in re-excavation of the enclosure over time. In particular the final two phases of recut identified within the ditch were roughly 1/10th of the volume of material of the earlier phases, suggesting a decrease in labour available, perhaps from a decline in social cohesion. The once important settlement at Lower Callerton perhaps only managed to gather a fraction of the labour that was once available for such communal tasks – which would then compound the issue of social disconnectedness and highlight the isolation of this community. The decline of Lower Callerton may be indicative of wider patterns of social isolation within communities at this time – once one settlement went out of use (if not replaced or rebuilt nearby) it could cause a cascade of failures of connected communities, and only the hardiest, most adaptable, or luckiest survived without external input. The changes and decline witnessed at many settlement sites are arguably occurring within an Iron Age social context. The latest Iron Age witnessed significant shifts in social relations, display, prestige and power, all of which likely contributed to the decline of the enclosed settlements and the rise of other settlement (Garland 2017).

Roman influence on settlement decline

There are many sites on the Northumberland coastal plain, such as West Brunton, West Shiremoor, and, as discussed above, the latest phase of Morley Hill, that showed signs of continued occupation into the late first and second centuries AD, and which would therefore have been contemporary with the huge Roman military presence in the area (see Fig. 2.15). Indeed, there is also some evidence for reoccupation or repurposing of sites from the late first century AD, such as at Pegswood Moor, Burradon and St George's Hospital. The middle Iron Age settlement at Pegswood Moor evolved into a substantial complex farmstead, though the final phase, dating from the late first to early second century AD, saw a reorganisation of the field system and abandonment of the area previously used for settlement – a change argued to have been brought about by the presence of the Roman military (Proctor 2009). The settlement at Burradon, located on a slight ridge on the coastal plain, was dated ceramically to the late first and second century AD, on the site of an earlier Iron Age settlement, though there is no explicit evidence for continuity (Jobey 1970). More recent excavations at St George's Hospital, Morpeth, revealed a middle Iron Age farmstead that was abandoned in the third century BC and also apparently reoccupied from the late first century AD (ARS Ltd 2016). In this case the settlement is suggested as continuing into 5th century, which marks it as unusual as elsewhere on the coastal plain there appears to have been a dramatic decline in settlement numbers after the second century AD (Brindle 2016, 315), though, as noted above, modern truncation may have removed some evidence for later activity. Its location a little further north than most of the excavated sites – and from the military on Hadrian's Wall – may, nevertheless, have been a contributing factor in its longevity.

There are also a number of upland sites that show signs of prolonged existence into the Roman Iron Age, although dating evidence is often very uncertain for these settlements, many of which were excavated by George Jobey in the second half of the twentieth century, without the benefits of radiocarbon dates. Such sites include Murton High Crags (Jobey and Jobey 1987, 181) from which samian pottery was identified under the floor of a stone-built structure. Indeed, the presence of stone-built structures has been predominantly shown to be an indicator of Roman Iron Age activity (Brindle 2016, 321). Reoccupation of upland settlements later into the Roman Iron Age occurred at sites such as Mid Hill (Oswald and McOmish 2002) and Castle Hill (Pearson *et al.* 2001a). It

is possible that Murton High Crags was also reoccupied at this time, perhaps indicating significant levels of disruption and movement to and from settlements.

The overall picture of settlement reoccupation, shift and abandonment points to a varied and complex period of social upheaval that may have started in the late Iron Age, as noted above, with abandonment of certain 'village' settlements like Lower Callerton. This social flux was almost certainly greatly accelerated by the direct impact of the Roman military from the later first century AD, which may have contributed to the settlement abandonment evidenced during the second century AD. Of course the concept of violence between Roman forces and local militias or even individual settlements is one scenario that may have caused a level of depopulation of the land. It may have been that an intentional and forceful depopulation of the frontier zone was undertaken, creating a buffer zone north of Hadrian's Wall as suggested by Hodgson *et al.* (2012). It is, however, also possible that this productive land was still of use to the Roman military constructing and manning Hadrian's Wall, and that utilising and pressuring local farmers into working the land would have been of great benefit to the occupiers. Whether this was mutually beneficial to the occupied population is another matter, though it may have been to some, perhaps just in the short-term while the frontier remained more mobile. Nevertheless, the eventual abandonment of the Antonine Wall in AD 162 and fossilisation of the frontier along the line of Hadrian's Wall – with its concentration of Roman *vici*, forts and military troops – may ultimately have applied increasing pressure on local populations and could have played a part in persuading communities to either move further south, to the relative yet controlled safety behind the wall; to move further north, or westwards into the uplands of Northumberland.

The physical impact of Hadrian's Wall in breaking contact between kinship groups north and south of the Tyne (Harding 2017, 216) may have been another factor in isolating communities and breaking down economic and cooperative networks. Brindle (2016, 315, fig. 9.8) demonstrated a sharp decline in the number of farmsteads north of the wall from the end of the second century AD, compared with those to the south. This may indicate a division in how Roman forces interacted with locals, perhaps ending or lessening their requirement for local produce, and therefore plunging northern settlements into economic collapse, with their late Iron Age social and trade networks already mostly lost.

Environmental factors

Another serious consideration in terms of Iron Age settlement decline is that of climate change. Considering the primary agricultural subsistence methods used by Iron Age communities, a decline in conditions for both crops and pastureland could have had a significant impact on settlement and population numbers. The peak of Iron Age Northumberland, in terms of complexity of settlement and population density, correlated with peak climatic conditions in the late Iron Age. As such, a corresponding decline may have negatively impacted Iron Age settlement and the ability to cope with the increased external pressures applied by other factors. Between AD 200–400 a significant phase of climatic instability has been identified, compared to three previous centuries of stable climate (McCormick *et al.* 2012).

In terms of other environmental factors, the impact on local resources may also have affected settlement activity. By the second century AD pollen evidence from throughout Northumberland suggests that significant deforestation had occurred, which would have made wood – the primary building material – particularly scarce (Dark 2000, 108; Rippon *et al.* 2015, 290). This would have affected lowland areas in particular, which had comparatively minimal stone resources. The pressure on resources would have been further impacted by Roman construction, which would have required massive quantities of both stone and wood, limiting local supplies further. Upland sites may have been less adversely affected by resource decline, instead adapting to stone-built architecture, for which resources were plentiful, perhaps indicating another gravitational factor for population movement in these directions.

The legacy of Iron Age Northumberland

The Iron Age settlements excavated by Headland Archaeology (UK) Ltd at Morley Hill and Lower Callerton present two new key datasets for exploring Iron Age settlement on the Northumberland Coastal Plain. The extensive settlement at Lower Callerton highlights the growing recognition of the diversity and complexity of settlement forms across the region first highlighted by the excavations at Pegswood Moor (Proctor 2009).

The approach adopted at Lower Callerton highlights the potential of sites with high numbers of features but with limited stratigraphy, artefactual and environmental assemblages. The detailed and rigorous programme of radiocarbon dating allowed for 70 samples to be submitted from a range of features making the most of the available material. Subsequently, multiple radiocarbon dates were available from single features and single contexts which could be modelled to address questions of settlement development, tempo of occupation and longevity. The site appears to follow the established development pattern from unenclosed to enclosed with likely continuous occupation. The resulting pattern when compared with other sites, including Morley Hill, provides further evidence for the range of broadly contemporary settlement forms. Iron Age settlement across the Northumberland Coastal Plain appear to be complex and diverse with a high level of connection and cooperation proposed between groups. The enclosures can be seen to represent the physical manifestation of cooperation, movement, adaptability and innovation during the Iron Age. The construction of the enclosures would have involved significant effort and resources with the results, whilst often not present today, remaining visible on the landscape for up to 1800 years after their abandonment, until the advent of intensive agriculture and redivision of the coastal plain landscape of the sixteenth to eighteenth centuries (Vervust *et al.* 2020).

Extensive settlements such as Lower Callerton with numerous roundhouses, sub-enclosures and specialist structures may have provided gathering places and the focal point of activity within the wider landscape. Enclosed settlements on the Northumberland Coastal Plain reached their peak in the mid- to late Iron Age with evidence for change and arguably decline moving into the first and especially second centuries AD. This decline appears at many sites to have its origins in an Iron Age context with the causes of such decline likely to be multi-faceted. An overuse of resources and subsequent lack of lowland building materials may have had an impact; a climate downturn may have limited or decreased the population capacity of existing agricultural techniques; and the collapse of long-standing local social, support and trade networks would have seriously impacted the viability of large lowland settlement.

Intertwined with all these variables is the impact of the Roman influence within the region from the later first century AD. The impact of Roman occupation and response of local communities along the northern frontier is an exciting topic which demands the collation of a broad range of datasets (Fernández-Götz *et al.* 2022). The perspective presented by this monograph is that while Roman impact may have been the final nail in the coffin for many communities, it was not the sole driver of change or cause of decline for the enclosed settlements of the Northumberland Coastal Plain.

Bibliography

AD Archaeology (2013) *Land at Morley Hill Farm, Hazlerigg, Newcastle upon Tyne. Archaeological Geophysical Survey.* Unpublished client report, AD Archaeology.

AD Archaeology (2014) *Additional Land at Morley Hill Farm, Hazlerigg, Newcastle upon Tyne. Archaeological Geophysical Survey.* Unpublished client report, AD Archaeology.

AD Archaeology (2015) *Land at Morley Hill Farm, Hazlerigg, Newcastle upon Tyne. Archaeological Evaluation.* Unpublished client report, AD Archaeology.

Ancient Technology Centre (ATC) (2021) *Iron Age Roundhouse.* https://ancienttechnologycentre.com/

Anderson-Whymark, H. (2012) 'Neolithic to early Bronze Age pit deposition practices and the temporality of occupation in the Upper Thames Valley'. In H. Anderson-Whymark and J. Thomas (eds.) 2012, 187–99.

Anderson-Whymark, H. and Thomas, J. (2012) *Beyond the Mundane: Regional Perspectives on Neolithic Pit Deposition.* Neolithic Studies Society Seminar Series 12, Oxford, Oxbow Books.

Aqua-calc (2021) *Calculate Weight of Compounds and Materials per Volume.* https://www.aqua-calc.com/calculate/volume-to-weight

Araus, J., Buxó, R. and Vegetal, D.D.B. (1993) 'Changes in carbon isotope discrimination in grain cereals from the North-Western Mediterranean basin during the past seven millennia'. *Australian Journal of Plant Physiology* 20 (1990), 117–28.

Araus, J., Febrero, A., Buxó, R., Rodríguez-Ariza, M., Molina, F., Camalich, M., Martín, D. and Voltas, J. (1997) 'Identification of ancient irrigation practices based on the carbon isotope discrimination of plant seeds: a case study from the South-East Iberian Peninsula'. *Journal of Archaeological Science* 24, 729–40.

Araus, J., Febrero, A., Catala, M., Molist, M., Voltas, J. and Romagosa, I. (1999) 'Crop water availability in early agriculture: evidence from carbon isotope discrimination of seeds from a tenth millennium BP site on the Euphrates'. *Global Change Biology* 5, 201–12.

Archaeological Research Services Ltd (ARS) (2016) *An Archaeological Excavation at St. George's Hospital, Morpeth, Northumberland.* Unpublished client report, Archaeological Research Services Ltd.

Archaeological Services Durham University (ASDU) (2013) *Callerton Park Newcastle upon Tyne, Tyne and Wear. Archaeological Desk-based Assessment.* Unpublished client report, Archaeological Services Durham University.

Archaeological Services Durham University (ASDU) (2014a) *Callerton Park Newcastle upon Tyne, Tyne and Wear. Geophysical Survey.* Unpublished client report, Archaeological Services Durham University.

Archaeological Services Durham University (ASDU) (2014b) *East Wideopen, North Tyneside, Tyne and Wear. Post-excavation Analysis.* Unpublished client report, Archaeological Services Durham University.

Archaeological Services Durham University (ASDU) (2015) *Lower Callerton Newcastle upon Tyne, Tyne and Wear. Archaeological Evaluation.* Unpublished client report, Archaeological Services Durham University.

Archaeological Services Durham University (ASDU) (2017a) *Morley Hill, Hazlerigg, Tyne and Wear. Archaeological Evaluation.* Unpublished client report, Archaeological Services Durham University.

Archaeological Services Durham University (ASDU) (2017b) *West Shiremoor (North), Shiremoor, North Tyneside. Archaeological Excavation.* Unpublished client report, Archaeological Services Durham University.

Archaeological Services Durham University (ASDU) (2019) *Arcot, Phase 1, Cramlington, Northumberland. Post-excavation Analysis.* Unpublished client report, Archaeological Services Durham University.

Armit, I. (2019) 'Enclosure, autonomy and anarchy in Iron Age Scotland'. In T. Romankiewicz, M. Fernández-Götz, G. Lock and O. Büchsenschütz (eds.) *Enclosing Space, Opening New Ground: Iron Age Studies from Scotland to Mainland Europe,* 101–10. Oxford, Oxbow Books.

Ashmore, P.J. (1999) 'Radiocarbon dating: avoiding errors by avoiding mixed samples'. *Antiquity* 73, 124–30.

Bakels, C. (2019) 'Baselines for δ 15 N values of cereals retrieved from archaeological excavations'. *Archaeometry* 61(2), 470–77. https://doi.org/10.1111/arcm.12424

Barclay, G., Brophy, K., MacGregor, G., Foster, S.M., Hogg, D.J., Miller, J., Ramsay, S., Saville, A., Sheridan, J.A., Smith, C. and Stevenson, J.B. (2003) 'Claish, Stirling'. *Proceedings of the Society of Antiquaries of Scotland* 132, 65–137. https://doi.org/10.9750/PSAS.132.65.137

Bevan, A., Colledge, S., Fuller, D., Fyfe, R., Shennan, S. and Stevens, C. (2017) 'Holocene fluctuations in human population demonstrate repeated links to food production and climate'. *Proceedings of the National Academy of Sciences* 114(49), E10524. https://doi.org/10.1073/pnas.1709190114

Biggins, J.A., Biggins, J., Coxon, R. and Watson, M. (1997) 'Survey of the prehistoric settlement at Gardner's House Farm, Dinnington'. *Durham Archaeological Journal* 13, 43–53.

Bishop, R. (2015a) 'Did Late Neolithic farming fail or flourish? A Scottish perspective on the evidence for Late Neolithic arable cultivation in the British Isles'. *World Archaeology* 47(5), 834–55. https://doi.org/10.1080/00438243.2015.1072477

Bishop, R. (2015b) 'Summed radiocarbon probability distributions from cereal grains: arable cultivation proxy or the 'archaeology of us'? (a reply to Stevens and Fuller 2015)'. *World Archaeology* 47(5), 876–81. https://doi.org/10.1080/00438243.2015.1093427

Bishop, R., Church, M., and Rowley-Conwy, P. (2010) 'Cereals, fruits and nuts in the Scottish Neolithic'. *Proceedings of the Society of Antiquaries of Scotland* 139, 47–103. http://journals.socantscot.org/index.php/psas/article/view/9746

Bogaard, A. (2004) *Neolithic Farming in Central Europe: An Archaeobotanical Study of Crop Husbandry Practices.* Abingdon, Routledge.

Bogaard, A. (2005) 'Garden agriculture' and the nature of early farming in Europe and the Near East'. *World Archaeology* 37(2), 177–96.

Bogaard, A. and Jones, G. (2007) 'Neolithic farming in Britain and central Europe: contrast or continuity?' In A. Whittle and C Cummings (eds.) *Going Over: The Mesolithic-Neolithic Transition in North-West Europe,* Oxford, Oxford University Press, 357–75. https://doi.org/10.5871/bacad/9780197264140.003.0019

Bogaard, A., Heaton, T.H.E., Poulton, P. and Merbach, I. (2007) 'The impact of manuring on nitrogen isotope ratios in cereals: archaeological implications for reconstruction of diet and crop management practices'. *Journal of Archaeological Science* 34, 335–43.

Boutoille, L. (2019) 'Cushion stones and company: British and Irish finds of stone metalworking implements from the Bell Beaker period to the Late Bronze Age'. In D. Brandherm (ed.) *Aspects of the Bronze Age in the Atlantic Archipelago and Beyond. Proceedings from the Belfast Bronze Age Forum 9–10 November 2013,* 203–17. Westfalen, Curach Bhán.

Brace, S., Diekmann, Y., Booth, T.J., van Dorp, L., Faltyskova, Z., Rohland, N., Mallick, S., Olalde, I., Ferry, M., Michel, M., Oppenheimer, J., Broomandkhoshbacht, N., Stewardson, K., Martiniano, R., Walsh, S., Kayser, M., Charlton, S., Hellenthal, G., Armit, I. and Barnes, I. (2019) 'Ancient genomes indicate population replacement in Early Neolithic Britain'. *Nature Ecology and Evolution* 3(5), 765–71. https://doi.org/10.1038/s41559-019-0871-9

Bradley, R. and Edmonds, M. (1993) *Interpreting the Axe Trade: Production and Exchange in Neolithic Britain.* Cambridge, Cambridge University Press.

Bradley, R., Watson, A. and Style, P. (2019) 'After the axes? The rock art at Copt Howe, North-west England, and the Neolithic sequence at Great Langdale'. *Proceedings of the Prehistoric Society* 85, 77–192. doi: 10.1017/ppr.2019.5.

Brindle, T. (2016) 'The North'. In A. Smith, M. Allen, T. Brindle and M. Fulford *The Rural Settlement of Roman Britain. New Visions of the Countryside of Roman Britain Vol 1.* Britannia Monograph Series 29, 308–30. London, Society for the Promotion of Roman Studies.

Bronk Ramsey, C. (1995) 'Radiocarbon calibration and analysis of stratigraphy: the OxCal program'. *Radiocarbon* 37, 425–30.

Bronk Ramsey, C. (1998) 'Probability and dating'. *Radiocarbon* 40, 461–74.

Bronk Ramsey, C. (2001) 'Development of the radiocarbon calibration program'. *Radiocarbon* 43, 355–63.

Bronk Ramsey, C. (2009) 'Bayesian analysis of radiocarbon dates'. *Radiocarbon* 51, 337–60.

Buck, C.E., Cavanagh, W.G., and Litton, C.D. (1996) *Bayesian Approach to Interpreting Archaeological Data.* Chichester, John Wiley and Sons, Ltd.

Burley, E. (1956) 'A catalogue and survey of the metal-work from Traprain Law'. *Proceedings of the Society of Antiquaries of Scotland* 89 (1955–6), 118–226.

Caffell, A., Gidney, L., Cotton, J., O'Brien, C. and Ranner, H. (2012) 'The biological remains'. In N. Hodgson *et al.* 2012, 163–82.

Carlton, R.J. (2011) 'Archaeological excavations at Harehaugh hillfort in 2002'. *Archaeologia Aeliana* 40(5), 85–115. https://doi.org/10.5284/1061234

Chapman, A. (2020) *Coton Park, Rugby, Warwickshire: A Middle Iron Age settlement with Copper Alloy Casting.* Oxford, Archaeopress Archaeology

Cheij, R. (1984) *McDonal Encyclopedia of Medicinal Plants.* London, McDonald.

Chevallier, A. (1996) *The Encyclopedia of Medicinal Plants.* London, Dorling Kindersley.

Cootes, K.V.E. and Quinn, P.S. (2017) 'Prehistoric settlement, mobility and societal structure in the Peak District National Park: new evidence from ceramic compositional analysis', *Archaeometry* 60, 678–94. https://doi.org/10.1111/arcm.12334

Cree, J. (1923). 'Account of the excavations on Traprain Law during the summer of 1922.' *Proceedings of the Society of Antiquaries of Scotland,* 57, 180–226.

Crellin, R., Fowler, C. and Tipping, R. (2016) 'Prehistory without borders: an introduction'. In R. Crellin, C. Fowler and R. Tipping (eds.) *Prehistory without Borders: The Prehistoric Archaeology of the Tyne-Forth Region,* 1–15. Oxford: Oxbow Books.

Cross, P.J (2011) 'Horse burial in first millennium AD Britain: issues of interpretation'. *European Journal of Archaeology* 14(1–2). 190–209.

Cruickshanks, G. (2020) 'Stone objects'. In G. Noble, N. Evans, D. Hamilton, C. MacIver, E. Masson-Maclean and J. O'Driscoll, Dunnicaer. Aberdeenshire, Scotland: a Roman Iron Age promontory fort beyond the frontier. *Archaeological Journal* 177(2), 293–96.

Cunliffe, B.W. (2005) *Iron Age Communities in Britain: An Account of England, Scotland and Wales from the Seventh Century BC until the Roman Conquest.* London, Routledge.

Curle, A.O. and Cree, J.E. (1916) 'Account of excavations on Traprain Law in the parish of Prestonkirk, county of Haddington, in 1915'. *Proceedings of the Society of Antiquaries of Scotland* 50, 64–144.

Dark, P. (2000) *The Environment of Britain in the First Millennium AD.* London, Bloomsbury.

Dickson, C. and Dickson, J. (2000) *People and Plants in Ancient Scotland.* Gloucestershire, NPI Media Group.

Dunbar, E., Cook, G.T., Naysmith, P., Tripney, B.G., and Xu, S. (2016) 'AMS ^{14}C dating at the Scottish Universities

Environmental Research Centre (SUERC) Radiocarbon Dating Laboratory'. *Radiocarbon* 58, 9–23.

English Heritage (2011) *Environmental Archaeology: A Guide to the Theory and Practice of Methods, from Sampling and Recovery to Post-excavation*, 2nd ed. Swindon, English Heritage Publishing.

Ertuğ, F. (2000) 'An ethnobotanical study in central Anatolia (Turkey)'. *Economic Botany* 54, 155–82.

Evans, J. (1995) 'Later Iron Age and 'native' pottery in the north-east'. In B. Vyner (ed) *Moorland Monuments: Studies in the Archaeology of North-East Yorkshire in Honour of Raymond Hayes and Don Spratt*. Council for British Archaeology Research Reports 101, 46–68. York, Council for British Archaeology.

Fairbairn, A. (2000) 'On the spread of crops across Neolithic Britain, with special reference to the southern England'. In A. Fairbairn (ed.) *Plants in Neolithic Britain and Beyond*, 107–121. Oxford, Oxbow Books.

Fell, D. (2009) 'Analytical earthwork survey of a hillfort near Whitley Crag, Asby, Cumbria'. *Transactions of the Cumberland and Westmorland Antiquarian and Archaeological Society* 9 (series 3), 5–20. https://doi.org/10.5284/1064182

Fernández-Götz, M., Cowley, D., Hamilton, D., Hardwick, I., and McDonald, S. (2022) 'Beyond walls: reassessing Iron Age and Roman encounters in Northern Britain'. *Antiquity* 1–9. doi:10.15184/aqy.2022.47

Ferrio, J., Araus, J., Buxo, R., Voltas, J. and Bort, J. (2005) 'Water management practices and climate in ancient agriculture: inferences from the stable isotope composition of archaeobotanical remains'. *Vegetation History and Archaeobotany* 14, 510–17.

Fiorentino, G., Ferrio, J.P., Bogaard, A., Araus, J.L. and Riehl, S. (2015) 'Stable isotopes in archaeobotanical research'. *Vegetation History and Archaeobotany* 24(1), 215–27. https://doi.org/10.1007/s00334-014-0492-9

Fitts, R.L., Haselgrove, C.C., Lowther, P.C. and Willis, S.H. (1999). 'Melsonby revisited: survey and excavation 1992–5 at the site of discovery of the "Stanwick", North Yorkshire, hoard of 1843'. *Durham Archaeological Journal*, 14–15, 1–52.

Flaherty, S., Wells, T., Andrews, P., Brook, E., Leivers, M., López-Dóriga, I. and Quinn, P.S. (2020) 'A ring ditch, later Bronze Age pottery and Iron Age settlement at Seabrook Orchards, Topsham Road, Exeter'. *Proceedings of the Devon Archaeological Society* 78.

Fraser, R., Bogaard, A., Heaton, T., Charles, M., Jones, G., Christensen, B.T., Halstead, P., Merbach, I., Poulton, P.R., Sparkes, D. and Styring, A.K. (2011) 'Manuring and stable nitrogen isotope ratios in cereals and pulses: towards a new archaeobotanical approach to the inference of land use and dietary practices'. *Journal of Archaeological Science* 38(10), 2790–804. https://doi.org/10.1016/j.jas.2011.06.024

Fraser, R.A., Bogaard, A., Charles, M., Styring, A.K., Wallace, M., Jones, G., Ditchfield, P. and Heaton, T.H.E. (2013) 'Assessing natural variation and the effects of charring, burial and pre-treatment on the stable carbon and nitrogen isotope values of archaeobotanical cereals and pulses'. *Journal of Archaeological Science* 40(12), 4754–66. https://doi.org/10.1016/j.jas.2013.01.032

Freestone, I. (1992) 'Petrology of the Bronze Age pottery'. In R.H. Bewley, I.H. Longworth, S. Browne, J.P. Huntley and G. Varndell, Excavation of a Bronze Age cemetery at Ewanrigg, Maryport, Cumbria. *Proceedings of the Prehistoric Society* 58, 325–54.

Freestone, I.C. and Middleton, A.P. (1991) 'Report on the petrology of pottery from Iron Age cemeteries at Rudston and Burton Fleming'. In I.M. Stead (ed.) *Iron Age Cemeteries in East Yorkshire: Excavations at Burton Fleming, Rudstone, Garton-on- the-Wolds, and Kirkburn*. English Heritage Archaeological Report 22, 162–64.

Frodsham, P.N.K. (ed.) (2004). *Archaeology in Northumberland National Park*. York, Council for British Archaeology.

Garland, N J. (2017) *Territorial Oppida and the Transformation of Landscape and Society in South-Eastern Britain from BC 300 to 100 AD*. Unpublished PhD thesis, University College London.

Garrow, D. (2011) 'Concluding discussion: pits and perspective'. In H. Anderson-Whymark and J. Thomas (eds.) *Regional Perspectives on Neolithic Pit Deposition: Beyond the Mundane*, 216–25. Oxford, Oxbow Books.

Garrow, D., Beadsmoore, E. and Knight, M. (2005) 'Pit clusters and the temporality of occupation: an earlier Neolithic site at Kilverstone, Thetford, Norfolk', *Proceedings of the Prehistoric Society* 71, 139–57.

Gates, T. (2009) 'Excavation of a late second/early first millennium B.C. unenclosed roundhouse at Halls Hill, near East Woodburn, Northumberland'. *Archaeologia Aeliana* 38(5), 43–85. https://doi.org/10.5284/1061206

Gidney, L.J. (2012) 'The animal bone'. In N. Hodgson *et al.* 2012, 163–6.

Green, H.S. (1980) *The Flint Arrowheads of the British Isles: A Detailed Study of Material from England and Wales with Comparanda from Scotland and Ireland*. British Archaeological Reports 75. Oxford, BAR Publishing.

Greene, K. (1978) 'Apperley Dene 'Roman fortlet': a re-examination, 1974-5'. *Archaeologia Aeliana* 6(5), 29–159.

Hallam, D. (2017) *The Bronze Age Funerary Cups of Northern England*. Unpublished MPhil thesis, University of Bradford. http://hdl.handle.net/10454/14861

Hamilton, D. (2010) The Use of Radiocarbon and Bayesian Modelling to (Re)write later Iron Age Settlement Histories in east-central Britain. Unpublished PhD thesis, University of Leicester.

Hamilton, D. (2012) 'Bayesian modelling'. In N. Hodgson *et al.*, 133–42.

Hamilton, D. and Kenney, J. (2015) 'Multiple Bayesian modelling approaches to a suite of radiocarbon dates from ovens excavated at Ysgol yr Hendre, Caernarfon, North Wales'. *Quaternary Geochronology* 25, 72–82.

Harding, D.W. (2017) *The Iron Age in Northern Britain: Britons and Romans, Natives and Settlers*. London, Routledge.

Haselgrove, C. (1984) 'The later pre-Roman Iron Age between the Humber and the Tyne', in P.R. Wilson, R.F.L. Jones and D.M. Evans (eds.) *Settlement and Society in the Roman North*, 9–25. Bradford and Leeds, Bradford University School of Archaeological Sciences and Roman Antiquities Section of the Yorkshire Archaeological Society.

Haselgrove, C. (2007) 'The age of enclosure: Late Iron Age settlement and society in northern France'. In C. Haselgrove and T. Moore (eds.) *The Later Iron Age in Britain and Beyond*, 492–552. Oxford, Oxbow Books.

Haselgrove, C. (ed.) (2009) *The Traprain Law Environs Project: Fieldwork and Excavations 2000–2004*. Edinburgh, Society of Antiquaries of Scotland.

Haselgrove, C. (2016) *Cartimandua's Capital? The late Iron Age Royal Site at Stanwick, North Yorkshire, Fieldwork and Analysis 1981–2011*. Digital Appendices [data-set]. York, Archaeology Data Service [distributor]. https://doi.org/10.5284/1036100

Haselgrove, C. and McCullagh, R. (2000) *An Iron Age Coastal Community in East Lothian: Excavations at Fishers Road, Port Seaton. 1994–95. Scottish Trust for Archaeological Research Monograph 6*. Edinburgh, Scottish Trust for Archaeological Research.

Hatherley, C. and Murray, R. (2021) *Culduthel: An Iron Age Craft Centre*. Edinburgh, Society of Antiquaries of Scotland.

Hayden, B. (2001) 'Fabulous feasts: a prolegomenon to the importance of feasting'. In M. Dietler and B. Hayden (eds.) *Feasts: Archaeological and Ethnographic Perspectives on Food, Politics, and Power*, 23–64. Washington, Smithsonian Institution Press.

Headland Archaeology (2019) *Enclosed Iron Age settlements on land east of Morley Hill Farm, Hazlerigg, Newcastle Upon Tyne*. Unpublished client report, Headland Archaeology.

Headland Archaeology (2020) *Lower Callerton Excavations, Newcastle*. Unpublished client report, Headland Archaeology.

Heslop, D.H. (1987) *The Excavation of an Iron Age Settlement at Thorpe Thewles, Cleveland, 1980–82*. Council for British Archaeology Research Report 65. York, Cleveland County Archaeology Section and the Council for British Archaeology.

Heslop, D.H. (2008) *Patterns of Quern Production, Acquisition and Deposition. A Corpus of Beehive Querns from Northern Yorkshire and Southern Durham*. Leeds, Yorkshire Archaeological Society.

Hill, J.D. (2006) 'Are we any closer to understanding how later Iron Age societies worked (or did not work)?'. In C. Haselgrove (ed.) *Les Mutations de la Fin de l'Age du Fer*, 169–79. Bibracte, Centre Archeologique Europeen.

Hill, J.D. (2011) 'How did British Middle and Late pre-Roman Iron Age societies work (if they did)?'. In T. Moore and X. Armad (eds.) *Atlantic Europe in the First Millennium BC: Crossing the Divide*, 242–63. Oxford, Oxford University Press.

Hodgson, N., Stobbs, G.C., Van der Veen, M., Croom, A.T. and Waddington, C. (2001) 'An Iron-Age settlement and remains of earlier prehistoric date beneath South Shields Roman Fort, Tyne and Wear'. *Archaeological Journal* 158(1), 62–160.

Hodgson, N., McKelvey, J. and Muncaster, W. (2012) *The Iron Age on the Northumberland Coastal Plain, Excavations in Advance of Development 2002–2010*. Tyne and Wear Museums Archaeological Monograph 3. Newcastle upon Tyne, TWM archaeology and the Arbeia Society.

Hunter, F. (2009) 'The finds assemblages in their regional context'. In C. Haselgrove *The Traprain Law Environs Project. Fieldwork and Excavations 2000–2004*, 140–56. Edinburgh, Society of Antiquaries of Scotland.

Ixer, R. and Vince, A. (2009) 'The provenance potential of igneous glacial erratics in Anglo-Saxon ceramics from Northern England'. In P.S. Quinn (ed.) *Interpreting Silent Artefacts: Petrographic Approaches to Archaeological Materials*, 11–23. Oxford, Archaeopress.

Jacobi, R. (1978) 'The Mesolithic of Sussex'. In P.L. Drewitt *Archaeology in Sussex to AD 1500*. Council for British Archaeology Research Report 29, 15–22. York, Council for British Archaeology.

Jobey, G. (1962) 'An Iron Age homestead at West Brandon, Durham'. *Archaeologia Aeliana* 40(4), 1–34. https://doi.org/10.5284/1060370

Jobey, G. (1963) 'Additional rectilinear settlements in Northumberland'. *Archaeologia Aeliana* 41, 211–15. https://doi.org/10.5284/1060404

Jobey, G. (1970) 'An Iron Age Settlement and Homestead at Burradon, Northumberland'. *Archaeologia Aeliana* 48(4), 51–95. https://doi.org/10.5284/1060525

Jobey, G. (1973) 'A Native Settlement at Hartburn and the Devil's Causeway, Northumberland 1971'. *Archaeologia Aeliana* 1(5), 11–53. https://doi.org/10.5284/1060585

Jobey, G. (1982) 'The settlement at Doubstead and Romano-British settlement on the coastal plain between Tyne and Forth'. *Archaeologia Aeliana* 5(10), 1–23. https://doi.org/10.5284/1060737

Jobey, G. (1983) 'Excavation of an unenclosed settlement on Standrop Rigg, Northumberland, and some problems related to similar settlements between Tyne and Forth'. *Archaeologia Aeliana* 11(5), 1–21. https://doi.org/10.5284/1060753

Jobey, G. (1984) 'A settlement on Boggle Hill, Thorneyburn (NY 783862)'. *Archaeologia Aeliana* 12(5), 241–42. https://doi.org/10.5284/1060778

Jobey, G. and Jobey, I. (1987) 'Prehistoric, Romano-British and later remains on Murton High Crags, Northumberland'. *Archaeologia Aeliana* 15(5), 151–98. https://doi.org/10.5284/1060815

Jobey, G. and Tait, J. (1966) 'Excavations on palisaded settlements and cairnfields at Alnham, Northumberland'. *Archaeologia Aeliana* 44(4), 5–48. https://doi.org/10.5284/1060449

Johnson, B., Waddington, C., Baker, P., Bronk Ramsey, C., Clogg, P., Cook, G., Cotton, J., Hamilton, D., Marshall, P. and Stern, B. (2008) 'Prehistoric and Dark Age settlement remains from Cheviot Quarry, Milfield Basin, Northumberland', *The Archaeological Journal*. 165, 107–264. https://doi.org/10.1080/00665983.2008.11020747

Kilbride-Jones, H.E. (1938) 'Excavation of a native settlement at Milking Gap, Northumberland'. *Archaeologia Aeliana* 15(4), 303–50. https://doi.org/10.5284/1060006

Lamdin-Whymark, H. (2010) 'Worked flint'. In K. Powell and A. Smith *Evolution of a Farming Community in the Upper Thames Valley: Excavation of a Prehistoric and Post-Roman Landscape at Cotswold Community, Gloucestershire and Wiltshire. Volume 2: Specialist Reports*. Thames Valley Landscaped Monograph 32, 53–73. Oxford, Oxford Archaeology.

Lightfoot, E. and Stevens, R.E. (2012) 'Stable isotope investigations of charred barley (*Hordeum vulgare*) and wheat (*Triticum spelta*) grains from Danebury Hillfort: implications for palaeodietary reconstructions'. *Journal of Archaeological Science* 39, 656–62. https://doi.org/10.1016/j.jas.2011.10.026

Lodwick, L., Campbell, G., Crosby, V. and Müldner, G. (2021) 'Isotopic evidence for changes in cereal production strategies in Iron Age and Roman Britain'. *Environmental Archaeology* 26, 13–28. https://doi.org/10.1080/14614103.2020.1718852

Mackenzie, E. (1825) *View of the County of Northumberland*. Newcastle Upon Tyne.

MacLauchlan, H. (1858) *Memoir Written During a Survey of the Roman Wall, Through the Counties of Northumberland and Cumberland, in 1852–1854*. Private circulation.

Malim, T., Morgan, D. and Panter, I. (2015) 'Suspended preservation: particular preservation conditions within the Must Farm–Flag Fen Bronze Age landscape'. *Quaternary International 368*, 19–30.

McCarthy, M. R. (2000) 'Prehistoric settlement in northern Cumbria'. In J. Harding and R. Johnston (eds.) *Northern Pasts: Interpretations of the Later Prehistory of Northern England and Southern Scotland.* British Archaeological Reports British Series, No. 302, 131–40. Oxford, Archaeopress.

McCarthy, M.R., Padley, T.G. and Henig, M. (1982). 'Excavations and finds from the Lanes, Carlisle'. *Britannia* 13, 79–89.

McCord, N. and Jobey, G. (1968) 'Notes on air reconnaissance in Northumberland and Durham I. Tyne to Wansbeck, Northumberland'. *Archaeologia Aeliana* 46(4), 51–68. https://doi.org/10.5284/1060484

McCord, N. and Jobey, G. (1971) 'Notes on air reconnaissance in Northumberland and Durham II'. *Archaeologia Aeliana* 49(4), 119–30. https://doi.org/10.5284/1060549

McCormick, M., Büntgen, U., Cane, M.A., Cook, E.R., Harper, K., Huybers, P.J., Litt, T., Manning, S.W., Mayewski, P.A., More, A.F., Nicolussi, K. and Tegel, W. (2012). 'Climate change during and after the Roman Empire: reconstructing the past from scientific and historical evidence'. *Journal of Interdisciplinary History* 43, 169–220.

Mercer, H.C. (1975) *Ancient Carpenters' Tools* (Fifth edition). Doylestown, PA, Bucks County Historical Society.

Miket, R. (1984) *The Prehistory of Tyne and Wear: An Inventory of Prehistoric Discoveries in the Metropolitan County of Tyne and Wear* 82. Newcastle, Northumberland Archaeological Group.

Miket, R., Edwards, B. and O'Brian, C. (2008) 'Thirlings: a Neolithic site in Northumberland'. *Archaeological Journal* 165, 1–106.

Millson, D. (2013) *Ceramics of the Tyne-Forth Region, c.3500 – 1500BC.* Unpublished PhD thesis, University of Durham. http://etheses.dur.ac.uk/7000/

Millson, D., Waddington, C. and Marshall, P. (2011) 'Towards a sequence for Neolithic ceramics in the Milfield Basin and Northumbrland'. *Archaeologia Aeliana* 50(5), 1–4.

Mitchell, A. (1880) *The Past in the Present: What is Civilisation?* Edinburgh, David Douglas.

Monaghan, J. (1994) 'An unenclosed Bronze Age house site at Lookout Plantation, Northumberland'. *Archaeologia Aeliana* 22(5), 29–41. https://doi.org/10.5284/1060935

Moore, T. (2007) 'Perceiving communities: exchange, landscapes and social networks in the later Iron Age of western Britain'. *Oxford Journal of Archaeology* 26(1), 79–102.

Moore, T. and Gonzalez-Alvarez, D. (2021) 'Societies against the Chief? Re-examining the value of `heterarchy' as a concept for examining European Iron Age societies.'. In T.L. Thurston and M. Manuel Fernández-Götz (eds.) *Power from Below in Pre-Modern Societies. The Dynamics of Political Complexity in the Archaeological Record*, 125–56. Cambridge: Cambridge University Press.

Morrison, J. (2016) *Specification for Archaeological Work at Land East of Morley Hill Farm and West of Hazlerigg.* Unpublished specification, Newcastle upon Tyne Newcastle City Council.

Morrison, J. (2017) *Specification for an Archaeological excavation at Lower Callerton, Newcastle upon Tyne.* Unpublished specification, Tyne and Wear Archaeology Service.

Muncaster, W. (2011) *Hoodsclose, Proposed Surface Mine: Coal and Fireclay Scheme. Archaeological Evaluation.* Unpublished client report, TWM Archaeology.

Mytum, H. and Meek, J. (2020) 'Experimental archaeology and roundhouse excavated signatures: the investigation of two reconstructed Iron Age buildings at Castell Henllys, Wales'. *Archaeological and Anthropological Sciences* 12(3), 1–19.

Neef, R., Cappers, R. and Bekker, R. (2012) *Digital Atlas of Economic Plants in Archaeology.* Groningen, Barkhuis and Groningen University Library.

NERC (2019) British Geological Survey

Nitsch, E.K., Charles, M. and Bogaard, A. (2015) 'Calculating a statistically robust δ13C and δ 15N offset for charred cereal and pulse seeds'. *Science and Technology of Archaeological Research* 1(1), STAR20151120548. https://doi.org/10.1179/2054892315Y.0000000001

Northern Archaeological Associates (NAA) (2008) *Delhi, Blagdon Hall, Northumberland. Post-excavation Assessment Report, Project No. 0367.* Unpublished client report, NAA.

Northern Archaeological Associates (NAA) (2016) *East Wideopen, Wideopen, Tyne and Wear Post-excavation Assessment Report.* Unpublished client report, NAA.

Oswald, A. and McOmish, D. (2002) *An Iron Age Hillfort on Mid Hill, Northumberland*, English Heritage Archaeological Investigation Report Series AI/2/2002.

Petts, D. and Gerrard, C. (2006) *The Archaeology of the East Midlands: An Archaeological Resource Assessment and Research Agenda.* Leicester Archaeology Monograph 13. Leicester, University of Leicester Archaeological services.

Palyvos A., Ginnever M. and McGalliard, S. (2017) *Dissington Garden Village, Ponteland. Archaeological Evaluation Trenching.* Unpublished client report, Headland Archaeology.

Pearson, T., Lax, A. and Ainsworth, S. (2001) *An Iron Age Hillfort and its Environs on Castle Hill, Alnham, Northumberland*, English Heritage Archaeological Investigation Report Series AI/2/2001.

Pollock, D. (1997) 'The excavation of Iron Age buildings at Ironshill, Inverkeilor, Angus.' *Proceedings of the Society of Antiquaries of Scotland* 127, 339–58.

Pope, R. (2003) *Prehistoric Dwelling, Circular Structures in North and Central Britain c. 2500 BC – AD 500.* Unpublished PhD thesis, University of Durham Department of Archaeology.

Pope, R. (2007) 'Ritual and the roundhouse: a critique of recent ideas on the use of domestic space in later British prehistory'. In C. Haselgrove and R. Pope (eds.) *The Earlier Iron Age in Britain and the Near Continent*, 204–28. Oxford, Oxbow Books.

Proctor, J. (2009) *Pegswood Moor, Morpeth: A Later Iron Age and Romano-British Farmstead Settlement.* Pre-Construct Archaeology Limited Monograph 11. London, Pre-construct Archaeology.

Pryor, F. (1996) 'Sheep, stockyards and field systems: Bronze Age livestock populations in the Fenlands of eastern England'. *Antiquity* 70, 313–24.

Pryor, F. (2006) *Farmers in Prehistoric Britain*. Stroud, Tempus.

Quinn, P.S. (2011) *Petrographic Analysis of Anglo-Saxon Ceramics from Shotton and Wallsend, England.* Unpublished report.

Quinn, P.S. (2013) *Ceramic Petrography: The Interpretation of Archaeological Pottery and Related Artefacts in Thin Section.* Oxford, Archaeopress.

Ray, K. and Thomas, J. (2018) *Neolithic Britain: The Transformation of Social Worlds*. Oxford, Oxford University Press.

Reimer, P.J., Austin, W.E.N., Bard, E., Bayliss, A., Blackwell, P.G., Ramsey, C.B., Butzin, M., Cheng, H., Edwards, R.L., Friedrich, M., Grootes, P.M., Guilderson, T.P., Hajdas, I., Heaton, T.J., Hogg, A.G., Hughen, K.A., Kromer, B., Manning, S.W., Muscheler, R., Palmer, J.G., Pearson, C., Plicht, J.v.d., Reimer, R.W., Richards, D.A., Scott, E.M., Southon, J.R., Turney, C.S.M., Wacker, L., Adolphi, F., Büntgen, U., Capano, M., Fahrni, S.M., Fogtmann-Schulz, A., Friedrich, R., Köhler, P., Kudsk, S., Miyake, F., Olsen, J., Reinig, F., Sakamoto, M., Sookdeo, A. and Talamo, S. (2020) 'The IntCal20 Northern Hemisphere Radiocarbon Age Calibration Curve (0–55 cal kBP)'. *Radiocarbon* 62, 725–57.

Reynolds, D.M. (1982) 'Aspects of later timber construction in south-east Scotland'. In D.W. Harding (ed.) *Later Prehistoric Settlement in South-East Scotland*. University of Edinburgh Department of Archaeology Occasional Paper 8, 44–56. Edinburgh, University of Edinburgh.

Reynolds, P.J. (1974) 'Experimental Iron Age storage pits: an interim report'. *Proceeding of the Prehistoric Society* 40, 118–131.

Reynolds, P. (2003) 'Butser Ancient Farm, Hampshire, UK'. In P.G. Stone and P.G. Planel (eds.) *The Constructed Past. Experimental Archaeology, Education and the Public*, 124–55. London, Routledge.

Rippon, S., Smart, C. and Pears, B. (2015) *Fields of Britannia: Continuity and Change in the Late Roman and Early Medieval Landscape*. Oxford, Oxford University Press.

Romankiewicz, T. (2019) 'Turf worlds: towards understanding an understudied building material in rural Iron Age architecture–some thoughts in a Scottish context'. In D. Cowley, M. Fernández-Götz, T. Romankiewicz and H. Wendling (eds.) *Rural Settlement: Relating Buildings, Landscape and People in the European Iron Age*, 135–142. Leiden, Sidestone Press.

Rye, O.S. (1976) 'Keeping your temper under control: materials and the manufacture of Papuan pottery'. *Archaeology and Physical Anthropology in Oceania* 11, 106–37.

Salaman, R.A. (1975) *Dictionary of Tools Used in the Woodworking and Allied Trades c.1700–1970*. London, George Allen and Unwin.

Scott, E.M. (2003) 'The Third International Radiocarbon Intercomparison (TIRI) and the Fourth International Radiocarbon Intercomparison (FIRI) 1990–2002: results, analysis, and conclusions'. *Radiocarbon* 45, 135–408.

Scott, E.M., Cook, G.T. and Naysmith, P. (2010) 'A report on phase 2 of the Fifth International Radiocarbon Intercomparison (VIRI)'. *Radiocarbon* 52, 846–58.

Sharples, N. (2007) 'Building communities and creating identities in the first millennium BC'. In C. Haselgrove and R. Pope (eds.) *The Earlier Iron Age in Britain and the Near Continent*, 174–84. Oxford, Oxbow Books.

Sheridan, A. (1997) 'Pottery production in Neolithic and Early Bronze Age Ireland: a petrological and chemical study'. In A. Middleton and I. Freestone (eds.) *Recent Developments in Ceramic Petrology*. British Museum Occasional Paper 81, 305–36. London, British Museum Press.

Sheridan, A. (2010) 'The Neolithization of Britain and Ireland: the "big picture."'. In B. Finlayson and G. Warren (eds.) *Landscapes in Transition,* 89–104. Oxford, Oxbow Books.

Stevens, C.J. and Fuller, D.Q. (2012) 'Did Neolithic farming fail? The case for a Bronze Age agricultural revolution in the British Isles'. *Antiquity* 86(333), 707–22. https://doi.org/ DOI: 10.1017/S0003598X00047864

Stevens, C.J. and Fuller, D.Q. (2015) 'Alternative strategies to agriculture: the evidence for climatic shocks and cereal declines during the British Neolithic and Bronze Age (a reply to Bishop)'. *World Archaeology* 47(5), 856–75. https://doi.org/10.1080/00438243.2015.1087330

Stone, P., Millward, D., Young, B., Merritt, J., Clarke, S., McCormac, M. and Lawrence, D. (2010) *Northern England*. Nottingham, British Geological Survey.

Stuiver, M. and Polach, H.A. (1977) 'Reporting of ^{14}C data'. *Radiocarbon* 19, 355–63.

Stuiver, M. and Reimer, P.J. (1993) 'Extended ^{14}C data base and revised CALIB 3.0 ^{14}C calibration program'. *Radiocarbon* 35, 215–30.

Styring, A.K., Manning, H., Fraser, R., Wallace, M., Jones, G., Charles, M., Heaton, T.H.E., Bogaard, A. and Evershed, R.P. (2013) 'The effect of charring and burial on the biochemical composition of cereal grains: investigating the integrity of archaeological plant material'. *Journal of Archaeological Science* 40(12), 4767–79. https://doi.org/10.1016/j.jas.2013.03.024

Swan, V., McBride, R. and Hartley, K. (2009) 'The coarse pottery'. In C. Howard-David (ed.) *The Carlisle Millennium Project: Excavations in Carlisle 1998-2001, Volume 2: Finds. Lancaster Imprints 15,* 566–660.

Thomas, J. (1991) *Rethinking the Neolithic*. Abingdon, Taylor and Francis.

Timpson, A., Colledge, S., Crema, E., Edinborough, K., Kerig, T., Manning, K., Thomas, M.G. and Shennan, S. (2014) 'Reconstructing regional population fluctuations in the European Neolithic using radiocarbon dates: a new case-study using an improved method'. *Journal of Archaeological Science* 52, 549–57. https://doi.org/https://doi.org/10.1016/j.jas.2014.08.011

Tinsley, A. and Waddington, C. (2009) *Prehistoric Ceramic Analysis of the Phase 1 Assemblage from Lanton Quarry*. Unpublished Report, Archaeological Research Services Ltd Report 2009/30.

Vaiglova, P., Snoeck, C., Nitsch, E., Bogaard, A. and Lee-Thorp, J. (2014) 'Impact of contamination and pre-treatment on stable carbon and nitrogen isotopic composition of charred plant remains'. *Rapid Communications in Mass Spectrometry* 28(23), 2497–510. https://doi.org/https://doi.org/10.1002/rcm.7044

Van der Veen, M. (1992) *Crop Husbandry Regimes: An Archaeobotanical Study of Farming in Northern England 1000 BC – AD 500*. Sheffield Archaeological Monographs 3. Sheffield, Collis Publications.

Van der Veen, M. (2007) 'Formation processes of desiccated and carbonized plant remains – the identification of routine practice'. *Journal of Archaeological Science* 34, 968–90.

Van der Veen, M. and Jones, G. (2006) 'A re-analysis of agricultural production and consumption: implications for understanding the British Iron Age'. *Vegetation History and Archaeobotany* 15, 217–28.

Van der Veen, M. and O'Connor, T. (1998) 'The expansion of agricultural production in Late Iron Age and Roman Britain'. In J. Bayley (ed.) *Science in Archaeology: An Agenda for the Future*. English Heritage Occasional Paper 1, 127–43. London, English Heritage.

Van Wessel, J. and Wilson, D. (2020) 'Iron Age settlement activity on the North-East coastal plain: excavations at Brenkley Lane Surface Mine, Tyne and Wear'. *Archaeologia Aeliana* 49(5), 25–63. https://doi.org/10.5284/1090424

Vervust, S., Kinnaird, T., Dabaut, N. and Turner, S. (2020) 'The development of historic field systems in northern England: a case study at Wallington, Northumberland'. *Landscape History* 41(2), 57–70. https://doi.org/10.1080/01433768.2020.1835183

Vince, A. (2005) 'Ceramic petrology and the study of Anglo-Saxon and later medieval ceramics'. *Medieval Archaeology* 49, 219–45.

Voltas, J., Ferrio, J., Alonso, N. and Araus, J. (2008) 'Stable carbon isotopes in archaeobotanical remains and palaeoclimate'. *Contributions to Science* 4(1), 21–31.

Waddington, C. (2009) 'A note on Neolithic, Bronze Age, Iron Age and Anglo-Saxon remains at Lanton Quarry near Milfield, Northumberland'. *Archaeologia Aeliana* 38, 23–9.

Waddington, C. (2011) 'Towards synthesis: research and discovery in Neolithic North-East England'. *Proceedings of the Prehistoric Society* 77, 279–319.

Waddington, C. and Davies, J. I. (2002) 'An Early Neolithic settlement and Late Bronze Age burial cairn near Bolam Lake, Northumberland: fieldwalking, excavation and reconstruction'. *Archaeologia Aeliana* 30, 1–47.

Wallace, M., Jones, G., Charles, M., Fraser, R., Halstead, P., Heaton, T.H.E. and Bogaard, A. (2013) 'Stable carbon isotope analysis as a direct means of inferring crop water status and water management practices'. *World Archaeology* 45(3), 388–409. https://doi.org/10.1080/00438243.2013.821671

Ward, G.K. and Wilson, S.R. (1978) 'Procedures for comparing and combining radiocarbon age determinations: a critique'. *Archaeometry* 20, 19–32.

Wardle, P. (1992) *Earlier Prehistoric Pottery Production and Ceramic Petrology in Britain.* British Archaeological Reports 225. Oxford, BAR Publishing.

Whitehouse, N.J., Schulting, R.J., McClatchie, M., Barratt, P., McLaughlin, T.R., Bogaard, A., Colledge, S., Marchant, R., Gaffrey, J. and Bunting, M.J. (2014) 'Neolithic agriculture on the European western frontier: the boom and bust of early farming in Ireland'. *Journal of Archaeological Science* 51, 181–205. https://doi.org/https://doi.org/10.1016/j.jas.2013.08.009

Wilkin, N. (2013) *Food Vessel Pottery from Early Bronze Age Funerary Contexts in Northern England: a Typological and Contextual Study.* Unpublished PhD thesis, University of Birmingham.

Williams, J. and Jenkins, D. (1999) 'A petrographic investigation of a corpus of Bronze Age cinerary urns from the Isle of Anglesey'. *Proceedings of the Prehistoric Society* 65, 189–22.

Willis, S. (2016) 'The Iron Age tradition and Roman pottery'. In C. Haselgrove *Cartimandua's Capital? The Late Iron Age Royal Site at Stanwick, North Yorkshire, Fieldwork and Analysis 1981–2011.* Council for British Archaeology Research Report 175, 207–55. York, Council for British Archaeology.

Woodward, A. (2008) 'Ceramic technologies and social relations'. In J. Pollard (ed.) *Prehistoric Britain*, 288–309. Oxford, Blackwell Publishing.